Gas Separation
by Adsorption Processes

Gas Separation
by Adsorption Processes

Ralph T. Yang
Professor of Chemical Engineering
State University of New York at Buffalo

Butterworths
Boston London Durban Singapore Sydney Toronto Wellington

Library of Congress Cataloging-in-Publication Data

Yang, R. T.
  Gas separation by adsorption processes.

  Bibliography: p.
  Includes indexes.
  1. Gases—Separation. 2. Gases—Absorption and
adsorption. I. Title.
TP242.Y36   1986   660.2′842   86-21584
ISBN 0-409-90004-4

Butterworth Publishers
80 Montvale Avenue
Stoneham, MA 02180

10 9 8 7 6 5 4 3 2 1

Printed in the United States of America

CONTENTS

PREFACE AND ACKNOWLEDGMENTS

The last two decades have witnessed a tremendous growth of gas adsorption processes that have made adsorption systems a key separations tool in chemical and petrochemical industries. The growth is a result of a series of significant scientific and engineering developments, initiated by the invention of synthetic zeolites and the pressure swing adsorption cycles. These inventions were followed by a succession of technological and theoretical advances. Among them are the developments of more efficient pressure swing adsorption (PSA) cycles, new and improved adsorbents, theories of adsorption from mixtures, theories on multicomponent adsorber dynamics, and modeling of PSA cycles.

The aim of this book is to present a comprehensive account and critical analysis of these developments. The presentation is made in a systematic manner with an emphasis on fundamental concepts and principles.

In Chapter 3 a detailed account is given on all theories and important experimental observations on adsorption from mixtures, as predicted by the pure-gas isotherms discussed in Chapter 2. Chapter 4 is a review of the important rate processes encountered in the fixed-bed adsorber, which is the workhorse in adsorption processes. The important aspects of the fixed-bed adsorber dynamics are summarized in Chapter 5 for both pure-component and multicomponent adsorptive gases. Chapter 6 reviews all cyclic adsorption processes for gas separation. A detailed analysis is given in Chapter 7 on the basic engineering concepts and designs of PSA cycles. Much of the information contained in this chapter is drawn from the patent literature; whenever possible, concepts rather than quantitative information are used. Chapter 8 is devoted to the theories and models of PSA cycles, along with experimental observations.

The book is intended for engineers and scientists, in industrial, government, or academic institutions, who are interested in gas separation processes. It could also form part of a one-semester graduate-level course for students in chemical engineering or related disciplines.

I assembled the greater part of the book during a sabbatical leave from the State University of New York at Buffalo in the spring of 1985.

In the early stage of my research and in organizing my thoughts on the subject, I have benefited greatly from discussions with a number of researchers in the field as well as colleagues at the university. In particular, I should mention Dr. Frank B. Hill and Dr. George E. Keller II. The untimely death of Frank Hill last October is a huge loss to the field, and his contribution and friendship are sorely missed.

Thanks are due to my past and present students and associates, with whom I have had so much pleasure in learning. The superb typing of Mrs. Darlene Innes and the highly efficient editing and publication by the staff at Butterworths are sincerely acknowledged. Finally, I would like to thank the U.S. Department of Energy and the National Science Foundation for supporting the research which substantially contributed to this book.

Ralph T. Yang
Buffalo, New York
August, 1985

CHAPTER 1

Introductory Remarks

Separation may be defined as a process that transforms a mixture of substances into two or more products that differ from each other in composition [1]. The process is difficult to achieve because it is the opposite of *mixing*, a process favored by the second law of thermodynamics. Consequently, the separation steps often account for the major production costs in chemical and petrochemical industries. Separation also plays a key role in chemistry and related scientific disciplines. Through the endeavor of human ingenuity, there exist a multitude of industrial separation processes [1] and laboratory separation techniques [2]. This book focuses on the industrial processes for separating gas mixtures which are accomplished by the preferential adsorption of certain constituents from the mixture.

The surface of a solid represents a discontinuity of its structure. The forces acting at the surface are unsaturated. Hence, when the solid is exposed to a gas, the gas molecules will form bonds with it and become attached. This phenomenon is termed *adsorption*. Direct exploitation of this phenomenon remained limited, until the early 1960s, to the purification of air and industrial vent gases. The picture has been drastically changed, however, by two major events: the development of a new adsorbent and the invention of a new process cycle. These events were followed by a series of significant developments in the past two decades that have made adsorption a key process for gas separation in the chemical and petrochemical industries.

The first major development was the invention of synthetic zeolites or molecular sieves by Milton at the Union Carbide Corporation [3]. This class of adsorbents is the only one known to adsorb a constituent from air preferentially. It preferentially adsorbs nitrogen over oxygen by a factor of approximately three [4]. The concurrent goal of research during the same time period was to develop an efficient process that used the new adsorbent to separate air, as an alternative to cryogenic means. The process had to be regenerative; that is, the adsorbent could be regenerated to permit reuse in further cycles as well as allowing recovery of the adsorbed gas. Regeneration by heating was not efficient because a heating-cooling cycle was necessarily time-consuming. Efficient pressure-swing cycles were invented concurrently by Skarstrom [5] and by Guerin de Montgareuil and Domine [6]. A series of developments followed. Various refined and sophisticated pressure-swing cycles were developed that allowed improvements on separation and energy requirements. Another new adsorbent, molecular sieve carbon, was developed. Like all new adsorbents, this allowed new applications that were not previously possible with other adsorbents.

1

Parallel with the commercial developments were the publications of the important fundamental theories underlying the separation processes. Starting with the ideal adsorbed solution theory [7], several significant theories have been developed for predicting the equilibrium adsorption of mixtures based on pure-gas isotherms. Major advances were made around 1970 on the equilibrium theories of adsorber dynamics for the adsorption of mixtures with nonlinear isotherms. More recently, modeling and simulation of the cyclic pressure-swing processes have been published that adequately describe the separation performance.

The objective of this book is to provide a comprehensive summary and analysis of these developments, both theoretical and commercial.

1.1   CRITERIA FOR WHEN TO USE ADSORPTION PROCESSES

Cryogenic separation — that is, liquefaction followed by distillation — remains the most frequently used process for large-scale applications. A comparison between distillation and adsorption for application in the chemical and petrochemical industries has been made by Keller [1, 8]. Some of his conclusions are followed here.

The widespread use of distillation is due to its process simplicity and scalability. It also yields high-purity products. The ease of separation by distillation is determined by the relative volatility, which for an ideal binary mixture is simply the ratio between the vapor pressures of the two components. The analogous parameter for adsorption is the separation factor defined by:

$$\alpha_{ij} = \frac{X_i/Y_i}{X_j/Y_j} \tag{1.1}$$

where X_i and Y_i are the equilibrium mole fractions of component i in, respectively, the adsorbed and gas phases. Despite the advantages associated with distillation, it is fundamentally an energy-intensive process. For this reason, there is interest in exploring alternatives for distillation. The following is a list of qualitative criteria [8] for deciding whether adsorption might be such an alternative.

1.   The relative volatility between the key components to be separated is in the order of 1.2 to 1.5 or less. An example for this case is the separation of isomers, where the separation factor for adsorption is practically infinity by using zeolites.

2.   The bulk of the feed is a relatively low-value, more volatile component, and the product of interest is in a relatively low concentration. In such situations large reflux ratios can be required in distillation and can result in high energy requirements.

3.   The two groups of components to be separated have overlapping boiling ranges. Several distillation columns are required for such a separation, even though various relative volatilities may be large. This separation may be efficiently

achieved by adsorption if the two groups contain chemically or geometrically dissimilar molecules — that is, with a high separation factor.

  4. A low temperature and a high pressure are required for liquefaction.

  5. Factors favorable for adsorption separation exist. The major cost for pressure swing adsorption is in the compressor costs. If the mixture is available at an elevated pressure, the costs for separation are substantially reduced. The gas throughput and product purities are also important considerations. The costs for adsorption separation are generally lower than distillation for small to medium throughputs, and when high-purity products are not required.

1.2   CATEGORIZATIONS OF ADSORPTIVE SEPARATION PROCESSES

1.2.1   Based on Method of Adsorbent Regeneration

The adsorbent can be regenerated by a number of methods, some of which are combined in the same process in practice. In the temperature swing adsorption (TSA) cycles, the adsorbent is primarily regenerated by heating. Heating is usually provided by preheating a purge gas. Each heating-cooling cycle usually requires a few hours to over a day. Thus TSA is used almost exclusively for purification purposes, in which the amounts of adsorptive gases being processed are small. The most rapidly growing process is pressure-swing adsorption (PSA). Regeneration of the adsorbent is accomplished by lowering the pressure. The throughput is high since rapid cycles, usually in minutes or seconds, are possible. In the inert-purge cycle, the adsorbent is regenerated by passing a nonadsorbing or weakly adsorbing gas through the adsorber. In the displacement-purge cycle, the purge gas adsorbs as strongly as the adsorbates contained in the mixture to be separated. The purge gas is referred to as the *desorbent*. This cycle is used only when the regeneration is not feasible by using the aforementioned three cycles — for example, when a high temperature in the TSA would damage the products. The desorbent must be separated from the purge stream for reuse.

1.2.2   Based on Feed Composition

The separation processes may also be divided into bulk separation and purification, depending on the concentration of the strongly adsorbed component in the mixture. This differentiation is desirable because the feed concentration is frequently an important factor in selecting the process cycle. There is no clear demarcation between the two categories. Keller has defined bulk separation as the point when 10 weight percent or more of the mixture is adsorbed [8]. In the commercial processes of hydrogen purification by PSA, however, the hydrogen content, which is nearly inert, is usually over 70% by volume.

1.2.3   Based on Mechanism of Separation

The adsorptive separation is achieved by one of the three mechanisms: steric, kinetic, or equilibrium effect. The *steric* effect derives from the molecular sieving property of zeolites. In this case only small and properly shaped molecules can diffuse into the adsorbent, whereas other molecules are totally excluded. *Kinetic* separation is achieved by virtue of the differences in diffusion rates of different molecules. A large majority of processes operate through the equilibrium adsorption of the mixture and hence are called *equilibrium* separation processes.

Steric separation is unique with zeolites because of the uniform aperture size in the crystalline structure. The aperture sizes of five synthetic zeolites are shown in Figure 1.1. Steric separations based on these well-defined aperture or micropore sizes are listed in Table 1.1. The two largest applications of steric separation are

Table 1.1   Steric Separations by Molecular-Sieve Zeolites

Molecular-Sieve Basic Type	Molecules Adsorbed[a]	Molecules Excluded	Typical Applications
3A	H_2O, NH_3, He (molecules with an effective diameter <3 Å)	CH_4, CO_2, C_2H_2, O_2, C_2H_5OH, H_2S (molecules with an effective diameter >3 Å)	Drying cracked gas, ethylene, butadiene, and ethanol
4A	H_2S, CO_2, C_2H_6, C_3H_6, C_2H_5OH, C_4H_6 (molecules with an effective diameter <4 Å)	C_3H_8, compressor oil (molecules with an effective diameter >4 Å)	Drying natural gas, liquid paraffins, and solvents. CO_2 removal from natural gas.
5A	n-Paraffins, n-olefins, n-C_4H_9OH (molecules with an effective diameter <5 Å)	Iso-compounds, all 4 + carbon rings (molecules with an effective diameter >5 Å)	n-Paraffin recovery from naphtha and kerosene
10X	Iso-paraffins, iso-olefins (molecules with an effective diameter <8 Å)	Di-n-butylamine and larger (molecules with an effective diameter >8 Å)	Aromatic separation
13X	Di-n-butylamine (molecules with an effective diameter <10 Å)	$(C_4F_9)_3$-N (molecules with an effective diameter >10 Å)	Desulfurization, general drying, simultaneous H_2O and CO_2 removal

Source: Collins [9]. Reprinted with permission.
[a]Each type adsorbs listed molecules plus those of preceding type.

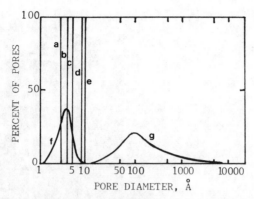

Figure 1.1   Micropore size distribution of (*a*) zeolite type 3A, (*b*) 4A, (*c*) 5A, (*d*) 10X, (*e*) 13X, (*f*) molecular-sieve carbon, and (*g*) activated carbon.

drying with 3A zeolite and the separation of normal paraffins from iso-paraffins and cyclic hydrocarbons using 5A zeolite.

Kinetic separation is possible only with molecular sieve carbon because of a distribution of pore sizes, as shown in Figure 1.1. Such a distribution of pores allows different gases to diffuse at different rates while totally avoiding exclusion of any gases in the mixture. Kinetic separation is used commercially for nitrogen generation from air. The separation is believed to be achieved as a result of a slight difference in the kinetic diameters of nitrogen and oxygen, which results in a relatively high diffusivity for oxygen. (Difference in kinetic diameters is not the only reason for the different diffusivities, however, as the phenomenon of restricted diffusion is not well understood.)

1.3   CURRENT STATUS AND FUTURE PROSPECTS

The past two decades have seen a tremendous growth in adsorption separation processes. Table 1.2 shows a list of representative commercial processes. Most of these processes employ pressure-swing adsorption cycles. A typical PSA system consists of three to four interconnected adsorbers, which allow a continuous flow of feed and products. Meanwhile, such a system is capable of accommodating complex and efficient PSA cycles. A picture of such a commercial unit is shown in Figure 1.2.

As noted earlier, distillation is still dominant in the chemical and petrochemical industries, and this situation is likely to continue. As with all new technologies, however, PSAs share of the separation task will continue to increase as the process is improved. For the production of oxygen or nitrogen from air, it is currently more economical to use PSA than cryogenic means for production rates below approximately 30 metric tons per day. Figure 1.3 shows the cost comparison of nitrogen produced from the two processes (liquid N_2 is from cryogenic processes). As further process improvements are made, PSA will compete more favorably at

Figure 1.2   A Union Carbide four-bed PSA system. Source: Kindly supplied by Mason Sze of Union Carbide Corporation.

still higher production rates. A similar situation also exists for hydrogen production [8]. High-purity (99.9999%) hydrogen can be produced by the PSA separation of steam reformer products. At present, PSA separation is more economical than cryogenic means at capacities approximately below 50,000 standard cubic meters per hour. An increase in the economical capacity limit from approximately 20,000 to 50,000 cubic meters per hour was recently made by the development of the seven- to ten-bed system. This allows more pressure equalization steps in the PSA cycle than does the three- to four-bed system.

New applications will also emerge as new or improved adsorbents are developed. The recently developed molecular sieve carbon is likely to result in lower-cost nitrogen. Separation of carbon dioxide from methane (for example, for landfill gas) or from hydrocarbons (for example, for tertiary oil recovery effluent gas) is also possible with this new adsorbent as a result of the relatively high diffusivity of carbon dioxide. The latter application currently employs membrane separation. A still more recent development is a so-called super A activated carbon, which has an adsorption capacity for most gases approximately two to six times

Table 1.2 Representative Commercial Gas-Adsorption Separations

Separation[a]	Adsorbent
I. Gas bulk separations	
Normal paraffins/iso-paraffins, aromatics	Zeolite
N_2/O_2	Zeolite
O_2/N_2	Carbon molecular-sieve
CO, CH_4, CO_2, N_2, A, NH_3/H_2	Zeolite, activated carbon
Acetone/vent streams	Activated carbon
C_2H_4/vent streams	Activated carbon
Separation of perfume components	—
II. Gas purification	
H_2O/olefin-containing cracked gas, natural gas, air, synthesis gas, etc.	Silica, alumina, zeolite
CO_2/C_2H_4, natural gas, etc.	Zeolite
Organics/vent streams	Activated carbon, others
Sulfur compounds/natural gas, hydrogen, liquefied petroleum gas (LPG), etc.	Zeolite
Solvents/air	Activated carbon
Odors/air	Activated carbon
NO_x/N_2	Zeolite
SO_2/vent streams	Zeolite
Hg/chlor-alkali cell gas effluent	Zeolite

Source: Keller [8]. Reprinted with permission.
[a] Adsorbates are listed first.

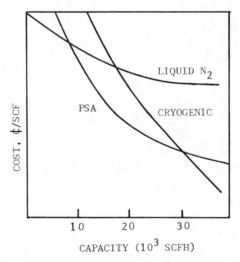

Figure 1.3 Cost comparison of nitrogen from PSA using 5A zeolite and cryogenic processes. Source: Brochure 522-301, reprinted with permission from Air Products and Chemicals, Inc.

higher than that of the commercial activated carbon [10]. A higher adsorption capacity would definitely improve the economics of separation. The development of a very hard, microspherical activated carbon by Kureha Chemical Company in Japan has made possible the commercialization of a new fluidized-bed/moving-bed adsorption process [8].

Keller concluded that although much growth is predictable for bulk separations by PSA processes, few innovations are likely to occur in purification processes.

REFERENCES

1. C.J. King, *Separation Processes*, 2nd ed. (New York: McGraw-Hill, 1980).
2. B.L. Karger, L.R. Snyder, and C. Horvath, *An Introduction to Separation Science* (New York: Wiley, 1973).
3. R.M. Milton, U.S. Patents 2,882,243 and 2,882,244 (1959).
4. R.M. Barrer, *Proc. Roy. Soc. (London)*, *A167*, 392 (1938).
5. C.W. Skarstrom, U.S. Patent 2,944,627 (1960) (filed in 1958).
6. P. Guerin de Montgareuil and D. Domine, U.S. Patent 3,155,468 (1964) (filed in 1958).
7. A.L. Myers and J.M. Prausnitz, *AIChE J.*, *11*, 121 (1965).
8. G.E. Keller II, in *Industrial Gas Separations* (T.E. Whyte, Jr., C.M. Yon, and E.H. Wagener, eds.), ACS Symp. Ser. No. 223 (Washington, D.C.: American Chemical Society, 1983), p. 145.
9. J.J. Collins, *Chem. Eng. Prog.*, *68*(8), 66 (1968).
10. A. Wennerberg and T. O'Grady, U.S. Patent 4,082,694 (1978), and paper presented at the 187th National ACS Meeting in St. Louis (April 1984).

CHAPTER 2

Adsorbents and Adsorption Isotherms

This chapter provides a review and analysis of the fundamental principles of adsorption on the basis of which adsorptive gas separation processes are operated. A wealth of knowledge exists on the adsorption of pure gases on solid surfaces, which has been reviewed in a number of monographs and texts [1–7]. Gas separation processes, however, are based on the different strengths of adsorption on a given sorbent for the constituents in the mixture. Our present knowledge on the equilibrium adsorption of mixtures is due largely to the more recent progress made in the last two decades. An updated review and analysis on the subject of mixture adsorption will be given in a separate chapter, Chapter 3.

2.1 INDUSTRIAL SORBENTS

In principle, all microporous materials can be used as sorbents for gas purification and separation. For example, bone chars, coal chars, calcined clays, iron oxide, calcined bauxite, and the like have all found commercial uses. The four sorbents to be discussed here, however, are those with well-controlled and high microporosity, and are produced in large quantities. Table 2.1 provides a perspective of the relative amounts used and the major gas separations performed in industry. In addition to the four sorbents listed in this table, a new sorbent, molecular sieve carbon, developed since about the mid-1970s, will also be discussed because of its unique ability to perform kinetic separation based on the different pore diffusion rates of different gas molecules.

Characterization of Sorbents.

The most important characteristic of a sorbent is its high porosity. Thus physical characterization is generally more important than chemical characterization.

The microporous structure of the sorbent can be characterized by standardized techniques. The most important physical characteristics include pore volume, pore size distribution, and surface area. Also of practical importance are bulk density, crush strength, and erosion resistance, but these will not be discussed.

Table 2.1   Applications and Annual Productions of Major Industrial Sorbents

Sorbent	Annual U.S. Production[a]	Major Uses for Gas Sorption
Activated carbon	90,000 (major)	Removal of nonpolar gases and organic vapors (e.g., solvents, gasoline vapor, odors, toxic and radioactive gases); H_2 purification; etc.
Zeolites:		
Synthetic	30,000[b] (major)	Drying; H_2 purification; air purification;
Natural	250,000[b] (minor)	air separation; separations based on molecular size and shape (e.g., n- and iso-paraffins, aromatics, etc.); gas chromatography
Silica gel	150,000 (minor)	Drying; gas chromatography
Activated alumina	25,000 (major)	Drying; gas chromatography

[a]Late 1970s figure in metric tons. The fraction used as sorbent is indicated in parentheses.
[b]Worldwide total figure.

The surface area of a sorbent can be determined by the BET method or estimated by a simpler *Point B* method [8]. Adsorption data for nitrogen at the liquid N_2 temperature, 77K, are usually used in both methods. The Brunaur-Emmett-Teller (BET) equation, which will be discussed in a later section of this chapter, is used to calculate the amount of N_2 for monolayer coverage. The surface area is taken as the area for monolayer coverage based on the N_2 molecular area, 16.2 $Å^2$, obtained by assuming liquid density and hexagonal close packing. In the Point B method, the initial point of the straight portion of the Type II isotherm is taken as the completion point for the monolayer. The corresponding amount adsorbed multiplied by molecular area yields the surface area.

In characterizing the pore volume, both total pore volume and its distribution over the pore diameter are needed. The total pore volume is usually determined by helium and mercury densities or displacements. Helium, because of its small atomic size and negligible adsorption, gives the total voids, whereas mercury does not penetrate into the pores at ambient pressure and gives interparticle voids. The total pore volume equals the difference between the two voids. The pore size distribution is measured by mercury porosimetry for pores larger than 100–150 Å and by N_2 desorption (or adsorption) for pores in the range 10–250 Å. For still smaller pores, molecular sieving is used to determine the size (the demarcation between the sizes of the gas molecules admitted and not admitted into the pores) while the admitted saturated amount is used to determine the pore volume (by using the simple Gurvitsch rule, assuming the pores are filled with liquid) [15]. The techniques of mercury porosimetry and N_2 desorption have been discussed in detail [5; 10; 11]. Mercury porosimetry essentially consists of measuring the extent of mercury penetration into the evacuated solid as a function of applied hydrostatic pressure. The pore radius (r) at a given pressure (P) is calculated by a balance between the applied pressure and the interfacial tension:

$$r = -\frac{2\sigma \cos \theta}{P} \tag{2.1}$$

where σ = interfacial tension
$\quad$ θ = contact angle

Generally σ is taken as 0.48 N/m and θ has an average value of 140°. Equation 2.1 reduces to $r = 7,500/P$ where P is in atmospheres and r is in Å. The N_2 desorption (or adsorption) technique takes advantage of the phenomenon where capillary condensation occurs at a relative pressure below unity because the equilibrium vapor pressure over a concave meniscus (P) is lower than that over a plane surface (P_0), as predicted by the Kelvin equation:

$$\ln \frac{P}{P_0} = \frac{-2\sigma V_m \cos \theta}{r_k RT} \tag{2.2}$$

where V_m = liquid molar volume
$\quad$ r_k = radius of curvature or Kelvin radius
R and T = gas constant and absolute temperature
$\quad$ θ = 0 for N_2

From an adsorption or desorption curve of N_2 at 77K, the pore-size distribution can be calculated on the basis of the Kelvin equation. (An easy-to-follow procedure can be found in reference 12).

2.1.1 Activated Carbon

Manufacturing Processes

The manufacture and use of activated carbon date back to the nineteenth century. The modern manufacturing processes basically involve the following steps: raw material preparation, pelletizing, low-temperature carbonization, and activation. The conditions are carefully controlled to achieve the desired pore structure and mechanical strength.

The raw materials for activated carbon are carbonaceous matters such as wood, peat, coals, petroleum coke, bones, coconut shell, and fruit nuts. Anthracite and bituminous coals have been the major sources. Starting with the initial pores present in the raw material, more pores, with desired size distributions, are created by the so-called activation process. After initial treatment and pelletizing, one activation process involves carbonization at 400–500°C to eliminate the bulk of the volatile matter, and then partial gasification at 800–1,000°C to develop the porosity and surface area. A mild oxidizing gas such as CO_2, steam, or flue gas is used in the gasification step because the intrinsic surface reaction rate is much slower than the pore diffusion rate, thereby assuring the uniform development of pores throughout the pellet. The activation process is usually carried out in fixed beds, but in recent years fluidized beds have also been used. The activated carbon created by this activation process is used primarily for gas and vapor adsorption processes. The other activation process that is used commercially depends on the action of inorganic additives to degrade and dehydrate the cellulosic materials and, simultaneously, to prevent shrinkage during carbonization. Lignin, usually the raw material that is blended with activators such as phosphoric acid, zinc chloride, potassium sulfide, or potassium thiocyanate, is carbonized at temperatures up to 900°C. The product, usually in powder form, is used for aqueous or gas purposes. The inorganic material contained in activated carbon is measured as ash content, generally in the range between 2 and 10%.

Surface Properties for Adsorption

The unique surface property of activated carbon, in contrast to the other major sorbents, is that its surface is nonpolar or only slightly polar as a result of the surface oxide groups and inorganic impurities. This unique property gives activated carbon the following advantages:

1. It is the only commercial sorbent used to perform separation and purification processes without requiring prior stringent moisture removal, such as is needed in air purification. (It is also useful in aqueous processes.)

2. Because of its large accessible internal surface, it adsorbs more nonpolar and weakly polar organic molecules than other sorbents do. For example, the amount of methane adsorbed by activated carbon at 1 atmosphere (atm) and room temperature is approximately twice that adsorbed by an equal weight of molecular sieve 5A (Figure 2.1).

3. The heat of adsorption, or bond strength, is generally lower on activated carbon than on other sorbents. Consequently, stripping of the adsorbed molecules is easier and results in lower energy requirements for regeneration of the sorbent.

It is not correct, however, to regard activated carbon as hydrophobic. The equilibrium sorption of water vapor on an anthracite-derived activated carbon is compared with that of other sorbents in Figure 2.2. The sorption of water vapor on activated carbon follows a Type V isotherm (according to the BDDT classification, reference 16) due to pore filling or capillary condensation in the micropores. (A detailed discussion of the special behavior of water in microporous sorbents is given in Chapter 5 of reference 5). Activated carbon is used, nonetheless, in processes dealing with humid gas mixtures and water solutions because the organic and nonpolar or weakly polar compounds adsorb more strongly, and hence preferentially, on its surface than water does.

Attempts have been made to modify the surface of activated carbon chemically for special applications. However, successful commercial operations

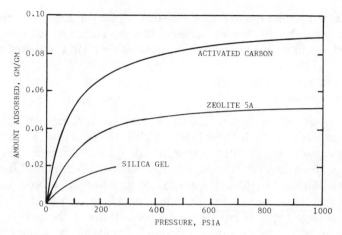

Figure 2.1 Equilibrium sorption of methane at 25°C on silica gel, zeolite 5A, and activated carbon. Sources: Saunders [13]; Yeh [89].

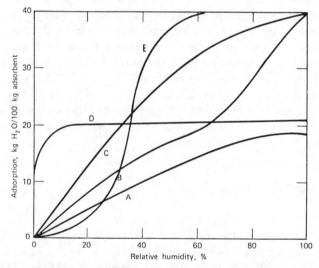

Figure 2.2 Equilibrium sorption of water vapor from atmospheric air at 25°C on (*A*) alumina (granular); (*B*) alumina (spherical); (*C*) silica gel; (*D*) 5A zeolite; (*E*) activated carbon. The vapor pressure at 100% R.H. is 23.6 Torr. Sources: (*D*) Breck [14]; (*E*) Stoeckli; Kraehenbuehl, and Morel [15].

have been limited to liquid-phase applications [17]. In gas-phase applications, it has been shown that by increasing the polarity of the surface, the amount of water vapor adsorbed at low relative pressures (below 4 Torr at 25°C; see Figure 2.2) can be drastically increased. For example, Walker and co-workers showed a hundred-fold increase in water vapor adsorption by activated carbon after surface oxidation by HNO_3 [18]. Exchange of the surface H-ions by cations (Li, Na, K, Ca) on the oxidized carbon further increased the moisture capacity at low vapor pressures to amounts comparable to that on zeolites. The ion-exchanged carbon was fully regenerated at 140°C, in contrast to temperatures over 350°C required for zeolite regeneration [18].

Pore Structure of Activated Carbon

Activated carbons are characterized by a large surface area between 300 and 2,500 m^2/g, as measured by the BET method, which is the largest among all sorbents. Commercial grades of activated carbon are designated for either gas phase or liquid phase, depending on its application. A majority of the pore volume is from pores near or larger than 30 Å in diameter for liquid-phase carbons, whereas the pores of gas-phase carbons are mostly in the range from 10 Å to 25 Å in diameter. The need for larger pores in liquid-phase carbons is due to the large size of many dissolved adsorbates, and the slower diffusion in liquid than in gas for molecules of the same size.

A polymodal pore-size distribution is generally found in activated carbon. The pore structure may be pictured as having many small pores branching off from larger ones, which are open through the entire particle. The larger pores are called *feeder* or *transport* pores; the smaller ones, which may be dead-end, are called *adsorption* pores. According to the International Union of Pure and Applied Chemistry (IUPAC) classification [19], the pores are subdivided by diameter (d) into *macropores* ($d > 500$ Å), *mesopores* (20 Å $< d < 500$ Å), and *micropores* ($d < 20$ Å). The cumulative pore-volume distribution of the fine pores for a typical gas-phase activated carbon is shown, along with four other sorbents, in Figure 2.3. The larger pores are mostly submicron in size, and their total volume amounts to a fraction of that found in the fine pores.

2.1.2   Molecular-Sieve Carbon

Since it is less hydrophilic than zeolites, molecular-sieve carbon (MSC) can be used more efficaciously in separation processes involving wet-gas streams. As a result of the foregoing and a number of other promising features [20], MSC has attracted considerable interest. Within the last decade, however, MSC has been commercially produced on the basis of proprietary processes. It has been largely used for the production of nitrogen from air.

The early research was focused on the preparation of MSC and its sieving properties. Three approaches were taken, in the following chronological order:

1. Carbonization of polymers such as poly(vinylidene chloride) (PVDC) [24–27]; Saran (90/10 mixture of vinylidene chloride and vinyl chloride); and cellulose, sugar, and coconut shell
2. Slightly carbonizing coals, especially anthracite [24, 28–30]
3. Coating of the pore mouths of the commercial activated carbon with a carbonized or coked thermosetting polymer [31]

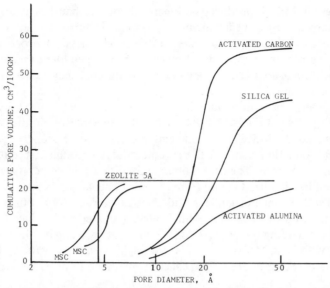

Figure 2.3   Pore-size distribution for activated carbon, silica gel, activated alumina, two molecular-sieve carbons, and zeolite 5A. Sources: For activated carbon and molecular-sieve carbons, Jüntgen [20]; for silica gel, Iler [21]; for activated alumina, MacZura, Goodboy, and Koenig [22]; for zeolite 5A, Breck [23].

Various interesting molecular sieving properties were found for these samples. For example, PVDC carbonized at 700°C was thought to have slit-shaped pores because it adsorbed flat molecules like benzene and naphthalene but not spherical ones like neopentane. Carbonized Saran had a pore entrance of about 6 Å and thus showed a striking separation between isobutane (with a kinetic diameter of 5.0 Å, which was admitted) and neopentane (with a kinetic diameter of 6.2 Å, which was rejected) [27]. With the carbonized PVDC, molecular-sieve effects with regard to neopentane were not seen until the carbonization temperature reached 1,200°C [24]. Anthracite heat-treated in hydrogen at 650°C adsorbed *n*-butane at an amount about five times larger than that of isobutane [29]. At carbon burnoff (by oxygen at 427°C) below 6.9%, anthracite admitted CO_2, less N_2 and almost no neopentane [30]. CO_2 is a linear molecule and is thought to have the smallest minimum diameter, 3.7 Å, among the three adsorbates [31]. For the coke coating technique, Walker et al. [31] prepared samples by forming carbon on activated carbons from furfuryl alcohol, polymerized with phosphoric acid. The pores were thought to be nearly 5 Å in diameter since the samples had a large capacity for *n*-butane (kinetic diameter = 4.3 Å), a small capacity for isobutane, and negligible capacity for neopentane. In a later work [32], carbon was deposited into the pores of a lignite char by cracking methane at 855°C. With nearly 3% carbon deposited, the samples showed a significant molecular sieving between CO_2 (admitted) and N_2 (hindered). The early development on MSC has been reviewed by Walker et al. [24] and by Spencer [33].

At present, MSC is produced commercially by Bergbau-Forschung GmbH in West Germany and by Takeda Chemical Company in Japan. Calgon Corporation has also started producing two types of MSC. The detailed procedures of the manufacturing processes, though not revealed in the open literature, are based on the carbonization of coal and coating of coke on the coal char, as described earlier. Carbonization of polymers such as PVDC is not used due to economic reasons.

The general procedure for the manufacture of MSC used by Bergbau-Forschung is shown in Figure 2.4 [34]. Two types of MSC are produced, although the type designated CMSN2 is the one with molecular-sieve properties and is used for nitrogen production from air. The raw material is a bituminous coal, ground to 90% passing 40 microns. The coal is first oxidized by air at temperatures below the ignition point in a fluidized bed to form *oxicoal*. Oxicoal is pelletized with a binder into granules 2–3 mm in diameter and then carbonized in a rotary drum. The uniform material formed at this point is further treated to produce two types of MSC: one by enlarging the pores (CMSH2) and one by partially blocking the pore mouths (CMSN2). CMSH2 is made by slight steam activation; CMSN2 is produced by cracking hydrocarbons such as methane in order to deposit a thin

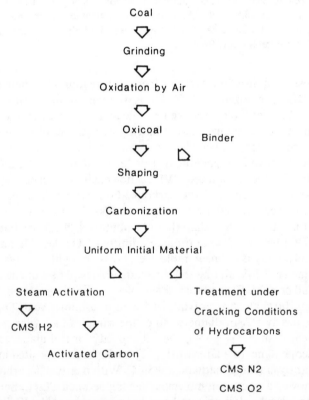

Figure 2.4   Procedures for the manufacture of molecular-sieve carbons. Source: Jüntgen, Knoblauch, and Harder [34]. Reprinted with permission.

layer of coke at the pore mouths. The former type is used for H_2 and He purification without predrying (which can also be done by activated carbon), whereas the latter is used for N_2 production from air. The sizes of the bottlenecks in CMSN2 are near 5 Å, as shown in Figure 2.3, which allow much faster penetration of oxygen than nitrogen into the pores. The pores of the two types of carbon are depicted in Figure 2.5. Using CMSN2 in pressure-swing adsorption, dry and CO_2-free nitrogen at 99.9% purity can be produced without the need to predry the air feed. The MSC manufactured by Takeda Chemical Company in Japan, designated MSC5A, has a micropore volume of 0.18 cm^3/g for pores with a nominal size of 5 Å, and a macropore volume of 0.38 cm^3/g for pores of 2.0 µm [35].

2.1.3 Activated Alumina

Activated alumina is one of the solids having the greatest affinity for water. An important industrial application for activated alumina continues to be the drying of gases and liquids, because of its hydrophilic property and large surface area. The term *activated alumina* refers to dehydrated or partially dehydrated alumina hydrates, both crystalline and amorphous, with high surface areas. It has been prepared by a variety of procedures [36].

Manufacturing Procedures and Surface Areas

Commercial production is exclusively by thermal dehydration or activation of aluminum trihydrate, $Al(OH)_3$ or gibbsite [22]. The oldest form, which is still widely used, is made from Bayer α-trihydrate, which is a by-product of the Bayer process for aqueous caustic extraction of alumina from bauxite. The trihydrate, in the form of gibbsite, is heated or activated in air to about 400°C to form crystalline γ/η-alumina with a minor amount of boehmite, and has a surface area of approximately 250 m^2/g. Alternatively, the trihydrate is heated very rapidly at

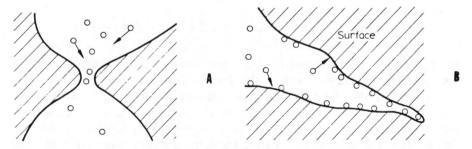

Figure 2.5 Molecular-sieve carbons made by Bergbau-Forschung: (A) Type CMSN2 with bottlenecks near 5 Å formed by coke deposition at the pore mouth; (B) Type CMSH2 formed by steam activation. Source: Jüntgen, Knoblauch, and Harder [34]. Reprinted with permission.

400–800°C to form an amorphous alumina with a higher surface area, 300–350 m^2/g. The major impurity in these products, besides water (typically 6%), is Na$_2$O at nearly 1%. The micropore volume is shown in Figure 2.3, but there is a considerable number of pores with sizes greater than 50 Å. A highly impure form of activated alumina is made by the thermal activation of bauxite, which contains alumina in the form of gibbsite.

Adsorption Applications

The major use of activated alumina as a sorbent is in drying. It also finds application in chromatography. A partial list of industrial gases that can be dried by activated alumina includes: Ar, He, H$_2$, low alkanes (mainly C$_1$–C$_3$) and hydrocarbons, Cl$_2$, HCl, SO$_2$, NH$_3$, and Freon fluorochloralkanes. It has been especially important in the drying of hydrocarbons produced by the thermal cracking of petroleum fractions. It, however, suffers a loss of adsorption capacity with prolonged use as a result of coking and contamination. This is a common problem for all sorbents. The moisture content can be reduced to below 1 ppm using activated alumina in suitably designed adsorbers.

2.1.4   Silica Gel

Silica gel is one of the synthetic amorphous silicas. It is a rigid, continuous network of spherical particles of colloidal silica. There are a number of preparation methods, which result in different pore structures [37].

Manufacturing Procedure

Commercially, silica gel is prepared by mixing a sodium silicate solution with a mineral acid such as sulfuric or hydrochloric acid. The reaction produces a concentrated dispersion of finely divided particles of hydrated SiO$_2$, known as silica hydrosol or silicic acid:

$$Na_2SiO_3 + 2HCl + nH_2O \rightarrow 2NaCl + SiO_2 \cdot nH_2O + H_2O$$

The hydrosol, on standing, polymerizes into a white jellylike precipitate, which is silica gel. The resulting gel is washed, dried and activated. Various silica gels with a wide range of properties such as surface area, pore volume and strength can be made by varying the silica concentration, temperature, pH and activation temperature [37]. Two typical types of silica gel are known as regular-density and low-density silica gels, although they have the same densities (true and bulk). The regular-density gel has a surface area of 750–850 m^2/g and an average pore diameter of 22–26 Å, whereas the respective values for the low-density gel are 300–350 m^2/g and 100–150 Å. The micropore volume of the regular-density gel is shown in Figure 2.3.

Silica gel, along with activated alumina, is a desirable sorbent for drying because of its high surface areas and unique surface properties. Silica gel contains 4–6% "water" by weight, which is the measured "loss on ignition." This so-called water is essentially a monolayer of hydroxyl groups bound to the silicon atoms on the surface, forming the silanol, Si–O–H, groups. The surface chemistry of silica gel has been extensively studied by infrared and near-infrared spectroscopic techniques, as it is a good infrared window and hence suitable for these techniques. Some of these studies on the interaction of water on silicas were reviewed by Klier and Zettlemoyer [38]. At a low surface coverage, evidence shows that the water molecule is bound to the silanol group "oxygen down":

$$\equiv Si\text{–}OH \cdots OH_2$$

At higher coverages, hydrogen bonding within clusters of water becomes predominant, with a bond strength or heat of adsorption approaching the liquefaction energy of water, 10.8 kcal/mole. Thus the heat of adsorption of water vapor on silica gel is approximately 11 kcal/mole — essentially the same as that on activated alumina. The relatively low heat of adsorption and, consequently, weakly held water are desirable for sorbent regeneration. Regeneration of silica gel is achieved by heating to approximately 150°C, as compared to 350°C for zeolites, where the heats of adsorption of water vapor are considerably higher [39]. A lower heat of adsorption is also desirable in separation processes because the temperature rise resulting from adsorption lowers the adsorption capacity, and a detrimental temperature drop occurs during desorption or regeneration. (Zeolites, however, have the advantage of higher water capacities at low relative pressures; hence they are used at high temperatures.)

The equilibrium water sorption capacity at 25°C for the regular-density gel is shown in Figure 2.2. The water capacity for the low-density gel is substantially lower.

2.1.5 Zeolites

Zeolites are crystalline aluminosilicates of alkali or alkali earth elements such as sodium, potassium, and calcium, represented by the stoichiometry:

$$M_{x/n}[(AlO_2)_x(SiO_2)_y]zH_2O$$

where x and y are integers with y/x equal to or greater than 1, n is the valence of cation M, and z is the number of water molecules in each *unit cell*. Unit cells are shown in Figure 2.6(b) and (c). The cations are necessary to balance the electrical charge of the aluminum atoms, each having a net charge of -1. The water molecules can be removed with ease upon heat and evacuation, leaving an almost

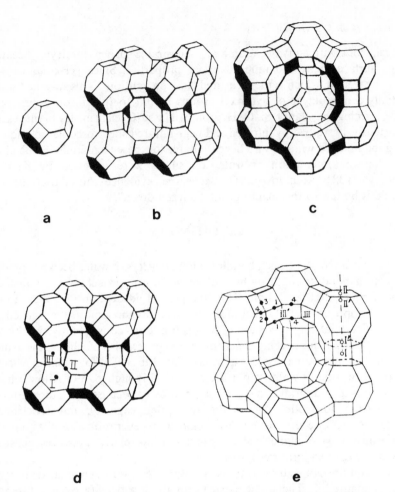

Figure 2.6 Line representations of zeolite structure: (a) sodalite cage, or truncated octahedron; (b) type A zeolite "unit cell"; (c) "unit cell" of types X and Y, or faujasite; (d) cation sites in type A (there are eight I, three II, and twelve III sites per unit cell); (e) cation sites in types X and Y (16 I, 32 I', 32 II, 32 II', 48 III, and 32 III' sites per unit cell).

unaltered aluminosilicate skeleton with a void fraction between 0.2 and 0.5. The skeleton has a regular structure of cages, which are usually interconnected by six windows in each cage. The cages can imbide or occlude large amounts of guest molecules in place of water. The size of the window apertures, which can be controlled by fixing the type and number of cations, ranges from 3 Å to 10 Å. The sorption may occur with great selectivity because of the size of the aperture (and to a lesser extent because of the surface property in the cages) — hence the name *molecule sieve*.

At least forty species of naturally occurring zeolites have been found. The principal ones are chabazite, $(Ca, Na_2)Al_2Si_4O_{12}(6\ H_2O)$; gmelinite, (Na_2, Ca)

$Al_2Si_4O_{12}(6 \ H_2O)$; mordenite, $(Ca, \ K_2, \ Na_2)$, $Al_2Si_{10}O_{24}(6.66 \ H_2O)$; levynite, $CaAl_2Si_3O_{10}(5 \ H_2O)$; and faujasite, $(Na_2, \ Ca, \ Mg, \ K_2)OAl_2Si_{4.5}O_{12}$ $(7 \ H_2O)$. More than 150 types of zeolites have been synthesized; they are designated by a letter or group of letters — Type A, Type X, Type Y, Type ZSM, and so on. The commercial production of synthetic zeolites started with the successful development of low-temperature (25–100°C) synthesis methods using very reactive materials such as freshly coprecipitated gels or amorphous solids [40, 41]. Two comprehensive monographs, by Barrer [42] and Breck [43], deal with all aspects of zeolites.

Structures and Cation Sites

The primary structural units of zeolites are the tetrahedra of silicon and aluminum, SiO_4 and AlO_4. These units are assembled into secondary polyhedral building units such as cubes, hexagonal prisms, octahedra, and truncated octahedra. The silicon and aluminum atoms, located at the corners of the polyhedra, are joined by a shared oxygen. The final zeolite structure consists of assemblages of the secondary units in a regular three-dimensional crystalline framework. The ratio Si/Al is commonly one to five. The aluminum atom can be removed and replaced by silicon in some zeolites, thereby reducing the number of cations; and the cations can also be exchanged. The inner atoms in the windows are oxygen. The size of the windows depends, then, on the number of oxygen atoms in the ring — four, five, six, eight, ten, or twelve. The aperture size, as well as the adsorptive properties, can be further modified by the number and type of exchanged cations. A description of the structures will be given only for the zeolites important in gas separation, Type A and Types X and Y.

Type A. The structural unit in Type A zeolite, as well as in Types X and Y, is the truncated octahedron, shown in Figure 2.6(a). This unit is also called sodalite cage, as sodalite is formed by directly fusing the four-member rings of the units. The four-member rings of the sodalite units can also be linked through four-member prisms, as shown in Figure 2.6(b), which is Type A zeolite. The unit cell of Type A zeolite, as shown in this figure, contains 24 tetrahedra, 12 AlO_4 and 12 SiO_4. When fully hydrated, 27 water molecules are contained in the central cage or cavity of the unit cell, and in the eight smaller sodalite cages. The free diameter in the central cavity is 11.4 Å, which is entered through six eight-member oxygen-ring apertures with a minimum diameter of 4.4 Å. There are twelve negative charges to be balanced by cations in each unit cell. The most probable locations for the cations are indicated in Figure 2.6(d). Type I is at the center of the six-member ring, thus at one of the eight corners of the cavity. Type II is at the eight-member aperture, directly obstructing the entrance. Type III is near the four-member ring inside the cavity. Type A zeolites are synthesized in the sodium form, with 12 sodium cations occupying all eight sites in I and three sites in II, plus one site in III. This is the commercial Type 4A zeolite, with an effective aperture size of 3.8 Å. The sodium form can be replaced by various other cations or by a hydrogen ion. The commercial Type 3A zeolite is formed by exchanging Na^+ with K^+, resulting in a smaller effective aperture size due to the larger K^+. The aperture size of the sodium form can also be increased by exchanging Na^+ with Ca^{+2} or Mg^{+2}, since $2 Na^+$ are replaced by one bivalent cation. The form of the exchanged Ca^{+2} or Mg^{+2} is Type 5A with rather unobstructed and larger apertures.

Types X and Y.   The skeletal structure of Types X and Y zeolites are the same as that of the naturally occurring faujasite. The sodalite units are linked through six-member prisms, as shown in the unit cell in Figure 2.6(c). Each unit cell contains 192 (Si, Al)O_4 tetrahedra. The number of aluminum ions per unit cell varies from 96 to 77 for Type X zeolite, and from 76 to 48 for Type Y zeolite. This framework has the largest central cavity volume of any known zeolite, amounting to about 50% void fraction in the dehydrated form. A unit cell, when fully hydrated, contains approximately 235 water molecules, mostly in the central cavity. The aperture is formed by the twelve-member oxygen rings with a free diameter of approximately 7.4 Å. Three major locations for the cations are indicated in Figure 2.6(e). The locations are: center of the six-member prism (I) and opposite to I in the sodalite cage (I'); similar to I and I' but further from the central cavity (II and II'); and at the twelve-member aperture (III and III'). The commercial 10X zeolite contains Ca^{+2} as the major cation, and Na^+ is the major cation for 13X zeolite. The distribution of Na^+, K^+, Ca^{+2}, other cations, and H_2O in X and Y zeolites among the sites have been discussed in detail by Barrer [44]. The BET surface area measured with N_2 for zeolites falls in the range between 500 and 800 m^2/g.

Manufacture Procedure and Applications for Gas Separation

Commercial zeolite pellets are made in the following sequence: synthesis, pelletizing, and calcination. Many alkali metal hydroxides and raw materials containing silica and alumina can be used in low-temperature synthesis. The steps involving the $Na_2O-Al_2O_3-SiO_2-H_2O$ system, which is used in synthesizing zeolites of types A, X, and Y, are as follows [43]:

$$NaOH(aq) + NaAl(OH)_4(aq) + Na_2SiO_3(aq)$$

$$\xrightarrow{T_1 \cong 25°C}$$

$$[Na_a(AlO_2)_b(SiO_2)_c \cdot NaOH \cdot H_2O]gel$$

$$\xrightarrow{T_2 \cong 25 - 175°C}$$

$$Na_x[(AlO_2)_x(SiO_2)_y] \cdot mH_2O + solution$$
$$(zeolite\ crystal)$$

The first step involves gel formation between sodium hydroxide, sodium silicate, and sodium aluminate in aqueous solution at room temperature. The gel is probably formed by the copolymerization of the silicate and aluminate species by a condensation-polymerization mechanism. Expressed in moles per mole of Al_2O_3

for $Na_2O/SiO_2/H_2O$, the compositions of the reactants are:

1. Type 4A zeolite, 2/2/35
2. Type X zeolite, 3.6/3/144
3. Type Y zeolite, 8/20/320

The gels are crystallized in a closed hydrothermal system at temperatures between 25°C and 175°C. Higher temperatures up to 300°C are used in some cases. The time for crystallization ranges from a few hours to several days.

The crystals formed are cubic single crystals with sizes ranging from 1 to 10 microns. For example, the commercial 5A zeolite contains cubic crystals with a mean size slightly greater than 2 microns. (The largest crystal synthesized is near 100 microns.) Types 3A and 5A zeolites are formed by ion exchange in the crystallization step by adding aqueous solutions of potassium and calcium salts, respectively. The crystals, after calcination at about 600°C, are further agglomerated and pelletized with or without a binder amounting to less than 20% of the pellets. The binder has a negligibly small capacity for the adsorption of gases. The characteristics of the major commercial zeolite sorbents in the pelletized forms are given in Table 2.2.

In Table 2.3, important industrial gases are grouped according to their molecular sizes, which are smaller than the apertures of the zeolite types, and hence can be sorbed. In principle, any mixture containing gases from different groups can be separated by molecular sieving. Many of the important zeolite-based gas separation processes currently practiced in industry, however, are not based on molecular-sieving action. They are based on the different strengths, or different equilibrium amounts adsorbed, of the constituents in the mixture. The important gas separation processes using zeolite sorbents are: air separation for the produc-

Table 2.2 Characteristics of Major Synthetic Zeolite Sorbents

Zeolite Type	Major Cation	Nominal Aperture Size, Å	Bulk Density,[a] lb/ft^3	Water[b] Capacity, wt%
3A (Linde)	K	3	40	20.0
3A (Davidson)	K	3	46	21.0
4A (Linde)	Na	4	41	22.0
4A (Davidson)	Na	4	44	23.0
5A (Linde)	Ca	5	45	21.5
5A (Davidson)	Ca	5	44	21.7
10X (Linde)	Ca	8	40	31.6
13X (Linde)	Na	10	38	28.5
13X (Davidson)	Na	10	43	29.5

[a] Based on 1/16 inch pellets or beads.
[b] The dried sorbent contains <1.5 weight-percent water in Linde products and 1.5 weight-percent in Davidson products.

Table 2.3 Molecules Admitted to Zeolites According to Molecular Dimensions and Zeolite Aperture Sizes

Molecular size increasing →

He, Ne, Ar, CO H₂, O₂, N₂, NH₃, H₂O	Kr, Xe CH₄ C₂H₆ CH₃OH CH₃CN CH₃NH₂ CH₃Cl CH₃Br CO₂ C₂H₂ CS₂	C₃H₈ n-C₄H₁₀ n-C₇H₁₆ n-C₁₄H₃₀ etc. C₂H₅Cl C₂H₅Br C₂H₅OH C₂H₅NH₂ CH₂Cl₂ CH₂Br₂ CHF₂Cl CHF₃ (CH₃)₂NH CH₃I B₂H₆	C₂F₆ CF₂Cl₂ᵃ CF₃Cl CHFCl₂	SF₆ iso-C₄H₁₀ iso-C₅H₁₂ iso-C₈H₁₈ etc. CHCl₃ CHBr₃ CHI₃ (CH₃)₂CHOH (CH₃)₂CHCl n-C₃F₈ n-C₄F₁₀ n-C₇F₁₆ B₅H₉	(CH₃)₃N (C₂H₅)₃N C(CH₃)₄ C(CH₃)₃Cl C(CH₃)₃Br C(CH₃)₃OH CCl₄ CBr₄ C₂F₂Cl₄	C₆H₆ C₆H₅CH₃ C₆H₄(CH₃)₂ Cyclopentane Cyclohexane Thiophene Furan Pyridine Dioxane B₁₀H₁₄	Naphthalene Quinoline, 6-decyl-1, 2, 3, 4-tetra- hydro- naphthalene, 2-butyl-1- hexyl indan C₆F₁₁CF₃	1, 3, 5-triethyl benzene 1, 2, 3, 4, 5, 6, 7, 8, 13, 14, 15, 16-decahydro- chrysene	(n-C₃F₉)₃N

Size limit for Ca- and Ba-mordenites and levynite about here (≈3·8 Å) — Type 5

Size limit for Na-mordenite and Linde sieve 4A about here (≈4·0 Å)

Size limit for Ca-rich chabazite, Linde sieve 5A, Ba-zeolite and gmelinite about here (≈4·9 Å) — Type 4

Size limit for Linde sieve 10X about here — Type 3

Size limit for Linde sieve 13X about here (≈10 Å) — Type 2

Type 1

Source: Barrer [42]. Reprinted with permission.

ᵃFreon-type molecules provide interesting borderline cases and can differentiate between certain of the zeolites grouped as type 3. Simple ketones and esters are also borderline cases.

tion of oxygen and nitrogen, hydrogen purification, recovery of *n*-paraffins from branched-chain and cyclic hydrocarbons, aromatic hydrocarbon separation, and drying. These and other uses have been discussed by Collins [88]. Except for the *n*-paraffin and aromatics separations, these processes employ the preferential adsorption of certain components. For example, nitrogen is preferentially adsorbed over oxygen (by approximately threefold in 5A zeolite) as a result of its quadruple moment, which forms a strong bond with the polar surface.

2.1.6 Selection of Sorbent

The selection of a proper sorbent for a given separation is a complex problem. The predominant scientific basis for sorbent selection is the equilibrium isotherm. The equilibrium isotherms of all constituents in the gas mixture, in the pressure and temperature range of operation, must be considered. As a first and possibly oversimplified approximation, the pure-gas isotherms may be considered additive to yield the adsorption from a mixture. The theories given in Chapter 3 should be used to provide better estimates for equilibrium adsorption. Based on the isotherms, the following factors that are important to the design of the separation process can be estimated:

1. Capacity of the sorbent, in the operating temperature and pressure range.
2. The method of sorbent regeneration — for example, thermal or pressure swing — and the magnitude of the required swing.
3. The length of the unusable (or unused) bed (LUB).
4. The product purities.

The LUB is approximately one-half of the span of the concentration wavefront, or the mass transfer zone. The LUB is primarily determined by the equilibrium isotherm, as will be discussed in Chapter 5. A sharp concentration front, or a short LUB, is desired because it results in a high sorbent productivity as well as a high product purity.

Consideration should also be given to other factors. As mentioned, activated carbon is the only commercial sorbent used for wet gas stream processing. (A predryer is required for other sorbents.) Sorbent deactivation, primarily by coke deposition, is an important consideration in the processing of hydrocarbon-containing gases. Coke is formed catalytically, and zeolites are excellent catalysts for these reactions. Pore-size distribution can play a role in the LUB, but not as important a role as that of the equilibrium isotherm, since the commercial sorbent pellets are designed to minimize the pore-diffusion resistance. Kinetic separation — that is, separation based on the difference between pore diffusivities of two gases — has found only one application: the production of nitrogen from air by molecular-sieve carbon. Dehydration of cracked gases with 3A zeolite and the separation of normal and iso-paraffins with 5A zeolite are based on selective molecular exclusion. All other commercial processes are based on the equilibrium isotherms. Temperature for activation and regeneration of the sorbent should also be considered. A high temperature of nearly 300°C is required for zeolites, whereas activated carbon usually requires the lowest temperature for regeneration.

The total void space in the bed, which varies with the sorbents, is also an important factor. A low void space is desired for high product recoveries since the gas mixture remaining in the void space in the saturated bed is usually not recovered as a useful product. Silica gel and activated alumina have the lowest void fractions, usually slightly below 70%; activated carbon has the highest void fraction, at nearly 80%.

2.2   EQUILIBRIUM ADSORPTION OF SINGLE GASES

For a given gas-solid pair, the amount adsorbed at equilibrium is described phenomenologically by:

$$v = f(P, T) \tag{2.3}$$

where v may be expressed in cc STP/g. At a fixed temperature, v is only a function of P, which is called an *adsorption isotherm*.

Based on the nature of the bonding between the adsorbate molecule and the solid surface, adsorption can be categorized as either physical adsorption or chemical adsorption, or *chemisorption*. Chemisorption involves electron transfer and is essentially a two-dimensional chemical reaction, whereas the bonds formed in physical adsorption are held by van der Waals and coulombic (or electrostatic) forces. The latter are much weaker, generally below 10–15 kcal/mole, and hence the process is easily reversed. The coulombic forces, as will be discussed in the next section, originate in the ionic atoms and polar groups on the surface. It should be noted that the surfaces of all commercial sorbents possess some degree of polarity. The oxygen-containing groups of activated carbon, for example, can only be removed *in vacuo* at temperatures near 900°C [45]. Furthermore, the π electrons on the graphite plane also contribute an electric field (see discussion in section 2.2.2).

Only physical adsorption is encountered in gas separation processes, on which our discussion will be focused. The capacity of a sorbent depends on two complementary factors: surface area and porosity. The driving force for all adsorptive gas separation processes lies in the departure from equilibrium (eq. 2.3). Information on this relationship, or on the isotherm, is therefore a prerequisite for design of the process.

2.2.1   Three Approaches for Isotherm Models

The great majority of the isotherms observed to-date can be classified into five types, as shown in Figure 2.7. Types I and II are the most frequently encountered in separation processes. Many theories and models have been developed to interpret

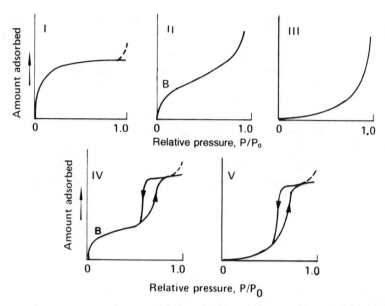

Figure 2.7 The five types of adsorption isotherms, according to the BDDT classification. P_0 is the saturation vapor pressure. Source: Bond [11]. Reprinted with permission.

these different types of isotherms. The resulting isotherm equations can then be used to predict the amounts adsorbed based on a limited number of experiments. A detailed discussion of the various models used to interpret each type of the isotherms has been given by Gregg and Sing [5].

The numerous isotherm models are based on three different approaches:

1. *The Langmuir approach:* The approach, given by Langmuir in 1918 [46], is originally a kinetic one, assuming the adsorption system is in dynamic equilibrium, where the rate of evaporation is equal to that of condensation. The Langmuir isotherm remains the most useful for data correlation in separation processes.

2. *The Gibbs approach:* This approach employs the Gibbs adsorption isotherm:

$$-Ad\pi + nd\mu = 0 \qquad (2.4)$$

and assumes a two-dimensional equation of state of the adsorbed film, relating $\pi - A - T$, where π is the spreading pressure, A is surface area, n is number of moles, and μ is the chemical potential. An integration of the Gibbs equation results in the desired isotherm. There are as many isotherms as the number of assumed equations of state, ranging from the ideal gas law to virial equations, which are truncated at a certain point.

3. *The potential theory:* As first formalized by Polanyi in about 1914 [47],

the adsorption system is viewed as a gradual concentration of gas molecules toward the solid surface due to a potential field, resembling the atmosphere of a planet. There is a relationship between the potential field, ε, and the volume above the surface, W, for a given gas-solid system. The relationship, empirically obtained for the system, is called the *characteristic curve*, which is assumed to be independent of temperature. In other words, the forces operative in adsorption are assumed to be temperature-independent dispersion forces. This is the reason that the potential theory is mostly applied to activated-carbon adsorption. The sorption potential is related to the work of isothermally compressing the gas from the gas pressure (P) to the saturation pressure (P_0) for liquefaction. Also, the volume (W) is converted to the amount adsorbed by assuming the adsorbed phase is a liquid. Thus an isotherm is obtained.

2.2.2   Physical Adsorption Forces

The forces holding the adsorbate molecule to the atoms on the surface have been extensively studied. The nature of the different forces is understood; however, quantitative calculations a priori, are not yet possible. The forces generally include dispersive and electrostatic or coulombic types, the latter exists only on polar surfaces.

   The dispersive forces exist between any two atoms or molecules, one being in the adsorbate and the other being on the surface of the adsorbent in the case of adsorption. These forces were first characterized by London [48]. They arise from the rapid fluctuation of electron density in each atom, which induces an electrical moment in the neighbor and thus creates an attraction between them. The name *dispersion* derives from its close relation with optical dispersion. The potential energy, ε, between two atoms separated by a distance, r, was first calculated by London and approximated by [49]:

$$\varepsilon(r) = -Cr^{-6} \tag{2.5}$$

where C is one of the dispersion constants associated with the dipole-dipole interactions. The negative sign implies attraction. A theoretical expression was derived for the short-range repulsive potential, an exponential function of r, exp $(-kr)$, which can be approximated by:

$$\varepsilon(r) = Br^{-12} \tag{2.6}$$

The total potential energy is the sum:

$$\varepsilon(r) = -Cr^{-6} + Br^{-12} \tag{2.7}$$

which is the familiar Lennard-Jones (6–12) potential. The curve is depicted in Figure 2.8. B is an empirical constant, whereas C can be theoretically calculated.

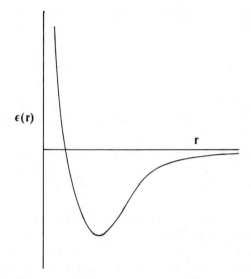

$\epsilon(r)$

Figure 2.8 The potential energy between two atoms separated by distance r. For a gas molecule near a solid surface, the potential is obtained by summing all interacting pairs of atoms, and yields the same shaped curve.

One of the best known relations for calculating C is that of Kirkwood and Müller [49, 50]:

$$C = \frac{6mc^2 \alpha_A \alpha_B}{(\alpha_A/\chi_A) + (\alpha_B/\chi_B)} \tag{2.8}$$

where c is the speed of light, α_A and α_B are polarizabilities, and χ_A and χ_B are the magnetic susceptibilities of atoms A and B. Other frequently used relations [51] include those by London [48], and Slater and Kirkwood [52].

For a gas molecule and a solid surface that are separated by distance z and measured between the center of the molecule and the plane going through the centers of the surface atoms, the potential function, $\phi(z)$, can be calculated by summing all interacting pairs of atoms:

$$\phi(z) = \phi_D + \phi_R = -\sum_i \left(C_{ij} \sum_j r_{ij}^{-6} \right) + \sum_i \left(B_{ij} \sum_j r_{ij}^{-12} \right) \tag{2.9}$$

For a polar surface, which induces a dipole in the adsorbate molecule, the interaction energy is [49]:

$$\phi_P = -\tfrac{1}{2}\alpha^2 F \tag{2.10}$$

where F is the field strength at the center of the adsorbate. If the adsorbate molecule has a permanent dipole, μ, an additional energy is due to the dipole-field interaction:

$$\phi_{F\mu} = -F\mu \cos \theta \tag{2.11}$$

where θ is the angle between the field and the axis of the dipole. For adsorbate molecules possessing a quadrupole moment, Q, another contribution, $\phi_{\dot{F}Q}$, results from the interaction with the field gradient, $\dot{F}$.

The total potential between the adsorbate molecule and the surface is:

$$\phi(z) = \phi_D + \phi_R + \phi_P + \phi_F + \phi_{\dot{F}Q} \tag{2.12}$$

At a fixed location above the surface, the $\phi(z)$ curve is qualitatively the same as Figure 2.8. The equilibrium distance from the surface at which the adsorbate will rest is at the curve minimum. Calculations have also been done on the potential energy as a function of the location on the xy plane, in addition to z [50]. These energy contour maps provide a good insight into the mobility and the possible mobility paths of the adsorbate on the surface by comparing the mean thermal energy, kT, with the energy barriers.

In considering the forces in adsorption, it is clear that the bond strength should be higher on a more polar surface for a given adsorbate molecule, and that for the same surface the bond strength is higher for gas molecules with permanent dipoles and quadrupoles. Comparing the commercial sorbents, activated carbon possesses the least polarity.

2.2.3   Isotherms Based on the Langmuir Approach

Langmuir Isotherm: Monolayer Adsorption on
Homogeneous Surfaces

The simplest and still the most useful isotherm, for both physical and chemical adsorption, is the Langmuir isotherm. Although Langmuir originally considered seven cases, including multilayer adsorption, adsorption on heterogeneous surfaces, and adsorption with dissociation [46], the Langmuir isotherm in its usual form is based on the following implicit assumptions:

1.   The adsorbed molecule or atom is held at definite, localized sites.
2.   Each site can accommodate one and only one molecule or atom.
3.   The energy of adsorption is a constant over all sites, and there is no interaction (for example, via van der Waals attraction) between neighboring adsorbates.

The isotherm equation that is derived is based on the concept of dynamic equilibrium between the rates of condensation (adsorption) and evaporation (desorption). Since the sites already occupied are no longer available for adsorption, the rate of adsorption per unit surface area is equal to $\alpha v(1 - \theta)$, where v is the collision frequency of gas molecules striking the surface, α is the sticking probability or accommodation coefficient for adsorption, and θ is the fractional coverage. As given by the kinetic theory of gases:

$$v = \frac{P}{(2\pi m k T)^{1/2}} \tag{2.13}$$

The rate of desorption per unit surface area (for physically adsorbed species) is:

$$\beta \theta e^{-E_d/RT} = \beta \theta e^{-Q/RT} \tag{2.14}$$

where β is the rate constant for desorption, and E_d is the activation energy for desorption which equals the heat of adsorption $(-\Delta H)$ for physically adsorbed species, Q.

At dynamic equilibrium,

$$\theta \left(= \frac{v}{v_m} \right) = \frac{BP}{1 + BP} \tag{2.15}$$

$$B = \frac{\alpha}{\beta (2\pi m k T)^{1/2}} e^{Q/RT} \tag{2.15a}$$

Equation 2.15 is the Langmuir isotherm and B is the Langmuir adsorption constant, or Langmuir constant. (In some literature, $1/B$ is called the Langmuir constant.) θ is the fraction of monolayer coverage. The Langmuir isotherm is useful for practical purposes because it fits Type I and the initial portion of Type II isotherms, Figure 2.7, which are frequently encountered. The isotherm reduces to a linear form, $\theta = BP$, or Henry's law form, for small P; and θ approaches unity for large P. (B is also called *Henry's law constant*, for the foregoing reason.) The temperature dependence of B is $e^{Q/RT} T^{-1/2}$, and its value decreases rapidly with increasing temperature because Q is always positive, or physical adsorption is always exothermic. The latter is true because the free energy (G) must decrease for the adsorption process to occur, and $\Delta G = \Delta H - T\Delta S$. The entropy change, ΔS, is negative because of the decrease in the number of degrees of freedom; hence ΔH must be negative.

The Langmuir isotherm can also be derived from statistical thermodynamics and by using Gibbs's isotherm. As pointed out by Fowler [53, 54], the assumptions implicitly made by Langmuir are not absolutely necessary. By equating the chemical potentials of the gas molecule and the adsorbed molecules (N molecules on S sites), where the chemical potentials are expressed in terms of the partition functions of the molecules and the sites, Fowler derives the same isotherm equation. The statistical thermodynamic derivation is based only on the whole set of states, gas-phase and adsorbed, accessible to the molecule. The assumptions are more general and also give an explicit definition of the constant B:

$$B = \frac{h^3}{(2\pi m)^{3/2}(kT)^{5/2}} \frac{f_a(T)}{f_g(T)} e^{Q/RT} \tag{2.16}$$

where $f_a(T)$ and $f_g(T)$ are the internal (mainly rotation and vibration) partition functions for a molecule in the adsorbed phase and the gas phase, respectively.

Langmuir Isotherm with Lateral Interactions

By using more realistic assumptions, many modifications have been made to the Langmuir isotherm. A simple modification is made by considering a lateral adsorbate-adsorbate interaction [54]. Such an interaction is largely due to the attractive van der Waals forces and therefore increases physical adsorption. (The interaction is usually repulsive for chemisorbed species.) A simple modification is made by assuming that a constant interaction energy is operative, and the resulting Langmuir constant is [55]:

$$B = \frac{\alpha}{\beta(2\pi mkT)^{1/2}} e^{(Q+zE)/RT} \tag{2.17}$$

where z = the number of occupied sites adjacent to an adsorbate
$\quad\quad E$ = the constant pair interaction energy

For the adsorption of argon on a graphitized carbon at 77.8K and 90.1K and at the θ range of 0.6 to 0.9, the value of zE is 380 cal/mole, compared to the Q value of 2,650 cal/mole [55]. To cover a wider range of θ, zE may be replaced by $z\theta\omega$, where ω is the constant lateral interaction energy.

Langmuir Isotherm on Nonuniform Surfaces: Freundlich Isotherm

In Langmuir's original paper [46], adsorption on "amorphous" surfaces is considered and the amount adsorbed is summed over all types of sites, each having its corresponding value of B, meaning corresponding bond energy or heat of adsorption. Zeldowitsch, assuming an exponentially decaying function of site density with respect to Q, obtained the classical empirical isotherm:

$$v = kP^{1/n} \tag{2.18}$$

which is known as the *Freundlich isotherm*.

The Langmuir equation for the sites with energy of adsorption between Q and $Q + dQ$ is:

$$\theta(Q) = \frac{bP \exp(Q/RT)}{1 + bP \exp(Q/RT)} \tag{2.19}$$

where b is assumed constant although it is weakly dependent on temperature. The number of sites with energy of adsorption between Q and $Q + dQ$ is $N(Q)dQ$, where $N(Q)$ is the distribution function. The overall fraction of sites covered is:

$$\theta = \frac{\int_0^\infty \theta(Q)N(Q)dQ}{\int_0^\infty N(Q)dQ} \tag{2.20}$$

By assuming:

$$N(Q) = ae^{-Q/Q_0} \tag{2.21}$$

where a and Q_0 are constants, Zeldowitsch derived the approximate solution, which is identical with equation 2.18. The solution becomes exact for small θ values.

Langmuir Isotherm on Nonuniform Surfaces: Langmuir-Freundlich Equation

Langmuir has also considered the dissociative adsorption for the case of each molecule occupying two sites [46]. In this case two sites are needed for both adsorption and desorption, and hence the rates are proportional to $(1 - \theta)^2$ and θ^2 for adsorption and desorption, respectively. The resulting isotherm is:

$$\theta = \frac{(BP)^{1/2}}{1 + (BP)^{1/2}} \tag{2.22}$$

When the adsorbate occupies n sites, it is straightforward to show [57, 58]:

$$\theta = \frac{(BP)^{1/n}}{1 + (BP)^{1/n}} \tag{2.23}$$

The same form of isotherm equation has also been derived by Miyamoto using a similar approach [59]. In this theory it is assumed that only the molecules in the gas phase that strike the solid surface with velocities greater than a limiting value u_0, and whose components are perpendicular to the surface, can be adsorbed. Also, the only molecules that can desorb are those whose energies (of vibration perpendicular to the surface) are greater than a limiting value, ε_0. The assumption is again made that the rate of adsorption is proportional to $(1 - \theta)^{1/n}$ and that of desorption to $\theta^{1/n}$. The value of n is greater than unity under normal conditions for physical adsorption.

In the foregoing derivations, the surface is assumed to be energetically uniform. This need not be true because the same treatment for the Freundlich isotherm can also be made for equation 2.23. That is, given the isotherm, equation 2.23, a distribution function for the energy of adsorption, $N(Q)$, can be found. This problem was first solved by Sips [60].

According to the Freundlich isotherm, the amount adsorbed will increase indefinitely with pressure. The following isotherm is consequently proposed [60], which is the same as equation 2.23:

$$\theta = \frac{BP^{1/n}}{1 + BP^{1/n}} \tag{2.24}$$

Recasting the Langmuir isotherm, and applying it to the sites with energy of adsorption in the range Q and $Q + dQ$, one obtains:

$$\theta(Q)dQ = \frac{N(Q)dQ}{1 + \left(\dfrac{a}{P}\right)\exp(-Q/RT)} \tag{2.25}$$

and the overall isotherm:

$$\theta = \int_{-\infty}^{\infty} \frac{N(Q)dQ}{1 + \left(\dfrac{a}{P}\right)\exp(-Q/RT)} \tag{2.26}$$

where a is again assumed constant and is the reciprocal of b as defined in equation 2.19. The $N(Q)$ function, necessary for equation 2.26 to reduce to equation 2.24, has been shown to be unique and is:

$$N(Q) = \frac{1}{nRT} \frac{\exp[(Q_m - Q)/nRT] \sin \dfrac{\pi}{n}}{1 + 2\left(\cos \dfrac{\pi}{n}\right)\exp[(Q_m - Q)/nRT] + \exp[2(Q_m - Q)/nRT]} \tag{2.27}$$

where Q_m is the maximum energy:

$$Q_m = nRT \ln(Ba^{1/n}) \tag{2.28}$$

The $N(Q)$ function given by equation 2.27 is extremely close to a Gaussian distribution [60]. The lower limit of the integration in equation 2.26 was later changed from $-\infty$ to 0; restrictions were found on the possible forms of the isotherm [61].

Both Langmuir and Freundlich isotherms contain two parameters. The hybrid isotherm (eq. 2.24) is a three-parameter one, since $v = \theta v_m$ and v_m is an additional constant. Consequently, equation 2.24 is superior for data correlation covering wide ranges of pressures and temperatures when both Langmuir and Freundlich isotherms fail. A good example is the adsorption of hydrocarbons such as ethane, ethylene, propane, and propylene on activated carbon at 100°–400°F, where n was found to be in the range from 1/2 to 2/3 [62].

Multilayer Adsorption: BET Isotherm

At temperatures below the critical temperature of the gas, the Type II isotherm predominates over Type I (Figure 2.7). This indicates that multilayer buildup occurs well before a complete monolayer is formed. To account for this fact, a two-parameter isotherm was developed by Brunauer, Emmett, and Teller [63], which was basically an extension of the Langmuir model.

In the BET model, each site can accommodate 0 to i (i approaches infinity) adsorbate molecules, which are not mobile on the surface. On the first layer, the rate of condensation on the bare sites is equal to the rate of evaporation from the sites that are covered by only one adsorbate molecule. Likewise, the equilibrium is established for all layers, and i equations result. The important assumption is then made that the heat of adsorption beyond the first layer is constant and equals the heat of liquefaction. In addition, the ratio of the adsorption and desorption constants, α/β (in eq. 2.14), is also assumed constant for layers beyond the first one. By summing over all layers, the BET equation is obtained:

$$\frac{P}{v(P_0 - P)} = \frac{1}{v_m c} + \frac{c-1}{v_m c}\left(\frac{P}{P_0}\right) \tag{2.29}$$

where the value of c is given by:

$$c = \frac{\alpha_1 \beta_2}{\alpha_2 \beta_1} \exp\left(\frac{Q_1 - Q_L}{RT}\right) \cong \exp\left(\frac{Q_1 - Q_L}{RT}\right) \tag{2.30}$$

where the subscripts indicate the number of layers from the surface, and L denotes liquefaction. The detailed derivation of the BET equation is given in most texts dealing with adsorption and surfaces. The values of c and v_m are experimentally determined. The constant c is usually large and is always greater than unity. The BET equation still prevails as the major tool for measuring the surface area. Using experimental data in the range of $P/P_0 = 0.05$ to 0.3, the left-hand side of equation 2.29 is plotted against the relative pressure, and the slope and intercept yield the values of v_m and c. Knowing the molecular area (e.g., 16.2 Å^2/molecule for nitrogen at 77K), the value of the surface area can be calculated directly from v_m.

The BET equation is seldom used for correlating adsorption data. One reason lies in the complexity involved in its mathematical form. Another reason is that the equation is not applicable to adsorption under supercritical conditions (i.e., at temperatures above the critical temperature). Under these conditions, the model reverts to the Langmuir model.

2.2.4 Isotherms Based on the Gibbs Approach

If the adsorbate is treated as a two-dimensional microscopic entity, the fundamental equations in classical thermodynamics are applicable. One of the four fundamental equations applied to the surface entity is [64]:

$$dG = -SdT + \mu dn + Ad\pi \qquad (2.31a)$$

or the Gibbs-Duhem equation:

$$SdT - Ad\pi + nd\mu = 0 \qquad (2.31b)$$

where A is surface area, π is spreading pressure, and n is the number of moles of adsorbate per unit mass of sorbent. At constant temperature, equation 2.31b yields the Gibbs adsorption isotherm:

$$-Ad\pi + nd\mu = 0 \qquad (T = \text{constant}) \qquad (2.31c)$$

The chemical potential of the adsorbed phase is equal to that of the gas phase at equilibrium. Assuming ideal gas behavior, μ is related to pressure, and:

$$\left(\frac{d\pi}{d \ln P} \right)_T = \frac{n}{A} RT \qquad (2.32)$$

The preceding equation has two underlying uses. It can transform by integration any adsorption isotherm into the corresponding two-dimensional equation of state, or the corresponding isotherm can be obtained from a proposed equation of state. Some of the isotherms thus derived will be discussed.

Equation 2.32 has been very useful in studying surface films on liquids [4], where π and other quantities can be measured. (Here π is the reduction of surface tension by the "adsorbed" film.) For adsorption on solid surfaces, if it is assumed that the adsorbed species can be treated as a two-dimensional film governed by a two-dimensional equation of state, relating $\pi - A - T$, equation 2.32 can be integrated with this equation of state to yield an adsorption isotherm. Since π is not a measurable quantity for an adsorbate on a solid surface, the equation of state is assumed, thus providing a large source of isotherms. This approach to obtaining the isotherm was first taken by Harkins and Jura [65]. This approach has also proved fruitful in recent developments of models for adsorption from mixed gases, as will be discussed in Chapter 3.

Analogous to the monomolecular films on liquids, Harkins and Jura assumed the following equation for the adsorbed phase:

$$\pi = b - a\sigma \qquad (2.33)$$

where σ is the area occupied by each adsorbate molecule and a and b are constants. Upon integration, and relating σ to v, the following isotherm is obtained:

$$\ln(P/P_0) = B - C/v^2 \qquad (2.34)$$

where B is a constant and C is related to A and T.

The Harkin-Jura isotherm is only one of a large number of isotherms developed by making use of the Gibbs equation and an assumed equation of state. The simplest is the ideal gas law:

$$\pi\sigma = RT \tag{2.35}$$

which leads to the Henry's law isotherm:

$$v = kP \tag{2.36}$$

which applies to dilute or low-pressure systems. The introduction of a co-volume in the ideal gas law:

$$\pi(\sigma - b) = RT \tag{2.37}$$

results in the isotherm:

$$P = k\frac{\theta}{1-\theta}\exp\frac{\theta}{1-\theta} \tag{2.38}$$

Equations of state (which contain both a co-volume and an attractive force term such as the van der Waals equation) and virial-type equations have also been used. The resulting isotherms are summarized in Table 2.4 [66].

The Gibbs approach has recently been used by Suwanayuen and Danner [67] to develop an isotherm which can readily be used for more than one adsorbate. In this approach the surface is considered to be composed of a *vacancy* (species *v*) and an adsorbed species (species 1), and the bulk "vacancy" solution is

Table 2.4 Isotherms Derived from Two-Dimensional Equations of State and the Gibbs Equation

Equation of State	Corresponding Isotherm
Ideal gas type	
$\pi\sigma = RT$	$\ln kP = \ln\theta$
$\pi(\sigma - \sigma^0) = RT$	$\ln kP = \theta/(1-\theta) + \ln[\theta/(1-\theta)]$
van der Waals type	
$(\pi + a/\sigma^2)(\sigma - \sigma^0) = RT$	$\ln kP = \theta/(1-\theta) + \ln[\theta/(1-\theta)] - c\theta$
$(\pi + a/\sigma^3)(\sigma - \sigma^0) = RT$	$\ln kP = \theta/(1-\theta) + \ln[\theta/(1-\theta)] - c\theta^2$
$(\pi + a/\sigma^3)(\sigma - \sigma^0/\sigma) = RT$	$\ln kP = 1/(1-\theta) + 1/2\ln[\theta/(1-\theta)] - c\theta, (c = 2a/\sigma^0 RT)$
Virial type	
$\pi\sigma = RT + \alpha\pi - \beta\pi^2$	$\ln kP = (\phi^2/2\omega) + (1/2\omega)(\phi + 1)[(\phi - 1)^2 + 2\omega]^{1/2}$ $-\ln\{(\phi - 1) + [(\phi - 1)^2 + 2\omega]^{1/2}\}, (\phi = 1/\theta, \omega = 2\beta RT/\alpha^2)$

Source: Adamson [66]. Reprinted with permission.

extremely dilute. The chemical potential for species, v, in the adsorbed phase is:

$$\mu = \mu_0 + RT \ln \gamma X + \pi \sigma \qquad (2.39)$$

where γ = the activity coefficient
X = the mole fraction
σ = the partial molar area

For the chemical potential of the same species in the gas phase, the last two terms in equation 2.39 vanish. Equating the chemical potentials in the two phases for species v, the following equation of state results:

$$\pi = -\frac{RT}{\sigma_v} \ln \gamma_v X_v \qquad (2.40)$$

They then use the Wilson equation to express the activity coefficient of the vacancy in the surface phase:

$$\ln \gamma_v = -\ln(X_v + \Lambda_{v1} X_1) - X_1 \left[\frac{\Lambda_{1v}}{X_1 + \Lambda_{1v} X_v} - \frac{\Lambda_{v1}}{X_v + \Lambda_{v1} X_1} \right] \qquad (2.41)$$

Using equations 2.40 and 2.41, equation 2.32 is integrated to give:

$$P = \left[\frac{n^\infty}{b_1} \frac{\theta}{1-\theta} \right] \left[\Lambda_{1v} \frac{1-(1-\Lambda_{v1})\theta}{\Lambda_{1v} + (1-\Lambda_{1v})\theta} \right]$$

$$\exp \left[-\frac{\Lambda_{v1}(1-\Lambda_{v1})\theta}{1-(1-\Lambda_{v1})\theta} - \frac{(1-\Lambda_{1v})\theta}{\Lambda_{1v} + (1-\Lambda_{1v})\theta} \right] \qquad (2.42)$$

where θ is the fractional coverage with respect to the limiting amount adsorbed, n^∞. The integration constant b_1 is defined such that agreement with Henry's law is assured at low pressures:

$$b_1 = \lim_{P \to 0} \left(\frac{n}{P} \right) \qquad (2.42a)$$

The pairwise interaction constants, Λ_{1v} and Λ_{v1}, must be empirically determined. Thus equation 2.42 contains four parameters. Using a least-square fitting scheme, values of these four parameters have been determined for O_2, N_2, CO, CO_2, and various hydrocarbon gases on activated carbon and zeolites 10X and 13X [67].

The model based on the Wilson activity coefficients has been improved and is now based on the Flory-Huggins activity coefficients [68], after realizing that the Wilson interaction parameters are highly correlated by $\Lambda_{1v}\Lambda_{v1} \cong 1$. Thus one of the parameters can be eliminated. By expressing the excess Gibbs free energy (g) equation derived by Flory and Huggins for polymer solutions in a two-dimensional form, one can apply it to the vacancy solution in the adsorbed phase. The activity coefficient of the vacancy species on the surface is (noting that $ng = RT \Sigma n_i \ln \gamma_i$):

$$\ln \gamma_v = \frac{\alpha_{1v}\theta}{1 + \alpha_{1v}\theta} - \ln(1 + \alpha_{1v}\theta) \tag{2.43a}$$

where

$$\alpha_{1v} = (a_1/a_v) - 1$$

Here a_1 and a_v are the molar areas of the adsorbed species.

Using equation 2.43a instead of equation 2.41, the adsorption isotherm is:

$$P = \left(\frac{n^\infty}{b_1} \frac{\theta}{1-\theta}\right) \exp\left(\frac{\alpha_{1v}^2\theta}{1 + \alpha_{1v}\theta}\right) \tag{2.43b}$$

Here α_{1v} is temperature dependent, which is empirically determined. Equation 2.43b has one less parameter than equation 2.42. It is also superior when extended to mixed-gas adsorption.

2.2.5 The Potential Theory

The isotherms derived from the potential theory have found utility in interpreting adsorption by capillary condensation, or pore filling. Thus they are especially useful for adsorption on microporous materials such as activated carbon. However, since the characteristic curve, to be described later, is assumed to be independent of temperature, which applies to adsorption by the temperature-independent dispersion forces, the resulting isotherms are applicable only to relatively nonpolar surfaces. The theory, nonetheless, is general in that it encompasses multilayer adsorption on energetically nonuniform surfaces.

Polanyi-Dubinin Isotherms

Polanyi [69] in 1914 first formalized the concept that the surface force field can be represented by equipotential contours above the surface, and that the space between each set of equipotential surfaces corresponds to a definite adsorbed volume (Figure 2.9). Consequently, the cumulated volume of the adsorbed space, W, is a function of the potential, ε:

$$W = f(\varepsilon) \tag{2.44}$$

This function is unspecified but is characteristic of the particular gas-solid system and hence is referred to as the *characteristic curve*. Furthermore, the characteristic curve is independent of temperature since the adsorption potential expresses the

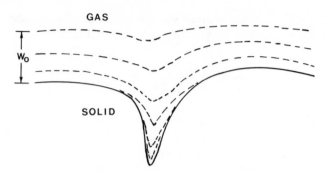

Figure 2.9   Schematic representation of adsorption according to the Polanyi potential theory.

work of temperature-independent dispersion forces. This proposition has been substantiated by voluminous experimental data involving the adsorption of gases and vapors on carbonaceous sorbents.

The potential theory is a uniquely powerful one in that once the characteristic curve is established at one temperature, it is possible to predict the adsorption at all temperatures for the same gas-solid system. (Extrapolation beyond the critical temperature will be discussed later in this section.)

Equation 2.44 is essentially an adsorption isotherm, since W represents the amount adsorbed and ε can be related to the pressure. The potential is equal to the work required to remove the molecule from its location in the adsorbed space to the gas phase. Thus for one mole of an ideal gas:

$$\varepsilon = \Delta F = \int_P^{P_0} V dP = RT \ln \frac{P_0}{P} \qquad (2.45)$$

where ΔF is the free energy change and P_0 is the saturated vapor pressure. The volume in the adsorbed space is:

$$W = nV_m \qquad (2.46)$$

where n = number of moles adsorbed per unit mass of sorbent
$\quad V_m$ = molar volume

The characteristic curve is plotted using equations 2.45 and 2.46 — that is, by plotting nV_m versus $RT \ln(P_0/P)$. Other methods of plotting have also been used, as will be discussed shortly.

The functional form of the characteristic curve (eq. 2.44) remains undefined. Dubinin [70] postulated semiempirically specific functions for two types of sorbents: microporous materials such as activated carbon and materials with large voids such as carbon black. The adsorption on the former type of sorbent is by capillary condensation, where the effect of increased adsorption potentials is dominant as a result of the overlapping force fields from opposite walls. The characteristic curve assumes the form [71, 72]:

$$W = W_0 \exp\left(-k\frac{\varepsilon^2}{\beta^2}\right)$$

(2.47)

where W_0 is the limiting volume of the adsorbed space, which equals micropore volume, and β is the affinity coefficient characterizing the polarizability of the adsorbate. Equation 2.47 is frequently referred to as the Dubinin-Radushkevich equation. It can be recast into the following isotherm:

$$v = v_0 \exp\left(-K\frac{\varepsilon^2}{\beta^2}\right)$$

or

$$\ln\frac{v}{v_0} = -D\left(\ln\frac{P_0}{P}\right)^2$$

(2.48)

where $D = KR^2T^2/\beta^2$.

The affinity coefficient, β, is intended as a shifting factor to bring the characteristic curves of all gases on the same sorbent into a single curve. Thus $\varepsilon = \beta f(W)$. Empirically, Dubinin and co-workers have found that the molar volume in the liquid state exhibits close proportionality to the β value [1] — that is:

$$\frac{\varepsilon_i}{\varepsilon_j} = \frac{\beta_i}{\beta_j} \cong \frac{V_i}{V_j}$$

(2.48a)

where V is the liquid molar volume of the adsorbate at the adsorption temperature. Although Dubinin and co-workers showed an excellent proportionality between β and V for a number of adsorbates, later data including nonpolar and weakly polar adsorbates did not bear this out, as will be shown in the next section. Thus equation 2.48a should be used with caution. Nevertheless, it is an excellent attempt to obtain a universal isotherm by which the adsorption data of one gas are extended to other gases.

For large-pore carbon sorbents where capillary condensation is not important, the following characteristic curve is used [70–72]:

$$W = W_0 \exp\left(-k\frac{\varepsilon}{\beta}\right)$$

(2.49)

which leads to the isotherm:

$$\ln\frac{v}{v_0} = -E\ln\frac{P_0}{P}$$

(2.50)

For nonideal gas behavior, $\ln(P_0/P)$ in equations 2.48 and 2.50 is replaced by $\ln(f_0/f)$, where f is the corresponding fugacity.

The Dubinin-Radushkevich (D-R) equation (eq. 2.47 or 2.48) fits the data well, with many nonpolar or weakly polar adsorbates below the critical temperature. The exponent of ε/β was later generalized to 2, 3, and noninteger numbers. A number of similar equations have been used for the sorption of polar compounds and especially for water on activated carbon [73, 74]. An example of experimental data fitting by the D-R equation is given in Figure 2.10. An example for data fitting equations similar to equation 2.50 is given by the adsorption of some hydrocarbons on activated carbon and silica [80]. The D-R equation has been applied in many instances to zeolites, and is especially useful in determining the limiting pore volume, W_0, at which all gases converge [9].

Extensive research has also been done by Marsh and colleagues [75, 76] to deduce the value for the monolayer adsorption volume, v_m, from the isotherm represented by equation 2.48, and thereby obtain the surface area. A good review of this work has been given by Thomas and Thomas [77]. More recently, Dubinin has developed a method, assuming slitlike pores, using benzene adsorption to calculate surface area from the isotherm [78].

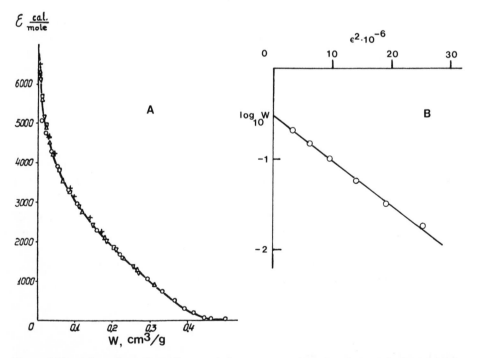

Figure 2.10   Adsorption of tetrafluoro-ethylene on an activated carbon at: 33.3°C (critical temperature, $+$); 0°C ($\square$); -28°C ($\triangledown$); -40°C ($\triangle$); -76.3°C ($\bigcirc$). (A) Characteristic curve: adsorbed volume, W, plotted against potential, ε, calculated from equation 2.45; (B) Plotted according to equation 2.47. Source: Dubinin [70]. Reprinted with permission.

Table 2.5 Proposed Methods of Plotting the Characteristic Curve and Calculating the Adsorbed Molar Volume and Saturated Pressure

Authors	Plotting A vs. B	Calculation of V_m	Calculation of f_0 or P_0
Polanyi/ Berenyi	nV_m vs. $RT \ln \dfrac{P_0}{P}$	As saturated liquid at $T < T_c$, as van der Waals constant b at $T > T_c$	Vapor pressure of liquid at $T < T_c$, 0.4 T/b for first trial at $T > T_c$ (b = van der Waals constant)
Dubinin [71]	nV_m vs. $\dfrac{RT}{V_m} \ln \dfrac{P_0}{P}$	Same as Polanyi	Vapor pressure of liquid at $T < T_c$, $T_r^2 P_0$ at $T > T_c$
Toth [79]	n vs. $RT \ln \dfrac{KP_0}{P}$		Vapor pressure of liquid at $T < T_c$, extrapolation of Clapeyron equation at $T > T_c$
Lewis et al. [80]	nV_m vs. $\dfrac{RT}{V_m} \ln \dfrac{f_0}{f}$	Saturated liquid at gas pressure P	Vapor pressure of liquid at $T < T_c$, extrapolation of Antoine equation at $T > T_c$
Maslan et al. [81]	nV_m vs. $\dfrac{RT}{V_m} \ln \dfrac{f_0}{f}$	At saturated pressure at T (by equation of state and compressibility factor)	Vapor pressure of liquid at $T < T_c$, curve "extrapolation" at $T > T_c$
Grant and Manes [82, 83]	nV_m vs. $\dfrac{RT}{V_m} \ln \dfrac{f_0}{f}$	Saturated liquid at normal boiling point	Vapor pressure of liquid at $T < T_c$, vapor pressure extrapolation at $T > T_c$
Cook and Basmadjian [84]	nV_m vs. $\dfrac{RT}{V_m} \ln \dfrac{f_0}{f}$	Saturated liquid at $T < T_b$, tangent to log V_m vs. log T plot at $T > T_b$	Vapor pressure of liquid at $T < T_c$, using known value of V and T for P using equation at state and compression factor
Reich et al. [85]	nV_m vs. $\dfrac{RT}{V_m} \ln \dfrac{f_0}{f}$	V_{nbp} at $T < T_{nbp}$, $V_{nbp}(T_c - T)/(T_c - T_{nbp})$ at $T_{nbp} < T \leqslant T_c$, $RT_c/(8P_c)$ at $T \geqslant T_c$	Reduced Kirchhoff equation for P at $T < T_c$, extrapolation of Kirchhoff equation for $T > T_c$

Polanyi-Dubinin Isotherm Extended to Supercritical Conditions

Under conditions above the critical temperature, theoretical treatments based on the potential theory become less amenable because the adsorbed phase is ill defined. However, since adsorption under such conditions is important in practical applications, many empirical or semiempirical correlations have been proposed, each fitting the experimental data of a particular adsorption system. A summary of the proposed correlations is given in Table 2.5. The proposed methods of calculating the molar volume and the saturated vapor pressure are given for the supercritical region as well as at temperatures below the critical temperature. The subscript "nbp" in the table stands for normal boiling point. More recently, the data of Reich et al. [85] and Ritter [86] on the adsorption of CH_4, C_2H_4, C_2H_6, CO_2, and CO on activated carbon, under wide ranges of conditions above the critical temperature, have been correlated by a generalized empirical characteristic function [87]. By using the following characteristic curve:

$$nV_{nbp}T_r^{0.6} = f\left(\frac{T}{V_{nbp}}\ln\frac{f_0}{f}\right) \tag{2.51}$$

where V_{nbp} denotes the molar volume at the normal boiling point and T_r is the reduced temperature, the individual characteristic curves of the above gases coalesce into a single one. The value for V_m is calculated from the BET surface area, A; and the monolayer adsorption, v_m, is measured from the Langmuir isotherm that usually fits the data for supercritical adsorption:

$$V_m = \left(\frac{1}{g}\frac{22,400A}{v_m N_0}\right)^{3/2} N_0 \tag{2.52}$$

where N_0 is Avogadro number and g is a packing factor, depending on the number of the nearest neighbors. For twelve neighbors in the bulk liquid and six on a plane (a common arrangement) the value of g is 1.091.

NOTATION

a	partial molar area
A	surface area of sorbent
b	Langmuir constant
B	Langmuir constant; dispersion constant
c	speed of light
C	dispersion constant; average number of sorbate molecules per cage in zeolite

E	interaction energy
f	fugacity; partition function
f_0	fugacity at saturation
F	field strength
G	Gibbs free energy
h	Planck constant
H	enthalpy
k	Boltzmann constant
m	mass
n	amount adsorbed in moles/g
N_0	Avogadro number
P	total pressure
P_0	saturation vapor pressure
P_c	critical pressure
Q	heat of adsorption; quadrupole moment
r	pore radius; distance of separation
r_k	Kelvin radius; radius of curvature
R	gas constant
S	entropy
T	temperature
T_c	critical temperature
T_r	reduced temperature
v	amount adsorbed in volume (STP)/g
v_m	monolayer amount adsorbed
V	liquid molar volume adsorbate
V_m	molar volume of adsorbate
V_{nbp}	liquid molar volume at normal boiling point
W	adsorbate volume above the surface
W_0	limiting volume of adsorbed space (=micropore volume)
X	mole fraction in adsorbed phase
Y	mole fraction in gas phase
α	polarizability; adsorption constant (=sticking probability)
β	desorption constant; affinity coefficient
γ	activity coefficient
ε	potential energy field over surface
θ	contact angle; fractional surface coverage; angle between field and dipole
Λ	pairwise interaction parameter
μ	chemical potential; permanent dipole
π	spreading pressure
ρ	density
σ	surface or interfacial tension; area occupied by an adsorbed molecule; partial molar area
ϕ	potential energy function
χ	magnetic susceptibility
ω	lateral interaction energy

REFERENCES

1. D.M. Young and A.D. Crowell, *Physical Adsorption of Gases* (London: Butterworths, 1962).
2. S. Ross and J.P. Olivier, *On Physical Adsorption* (New York: Wiley, 1964).
3. V. Ponec, Z. Knor, and S. Cerny, *Adsorption on Solids* (London: Butterworths, 1974).
4. A.W. Adamson, *Physical Chemistry of Surfaces*, 3rd ed. (New York: Wiley-Interscience, 1976).
5. S.J. Gregg and K.S.W. Sing, *Adsorption, Surface Area and Porosity*, 2nd ed. (New York: Academic Press, 1982).
6. J. Oscik, *Adsorption* (New York: Wiley-Interscience, 1983).
7. D.M. Ruthven, *Principles of Adsorption and Adsorption Processes* (New York: Wiley-Interscience, 1984).
8. S.J. Gregg and K.S.W. Sing, *Adsorption, Surface Area and Porosity*, 2nd ed., Chap. 5, (New York: Academic Press, 1982).
9. S. Brunauer, *The Adsorption of Gases and Vapors* (Princeton, N.J.: Princeton University Press, 1945), pp. 68–82.
10. E.P. Barrett, L.G. Joyner, and P.H. Halenda, *J. Am. Chem. Soc.*, *73*, 373 (1951).
11. R.L. Bond, ed., *Porous Carbon Solids* (New York: Academic Press, 1967), Chaps. 1, 5, and 6.
12. C.N. Satterfield, *Heterogeneous Catalysis in Practice* (New York: McGraw-Hill, 1980), pp. 108–110.
13. J.T. Saunders, M.S. thesis, State University of New York, Buffalo (1982).
14. D.W. Breck, *Zeolite Molecular Sieves*, p. 600, reprint ed. (Malabar, Fl.: Krieger Publishing Company, 1984). Originally published by Wiley-Interscience, New York, 1974.
15. H.F. Stoeckli, F. Kraehenbuehl, and D. Morel, *Carbon*, *21*, 589 (1983).
16. S. Brunauer, L.S. Deming, W.E. Deming, and E.J. Teller, *J. Am. Chem. Soc.*, *62*, 1723 (1940).
17. J.T. Cookson, Jr., "Adsorption Mechanisms: The Chemistry of Organic Adsorption on Activated Carbon," in *Carbon Adsorption Handbook* (P.N. Cheremisinoff and F. Ellerbusch, eds.) (Ann Arbor, Mich.: Ann Arbor Science, 1978).
18. O.P. Mahajan, A. Youssef, and P.L. Walker, Jr., *Sep. Sci. Tech.*, *17*, 1019 (1982).
19. *IUPAC–Manual of Symbols and Terminology for Physicochemical Quantities and Units* (London: Butterworths, 1972).
20. H. Jüntgen, *Carbon*, *15*, 273 (1977).
21. R.K. Iler, *The Chemistry of Silica* (New York: Wiley, 1979), p. 478.
22. G. MacZura, K.P. Goodboy, and J.J. Koenig, in *Kirk-Othmer Encyclopedia of Chem. Tech.*, Vol. 2, 3rd ed. (New York: Wiley-Interscience, 1977).
23. D.W. Breck, *Zeolite Molecular Sieves*, Chap. 5, (Malabar, Fla.: Krieger, 1984). Originally published by Wiley-Interscience, New York, 1974.
24. P.L. Walker, Jr., L.G. Austin, and S.P. Nandi, in *Chemistry and Physics of Carbon* (P.L. Walker, Jr., ed.), Vol. 2 (New York: Marcel Dekker, 1966).
25. J.R. Dacey and D.G. Thomas, *Trans. Faraday Soc.*, *50*, 740 (1954).
26. M.M. Dubinin, O. Kadlec, I. Botlik, E.D. Zaverina, A. Zukal, and B. Sumec, *Dokl. Akad. Nauk SSSR*, *157*, 656 (1964).
27. T.G. Lamond, J.E. Metcalfe III, and P.L. Walker, Jr., *Carbon*, *3*, 59 (1965).
28. J.E. Metcalfe, M. Kawahata, and P.L. Walker, Jr., *Fuel*, *42*, 233 (1963).
29. R.B. Mason and P.E. Eberly, Jr., U.S. Patent 3,222,412 (1965).

30. R.L. Patel, S.P. Nandi, and P.L. Walker, Jr., *Fuel, 51*, 47 (1972).
31. P.L. Walker, Jr., T.G. Lamond, and J.E. Metcalfe III, *2nd Conf. Ind. Carbon Graphite*, p. 7, Society of Chemistry and Industry, London (1966).
32. M. Kamishita, O.P. Mahajan, and P.L. Walker, Jr., *Fuel, 56*, 444 (1977).
33. D.H.T. Spencer, in *Porous Carbon Solids* (R.L. Bond, ed.) (New York: Academic Press, 1967), pp. 87–154.
34. H. Jüntgen, K. Knoblauch, and K. Harder, *Fuel, 60*, 817 (1981).
35. K. Kawazoe, M. Suzuki, and K. Chihara, *J. Chem. Eng. Japan, 7*, 151 (1974).
36. K. Wefers and G.M. Bell, *Oxides and Hydroxides of Aluminum*, Technical Paper No. 19, Alcoa, Pittsburgh, Pa. (1972).
37. R.K. Iler, *The Chemistry of Silica* (New York: Wiley, 1979), p. 510.
38. K. Klier and A.C. Zettlemoyer, *J. Coll. Interf. Sc., 58*, 216 (1977).
39. D.W. Breck, *Zeolite Molecular Sieves* (Malabar, Fla.: Krieger, 1984), Chap. 8.
40. R.M. Milton, U.S. Patent 2,882,243 (1959), to Union Carbide Corporation.
41. R.M. Milton, U.S. Patent 2,882,244 (1959), to Union Carbide Corporation.
42. R.M. Barrer, *Zeolites and Clay Minerals as Sorbents and Molecular Sieves* (New York: Academic Press, 1978).
43. D.W. Breck, *Zeolite Molecular Sieves* (Malabar, Fla.: Krieger, 1984). Originally published by Wiley, New York, 1974.
44. R.M. Barrer, *Zeolites and Clay Minerals as Sorbents and Molecular Sieves* (New York: Academic Press, 1978), pp. 78–79.
45. N.R. Laine, F.J. Vastola, and P.L. Walker, Jr., *J. Phys. Chem., 67*, 2030 (1964).
46. I. Langmuir, *J. Amer. Chem. Soc., 40*, 1361 (1918).
47. A.W. Adamson, *Physical Chemistry of Surfaces*, 3rd ed. (New York: Wiley-Interscience, 1976), Chap. 14.
48. F. London, *Z. Physik, 63*, 245 (1930).
49. J.G. Kirkwood, *Phys. Zeits., 33*, 57 (1932).
50. A. Müller, *Proc. Roy. Soc., 154A*, 624 (1936).
51. S.J. Gregg and K.S.W. Sing, *Adsorption, Surface Area and Porosity*, 2nd ed. (New York: Academic Press, 1982), Chap. 1.
52. J.C. Slater and J.G. Kirkwood, *Phys. Rev., 37*, 682 (1931).
53. R.H. Fowler, *Proc. Camb. Phil. Soc., 31*, 260 (1935).
54. R.H. Fowler and E.A. Guggenheim, *Statistical Thermodynamics* (Cambridge: Cambridge University Press, 1952).
55. S. Ross and W. Winkler, *J. Colloid Sci., 10*, 319 (1955).
56. J. Zeldowitsch, *Acta Physicochim. U.R.S.S., 1*, 961 (1934).
57. A. Ganguli, *Kolloidzeitschrift, 60*, 180 (1932).
58. A. Boutaric, *J. Chim. Phys., 35*, 158 (1938).
59. S. Miyamoto, *Kolloidzeitschrift, 70*, 275 (1935).
60. R. Sips, *J. Chem. Phys., 16*, 490 (1948).
61. R. Sips, *J. Chem. Phys., 18*, 1024 (1950).
62. R.A. Koble and T.E. Corrigan, *Ind. Eng. Chem., 44*, 383 (1952).
63. S. Brunauer, P.H. Emmett, and E. Teller, *J. Am. Chem. Soc., 60*, 309 (1938).
64. H.C. Van Ness, *Ind. Eng. Chem. Fundam., 8*, 465 (1969).
65. W.D. Harkins and G. Jura, *J. Am. Chem. Soc., 66*, 919 (1944).
66. A.W. Adamson, *Physical Chemistry of Surfaces*, 3rd ed. (New York: Wiley, 1976), p. 574.
67. S. Suwanayuen and R.P. Danner, *AIChE J., 26*, 68 (1980); S.H. Hyun and R.P. Danner, *J. Chem. Eng. Data, 27*, 196 (1982).
68. T.W. Cochran, R.L. Kabel, and R.P. Danner, *AIChE J., 31*, 268 (1985).

69. M. Polanyi, *Trans. Faraday Soc.*, *28*, 316 (1932).
70. M.M. Dubinin, *Chem. Rev.*, *60*, 235 (1960).
71. M.M. Dubinin, *P. Acad. Sc. USSR* (international ed.), *55*, 137 (1947).
72. M.M. Dubinin and L.V. Radushkevich, *Dokl. Akad. Nauk. SSSR*, *55*, 327 (1947).
73. P.J. Reucroft, W.H. Simpson, and L.A. Jonas, *J. Phys. Chem.*, *75*, 3526 (1971).
74. R. Wojsz and M. Rozwadowski, *Carbon*, *22*, 437 (1984).
75. H. Marsh and W.F.K. Wynne-Jones, *Carbon*, *1*, 269 (1964).
76. T.G. Lamond and H. Marsh, *Carbon*, *1*, 293 (1964).
77. J.M. Thomas and W.J. Thomas, *Introduction to the Principles of Heterogeneous Catalysis* (New York: Academic Press, 1967), Chap. 2.
78. M.M. Dubinin, *Carbon*, *18*, 355 (1980).
79. J. Toth, *Acta Chim. Hung.*, *30*, 415 (1962).
80. W.K. Lewis, E.R. Gilliland, B. Chertow, and W.P. Cadogan, *Ind. Eng. Chem.*, *42*, 1326 (1950).
81. F.D. Maslan, M. Altman, and E.R. Aberth, *J. Phys. Chem.*, *57*, 106 (1953).
82. R.J. Grant, M. Manes, and S.B. Smith, *AIChE J.*, *3*, 403 (1962).
83. R.J. Grant and M. Manes, *Ind. Eng. Chem. Fundam.*, *3*, 221 (1964).
84. W.H. Cook and D. Basmadjian, *Can. J. Chem. Eng.*, *42*, 146 (1964).
85. R. Reich, W.T. Ziegler, and K.A. Rogers, *Ind. Eng. Chem. Proc. Des. Dev.*, *19*, 336 (1980).
86. J.A. Ritter, Thesis, State University of New York at Buffalo (1985).
87. W.N. Chen and R.T. Yang, in *Recent Developments in Separation Science*, Vol. 9 (N.N. Li and J.M. Calo, eds.) (Cleveland: CRC Press, 1986), Chap. 7.
88. J.J. Collins, *Chem. Eng. Prog.*, *64*(8), 66 (1968).
89. Y.T. Yeh, unpublished results, State University of New York at Buffalo (1985).

CHAPTER 3

Equilibrium Adsorption
of Gas Mixtures

Models or correlations for mixed-gas adsorption are crucial to the design of adsorptive gas separation processes. They should be capable of predicting the equilibrium amount adsorbed from pure gas isotherms for each constituent in the mixture, within given ranges of operating temperature and total pressure. Significant progress in the theoretical aspect of the problem has been made in the last two decades, parallel to the growing interest in new adsorptive separation processes. Because of the paucity of experimental data, however, none of the theories or models has been extensively tested.

The measurement of mixed-gas adsorption is not necessarily difficult, but it is certainly tedious. With the additional measurement of equilibrium gas-phase composition, essentially all experimental techniques used for measuring single-gas isotherms can be used for mixed-gas adsorption. A brief description of experimental techniques is given later in this chapter.

The theories for mixed-gas adsorption fall into the same three categories as the single-gas adsorption isotherms. Thus they are discussed accordingly.

3.1 LANGMUIR-TYPE EQUATIONS AND CORRELATION

3.1.1 Extended Langmuir Equation

The Langmuir isotherm for single-gas adsorption can readily be extended to an n-component mixture. For the convenience of discussion, the derivation for a binary mixture, after Markham and Benton [1], is given next. The same assumption of an ideal localized monolayer is made. The system is defined as containing partial pressures P_1 and P_2 in the gas phase, which is in equilibrium with coverages θ_1 and θ_2 on the surface. The rate of condensation for gas 1, r_1, is given by:

$$r_1 = \alpha_1 v_1 (1 - \theta_1 - \theta_2) = \alpha'_1 P_1 (1 - \theta_1 - \theta_2) \tag{3.1}$$

where α is the sticking probability and v is given by equation 2.13. The rate of evaporation for gas 1 is $\beta_1' \theta_1$, which is given by equation 2.14. At equilibrium,

$$\alpha_1' P_1 (1 - \theta_1 - \theta_2) = \beta_1' \theta_1 \tag{3.2}$$

or

$$\theta_1 = \frac{B_1 P_1 (1 - \theta_2)}{1 + B_1 P_1} \tag{3.3}$$

With the corresponding equation for θ_2, we have:

$$\theta_1 = \frac{B_1 P_1}{1 + B_1 P_1 + B_2 P_2} \tag{3.4}$$

For an n-component mixture:

$$\theta_i = \frac{B_i P_i}{1 + \sum_{j=1}^{n} B_j P_j} \tag{3.5}$$

Equation 3.5 is the Langmuir equation for an n-component mixture. The total surface coverage, θ_t, is:

$$\theta_t = \sum_{i=1}^{n} \theta_i = \frac{\sum B_i P_i}{1 + \sum_{j=1}^{n} B_j P_j} \tag{3.6}$$

Equation 3.5 gives fractional coverage for the i species. The monolayer coverage for i in the mixed adsorbed phase remains undefined. If, however, each species maintains its own molecular area (the area covered by one molecule that is not influenced by the presence of other species on the surface, as in single-gas adsorption) the amount adsorbed for i in the mixture is:

$$v_i = \frac{v_{mi} B_i P_i}{1 + \sum_{j=1}^{n} B_j P_j} \tag{3.7}$$

where v_{mi} is the monolayer amount for i. The fractional surface uncovered is $1/(1 + \Sigma B_j P_j)$.

The lateral interactions among the adsorbed molecules in the single-gas adsorption can be accounted for by an interaction energy that results in a modified Langmuir constant B, as shown in equation 2.17. This is an experimentally measured value. For the adsorption of mixed species, the lateral interactions among the species are expected to differ from the self-interactions. Thus the interaction energies, zE in equation 2.17, could be different and would simply result in a different Langmuir constant for the species. The interspecies interactions can be accounted for by:

$$v_i = \frac{v_{mi}(B_i/\eta_i)P_i}{1 + \sum\limits_{j=1}^{n} (B_j/\eta_j)P_j} \tag{3.8}$$

where η_i describes the changes in the interaction energies in the mixed adsorbates, which can be either greater or less than unity. Equation 3.8 has been used by Schay et al. [2]. The value of η_i can be expected to vary with the composition of the adsorbed phase. However, as with the modified Langmuir constants for single adsorbates given in equation 2.17, constant η_i values are adequate to describe experimental data at moderate surface coverages.

The thermodynamic consistency of equation 3.7 has been discussed by Broughton [3] and Kemball et al. [4], with both arriving at the same conclusion. Following a reversible isothermal cycle in a system undergoing adsorption-displacement-desorption, it is shown that the monolayer adsorption must be equal for all species, or $v_{mi} = v_{mj}$ [3]. For binary mixtures, Innes and Rowley [5, 6] have used the following averaged v_m value for both species:

$$\frac{1}{v_m} = \frac{X_1}{v_{m1}} + \frac{X_2}{v_{m2}} \tag{3.9}$$

Good agreements with experimental data are obtained by using the averaged value for mixtures with widely different (e.g., over twofold) monolayer adsorbed amounts.

The simple form of equation 3.7 makes it amenable to mathematical treatment. It has been the major model used in calculations of adsorber dynamics for multicomponent adsorption (see Chapter 5 for a detailed discussion).

3.1.2 Loading Ratio Correlation

As in the extended Langmuir equation for mixtures, the hybrid Langmuir-Freundlich equation (eq. 2.24) can also be extended to an n-component mixture [7].

$$v_i = \frac{v_{mi}B_iP_i^{1/n_i}}{1 + \sum\limits_{j=1}^{n} B_jP_j^{1/n_j}} \tag{3.10}$$

A similar equation can be written with the lateral interaction parameters, η_i, as:

$$v_i = \frac{v_{mi}(B_i/\eta_i)P_i^{1/n_i}}{1 + \sum\limits_{j=1}^{n} (B_j/\eta_j)P_j^{1/n_j}} \tag{3.11}$$

The ratio v/v_m was referred to as loading ratio, hence the term *loading ratio correlation* (LRC) for equations 3.10 and 3.11 [7]. Similar to the extended Langmuir equation, the LRC equations lack a rigorous theoretical foundation. Because of their mathematical simplicity, however, the extended Langmuir and LRC equations have been predominantly used in the modeling and design of adsorbers and cyclic gas separation processes for concentrated mixtures. Detailed discussions of the applications and comparisons of the isotherm equations for mixed-gas adsorption are deferred until later sections.

Because of the lack of a rigorous theoretical foundation, the LRC equations are used only for empirical correlation and design purposes. The temperature dependence of the LRC parameters is:

$$v_m = k_1/T^{k_2} \qquad \text{(or a linear function)} \tag{3.12}$$

$$B = k_3 \exp(k_4/T) \tag{3.13}$$

$$1/n = k_5 + k_6/T \tag{3.14}$$

where the empirical constants usually assume the following values:

$k_2 \leqslant 1$
$k_4 \cong Q/R$
$k_6 \cong 0$

Equation 3.10 can be recast into:

$$\frac{\theta_i}{\theta_t} = \frac{B_i P_i^{1/n_i}}{\displaystyle\sum_{j=1}^{n} B_j P_j^{1/n_j}} \tag{3.15}$$

This correlation has been widely used for modeling adsorber dynamics involving liquid solutions [8], where $1/n$ frequently exceeds unity.

3.1.3   Other Theories

The Freundlich isotherm for a binary mixture has been derived by Glueckauf [9] for the specific case when the exponents $1/n$ in equation 2.18 are equal. Glueckauf [10] was also able to derive isotherm equations for the mixed monolayer adsorption of two species on a surface containing sites where the number falls off exponentially with their adsorption energy. These equations, however, have not been used in the literature except in one case by Tompkins and Young [11] for the adsorption of argon-oxygen on cesium iodide at 77K. The extended Langmuir equation for mixtures, which is also derived for monolayer adsorption, has proved far more useful than Glueckauf's equations.

The BET theory for multilayer adsorption has also been extended to mixtures

[12]. The resulting equations are complex because it is necessary to account for the various possible heats of adsorption between the mixed layers. Like the extended Freundlich isotherm, it has very limited use. A simplified version of the BET model for mixture adsorption has been developed by Gonzalez and Holland [13]. By assuming that the ratio between the Langmuir constant of the $(n + 1)$th layer and the nth layer is a constant for all components in the mixture:

$$\frac{B_{n+1}}{B_n} = v \tag{3.16}$$

the amount of i adsorbed is:

$$v_i = v_{mi} P_i \sum_j \frac{B_i v^{j(j-1)/2} \phi^{j-1}}{(1 + \phi)(1 + v\phi)(1 + v^2\phi) \dots (1 + v^{j-1}\phi)} \tag{3.17}$$

where j is the number of the layer of adsorbate, and

$$\phi = \sum_m B_m P_m \tag{3.18}$$

When $j = 1$, equation 3.17 reverts to the extended Langmuir equation, (eq. 3.7), Gonzalez and Holland have shown that $j = 2$ is adequate for mixtures of paraffins on activated carbon and silica gel.

The theories described in the next two sections, all accounting for multilayer adsorption, have proven more useful than the extended BET model.

3.2 THE POTENTIAL-THEORY APPROACH

3.2.1 Direct Extension of the Dubinin-Radushkevich (D-R) Equation

The D-R equation is extended to the adsorption of mixed gases by Bering et al. [14, 15]:

$$n_t = \sum n_i = \frac{W_0}{\sum X_i V_{mi}} \exp\left[-\frac{kT^2}{(\sum X_i \beta_i)^2} \left(\sum X_i \ln \frac{P_{0i}}{P_i} \right)^2 \right] \tag{3.19}$$

where n_t = total amount of mixture adsorbed, in moles/g
V_m = molar volume or partial molar volume of the adsorbed phase

The mole fractions in the adsorbed phase are related by:

$$\sum X_i = 1 \tag{3.20}$$

Equations 3.19 and 3.20 are not sufficient for solving the values of n_i and n_t.

For binary mixtures, the following relationship first found empirically by Lewis et al. [16] provides the additional equation needed:

$$\frac{n_1}{n_1^0} + \frac{n_2}{n_2^0} = 1 \tag{3.21}$$

or

$$\frac{X_1}{n_1^0} + \frac{X_2}{n_2^0} = \frac{1}{n_t} \tag{3.22}$$

where n_i^0 represents the amount of i adsorbed from the pure gas at the same total pressure. A theoretical basis for this relationship will be given following this section.

Equations 3.19, 3.20, and 3.22 have been used to give good predictions of adsorption from several binary mixtures below the critical temperature, with errors averaging approximately 2% [14, 15].

The prerequisite for using this model is an adequate representation of the single-gas adsorption data by the Dubinin-Radushkevich equation. The Lewis relation (eq. 3.21) must also hold. This relation indeed agrees well ($\pm 6\%$) with experimental data for mixtures of C_1 to C_4 paraffins and olefins on activated carbon and silica gel [16]. It does not fit the data well, however, in some other cases, such as H_2-N_2 [17] and $CH_4-C_2H_4$ on activated carbon [16], and $CO_2-C_3H_8$ on porous glass [18].

3.2.2   Theoretical Basis for the Lewis Relationship

The Lewis relationship (eq. 3.21) was found empirically by Lewis et al. [16] for binary-mixture adsorption:

$$\frac{n_1}{n_1^0} + \frac{n_2}{n_2^0} = 1 \tag{3.23}$$

The relationship is illustrated by Lewis et al. in Figure 3.1 for a variety of binary hydrocarbon mixtures on silica gel and two activated carbons.

Equation 3.23 is an important one because it provides a simple relationship between pure-gas adsorption (n_i^0) and mixture adsorption (n_i). It is subsequently used as the basic assumption in several models for predicting mixture adsorption, some of which are included in this chapter.

A theoretical derivation for the binary adsorption equation is given by Lee [19]. The derivation given next is a generalized version for multicomponent adsorption.

The maximum capacity for micropore filling is W_0, which is the same for all

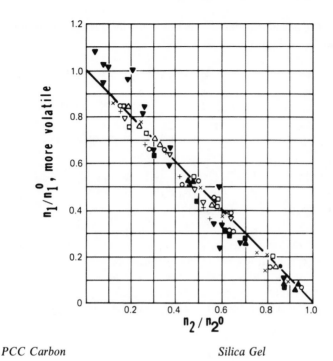

PCC Carbon

○ $C_2H_4 + C_3H_8$
△ $C_2H_6 + C_3H_8$
☐ iso-$C_4H_{10} + 1$-C_4H_8

Silica Gel

▼ $CH_4 + C_2H_4$
+ $C_2H_6 + C_3H_8$
× iso-$C_4H_{10} + 1$-C_4H_8

Columbia G Carbon

▽ $CH_4 + C_2H_4$
● $C_2H_4 + C_2H_6$

■ $C_2H_4 + C_3H_6$
▲ $C_3H_6 + C_3H_8$

Figure 3.1 The Lewis relationship for binary-mixture adsorption. Source: Lewis, Gilliland, Chertow, and Cadogan [16]. Reprinted with permission.

pure gases. Thus the total number of moles of adsorbed mixture is:

$$n_t = \frac{W_0}{V_m} \tag{3.24}$$

where V_m is the molar volume of the mixed adsorbate, and W_0 is given by the potential-theory plot of any of the pure-gas adsorption data. The number of moles of component i in the mixed adsorbate is given by:

$$n_i = n_t X_i \tag{3.25}$$

The assumption is then made that there is no volume change when mixing takes place in the adsorbed phase, which is equivalent to assuming ideal solution. The partial molar volumes are hence additive:

$$V_m = \sum X_i V_i^0 \tag{3.26}$$

where V_i^0 is the molar volume of i for pure-gas adsorption at temperature T and total pressure P.

Dividing equation 3.26 by V_m and substituting equations 3.24 and 3.25, we have:

$$\sum (n_i/n_i^0) = 1 \tag{3.27}$$

where $n_i^0 = W_0/V_i^0$.

Equation 3.27 is the Lewis relationship for multicomponent mixture adsorption. The required conditions are: (1) gases are adsorbed by micropore filling, and (2) there is no volume change when mixing the adsorbates, or ideal adsorbed solution behavior holds. The equation may then apply for activated carbon, zeolites, silica gel, and gases with no strong interactions.

3.2.3   The Model of Grant and Manes

The Grant-Manes model [20] originates to some extent, from the method of correlation for single-gas data by Lewis et al. [21]. Using the affinity coefficients approximated by liquid molar volumes at the adsorption temperature (i.e., Dubinin's approximation in equation 2.48a), Lewis et al. found substantial deviations (up to 50%) among the characteristic curves for single-gas adsorption. The systems studied were the lower hydrocarbons from methane to C_4s on silica gel and several activated carbons. They had a wide temperature and pressure range and included supercritical conditions. The crucial step in their correlation is using the molar volume of the saturated liquid as the affinity coefficient at a vapor pressure equal to adsorption pressure. By the use of this step, the characteristic curves can be brought substantially closer. In mathematical forms using binary mixture as an example, the *equipotential* concept of Dubinin, in its original form and for equal volume adsorbed, can be expressed as:

$$\left[\frac{RT}{V'} \ln \frac{P_0}{P} \right]_1 = \left[\frac{RT}{V'} \ln \frac{P_0}{P} \right]_2 \tag{3.28}$$

where V' is the molar volume of saturated liquid at the adsorption temperature.

The corresponding correlation by Lewis et al. is:

$$\left[\frac{RT}{V} \ln \frac{f_0}{f} \right]_1 = \left[\frac{RT}{V} \ln \frac{f_0}{f} \right]_2 \tag{3.29}$$

where V is the molar volume of saturated liquid at a vapor pressure equal to adsorption pressure. Here fugacity has replaced pressure to account for nonideality.

The value of V corresponds to an imaginary temperature which would make the vapor pressure of the pure liquid equal to the adsorption pressure of the gas mixture. This imaginary temperature and the real adsorption temperature differ by over 100°C, while the difference in V' and V may be as great as 50%. By using V at the imaginary temperature, the problem of making an approximation for the liquid molar volume above critical temperature is also solved.

Using the correlation by Lewis et al. for adsorption of nitrogen, methane, argon, hydrogen, and neon on activated carbon, Grant and Manes found a systematic temperature-dependent shift among the characteristic curves [22]. To reduce the shift, they chose the molar volume of liquid at the normal boiling point as the affinity coefficient. This pressure-independent molar volume improved the correlation of their data.

To apply the equipotential concept to mixed-gas adsorption, Grant and Manes [20] consider the liquidlike adsorbate as a mixture in which the adsorption potential of each pure adsorbed component is determined by the total adsorbate volume of the mixture. In addition, the following assumptions are made: (1) Raoult's law is valid as the relationship between the partial pressure of each component and its mole fraction in the adsorbate, and (2) the adsorbate volumes are additive, or the adsorbate forms an ideal solution. With these assumptions, the amount and composition of adsorbate corresponding to a given set of partial pressures can be calculated from the known single-gas characteristic curves. Furthermore, the characteristic curves do not have to coalesce into a single curve.

The Grant-Manes model can be summarized by the characteristic curve of component i in the mixture:

$$F_i(n_t V_m) = \left[\frac{\varepsilon}{V_{nbp}} \right]_i = \left[\frac{RT}{V_{nbp}} \ln \frac{Xf_0}{f} \right]_i \qquad (3.30)$$

where V_m is the liquid molar volume of the adsorbed mixture, V_{nbp} is the liquid molar volume at the normal boiling point, f_0 is the fugacity of pure i at its saturation vapor pressure at adsorption temperature, T, and f is the fugacity of i in the gas-phase mixture at P, T, and Y_i. The F function does not have to be the same for the pure components; it is important, however, that the same value of $n_t V_m$ be given by all components in the mixture. The detailed calculation thus follows.

1. Raoult's law holds for each component:

$$Y_i P = X_i P_i^*$$

or

$$f_i = X_i f_i^* \qquad (3.31)$$

where f_i is the fugacity of component i in the gas phase and f_i^* is the fugacity that the component would exert as a pure adsorbate at the total adsorbed volume of the mixture $(n_t V_m)$.

2.   The adsorption potential, ε_i, of component i is:

$$\varepsilon_i = RT \ln \left(\frac{f_0}{f^*} \right)_i \tag{3.32}$$

which, upon substitution of equation 3.31, becomes:

$$\varepsilon_i = RT \ln \left(\frac{X f_0}{f} \right)_i \tag{3.33}$$

V_{nbp} is then used as the empirical affinity coefficient, which is not required to make all single-component characteristic curves collapse into a single one.

Applying the equipotential concept, we have:

$$F_i(n_t V_m) = \left[\frac{RT}{V_{nbp}} \ln \frac{X f_0}{f} \right]_i \tag{3.30}$$

Equation 3.30 is subject to:

$$\sum X_i = 1 \tag{3.34}$$

With the known single-gas adsorption data, equations 3.30 and 3.34 can be used to calculate X_i from the given values of f_i, $(f_0)_i$ and $(V_{nbp})_i$ by the following procedure. The single-gas adsorption data are plotted according to equation 3.30. A set of X_i is assumed, which is modified by successive approximation until the same value for the adsorbed volume in all components is obtained. Having determined the adsorbate composition and total volume, the number of moles of each component is calculated by the following equations:

$$\sum X_i V_{m,i} = V_{m,mix} \tag{3.35}$$

and

$$n_i = X_i n_t \tag{3.36}$$

where $V_{m,i}$ is the molar volume of pure component i. Grant and Manes [20] calculate $V_{m,i}$ as the saturated liquid molar volume at the temperature that corresponds to the vapor pressure, P_i^*, where

$$P_i^* = \frac{Y_i P}{X_i} \tag{3.37}$$

The value of n_t is obtained by dividing the value of $n_t V_m$ by $V_{m,mix}$.

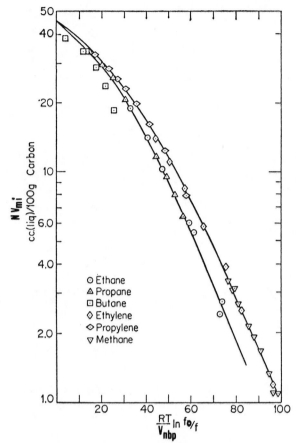

Figure 3.2 Characteristic curves for pure-gas adsorption (eq. 3.30) for hydrocarbons on activated carbon at 20°C. Nuxit-AL carbon, data from Szepesy and Illes [23]. Source: Grant and Manes [20]. Reprinted with permission.

The data of Szepesy and Illes [23, 24] have been treated by Grant and Manes [20]. The characteristic curves for the single gases are plotted in Figure 3.2. The binary mixture data are compared with the predictions of the Grant-Manes model in Figure 3.3. The predictions for mixtures involving methane are less satisfactory because of the approximation used for calculating the liquid molar volume of methane above its critical temperature. The fugacities are calculated assuming the fugacity-pressure ratio of methane applies to other gases. Other appropriate methods or equations of state may also be used for evaluating the thermodynamic properties.

The Grant-Manes model has been used by Reich et al. [25] to interpret their data for adsorption of a number of binary and ternary mixtures of methane, ethane, ethylene, and carbon dioxide on activated carbon at 212.7, 260.2, and 301.4K, and at pressures up to about 35 atm. The conditions cover below and above the critical

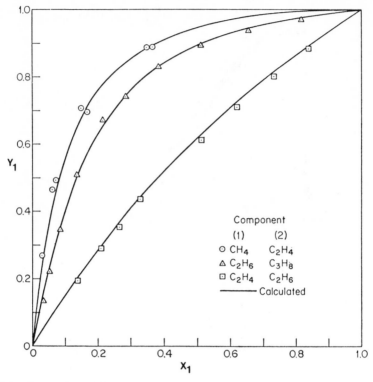

Figure 3.3 Comparison of binary-mixture adsorption data (from Szepesy and Illes [24]) and model predictions (from Grant and Manes [20]). Reprinted with permission.

temperatures (for methane and ethylene). It is of interest to list here the equations used in their evaluations of thermodynamic properties.

For the adsorbate (liquid) molar volume, the following equations first proposed by Nikolaev and Dubinin [26], based on the system temperature, are used:

$$V_m = V_{nbp} \qquad T < T_{nbp} \tag{3.38}$$

$$V_m = V_{nbp} \frac{T_c - T}{T_c - T_{nbp}} \qquad T_{nbp} \leqslant T < T_c \tag{3.39}$$

$$V_m = b = \frac{RT_c}{8P_c} \qquad T \geqslant T_c \tag{3.40}$$

The quantity b is one of the constants used in the van der Waals equation of state.

The fugacities are computed using the appropriate Benedict-Webb-Rubin (BWR) equation of state [27]. The vapor pressures, for below and above critical temperature, are calculated by using the reduced Kirchhoff equation [28]:

$$P = P_c \exp\left[h\left(1 - \frac{1}{T_r}\right)\right] \tag{3.41}$$

where

$$h = \frac{T_{nbp}}{T_c}\left(\frac{\ln P_c}{1 - T_{nbp}/T_c}\right) \tag{3.42}$$

The Grant-Manes model can be used in adsorber and gas separation process modeling provided the characteristic curves are fitted with equations. An example for the curve fitting may be found in Reich et al. [25], where the data in Figure 3.2 can be fitted well by a linear relationship for an abscissa less than 60 cal/cm^3, and by the Dubinin-Radushkevich equation for an abscissa greater than 60 cal/cm^3 [25].

3.3 OTHER THERMODYNAMIC MODELS

3.3.1 The Method of Lewis et al. for Binary Mixtures

The thermodynamic method of Lewis et al. [16] is intended particularly for the calculation of *relative volatility*, α, which is later called *selectivity ratio* or *separation factor*,

$$\alpha = \frac{Y_1/X_1}{Y_2/X_2} \tag{3.43}$$

from single-gas isotherms. The method is based on the second-law relationship derived by Broughton [3]. By carrying out the reversible thermodynamic cycle (i.e., adsorption of species 1 at P, replacement of 1 by 2 at constant total pressure P and desorption of 2 to close the cycle), the following relationship results:

$$\int_0^{n_1^0} \ln P_1^0 dn_1^0 - \int_0^{n_1^0} \ln P_1 dn_1 = \int_0^{n_2^0} \ln P_2^0 dn_2^0 - \int_0^{n_2^0} \ln P_2 dn_2 \tag{3.44}$$

The superscript zero refers to the isotherms of the pure gas, and the absence of a superscript refers to adsorption of the component in a mixture at a constant total pressure P.

The Lewis relationship:

$$\frac{n_1}{n_1^0} + \frac{n_2}{n_2^0} = 1 \tag{3.45}$$

and the empirical observation:

$$\alpha = \text{constant} \tag{3.46}$$

are then introduced. Combining equations 3.43, 3.44, 3.45, and 3.46 yields the following expression at constant temperature and total pressure:

$$\left(\frac{\alpha - 1}{\alpha\beta - 1}\right) n_1^0 \ln \alpha\beta = (n_2^0 - n_1^0)\ln P$$

$$- \int_0^{n_2^0} \ln P_2^0 dn_2^0 + \int_0^{n_1^0} \ln P_1^0 dn_1^0 \tag{3.47}$$

where $\beta = n_1^0/n_2^0$
$P = P_1 + P_2$

With the single-gas isotherms, all terms in equation 3.47 can be evaluated and α can be calculated by trial and error. Knowing α, equation 3.45 can be used to obtain the complete binary mixture isotherms.

The method has been used with some success by Lewis et al. [16] for the adsorption of hydrocarbons on activated carbon and silica gel, and by Maslan et al. [29] for oxygen-nitrogen on activated carbon. Caution must be exercised, however, since equation 3.46 is not always valid. The value of α frequently varies with composition, temperature, and total pressure. Examples of systems with varying α are given in Table 1 of Cook and Basmadjian [17]. In addition, the validity of equation 3.45 requires no volume change upon mixing of adsorbates, and adsorption by micropore filling as already discussed.

3.3.2   The Method of Cook and Basmadjian for Binary Mixtures

This method is semiempirical, and is basically a graphical one [17]. The method is founded on the equation derived by Basmadjian [30] for predicting selectivity ratios based on the integration of P_1^0/P_2^0 over v^0, which can readily be made from pure-gas isotherm data:

$$\log \alpha = \frac{1}{v_1^0} \int_0^{v_1^0} \log\left(\frac{P_1^0}{P_2^0}\right) dv^0 \tag{3.48}$$

Equation 3.48 is used to find, by extrapolation, the limiting selectivity ratio at $X_1 = 1$ and $X_2 = 1$:

$$\log(\alpha)_{X_1 = 1} = \frac{1}{v_1^0} \int_0^{v_1^0} \log\left(\frac{P_1^0}{P_2^0}\right) dv^0 \tag{3.49}$$

$$\log(\alpha)_{X_2=1} = \frac{1}{v_2^0} \int_0^{v_2^0} \log\left(\frac{P_1^0}{P_2^0}\right) dv^0 \tag{3.50}$$

The limiting αs are used to evaluate the limiting ratios of P/X, via the definition of α in equation 3.43:

$$\left(\frac{P_1}{X_1}\right)_{X_2=1} = P(\alpha)_{X_2=1} \tag{3.51}$$

$$\left(\frac{P_2}{X_2}\right)_{X_1=1} = \frac{P}{(\alpha)_{X_1=1}} \tag{3.52}$$

Given the total pressure, P, equations 3.51 and 3.52 yield points C and D, entered in Figure 3.4, which also shows pure-gas isotherms 1 and 2. Points A and B are also located from total pressure P. Lines AC and BC represent the binary mixture isotherms, and are empirically found to be linear.

Given partial pressures P_1 and P_2, it is possible to evaluate v_t, X_1, and X_2. A value for v_t is first assumed. The values of P_1/X_1 and P_2/X_2 are read off Figure 3.4, as indicated in the figure. The correct v_t is obtained when $X_1 + X_2 = 1$.

This method is suited for adsorption in the monolayer coverage range. It has been used with success by Cook and Basmadjian for the adsorption of a number of binary mixtures on charcoal, silica gel, porous glass, and molecular sieve 5A [17]. The method, however, lacks thermodynamic consistency, as discussed by Sircar and Myers [32].

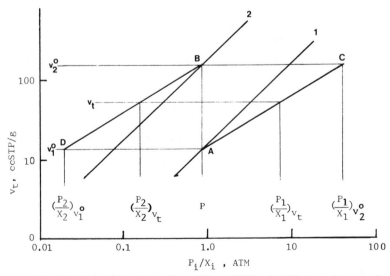

Figure 3.4 Graphical method of Cook and Basmadjian for binary-mixture adsorption. Curves 1 and 2 are pure-gas isotherms, and AC and BD are mixture isotherms. Source: Cook and Basmadjian [17]. Reprinted with permission.

3.3.3   The Adsorbed Solution Theory of Myers and Prausnitz

The familiar ideal adsorbed solution (IAS) theory is a special case in the treatment, by Myers and Prausnitz [31], of the mixed adsorbate as a solution in equilibrium with the gas phase. The fundamental thermodynamic equations for liquids are applied to the adsorbed phase. For example, the total internal energy, U, and the total Gibbs free energy, G, of the adsorbed phase are given by:

$$dU = TdS - \pi dA + \sum \mu_i dn_i \qquad (3.53)$$

$$dG = -SdT + Ad\pi + \sum \mu_i dn_i \qquad (3.54)$$

where π and A, respectively, replace P and V, and the adsorbed mixture is treated as a two-dimensional phase that is not necessarily a monolayer. The quantity A is the surface area, and π is spreading pressure. Spreading pressure thus plays a central role in applying solution equilibria to mixture adsorption. The physical meaning of spreading pressure is analogous to that of a monomolecular film at the gas-liquid interface:

$$\pi = \sigma^0 - \sigma \qquad (3.55)$$

where σ^0 and σ are the surface or interfacial tensions of the clean and monolayer-covered surfaces, respectively. Thus π defines the lowering of the surface tension at the solid-gas interface upon adsorption. Though not a measurable quantity, it is defined by:

$$\pi = -\left(\frac{\partial U}{\partial A}\right)_{S,n_i} \qquad (3.56)$$

from equation 3.53. It can also be calculated from measurable quantities. The isothermal Gibbs adsorption isotherm from equation 3.54 is:

$$Ad\pi = \sum n_i d\mu_i \qquad (3.57)$$

which is analogous to the Gibbs-Duhem equation. For pure-gas adsorption and assuming ideal gas behavior:

$$Ad\pi = nRTd \ln P$$

or

$$\frac{\pi A}{RT} = \int_0^P \frac{n}{P} dP \qquad (3.58)$$

Equation 3.58 can be used to calculate spreading pressure from the pure-gas isotherm.

In equation 3.54 the intensive variables are π, T, and composition. Myers and

Prausnitz propose that activity coefficients for the mixed adsorbate be defined in the same way as for solution. Thus the molar Gibbs free energy for mixing the adsorbates at constant T and π is:

$$g^m(T, \pi, X_i) = RT \sum X_i \ln (\gamma_i X_i) \qquad (3.59)$$

where γ_i is the activity coefficient of i in the mixed adsorbate. Using the activity coefficient defined in equation 3.59, along with the equilibrium criterion, which states that the chemical potential for each component in the adsorbed phase is equal to that in the gas phase, it can be shown that:

$$PY_i = P_i^0(\pi)X_i\gamma_i \qquad (3.60)$$

where P_i^0 is the equilibrium "vapor pressure" for pure i adsorption at the same spreading pressure, π, and the same T as the adsorbed mixture. This equation reduces to Raoult's law when γ_i is unity.

Using the same proposition, which is based on equation 3.59, the molar area of the mixed adsorbates is:

$$\frac{1}{n.} = \sum \frac{X_i}{n_i^0} + \frac{RT}{A} \sum X_i \left(\frac{\partial \ln \gamma_i}{\partial \pi} \right)_{X_i} \qquad (3.61)$$

where n_t is the total number of moles of adsorbed mixture, whereas n_i^0 is the number of moles of i when adsorbed from pure gas at the same π and T as the adsorbed mixture. The last term in equation 3.61 represents the molar area for mixing. Note that n_i^0 here is different from that defined in the Lewis relationship (eq. 3.27) and hence equation 3.61 or 3.64 is different from the Lewis equation. Finally, the number of moles of each component adsorbed is:

$$n_i = n_t X_i \qquad (3.62)$$

Equations 3.60, 3.61, and 3.62 are needed for predicting mixture adsorption from single-gas isotherms. In addition, equation 3.58 is used to evaluate P_i^0. If the gas phase is nonideal, such as in the case of high pressure, fugacities should replace pressures in all equations. The foregoing equations are the basis for the adsorbed solution theory.

For the special case of ideal solution, the activity coefficients are unity. Hence equation 3.60 reverts to Raoult's law:

$$PY_i = P_i^0(\pi)X_i \qquad (3.63)$$

and equation 3.63 simplifies to:

$$\frac{1}{n_t} = \sum \frac{X_i}{n_i^0} \qquad (3.64)$$

Equations 3.58, 3.62, 3.63, and 3.64 form the ideal adsorbed solution theory, by which mixed-gas adsorption can be predicted from single-gas isotherms. An example for the calculations procedure using IAS theory is given next for a binary mixture. The single-gas isotherms for the binary mixture are given by $n_1(P)$ and $n_2(P)$. The spreading pressure is the same for both species and the mixture. From equation 3.58:

$$\int_0^{P_1^0} \frac{n_1}{P} dP = \int_0^{P_2^0} \frac{n_2}{P} dP \qquad (3.65)$$

Equation 3.63 is written for both species:

$$PY_1 = P_1^0 X_1 \qquad (3.66)$$

$$PY_2 = P_2^0 X_2 = P_2^0(1 - X_1) \qquad (3.67)$$

These three equations (eqs. 3.65, 3.66, and 3.67) define the adsorbed mixture. For example, if P and Y_1 (and Y_2) are given (T is already given), the three equations are solved for P_1^0, P_2^0, and X_1. Equation 3.65 can be integrated to yield an algebraic equation if the isotherms have certain forms like Langmuir and Freundlich equations. Otherwise, equation 3.65 is solved graphically. With the values of P_1^0, P_2^0 and X_1 determined, the following equations are used to calculate n_1, n_2, and n_t from equations 3.62 and 3.64:

$$\frac{1}{n_t} = \frac{X_1}{n_1(P_1^0)} + \frac{X_2}{n_2(P_2^0)} \qquad (3.68)$$

$$n_1 = n_t X_1 \quad \text{and} \quad n_2 = n_t X_2 \qquad (3.69)$$

The results calculated by the IAS model for the methane-ethane adsorption on Nuxit-AL activated carbon at 20°C and 1 atm [23, 24] are shown in Figures 3.5 and 3.6.

The IAS theory has been extended to a high relative pressure region where multilayer condensation occurs [32]. In this region, the limiting value of spreading pressure at saturation (π_s) is ensured by mixing the adsorbates at a constant value of the reduced spreading pressure: π/π_s, which is the standard state.

It is interesting to compare the similarity between the potential theory of Grant and Manes (section 3.2.3) and IAS theory. Both theories assume ideal solution behavior for the adsorbate mixture, and apply Raoult's law as the relationship between the gas and adsorbed phases. It is, therefore, not surprising that similarities between the two theories exist. Both Grant and Manes [20] and Belfort [40] have shown that the link between the two theories is:

$$\varepsilon = A\pi \qquad (3.70)$$

This relation simply equates adsorption potential with the work needed to change

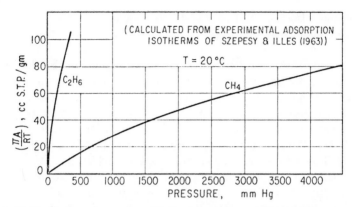

Figure 3.5 Spreading pressure of methane and ethane on Nuxit-AL activated carbon. Source: Myers and Prausnitz [31]. Reprinted with permission.

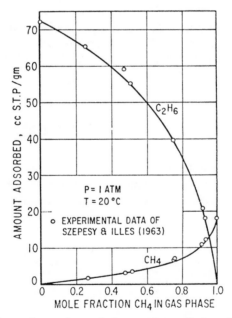

Figure 3.6 Comparison of experimental data with predictions by the ideal adsorbed solution theory. Source: Myers and Prausnitz [31]. Reprinted with permission.

spreading pressure from the bare surface to the adsorbed surface at a constant molar area A. Grant and Manes [20] also pointed out that IAS requires integration from zero pressure, whereas potential theory only requires information at the conditions of interest — namely, the vapor pressure of the liquid. Thus the potential theory requires extrapolation into regions where vapor pressure is undefined, when applied to supercritical conditions.

3.3.4   Nonideal Adsorbed Solution Models: Predictions of Activity Coefficients

Good agreements between experimental data and predictions by the IAS theory have been shown for many systems, including binary and ternary mixtures on activated carbon, silica gel, and zeolites [19, 31–39]. Deviations, some of them severe, have also been shown for many systems on the same sorbents [19, 41–46]. The most severe deviations are shown in the adsorption of CO_2–C_3H_8 on H-mordenite, where three- to tenfold differences are reported [46, 113]. (Poor fit has also been cited for CO_2–SO_2 on H-mordenite by Lee [19].)

In principle, it is possible to predict the deviation from ideal solution behavior. Attempts have been made to do so by using bulk solution theories to calculate the activity coefficients of the mixed adsorbed species. However, these have been done without consideration for the adsorbate-solid interactions, with the exception of the vacancy solution theory, which will be discussed in the next section.

Many semiempirical equations are available for calculating the activity coefficients in a liquid mixture. The Wilson equation [47] and the universal quasi-chemical (UNIQUAC) equation [48] have been used by Costa et al. to correlate their data on binary- and ternary-mixture adsorbates [45]. Using the Wilson equation, the activity coefficient for species i is:

$$\ln \gamma_i = 1 - \ln \left(\sum_j X_j \Lambda_{ij} \right) - \sum_k \frac{X_k \Lambda_{ki}}{\sum_j X_j \Lambda_{kj}} \tag{3.71}$$

where the binary constants Λ_{ij}, Λ_{ki}, and Λ_{kj} are empirical constants to be determined from binary-mixture data. These constants can then be used for predicting multicomponent mixtures. The activity coefficient according to the UNIQUAC equation is:

$$\ln \gamma_i = \ln \frac{\phi_i}{X_i} + \frac{z}{2} s_i \ln \frac{\theta_i}{\phi_i} + l_i - \frac{\phi_i}{X_i} \sum_j X_j l_j$$
$$+ s_i \left[1 - \ln \left(\sum_j \theta_j \tau_{ji} \right) - \sum_j \frac{\theta_j \tau_{ij}}{\sum_k \theta_k \tau_{kj}} \right] \tag{3.72}$$

with

$$\theta_i = \frac{s_i X_i}{\sum_j s_j X_j} ; \qquad \phi_i = \frac{r_i X_i}{\sum_j r_j X_j} ; \qquad l_j = \frac{z}{2}(r_j - s_j) - (r_j - 1) \tag{3.73}$$

where r_i and s_i are the structural parameters and z is the coordination index pertaining to the individual molecules. The binary constants τ_{ij} and τ_{ji} are empirical constants to be determined by binary data and used for multicomponent mixtures.

Costa et al. [45] have measured adsorption of binary and ternary mixtures of methane, ethane, ethylene, and propylene at 20°C and nearly 1 atm on a Spanish-made activated carbon (type AC-40). Using the nonideal adsorbed solution theory, activity coefficients in the binary adsorbates are calculated from the experimental data. (It should be noted, however, that the ideal solution equation for mixing [eq. 3.64], is apparently used in their calculations.) Typical results are shown in Figure 3.7 for the methane-ethane mixture. The empirical binary constants in the Wilson and UNIQUAC equations are then used to predict ternary-mixture equilibria. The predicted ternary adsorptions are indeed better than those predicted by IAS theory and the vacancy solution theory, although the predictions by the two latter theories are already within 10% of the experimental values [39, 45]. A detailed comparison will be given in a later section.

Talu [46] has used an equation similar to the UNIQUAC equation derived by Mauer and Prausnitz [49] in which a two-fluid theory is used. The dependence of activity coefficients on spreading pressure is expressed in terms of pure-component isosteric heats of adsorption.

Fundamental questions remain, however, on the validity of treating the adsorbate as a liquid solution. These questions should be addressed carefully before further developments are made on the nonideal adsorbed solution theory.

Consider the following anomalous and puzzling facts:

1. Adsorption of many mixtures can be predicted successfully by the ideal adsorbed solution theory; that is, the adsorbates obey Raoult's law. However, many of the same mixtures in the bulk liquid phase are nonideal [50].

2. As typically shown by Figure 3.7, deviations from Raoult's law reported for the mixed adsorbates are negative (i.e., $\gamma_i < 1$, based on calculations of limited

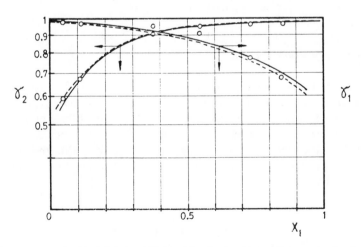

Figure 3.7 Experimental activity coefficients in the methane-ethane mixed adsorbate on activated carbon (Type AC-40) at 20°C. Circles are calculated from experimental data. Also shown are the empirically fitted Wilson equation (solid line) and UNIQUAC equation (dashed line). Source: Costa, Sotela, Calleja, and Marron [45]. Reprinted with permission.

data [51], however), whereas bulk liquid mixtures for some (or many) of the compounds display positive deviations. Good examples of this anomaly are seen in the adsorption of hydrocarbons [51]. Also, although the activity coefficients in the bulk liquids are nearly symmetric, centered at $X_1 = 0.5$, the distributions in the adsorbates are asymmetric, as shown in Figure 3.7.

These two facts point to the importance of the strong interactions between the adsorbate mixture and the solid surface. These interactions must be considered before meaningful correlations between the mixed adsorbates and liquid solutions can be made. The vacancy solution theory accounts for the solid-sorbate interactions by treating the solid surface as a thermodynamic entity, called *vacancy*. However, additional empirical constants are needed to account for such interactions.

Myers [51] suggests that the nonideality of the adsorbate can be an artifact caused by (incorrectly) considering a heterogeneous surface as a homogeneous one and applying the adsorbed solution model. This has been demonstrated for a surface consisting of two types of sites, each with a different heat of adsorption, as well as a pure-gas adsorption on both sites following the Langmuir isotherm. By comparing the mixture adsorption calculated by the extended Langmuir model, (incorrectly) assuming a homogeneous surface and applying the nonideal adsorbed solution model, false activity coefficients similar to those shown in Figure 3.7 are obtained [51]. However, it remains to be shown that the negative deviations from Raoult's law are associated with decreasing isosteric heats of adsorption when surface coverage increases. The latter can readily be calculated from the literature data (on isotherms at two temperatures). Surface heterogeneity is likely not the only reason for highly nonideal behaviors, such as the data reported by Talu. The most satisfactory model should encompass both nonideal solution behavior and surface heterogeneity, the latter being measurable.

3.3.5   Vacancy Solution Theory

The vacancy solution theory [52], described by equations 2.41 to 2.43, is also applicable to an n-component mixture by considering $n + 1$ species. The derivation of the model for multicomponent mixtures, with repetition of some of the equations for pure component, is given next for two versions: the vacancy solution model using the Wilson equation, which will be referred to as VSM, and the vacancy solution model using Flory-Huggins activity coefficient equations, which will be referred to as F-H VSM.

The VSM is extended first [53]. The single-component VSM isotherm is:

$$P = \left[\frac{n^\infty}{b_1} \frac{\theta}{1-\theta} \right] \left[\Lambda_{1v} \frac{1 - (1 - \Lambda_{v1})\theta}{\Lambda_{1v} + (1 - \Lambda_{1v})\theta} \right]$$
$$\exp\left[-\frac{\Lambda_{v1}(1 - \Lambda_{v1})\theta}{1 - (1 - \Lambda_{v1})\theta} - \frac{(1 - \Lambda_{1v})\theta}{\Lambda_{1v} + (1 - \Lambda_{1v})\theta} \right] \tag{3.74}$$

where subscripts 1 and v denote species 1 and vacancy, respectively, and θ is the fractional coverage with respect to the limiting amount adsorbed, n^∞.

The activity coefficients for i and v are given by the general form of the Wilson equation:

$$\ln \gamma_k = 1 - \ln \left[\sum_j X_j \Lambda_{kj} \right] - \sum_i \left[\frac{X_i \Lambda_{ik}}{\sum_j X_j \Lambda_{ij}} \right] \tag{3.75}$$

There are $n + 1$ equations for an n-component mixture.

An equilibrium relationship governing the distribution of species i between the adsorbed and gas phases is needed. Such a relationship can be derived by equating the chemical potentials of i in the two phases. (Raoult's law will result for ideal behavior and by using the same standard state for the two chemical potentials.) By further applying the relationship to infinite dilution, the following is obtained:

$$\phi_i Y_i P = \gamma_i X_i n_t \frac{n_i^\infty \Lambda_{iv}}{n_t^\infty b_i} \exp(\Lambda_{vi} - 1) \exp\left(\frac{\pi a_1}{RT}\right) \tag{3.76}$$

where ϕ_i = fugacity coefficient
$\quad n_t$ = total number of moles adsorbed
$\quad a_i$ = partial molar area of i

and the superscript denotes the limiting or maximum value.

The values of n_t^∞ and $\pi a_i / RT$ can be calculated by:

$$n_t^\infty = \sum X_i n_i^\infty \tag{3.77}$$

$$-\frac{\pi a_i}{RT} = \left[1 + \frac{n_t^\infty - n_i^\infty}{n_t} \right] \ln \gamma_v X_v \tag{3.78}$$

With the conditions,

$$\sum X_i = \sum Y_i = 1 \qquad (i \neq v) \tag{3.79}$$

Equations 3.74–3.79 are a complete set of equations that can be used for predicting multicomponent mixture adsorption from single-component isotherms. The adsorbate-surface interaction parameters, Λ_{iv} and Λ_{vi}, are empirical constants obtained from single-component data. The adsorbate-adsorbate interaction parameters, Λ_{ij} and Λ_{ji}, can be estimated by using equations similar to those used for bulk liquid mixtures. For similar adsorbates, the interactions may be neglected, or $\Lambda_{ij} = \Lambda_{ji} = 1$. The equations for estimating Λ_{ij} are:

$$\Lambda_{ij} = \frac{n_i^\infty}{n_j^\infty} \exp\left[-\frac{\lambda_{ij} - \lambda_{ii}}{RT} \right] \tag{3.80}$$

where

$$\lambda_{ii} = \frac{2}{z}(q + RT) \tag{3.81}$$

and

$$\lambda_{ij} = (\lambda_{ii}\lambda_{jj})^{1/2} \tag{3.82}$$

Here q is the isosteric heat of adsorption and z is the coordination number of the molecule in the adsorbate, which is evaluated empirically. The value of z in the zeolite cavity for several mixtures is assumed to be 3 [53].

With a given gas composition, T, P, and pure-gas isotherms, the procedure for calculating the equilibrium adsorbates is as follows:

1. Use equation 3.74 to obtain the constants n_i^∞, b_i, Λ_{iv}, and Λ_{vi} for each gas from pure-gas data.
2. Select a set of X_i and calculate n_t^∞ from equation 3.77.
3. Use equation 3.75 to calculate the activity coefficients.
4. Use equation 3.76 and 3.78 to calculate Y_i and n_t, noting that $\sum Y_i = 1$.

Steps 2–4 are iterated until the correct values for Y_i are reached.

The VSM has been applied with good results by Danner and co-workers as well as by other authors. Among the systems predicted by the VSM are binary mixtures on activated carbon [53] and zeolites [53, 54], and binary to quaternary mixtures on activated carbon [55]. To yield good predictions, the adsorbate-adsorbate interactions are neglected for activated carbon [53, 55], but must be included for certain gases (O_2, N_2, and CO) while excluded for others on zeolites [53, 54].

An interesting application of VSM is in the prediction of the adsorption azeotrope, as shown in curves B and C in Figure 3.8. The azeotropic behavior has been previously reported [56–59]. It indicates a reversal in selectivity, which occurs frequently when the two pure-gas isotherms cross over each other. Brunauer [56] has interpreted the phenomenon based on multilayer adsorption in which selectivity is reversed on second and higher layers, where the latent heat of condensation becomes the determining factor. Hyun and Danner [54] have shown that VSM is the only model capable of predicting the adsorption azeotrope among the models tested: extended Langmuir, IAS, and the simplified statistical thermodynamic model of Ruthven. The test is, however, not exhaustive. The azeotrope can also be predicted by other models [56], including the two-dimensional gas model to be discussed following this section.

The VSM has been modified to the F-H VSM [60], which contains one less constant for each gas component without a loss in accuracy. As given in equation 2.43a,b, the pure-gas isotherms are:

$$P = \left(\frac{n_1^\infty}{b_1}\frac{\theta}{1-\theta}\right)\exp\left(\frac{\alpha_{1v}^2\theta}{1+\alpha_{1v}\theta}\right) \tag{3.83}$$

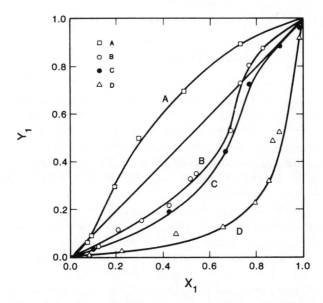

Figure 3.8 Adsorption phase diagrams for binary mixtures on zeolite 13X at 137.8 kPa: (A) $C_2H_4(1)$–$CO_2(2)$ at 298K, (B) i–$C_4H_{10}(1)$–$C_2H_4(2)$ at 298K, (C) i–$C_4H_{10}(1)$–$C_2H_4(2)$ at 373K, (D) i–$C_4H_{10}(1)$–$C_2H_6(2)$ at 298K. Source: Hyun and Danner [54]. Reprinted with permission.

where

$$\alpha_{1v} = \frac{a_1}{a_v} - 1 \tag{3.84}$$

and a is the molar area.

For a multicomponent system, the activity coefficients are given by the Flory-Huggins equation:

$$\ln \gamma_i = -\ln \sum_j \frac{X_j}{\alpha_{ij} + 1} + \left[1 - \left(\sum_j \frac{X_j}{\alpha_{ij} + 1} \right)^{-1} \right] \tag{3.85}$$

where $\alpha_{ii} = 0$ and the summations are over all components, including the vacancy. Equation 3.76 can be rewritten with the activity coefficients defined by equation 3.85 to give:

$$Y_i \phi_i P = \gamma_i X_i \frac{n_t}{n_t^\infty} \frac{n_i^\infty}{b_i} \left[\frac{\exp \alpha_{iv}}{1 + \alpha_{iv}} \right] \exp \left\{ \left[\left(\frac{n_i^\infty - n_t^\infty}{n_t} \right) - 1 \right] \ln \gamma_v X_v \right\} \tag{3.86}$$

From the definition of α, given in equation 3.84,

$$\alpha_{ij} = \frac{\alpha_{iv} + 1}{\alpha_{jv} + 1} - 1 \tag{3.87}$$

As in the VSM,

$$n_t^\infty = \sum X_i n_i^\infty \qquad (3.88)$$

Equations 3.83 to 3.88 are sufficient for predicting multicomponent mixture adsorption from pure-gas isotherms. The pure-gas isotherm requires three fitting parameters rather than four in the VSM. The calculation procedure starts with fitting three parameters from the pure-gas data for each component. The binary parameters, α_{ij}, are determined by using equation 3.87. A trial-and-error scheme is then needed, as for the VSM, by using equations 3.85, 3.86, and 3.88 to iterate for Y_i and determine n_t, noting that $\sum Y_i = 1$.

The F-H VSM has been tested for a number of systems [60]. Equally excellent predictions are obtained by the VSM and the F-H VSM. (There is, of course, no obvious reason to expect the F-H VSM to give better predictions than the VSM except that F-H avoids regression problems caused by cross-correlation of VSM parameters.) The least satisfactory predictions by both models are for quaternary [55] and some ternary mixtures [55, 60]. One such prediction is shown for the O_2–N_2–CO adsorption on zeolite 10X, from the data of Dorfman and Danner [61] in Figures 3.9a and 3.9b. In this case, the F-H VSM is actually better than the VSM.

3.3.6   Two-Dimensional Gas Model

An interesting alternative approach to adsorption is to consider the adsorbed phase as a nonideal compressed gas. Extensive work has been done on this concept by Ross and Olivier [62]. By applying the mixing rules, Hoory and Prausnitz [63] extended the isotherm for mixed gases. The resulting model is best suited for adsorption below monolayer coverage on homogeneous surfaces.

Ross and Olivier [62] have found that for submonolayer adsorption, the properties of the adsorbed phase can be adequately represented by a two-dimensional form of the van der Waals equation of state:

$$\pi = \frac{kT}{\sigma - \beta} - \frac{\alpha}{\sigma^2} \qquad (3.89)$$

where π = spreading pressure
σ = area occupied by each molecule at π
α = constant

The two-dimensional van der Waals constant, β, has been shown to be approximately equal to the molecular area at monolayer coverage [64]. The following corresponding isotherm can be obtained by means of the Gibbs transformation:

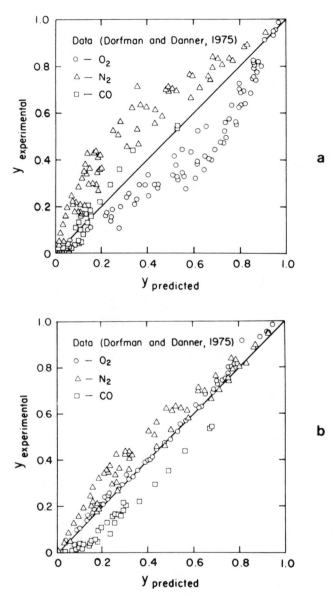

Figure 3.9 Predictions of gas-phase mole fractions for O_2–N_2–CO mixtures adsorbed on zeolite 10X at 144.3K and 1 atm from single-gas isotherms by (a) the VSM, and (b) the F-H VSM. Source: Cochran, Kabel, and Danner [60]. Reprinted with permission.

$$P = \frac{K\theta}{1-\theta} \exp\left[\frac{\theta}{1-\theta} - \frac{2\alpha\theta}{kT\beta}\right]$$

(3.90)

In equation 3.90, P is replaced by fugacity if the gas is nonideal.

For a binary mixture, it is assumed that the binary van der Waals constants, α_M and β_M, are related to those of pure components by [63]:

$$\beta_M = X_1\beta_1 + X_2\beta_2 \qquad (3.91)$$

and

$$\alpha_M = \alpha_1 X_1^2 + 2\alpha_{12}X_1X_2 + \alpha_2 X_2^2 \qquad (3.92)$$

where α_{12} is a constant characteristic of the interaction between the two components, and is assumed to be:

$$\alpha_{12} = (\alpha_1\alpha_2)^{1/2} \qquad (3.93)$$

By using the same transformation, and by assuming ideal gas behavior, the mixed isotherms are:

$$\ln PY_1 = \ln\left(\frac{X_1 K_1 \beta_1}{\sigma - \beta_M}\right) + \frac{\beta_1}{\sigma - \beta_M} - \frac{2}{\sigma kT}(\alpha_1 X_1 + \alpha_{12}X_2) \qquad (3.94)$$

$$\ln PY_2 = \ln\left(\frac{X_2 K_2 \beta_2}{\sigma - \beta_M}\right) + \frac{\beta_2}{\sigma - \beta_M} - \frac{2}{\sigma kT}(\alpha_2 X_2 + \alpha_{12}X_1) \qquad (3.95)$$

The molecular areas are calculated from the surface area of the solid, A,

$$\beta_i = \frac{A}{n_{mi}N_0} \qquad (3.96)$$

where n_m = monolayer adsorbed amount

N_0 = Avogadro number

Given the pure-component isotherms, equation 3.90 is used to evaluate the three constants for each component: K, α, and β. At the same T, for a given set of P and Y_i, equations 3.94 and 3.95 are used to solve for σ and $X_1(X_2 = 1 - X_1)$. The total number of moles adsorbed, n_t, is related to σ by:

$$\sigma = \frac{A}{n_t N_0} \qquad (3.97)$$

The model described can readily be generalized to multicomponent mixtures. An extension has been made to heterogeneous surfaces by considering that the surface consists of patches [63].

A similar model has been developed by Friederich and Mullins [35], but the use of the model requires experimental isotherms measured at constant gas composition and considerable iteration.

The Hoory-Prausnitz model has been tested against experimental data on adsorption of binary mixtures of ethane-ethylene-propane-propylene on carbon black at 25°C [35], and ethane-ethylene on zeolite 13X [36]. The carbon black used here is a graphitized powder which yields rather constant isosteric heats of adsorption below monolayer coverage [65]. In both cases, the model gives excellent predictions, nearly as good as those by the IAS. The model has also been used by Hoory and Prausnitz [63] to predict binary adsorption from pure-component data on a graphitized carbon, and some interesting results emerge. These predictions have not been confirmed, however, because no mixture data are available on the system. They show that the two-dimensional gas model is capable of predicting: (1) positive deviations from Raoult's law (activity coefficients greater than unity) and (2) adsorption azeotrope. The adsorbed solution models except the VSM are not capable of making such predictions.

For the adsorption of $CFCl_3$–$CHCl_3$ on graphitized carbon, the two-dimensional gas model and the IAS model yield the same predictions. The agreement is not surprising because these two molecules have similar values of α and β and consequently form an ideal mixture. The two models give different predictions, however, for the $CFCl_3$–C_6H_6 and N_2–Ar mixtures on the same sorbent. The binary results on the $CFCl_3$–C_6H_6 adsorption predicted by the two-dimensional gas model yield activity coefficients greater than unity as shown in Figure 3.10. The activity coefficients are calculated according to the same definition used in the adsorbed solution theory [31, 63]. For adsorption of N_2–Ar on graphitized carbon at 90.1K, adsorption azeotrope is predicted by the two-dimensional gas model.

3.3.7 Simplified Statistical Thermodynamic Model of Ruthven

The regular cagelike structure of zeolites makes them amenable for treatment by the statistical thermodynamic method. The models derived in this section apply only to zeolites.

For pure-component sorption in zeolites, several isotherms have been derived by different authors [66–70] and have been reviewed by Barrer [71] and Ruthven [72]. The following derivation is taken from Ruthven and Wong [73].

The zeolite contains B identical cages, each capable of sorbing up to m gas molecules. It is assumed that the interactions and interchange between the molecules in neighboring cages are negligible. A single cage is used to represent the whole system. The grand partition function (Ξ) for the cage is:

$$\Xi = 1 + Z_1 a + Z_2 a^2 + \cdots + Z_m a^m \tag{3.98}$$

where Z_s is the configuration integral of the cage containing s molecules and is defined by:

$$Z_s = \frac{1}{s!} \int \exp[-U_s(r_1, r_2, \ldots r_s)/kT] dr_1 dr_2 \ldots dr_s \tag{3.99}$$

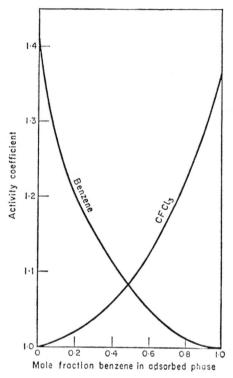

Figure 3.10 Activity coefficients for adsorbed mixtures of $CFCl_3$–C_6H_6 on graphitized carbon at 273.2K and 6 Torr, as predicted by the two-dimensional gas model. Source: Hoory and Prausnitz [63]. Reprinted with permission.

where U_s is the potential of the molecules located at position vectors $r_1, r_2, \ldots r_s$ and the integration is carried out over the entire volume of the cage. The quantity a is the activity, $a = \lambda(2\pi mkT/h^2)^{3/2}$, which is P/kT for an ideal gas.

The average number of sorbate molecules per cage, C, is given by:

$$C = \frac{\partial \ln \Xi}{\partial \ln a} = \frac{Z_1 a + 2Z_2 a^2 + \cdots + mZ_m a^m}{1 + Z_1 a + Z_2 a^2 + \cdots + Z_m a^m} \qquad (3.100)$$

The same expression for C can be derived if the system is considered to consist of B cages.

The isotherm given by equation 3.100 is general, but evaluating the exact configuration integrals is difficult, especially for a large s. Calculations of the integrals by several authors have been reviewed by Barrer [71]. Ruthven [68] assumes that the sorbate behaves as a van der Waals gas, and thus:

$$Z_s = \frac{Z_1^s}{s!}(1 - sb/v)^s \exp\left(\frac{sb\varepsilon}{vkT}\right) \qquad (3.101)$$

where b = van der Waals co-volume
$\qquad v$ = volume of the cage
$\qquad \varepsilon$ = constant

The factor $1 - sb/v$ corrects for the reduction in free volume, and the exponential factor represents the mutual interaction of sorbates. For practical application, these two factors can be combined as a single empirical constant:

$$Z_s = \frac{Z_1^s}{s!} R_s \qquad (3.102)$$

where R_s is now a temperature-dependent constant characteristic of the sorbate-sorbate system. Values of $R > 1.0$ represent attractive interactions; those with $R < 1.0$ represent repulsive forces between molecules. (Empirically, $R < 1.0$ indicates that repulsive forces dominate.) For $s = 1$, $Z_1 a = KP$ where K is the Henry constant. With the foregoing simplifications, the following semiempirical isotherm results:

$$C = \frac{KP + (KP)^2 R_1 + \cdots + \dfrac{(KP)^m}{(m-1)!} R_m}{1 + KP + \dfrac{1}{2!}(KP)^2 R_1 + \cdots + \dfrac{(KP)^m}{m!} R_m} \qquad (3.103)$$

This isotherm is extended to multicomponent adsorption by Ruthven and co-workers [73, 74]. A further simplifying assumption needs to be made in the configuration integral for a mixture. For a cage containing i molecules of A and j molecules of B, $i + j = s$, the configuration integral is assumed to be:

$$Z_{ij} a_A^i a_B^j = \frac{(K_A P_A)^i (K_B P_B)^j}{i!j!} (R_{As}^i R_{Bs}^j)^{1/(i+j)} \qquad (3.104)$$

This assumption is equivalent to using the mixing rule. The assumption is good for molecules of similar sizes and with weak interactions (e.g., nonpolar molecules). The mixed-gas isotherms using the foregoing configuration integral are:

$$C_A = \frac{K_A P_A + \sum_j \sum_i \dfrac{(K_A P_A)^i (K_B P_B)^j}{(i-1)!j!}(R_{As}^i R_{Bs}^j)^{1/(i+j)}}{1 + K_A P_A + K_B P_B + \sum_j \sum_i \dfrac{(K_A P_A)^i (K_B P_B)^j}{i!j!}(R_{As}^i R_{Bs}^j)^{1/(i+j)}} \qquad (3.105)$$

With a corresponding equation for B, the summation is carried out over all possible values of i and j that are subject to $i + j \leqslant s$.

Equations 3.103 and 3.105 can be used to predict mixture adsorption from single-gas isotherms. Equation 3.103 is first used to evaluate the constants K, R_1,

$R_2, \ldots, R_s$ for each component. Equation 3.105 is then used to directly calculate mixture adsorption. In using equation 3.103, the Henry constant, K, should be evaluated first by using data at low pressures, or by extrapolating a plot of $\log(P/C)$ versus C as recommended by Barrer and Lee [75].

To make the data fitting manageable, the value of s, or the number of Rs, should be limited to less than 3 or 4. A practical way of limiting s is by choosing a smaller subsystem — that is, by using a fraction of the cage as the representative subsystem. An example of using a fractional cage is given by Ruthven and Wong [73] in fitting the data of Danner and Choi on C_2H_4–C_2H_6 adsorption in 13X zeolite [36]. The parameters for fitting equation 3.103 are given in Table 3.1. The comparison between the predictions for mixture adsorption given by both sets of parameters (whole-cage and half-cage), based on equation 3.105, and the experimental data is excellent. Also, the two sets of parameters yield predictions within a few percentage points [73]. In this system the saturation adsorption for both components is nearly 5 molecules/cage; hence $s = 5$ and 5 Rs are needed. By using a half-cage subsystem, s is reduced to 2. The calculated concentration, of course, must be doubled to give the whole-cage value.

The simplified statistical thermodynamic model (SSTM) by Ruthven has been tested for a number of binary mixture systems on zeolites. They include: C_2 to C_4 hydrocarbons and CO_2 on zeolite 5A [73, 74, 76], O_2–N_2–CO–CH_4 on zeolite 5A [77], C_2H_4–C_2H_6 on zeolite 13X [36, 73] and cyclohexane-n-heptane on zeolite 13X [73]. Good agreements are shown for all systems with the exception of Holborow's data [73, 74, 76].

The SSTM is best suited for large (so s is small), nonpolar molecules of similar

Table 3.1 Parameters for Fitting Equation 3.103 for Adsorption of C_2H_4–C_2H_6 on Zeolite 13X

	C_2H_4		C_2H_6	
	298K	*323K*	*298K*	*323K*
1. Based on subsystem = 1 cage				
K^a	0.16	0.1	0.018	0.0089
R_1	0.99	1.304	0.967	1.013
R_2	1.167	0.337	1.102	1.024
R_3	0.537	0.012	1.10	0.543
R_4	0.147	0.042	0.636	0.225
R_5	0.018	0	0	0.172
2. Based on subsystem = 1/2 cage				
K^b	0.08	0.05	0.0089	0.0045
R_1	1.112	0.40	1.686	0.897
R_2	0.233	0.057	0.44	0.564

Source: Ruthven and Wong [73]. Reprinted with permission.
[a]Molecules/cage/Torr.
[b]Molecules/half cage/Torr.

sizes. In addition, the fractional-cage subsystem (for reducing s) cannot be used for mixtures containing small molecules or those with different sizes.

The model appears to be empirical when applied, but it has a sound theoretical base. For $m = 1$, equation 3.103 reduces to a Langmuir isotherm, whereas equation 3.105 reduces to an extended Langmuir isotherm for binary mixtures. For sorbates of equal molecular volume, it is reduced to the IAS model [74].

An encouraging note on the SSTM is its potential application in design and modeling of gas separation processes. The SSTM and the LRC are the only two models that do not require iteration in calculating mixed-gas adsorption (in fact, their mathematical forms are similar). Hence a considerable amount of computation is saved by using these models. Although it lacks the rigorous theoretical basis of SSTM, the LRC has already been widely used for design and modeling.

3.3.8   Lattice Solution Model of Lee

Lee [19] has developed a model based on the lattice theory of solutions with the assumption that adsorption occurs by micropore filling. As such, it is suited for all microporous sorbents, although it is intended for zeolites and should work best at subcritical conditions.

For pore filling, the maximum volume for adsorption, W_0, is the same for all adsorbates. The molar volume for pure component, i, at T and P_i, is:

$$(V_i^0)_{P_i} = \frac{W_0}{(n_i)_{P_i}} \qquad (3.106)$$

and the free energy for adsorption is:

$$G_i = RT \ln \frac{(V_i^0)_{P_i}}{V_{gi}} = RT \ln \frac{(V_i^0)_{P_i} P_i}{RT} \qquad (3.107)$$

where V_{gi} is the gas molar volume, and the second equation applies to an ideal gas.

The pure gases are now mixed along with their respective adsorbed phases, each at its partial pressure P_i, to give a total pressure P, at temperature T. The molar free energy of adsorption of the mixture for a binary system is:

$$G_m = X_1 G_1 + X_2 G_2 + \Delta G_m \qquad (3.108)$$

where ΔG_m represents the free energy of mixing in the adsorbed phase. This quantity can be obtained according to the lattice theory of solutions:

$$\Delta G_m = X_1 RT \ln \phi_1 + X_2 RT \ln \phi_2 + (X_1 X_2 \phi_1 \phi_2)^{1/2} A_{12} \qquad (3.109)$$

where ϕ_1 and ϕ_2 are the volume fractions in the adsorbed phase, which can be obtained from the mole fractions and molar volumes.

The quantity A_{12} is the *interchange energy* of adsorption and is important. It contains not only the interchange energy of the mixture, but also that between the adsorbates and surface.

By assuming there is no volume change upon the mixing of adsorbates, the molar volume of the mixture is:

$$V_m = X_1(V_1^0)_P + X_2(V_2^0)_P \qquad (3.110)$$

where

$$(V_i^0)_P = \frac{W_0}{(n_i^0)_P} \qquad (3.111)$$

Since the molar free energy of adsorption for the mixture is:

$$G_m = RT \ln \frac{V_m}{V_{gm}} \qquad (3.112)$$

where subscript g indicates gas phase, which is assumed ideal, equation 3.108 gives us:

$$V_m = \frac{RT}{P} \exp[(X_1 G_1 + X_2 G_2 + \Delta G_m)/RT] \qquad (3.113)$$

Equation 3.113 is an implicit expression of the Y-X phase diagram, with A_{12} being a parameter in ΔG_m.

The number of moles adsorbed is:

$$n_t = \frac{W_0}{V_m} \qquad (3.114)$$

and for each component

$$n_i = X_i n_t \qquad (3.115)$$

For a given set of T, P, and Y_i, the calculation procedure is as follows:

1. W_0 is obtained from any set of pure-gas data by a potential-theory plot (e.g., Figure 2.10).
2. From pure-gas data, calculate n_1^0 and n_2^0 at, respectively, P_1 and P_2, and both at T.
3. Calculate $(V_1^0)_{P_1}$ and $(V_2^0)_{P_2}$ from equation 3.106, G_1 and G_2 from equation 3.107 and $(V_1^0)_P$ and $(V_2^0)_P$ from equation 3.111.

4. Assume values for X_1 and X_2, calculate V_m from equation 3.110 and ΔG_m from equation 3.109.
5. Use equation 3.113 to check the value of V_m. Steps 4 and 5 are iterated until the values of V_m match.

Attempts to calculate A_{12} from molecular properties have failed [19]. A_{12} should be a function of T, P, and composition (X) for a given system. Lee states that at constant T and P, the values of A_{12} are nearly constant over the entire range of X for several binary mixtures [19]. Thus A_{12} can be determined by one experimental mixture data point. Ten binary-gas-zeolite systems have been studied by Lee, and the results are all superior to the models of Cook and Basmadjian and the IAS. The values of A_{12}/RT range from 6 to 19 for these systems. The gases studied by Lee include O_2, N_2, CO, and the highly polar H_2S and SO_2; the zeolites are 5A, 10X, and H-mordenite.

Danner and Choi [36] have tested Lee's model with their data on C_2H_4–C_2H_6 on zeolite 13X at 25°C and 50°C, and found the model to be inferior to the other three tested: IAS, two-dimensional gas and SSTM (in descending order for best agreement). The disappointing result was that A_{12} varies with composition in the range between 5 and 3.5 kcal/gmole, or approximately between 8 and 6 for A_{12}/RT. This is not in agreement with Lee's finding that A_{12} is a constant over composition. A possible reason for the disagreement is that the temperature is above or near the critical temperatures of C_2H_4 ($T_c = 283.05K$) and C_2H_6 ($T_c = 305.38K$); Lee's best results are obtained under subcritical conditions.

3.3.9 Law-of-Mass-Action Models

The equilibrium adsorption of a binary mixture, A–B, on a surface, S, is treated as a substitution reaction:

$$A + \delta_{BA}BS \rightleftarrows AS + \delta_{BA}B \tag{3.116}$$

where δ_{BA} is the stoichiometric coefficient, which indicates the selectivity. At equilibrium,

$$K = \frac{C_{AS}C_B^\delta}{C_A C_{BS}^\delta} = \frac{n_A C_B^\delta}{C_A n_B^\delta} \tag{3.117}$$

where C denotes molar concentration and δ has replaced δ_{BA}. Equation 3.117 is written for adsorption from both gas and liquid phases. To account for nonideal behavior, K is expressed by [78–80]:

$$\ln K = \ln \frac{n_A(C_B\gamma_B)^\delta}{(C_A\gamma_A)n_B^\delta} = \ln K_s - \ln \gamma_{sA} + \delta \ln \gamma_{sB} \tag{3.118}$$

where γ is the activity coefficient, the subscript s indicates adsorbed state, and K_s is given by:

$$K_s = \frac{C_{sA}\gamma_{sA}(C_B\gamma_B)^\delta}{C_A\gamma_A(C_{sB}\gamma_{sB})^\delta} \tag{3.119}$$

The problem of determining equilibrium mixture adsorption is thus reduced to the determination of K, or the determination of K_s, γ_{sA} and γ_{sB}. It is possible to determine these three parameters from fundamental thermodynamic principles. For example, K_s can be calculated by using statistical methods — that is, using the partition functions when knowing the exact states of the adsorbed phase; and γ_{sA} and γ_{sB} can be calculated from solution thermodynamics, as shown in sections 3.3.4 and 3.3.5. These coefficients become unity for an ideal solution. This approach is referred to as the "law of mass action" by earlier authors [81], and as "stoichiometry theory" by Tolmachev et al. [78–80]. It is essentially the same as the concept of dynamic equilibrium between gas and adsorbed phases that is used to derive the Langmuir isotherm.

The three parameters, K_s, γ_{sA}, and γ_{sB}, have been calculated for a number of binary systems using basic thermodynamic relations and the Dubinin-Polanyi potential theory. The equilibrium constant, K_s, can be related to the individual affinity coefficients, β_A and β_B, which are defined in Chapter 2. The resulting relationship is:

$$\ln K_s = \ln\left[\frac{n_A^0 C_{BO}^\delta}{C_{AO}(n_B^0)^\delta}\right]_T - (\delta\beta_B - \beta_A)\frac{2.303\Gamma(1/k)}{T^k B^{1/2}} \tag{3.120}$$

where C_{AO} and C_{BO} are the molar concentrations of saturated vapor, $\Gamma(1/k)$ is the gamma function and n^0 is the limiting amount adsorbed (when all pores are filled), given by:

$$n_i^0 = \frac{W_0}{V_i} \tag{3.121}$$

W_0 can be obtained from any pure-component data by extrapolation (see Figure 2.10). V_i is the temperature-dependent molar volume, which can be calculated [17]. The constants k and B are determined from the pure-component data by using the general kth power Dubinin-Astakhov equation [82, 83]. The affinity coefficients are expressed relative to a standard vapor for which $\beta = 1$. Benzene is used as the standard and β_i is determined by the pure-component data. The value of δ is:

$$\delta_{BA} = \frac{n_B^0}{n_A^0} = \frac{V_A}{V_B} \tag{3.122}$$

which is the ratio of molar volumes. Thus K_s can be evaluated by equation 3.120 from the pure-component data.

As mentioned earlier, a number of models can be used to calculate the activity coefficients of *A* and *B* in the adsorbed mixture. Tolmachev et al. [80] have used the potential theory and the Gibbs-Duhem equation to calculate γ_{sA} and γ_{sB}, which is based on the experimental data of another binary mixture adsorption system — that is, *M-N* adsorption on another sorbent. For the calculation, a similarity assumption is made between the characteristic curves of the mutual replacement for *A* and *B* and those for *M* and *N*.

Tolmachev and co-workers have used their calculation procedure for a number of binary mixtures on activated carbon and zeolites. Deviations for *K* from experimental data not exceeding 10–20% are reported [80].

3.4 COMPARISON OF MODELS AND EXPERIMENTS

Compared to the number of models that have been proposed, experimental data for mixture adsorption are indeed scarce. Consequently, most of the models have been tested only by very few sets of experimental data, and these experimental data are primarily for binary mixtures at low coverages or at low pressures. In addition, the experimental error can be substantial as a result of the experimental complexity. A degree of confidence may be gained, however, if the data can satisfy any one of the thermodynamic consistency tests [116].

The most commonly used set of experimental data for model testing is that of Szepesy and Illes [23, 24] on the pure-gas and binary adsorption of methane, ethane, ethylene, acetylene, propane, propylene, butane, and carbon dioxide on carbon at 20–90°C and pressures up to 900 Torr for pure-gas and nearly 760 Torr for binary mixtures. Because their data are complete and reported in tabulated forms, almost all models have been compared with the data. An experimental error was involved, however, which should be kept in mind whenever their data are used. The error was caused by assuming that the adsorption of hydrogen on activated carbon was negligible [24], and consequently using hydrogen instead of helium to measure the dead-space volumes [23, 84]. Hydrogen was also used as an "inert" carrier gas in two of the binary adsorption experiments [24]. A recalculation of their data is possible if all the raw data are available. Without the detailed raw data, an assessment of the approximate errors in their results is given next. The volume of the dead space was 19–26 cm³, which was the volume surrounding the carbon sample and enclosed by stopcocks 3, 5, and 6 in Figure 2 of reference 23. The amount of carbon sample was approximately 5 g. The amount of hydrogen adsorbed can be estimated from their mixture data [24, Tables XI, XII], which was 1.17 ccSTP/g H_2 at approximately 0.8 atm H_2 pressure. (This value agrees with the H_2 isotherm on PCB activated carbon measured by Saunders [34].) The reservoir was burette B_1 [23, Fig. 2], which had a maximum volume of 100 cm³. The approximate errors for pure-gas data are given later on by assuming a reservoir volume of 100 cm³, which would yield the minimum errors. For methane adsorption, their reported amount adsorbed was low by approximately 6% at 20°C and 330 Torr, and low by approximately 12% at 90°C and 330 Torr. For the amount of propylene adsorbed, the approximate errors were 0.2% too low at 20°C and 107 Torr; and 1.5% at 90°C and 117 Torr. The error was greater for the less strongly adsorbed species and higher temperatures. Thus the errors for other gases would fall between those for methane and propylene. The total amounts of mixtures adsorbed were also low. The error in the dead-space measurement also resulted in an error in the X-Y phase diagram. Since the amount and the composition of the adsorbed phase were calculated as the difference between the gases before and after adsorption took place, the corrected selectivity for their data should be shifted toward unity. Although it is not possible to calculate the percentage errors in their X-Y diagrams, a few percentage points would be a reasonable estimate.

The most commonly used plot for reporting binary mixture data is the X-Y phase diagram. It should be noted, however, that the X-Y diagram represents only half of the data, and it frequently can be misleading. The data are complete only when the total amount is reported, which is a function of composition, $n_t(X)$. It is not unusual that a good fit on the X-Y diagram between theory and experiment is obtained, but the actual amounts adsorbed deviate significantly. Examples of this can be found in oxygen-carbon monoxide adsorption on zeolite 10X [19, Figs. 5, 12]; ethane-ethylene on zeolite 13X [36, Figs. 4, 5]; and oxygen-carbon monoxide on zeolite 10X [60, Figs. 8, 9].

3.4.1   Comparison between Literature Data and Models

The data in the literature on mixture adsorption primarily concern two sorbents: activated carbon and zeolites. The experimental data are compared with various theories and models, as shown in Tables 3.2 and 3.3. The comparisons are shown as approximate percentage differences, either positive or negative, between experiment and theory.

The list of publications on experimental data for mixture adsorption is short. The data are primarily on binary mixtures at subatmospheric pressures. In addition, the binary mixtures frequently consist of similar molecules, the ideal pair being C_2H_4–C_2H_6. Under these circumstances most of the theories give reasonably good predictions. At higher pressures (20°C and above 1 atm) the adsorbate concentrations are higher, and deviations between theory and experiments over 20% are generally observed. Replacement of pressure by fugacity does not significantly improve the model predictions [95].

Experimental data for mixtures containing more than two components are quite rare. From the limited amount of data, however, it generally becomes clear that as the number of components increases, the model predictions become worse. Ternary mixture data are available [7, 25, 45, 46, 61, 55, 95]. The last two references also contain data on four- and five-component mixtures. All experimental data show increasingly poor model predictions as the number of components in the mixture increases. The extensive data by Ritter [95] are shown in Figures 3.11 and

Table 3.2 Approximate Deviations between Experimental Data and Theories for Adsorption on Activated Carbon

Mixture, T, P	Langmuir + LRC	Potential	IAS[a]	VSM [53, 60]	Cook + Basmadjian[b]	2-D Gas
CH_4–C_2H_6, 20°C, 1 atm [24][c]		10% [20]	<5% [31]	<5% [53, 60]		
CH_4–C_2H_6, 212; 301K, 20 atm [25]	20% [41]		20% [41]			
CH_4–C_2H_4, 20°C, 1 atm [24][c]		<5% [20]			5% [32]	
CH_4–C_2H_4, 212; 301K, 20 atm [25]	20% [41]	20% [25]	20% [41]			
C_2H_4–C_2H_6, 20°C, 1 atm [24][c]	5% [41]	<5% [20]	<5% [35]	<5% [53, 60]		
C_2H_4–C_2H_6, 212; 301K, 20 atm [25]	15%	20% [25]	5% [41]			<5% [35]
H_2–CH_4, 22–207°C, 1–40 atm [34, 93][c]		15%	15%			
C_2H_6–C_3H_8, 20°C, 1 atm [24][c]	5% [13, 32]	<5% [20]	5% [32, 35]	<5% [53, 60]		<5% [35]
C_3H_6–C_3H_8, 20°C, 1 atm [24, 35][c]		10% [20]	10% [35]	<5% [60]	5% [32]	<5% [35]
C_3H_8–nC_4H_{10}, 20°C, 1 atm [24][c]		10% [20]		<5% [53]		
CO_2–C_2H_4, 20°C, 1 atm [24][c]						
CH_4–C_2H_4–C_2H_6, 20°C, 1 atm [45]			10% [39]	10% [39]		
H_2–CO–CO_2–CH_4, 25°C, 3.4 atm [55]			2–40% [55]	2–50% [55]		
H_2S–CO–CO_2–CH_4, 22; 102°C, 8–35 atm [95]	50%		50%			
H_2S–CO–CO_2–CH_4–H_2, 22; 102°C, 8–35 atm [95]	50%		50%			

CH_4–C_2H_6, CH_4–CO, CH_4–CO_2, CH_4–N_2, 25°C, 0–30 atm [91]. Excellent correlations by potential theory, except for CH_4–CO_2 with 20%. H_2O with C_6H_6 or acetone or methanol or toluene, 30°C, 1 atm [93]. Correlations within 15% by potential theory with capillary condensation. H_2O with water-immiscible hydrocarbons, 25°C, 1 atm [114, 115]. Correlations within 30% by potential theory.

Note: The reference numbers are shown in square brackets.
The approximate deviations in Tables 3.2 and 3.3 are based on the amounts adsorbed, when available. X–Y diagrams are used when the amounts are not reported.

[a] The binary mixture data of CH_4, C_2H_4, C_2H_6, and C_3H_6, except C_2H_4–C_2H_6, at 20°C and 1 atm, showed deviations of up to 40% with IAS [45].
[b] Data of Lewis et al. [16] on binary mixtures of hydrocarbons from CH_4 to C_4H_{10} at 20°C and 1 atm fit Cook and Basmadjian to within 5%, and fit the Lewis correlation to within 10%.
[c] An experimental error has been found (see section 3.4) in Szepesy and Illes [23, 24]. The amounts adsorbed were too low by approximately 0.2–12%.

Table 3.3 Approximate Deviations between Experiments and Theories for Adsorption on Zeolites

Mixture, Zeolite, T, P	Langmuir +LRC	IAS	VSM [53, 60]	SSTM	Basmadjian +Cook	Lee
O₂-N₂; 5A, 144K, 1 atm [42]				<10% [77]		0–10% [19]
O₂-CO, 10X, 144K, 1 atm [42]		20% [39]	30% [39, 53]ª; 5% [60]			
O₂-CO, 10X, 228K, 1 atm [85]			<10% [53]	<10% [53]		
O₂-N₂; 5A, 278–303K, 1.7–4.4 atm [86]		<5% [86]	5% [86]	<5% [86]	<5% [86]	0–10% [19]
O₂-N₂; 5A, 144K, 1 atm [42]				<10% [77]		
O₂-N₂; 10X, 228K, 1 atm [85]			<10% [53]	<10% [53]		
N₂-CO₂; 4A; 10X, 201–325K, 1–100 atm [101]	15% [101]					
N₂-CH₄, 5A, 123–295K, 1 atm [87]	15% [7]	30% [7] Poorᵇ				
NH₃-nC₆H₁₄, NaCaA, 50–250°C, <1 atm [92]						
CO₂-H₂S, 5A, 10X, 295K, 1 atm [19]		>10% [19]			>10% [19]	<10% [19]
CO₂-SO₂, H-mordenite, 0–100°C, 1 atm [88]		Poor [19]			Poor [19]	10% [19]

C₂H₄–C₂H₆, 13X, 25; 50°C, 1.36 atm [36]	<5% [89]	<5% [36]		<10% [36]	5–50% [19]
C₂H₄–iC₄H₁₀, 13X, 393K, 1.36 atm [54]		c	<5% [54]	c	
CO₂–C₂H₄, 5A, 50°C, 8 Torr [76]		20% [76]		<10% [76]	
C₂H₄–C₃H₈, 5A, 50°C, 8 Torr [76]		20% [76]		<10% [76]	
O₂–CO–N₂, 10X, 144K, 1 atm [61]		20% [39]	40% [39, 53]ᵃ; 20% [60]		
CO₂–N₂–O₂, 5A, −98–316°F, 1–100 atm [7]	15% [7]	50% [7]			

CH₄–C₂H₆, CH₄–CO, CH₄–CO₂, CH₄–N₂, 5A, 298K, 0–30 atm [91]. Excellent correlation with potential theory, except CH_4–CO_2 with 10%. Binary and ternary mixtures of CO_2–H_2S–C_3H_8 in H-mordenite, 30°C, <100 Torr [46]. Experimental activity coefficients were 0.1–0.5, indicating highly nonideal adsorbate [46].

The reference numbers are shown in square brackets.

ᵃThe deviation can be reduced by including a sorbate-sorbate interaction parameter obtained from one mixture data point [39, 53].

ᵇResults expressed in average separation factor (α), which deviates from IAS by 40–600% [92].

ᶜAzeotrope not predicted.

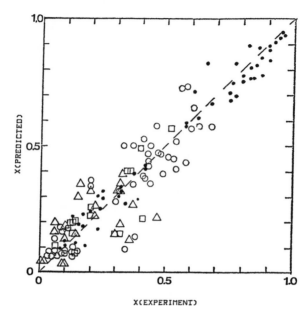

X(EXPERIMENT)

Figure 3.11 Comparison of adsorbed-phase mole fraction with that predicted by the IAS theory for 2-(●), 3-(○), 4-(□), and 5-(△) component mixtures of H_2, CO, CH_4, CO_2, and H_2S on activated carbon at two temperatures (22 and 102°C) and 8–35 atm pressure. Source: Ritter [95].

3.12. The model predictions for binary mixtures are generally satisfactory. Deviations of 50% or more are seen for four- and five-component mixtures.

3.4.2   Comparison and Use of Models

As seen in Tables 3.2 and 3.3, the agreement between experiments and theory is generally better for activated carbon than for zeolites. This is not surprising because for adsorption on activated carbon the van der Waals forces dominate, whereas for zeolites the electrostatic forces are also important. As a result, the adsorbate mixture is less ideal on zeolites, and experimental activity coefficients for adsorbate mixtures of polar molecules of less than 0.1 have been measured [46].

The potential theory, described in section 2.2.5 of Chapter 2, is ideally suited for adsorption on activated carbon. The characteristic curve, which is obtained empirically, is assumed to be independent of temperature and is thus applicable only to the temperature-independent dispersion forces. The application of the potential theory to zeolites is not as successful for either pure-gas or mixture adsorptions. As pointed out by Barrer [71], some adjustment of the adsorbate molar volume at various temperatures is needed in order to fit the experimental results to a single characteristic curve. This has been done by Dubinin et al. [98] for adsorption of water on zeolite NaX.

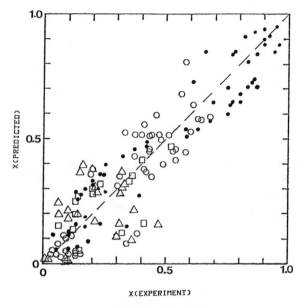

Figure 3.12 Comparison of adsorbed-phase mole fraction with that predicted by the extended Langmuir isotherm for 2-(●), 3-(○), 4-(□), and 5-(△) component mixtures of H_2, CO, CH_4, CO_2, and H_2S on activated carbon at 22 and 102°C, and 8–35 atm. Source: Ritter [95].

For adsorption of molecules with similar sizes in zeolites, especially for large molecules, the SSTM theory has been among the most satisfactory. Again, this is based on limited testing. The calculation becomes untractable, however, for mixtures containing molecules with widely different sizes. The VSM theory is unique because it contains both sorbate-surface and sorbate-sorbate interactions. The Flory-Huggins version of the VSM is a three-constant model that makes regression of the constants from pure-gas data considerably simpler than does the four-constant version. The VSM appears to work well for both activated carbon and zeolites. The IAS theory, on the other hand, contains only two constants (if the Langmuir or Freundlich isotherm is used for pure gases) and hence is simpler to use. It is the most tested theory for the adsorption of mixtures. For the reason discussed in the foregoing, it is good for activated carbon but not as good for zeolites. The IAS theory has recently been extended to include the sorbate-surface [99] and sorbate-sorbate interactions [100]. The extended theory should work well for all sorbents. It, however, becomes a four-constant model with the inclusion of an energy distribution parameter (to account for the sorbate-surface interactions) and a lateral interaction energy.

Because of the noniterative procedure for calculation, the extended Langmuir isotherm and the LRC model are uniquely suited for the modeling of adsorber behavior and cyclic gas separation processes [Chapter 5 on adsorber dynamics; 101; 102]. They suffer, nonetheless, from the lack of a rigorous thermodynamic basis. In modeling a pressure-swing adsorption process that separates a three-component gas mixture, the computer time is approximately 70% longer by using IAS in the model than by using the LRC equations [103]. Since the mathematical forms of the simplified version of SSTM [73] and the LRC are similar, the SSTM should also find use in modeling for gases of large and similar molecular sizes.

3.5 EXPERIMENTAL TECHNIQUES

The measurement of pure-gas isotherms is rather straightforward. The amount adsorbed at equilibrium can be determined by two commonly used methods: (1) the volumetric method, where the pressure drop before and after adsorption in a closed system is measured, and (2) the gravimetric method, in which the amount adsorbed is directly determined by the weight gain in a flow system. For mixed-gas isotherms, additional measurements are necessary for determining the compositions of both gas and adsorbed phases. A summary of four methods for measuring mixed-gas adsorption will be given.

3.5.1 Constant-Volume Method

The amount and composition of the gas mixture are measured before and after the adsorption takes place. The amount and composition of the adsorbed phase are then calculated by the difference. The total gas mixture amount can be determined by the pressure and volume, using an appropriate *P-V-T* relationship. The experimental apparatus contains two compartments: reservoir and sample, the latter containing a dead space. Volumes of both compartments can be predetermined by helium displacement. The sample compartment is outgassed before each adsorption measurement. The gas mixture in the reservoir is admitted to the sample compartment, and equilibrium is indicated by the constancy of the pressure and composition in the gas mixture. The gas-phase composition can be measured by a number of ways. Usually a small amount of gas is withdrawn for analysis by gas chromatography.

The difficulty involved in the volumetric method lies in the slow attainment of equilibrium, caused by the diffusion resistance in the adsorbent bed as well as in the small-diameter tubings. Thus the time required for equilibration in a static system is usually in the order of days. The equilibration time can be substantially reduced to below one hour by circulating the gas mixture through the sample by using a circulating pump.

The volumetric method with internal circulation has been used by a number of groups for both sub- and superatmospheric pressure measurements on activated carbon, silica gel, and zeolites. The simplest circulation was achieved by Lewis et al. [16] and Szepesy and Illes [24], by periodically displacing a slug of gas mixture between two variable-volume mercury-filled burettes. Circulating pumps were used in more recent experiments by Danner and co-workers [61], Costa et al. [45], Sorial et al. [86], Veyssiere et al. [91], and Ruthven and Wong [73]. The flow method has been used primarily for subatmospheric pressure measurements, except for the work of Veyssiere et al. [91] where adsorption of binary mixtures at pressures up to 30 atm was measured, and Sorial et al. [86] at 4.4 atm.

3.5.2 Dynamic Method

A method that is as popular as the constant volume method may be referred to as the *dynamic method*. It is a flow method in which the equilibrium is attained after the breakthrough, as indicated by the constancy of the effluent gas composition. The sample compartment is then isolated, and the adsorbate mixture is sub-sequently desorbed quantitatively by evacuation and/or heating. The desorbed mixture, usually trapped in a vessel maintained at the liquid-nitrogen temperature, is measured and analyzed after warming to ambient temperatures. Thus the total amount and the composition of the adsorbed mixture are measured directly.

This method has been used by a number of groups, many of which were involved in high pressure, for both activated carbon and zeolites. The recent groups using this technique included: Danner and Wenzel [42], Fernbacher and Wenzel [44], Gonzalez and Holland [13], Rogers [96], Reich et al. [25], Talu [46], Bulow et al. [92], and Okazaki et al. [93].

The simplest technique of this type is that developed by Rogers [96]. The saturated bed is repeatedly desorbed into an empty vessel, which is degassed before each equilibration. The desorbed gas in the vessel is measured (by pressure reading) and analyzed after each equilibration, and finally summed to yield the total adsorbed mixture.

3.5.3 Gravimetric Method

In the gravimetric technique, only the measurement of the total amount of adsorbate is required. The adsorbate composition can be calculated by a rigorous thermodynamic technique suggested by Van Ness [90], using the Gibbs adsorption isotherm.

The Gibbs adsorption isotherm for mixtures is:

$$-\frac{A}{n_t RT} d\pi + d \ln P + \sum (X_i d \ln Y_i) = 0 \tag{3.123}$$

If the gas phase is held at constant composition in an experiment where the gas pressure is increased from zero to P and the spreading pressure from zero to π, the Gibbs isotherm can be integrated to give:

$$\frac{\pi}{RT} = \int_0^P \frac{n_t}{AP} dP \qquad \text{(constant } Y) \tag{3.124}$$

Equation 3.124 is applicable to both pure and mixed gases and can be used for the evaluation of π from experimental data.

If π/RT is evaluated from equation 3.124 for various values of Y_1, but all for the same T and P, we may set $d \ln P = 0$ in equation 3.123 for a binary adsorbate mixture in equilibrium with an ideal gas. Thus:

$$\frac{A}{n_t}\left(\frac{\partial \dfrac{\pi}{RT}}{\partial Y_1}\right)_{T,P} = \frac{X_1 - Y_1}{Y_1(1 - Y_1)} \tag{3.125}$$

Equations 3.124 and 3.125 can be used to calculate the composition of the adsorbate. The required experimental data are the total amount adsorbed, n_t in gmoles/g sorbent, at a series of constant gas compositions while varying the total pressure. These data can be readily obtained gravimetrically by using premixed gases (with fixed compositions) at several total pressures. Volumetric methods can also be used to measure n_t, but it is difficult to keep the gas composition constant. When the gravimetric method is used, the average molecular weight of the adsorbate can be calculated from:

$$M = X_1 M_1 + (1 - X_1)M_2 \tag{3.126}$$

where M is molecular weight. Clearly an iterative procedure is required to calculate X_1 in solving equations 3.124, 3.125, and 3.126. This method can be extended to n-component mixtures, where data for $n - 1$ gas compositions are needed for $n - 1$ equations in equation 3.125.

The Van Ness method can yield tremendous savings in experimental equipment and time. The total amount adsorbed can readily be measured by a simple flow apparatus, in which the sample is sealed off, disconnected, and weighed after equilibrium is reached. When the gas phase is not ideal, compressibility factors may be used. Thus this simple method can be used for high pressure and temperature with no difficulty. This promising method has apparently caught little attention, however. Friederich and Mullins have applied the technique, using a commercial microbalance, to measure binary-mixture adsorption on carbon black at 25°C and 10–700 Torr pressure [35].

3.5.4   Chromatographic Methods

The chromatographic methods have been used for decades for measuring pure-gas isotherms, and more recently have been developed for mixture adsorption. These methods have the advantage of simplicity and speed in producing data, but suffer from the difficulty in accurate data analysis.

Adsorption from mixture can be calculated from the breakthrough curves, or, the column response at the outlet after a stepped change in the feed — that is, frontal chromatography and elution chromatography. A recent example of the use of this technique is the work of Siddiqi and Thomas [97]. A detailed discussion of the analysis of the breakthrough curves will be given in Chapter 5. The analysis can be accurate only under idealized conditions: dilute mixtures, isothermal operation, plug flow, instantaneous equilibrium between fluid and solid phases for both concentration and temperature, no pressure drop, and so on. Because these conditions are never guaranteed, the results obtained are estimates at best.

More recently an improved chromatographic technique, referred to as *perturbation chromatography*, has received attention. The technique requires a small perturbation (by the injection of a small dose of mixture in the feed), and the measurement of the retention time. A retention volume, caused by the exchange between the gas and the adsorbed phases, can be calculated from the retention time. The retention volume then yields, through a mathematical analysis, the desired equilibrium relationship (distribution coefficient) between the gas and adsorbed phases. As long as the perturbation is small, the technique can be used for high concentrations.

In perturbation chromatography, the column is initially brought to equilibrium with a flowing mixture. One of two types of perturbation is used: either a pulse of the pure components or a pulse of the radioactive isotope (of one or more components). The former is referred to as the *concentration pulse method*, the latter as the *tracer pulse method*. The concentration pulse method has been used and discussed by a number of workers [104–107]. In the concentration pulse method, one measures the propagation velocity of the concentration front. Whereas in the tracer pulse method, the movement of the tracer, which does not introduce any change in the equilibrium adsorption, is measured. The concentration pulse method has been critically analyzed by Hyun and Danner [107]. They have shown that, even under idealized assumptions, the mathematical analysis of the data becomes intractable for mixtures containing three or more components. The tracer pulse method is a more promising one as shown by Kobayashi and co-workers [108–110], and Danner and co-workers [111, 112]. Nevertheless, the method also resorts to the equilibrium assumption (i.e., no mass transfer resistance) as well as other idealized conditions. The results obtained by using this method have been shown to be close to those by the dynamic and static methods [110, 112].

NOTATION

a	partial molar area; activity
A	surface area of sorbent; interchange energy
b	Langmuir constant; van der Waals co-volume
B	Langmuir constant
C	molar concentration; average number of sorbate molecules per cage in zeolite
E	interaction energy; energy
f	fugacity; partition function

f_0	fugacity at saturation
G	Gibbs free energy
h	Planck's constant
H	enthalpy
k	Boltzmann constant
K	Henry's law constant
m	mass
n	amount adsorbed in moles/g
n_i^0	amount of i adsorbed from pure gas at the same total pressure
N_0	Avogadro number
n_t	total amount adsorbed
P	total pressure
P_0	saturation vapor pressure
P_c	critical pressure
P_i	partial pressure of species i
P_i^0	equilibrium vapor pressure for pure i adsorbed at the same spreading pressure and temperature as the mixture
q	isosteric heat of adsorption
Q	heat of adsorption
r	pore radius; radial distance
R	gas constant; interaction constant (eq. 3.102)
S	entropy
T	temperature
T_c	critical temperature
T_r	reduced temperature
u	internal energy
v	amount adsorbed in volume (STP)/g
v_i^0	amount of i adsorbed (in volume) from pure gas at the same total pressure
v_m	monolayer amount adsorbed
V	liquid molar volume of adsorbate
V'	molar volume of saturated liquid at the adsorption temperature
V_m	molar volume of mixed adsorbate
V_{nbp}	liquid molar volume at normal boiling point
W	adsorbate volume above the surface
W_0	limiting volume of adsorbed space ($=$ micropore volume)
X	mole fraction in adsorbed phase
Y	mole fraction in gas phase
α	adsorption constant ($=$ sticking probability); separation factor, selectivity ratio
α_{ij}	separation factor $= (Y_i/X_i)/(Y_j/X_j)$; or defined in equation 3.84
β	desorption constant; affinity coefficient in potential theory; van der Waals constant
γ	activity coefficient
δ	stoichiometric coefficient
ε	potential energy field over surface

η correction factor to account for lateral interaction
θ fractional surface coverage
Λ pairwise interaction parameter
μ chemical potential
ν frequency of vibration; ratio of Langmuir constants
π spreading pressure
ρ density
σ surface or interfacial tension; area occupied by an adsorbed molecule
ϕ fugacity coefficient; or defined by equation 3.18
ω lateral interaction energy

Subscripts

i species i
m monolayer value; molar value; mixing in sorbate
0   saturated value
t total
v vacancy

Superscripts

0   for pure gas at the same total pressure as the mixture
*   equilibrium value; pure component; or where defined
∞ limiting value

REFERENCES

1. E.D. Markham and A.F. Benton, *J. Am. Chem. Soc.*, *53*, 497 (1931).
2. G. Schay, P. Fejes, and J. Szethmary, *Acta Chem. Acad. Sc. Hungary*, *12*, 299 (1957).
3. D.B. Broughton, *Ind. Eng. Chem.*, *40*, 1506 (1948).
4. C. Kemball, E.K. Rideal, and E.A. Guggenheim, *Trans. Faraday Soc.*, *44*, 948 (1948).
5. W.B. Innes and H.H. Rowley, *J. Phys. Chem.*, *51*, 1154 (1947).
6. W.B. Innes, R.B. Olney, and H.H. Rowley, *J. Phys. Chem.*, *55*, 1324 (1951).
7. C.M. Yon and P.H. Turnock, *AIChE Symp. Ser.*, No. 117, *67*, 3 (1971).
8. C.D. Holland and A.I. Liapis, *Computer Methods for Solving Dynamic Separation Problems* (New York: McGraw-Hill, 1983), Chap. 12.
9. E. Glueckauf, *J. Chem. Soc.*, 1321 (1947).
10. E. Glueckauf, *Trans. Faraday Soc.*, *49*, 1066 (1953).
11. D.M. Young and A.D. Crowell, *Physical Adsorption of Gases* (London: Butterworths, 1962), Chap. 11.
12. T.L. Hill, *J. Chem. Phys.*, *14*, 46, 268 (1946).
13. A.J. Gonzalez and C.D. Holland, *AIChE J.*, *16*, 718 (1970).

14. B.P. Bering, V.V. Serpinsky, and S.I. Surinova, *Dokl. Akad. Nauk. SSSR, 153,* 129 (1963).
15. B.P. Bering, V.V. Serpinsky, and S.I. Surinova, *Izv. Skad. Nauk. SSSR, Otd. Khim. Nauk,* 769 (1965).
16. W.K. Lewis, E.R. Gilliland, B. Chertow, and W.P. Cadogan, *Ind. Eng. Chem., 42,* 1319 (1950).
17. W.H. Cook and D. Basmadjian, *Can. J. Chem. Eng., April,* 78 (1965).
18. J.D. Kaser, L.O. Rutz, and K. Kammermeyer, *J. Chem. Eng. Data, 7,* 211 (1962).
19. A.K.K. Lee, *Can. J. Chem. Eng., 51,* 688 (1973).
20. R.J. Grant and M. Manes, *Ind. Eng. Chem. Fundam., 5,* 490 (1966).
21. W.K. Lewis, E.R. Gilliland, B. Chertow, and W.P. Cadogan, *Ind. Eng. Chem., 42,* 1326 (1950).
22. R.G. Grant and M. Manes, *Ind. Eng. Chem. Fundam., 3,* 221 (1964).
23. L. Szepesy and V. Illes, *Acta Chim. Hung., 35,* 37 (1963).
24. L. Szepesy and V. Illes, *Acta Chim. Hung., 35,* 245 (1964).
25. R. Reich, W.T. Zeigler, and K.A. Rogers, *Ind. Eng. Chem. Proc. Des. Dev., 19,* 336 (1980).
26. K.M. Nikolaev and M.M. Dubinin, *Bull. Acad. Sci. USSR, Div. Chem. Sci.,* No. 10, 1124 (1958).
27. M. Benedict, G.B. Webb, and L.C. Rubin, *Chem. Eng. Prog., 47,* 419 (1951).
28. R.C. Reid and T.K. Sherwood, *The Properties of Gases and Liquids,* 2nd ed. (New York: McGraw-Hill, 1966).
29. F.D. Maslan, M. Altman, and E.R. Aberth, *J. Phys. Chem., 57,* 106 (1953).
30. D. Basmadjian, *Can. J. Chem., 38,* 149 (1960).
31. A.L. Myers and J.M. Prausnitz, *AIChE J., 11,* 121 (1965).
32. S. Sircar and A.L. Myers, *Chem. Eng. Sci., 28,* 489 (1973).
33. D.M. Ruthven, *Principles of Adsorption and Adsorption Processes* (New York: Wiley, 1984), Chap. 4.
34. J.T. Saunders, M.S. thesis, State University of New York at Buffalo (1982).
35. R.O. Friederich and J.C. Mullins, *Ind. Eng. Chem. Fundam., 11,* 439 (1972).
36. R.P. Danner and E.C.F. Choi, *Ind. Eng. Chem. Fundam., 17,* 248 (1978).
37. G.A. Sorial, W.H. Granville, and W.O. Daly, *Chem. Eng. Sci., 38,* 1517 (1983).
38. R.J. Wilson and R.P. Danner, *J. Chem. Eng. Data, 28,* 14 (1983).
39. B.K. Kaul, *Ind. Eng. Chem. Proc. Des. Dev., 23,* 711 (1984).
40. G. Belfort, *AIChE J., 27,* 1021 (1981).
41. W.N. Chen and R.T. Yang, in *Recent Developments in Separation Science,* vol. 9 (N.N. Li and J.M. Calo, eds.) (Cleveland: CRC Press, 1986).
42. R.P. Danner and L.A. Wenzel, *AIChE J., 15,* 515 (1969).
43. C. Minka and A.L. Myers, *AIChE J., 19,* 453 (1973).
44. J.M. Fernbacher and L.A. Wenzel, *Ind. Eng. Chem. Fundam., 11,* 457 (1972).
45. E. Costa, J.L. Sotela, G. Calleja, and C. Marron, *AIChE J., 27,* 5 (1981).
46. O. Talu, Ph.D. dissertation, Arizona State University, Tempe (1984).
47. G.M. Wilson, *J. Am. Chem. Soc., 86,* 127 (1964).
48. D.S. Abrams and J.M. Prausnitz, *AIChE J., 21,* 116 (1975).
49. G. Mauer and J.M. Prausnitz, *Fluid Phase Equil., 2,* 91 (1978).
50. A.L. Myers, C. Minka, and D.Y. Ou, *AIChE J., 28,* 97 (1982).
51. A.L. Myers, *AIChE J., 29,* 691 (1983).
52. S. Suwanayuen and R.P. Danner, *AIChE J., 26,* 68 (1980).
53. S. Suwanayuen and R.P. Danner, *AIChE J., 26,* 76 (1980).

54. S.H. Hyun and R.P. Danner, *J. Chem. Eng. Data*, *27*, 196 (1982).
55. R.J. Wilson and R.P. Danner, *J. Chem. Eng. Data*, *28*, 14 (1983).
56. S. Brunauer, *The Adsorption of Gases and Vapors* (Princeton, N.J.: Princeton University Press, 1945).
57. G. Damkohler, *Z. Phys. Chem.*, *B23*, 58 (1933).
58. G. Damkohler, *Z. Phys. Chem.*, *B23*, 69 (1933).
59. J.N. Reeds and K. Kammermeyer, *Ind. Eng. Chem.*, *51*, 707 (1959).
60. T.W. Cochran, R.L. Kabel, and R.P. Danner, *AIChE J.*, *31*, 268 (1985).
61. L.R. Dorfman and R.P. Danner, *AIChE Symp. Ser.*, 152, 71, *30* (1975).
62. S. Ross and J.P. Olivier, *On Physical Adsorption* (New York: Wiley, 1964).
63. S.E. Hoory and J.M. Prausnitz, *Chem. Eng. Sci.*, *22*, 1025 (1967).
64. J.H. DeBoer, *The Dynamic Character of Adsorption*, 2nd ed. (London: Oxford University Press, 1968).
65. S.J. Gregg and K.S.W. Sing, *Adsorption, Surface Area and Porosity*, 2nd ed. (New York: Academic Press, 1982).
66. L. Riekert, *Adv. Catalysis*, *21*, 287 (1970).
67. V.A. Bakajev, *Dokl. Akad. Nauk USSR*, *169*, 369 (1966).
68. D.M. Ruthven, *Nature Phys. Sci.*, *232*(29), 70 (1971).
69. P. Brauer, A.A. Lopatkin, and G.Ph. Stepanez, in *Molecular Sieve Zeolites, Adv. Chem. Ser.*, ACS, *102*, 97 (1971).
70. R.M. Barrer and D.E.W. Vaughan, *J. Phys. Chem. Solids*, *32*, 731 (1971).
71. R.M. Barrer, *Zeolites and Clay Minerals as Sorbents and Molecular Sieves* (New York: Academic Press, 1978), Chap. 3.
72. D.M. Ruthven, *Principles of Adsorption and Adsorption Processes* (New York: Wiley, 1984), Chap. 3.
73. D.M. Ruthven and F. Wong, *Ind. Eng. Chem. Fundam.*, *24*, 27 (1985).
74. D.M. Ruthven, K.F. Loughlin, and K.A. Holborow, *Chem. Eng. Sci.*, *28*, 701 (1973).
75. R.M. Barrer and J.A. Lee, *Surf. Sci.*, *12*, 354 (1968).
76. K.A. Holborow and K.F. Loughlin, *Am. Chem. Soc. Symp. Ser.*, *40*, 379 (1977).
77. D.M. Ruthven, *AIChE J.*, *22*, 753 (1976).
78. A.M. Tolmachev, *Zh. Fiz. Khimii*, *52*, 1050 (1978).
79. A.M. Tolmachev and I.B. Trubnikov, *Zh. Fiz. Khimii*, *52*, 1059 (1978).
80. A.M. Tolmachev, I.B. Trubnikov, and G.G. Artyushina, *Carbon*, *22*, 459 (1984).
81. A. Boutaric, *J. Chim. Phys.*, *35*, 158 (1938).
82. M.M. Dubinin and V.A. Astakhov, *Izv. Skad. Nauk SSSR, Ser. Khim.*, 5; 11; 17 (1971).
83. M.M. Dubinin, *Carbon*, *17*, 505 (1979).
84. L. Szepesy and V. Illes, *Acta Chim. Hung.*, *35*, 53 (1963).
85. J.T. Nolan, T.W. McKeehan, and R.P. Danner, *J. Chem. Eng. Data*, *26*, 112 (1981).
86. G.A. Sorial, W.H. Granville, and W.N. Daly, *Chem. Eng. Sc.*, *38*, 1517 (1983).
87. P.B. Lederman and B. Williams, *AIChE J.*, *10*, 30 (1964).
88. J.I. Joubert, Ph.D. thesis, Worcester Polytechnic Institute, Worcester, Mass., (1971).
89. P.L. Cen and R.T. Yang, unpublished results (1985).
90. H.C. Van Ness, *Ind. Eng. Chem. Fundam.*, *8*, 465 (1969).
91. M.C. Veyssiere, P. Cartraud, C. Clavaud, and A. Cointot, *J. Chimie Phys.*, *78*, 543 (1981).
92. M. Bulow, V.K. Cuikina, and W. Shirmer, *Z. Phys. Chemie., Leipzig*, *258*, 321 (1977).
93. M. Okazaki, H. Tamon, and R. Toei, *J. Chem. Eng. Japan*, *11*, 209 (1978).
94. J.T. Saunders, B.M. Tsai, and R.T. Yang, *Fuel*, *64*, 621 (1985).
95. J.A. Ritter, M.S. thesis, State University of New York at Buffalo (1985).

96.   K.A. Rogers, Ph.D. thesis, Georgia Institute of Technology, Atlanta, Georgia (1973).
97.   K.S. Siddiqi and W.J. Thomas, *Carbon*, *20*, 473 (1982).
98.   M.M. Dubinin, O. Kadlec, and A. Zukal, *Coll. Czech. Chem. Comm.*, *31*, 406 (1966).
99.   J.A. O'Brien and A.L. Myers, *AIChE Symp. Ser.*, *81*(No. 242), 51 (1985).
100.   J.A. O'Brien and A.L. Myers, *J. Chem. Soc. Faraday Trans.*, in press (1985).
101.   R.T. Mauer, *ACS Symp. Ser.*, *135*, 73 (1980).
102.   R.T. Yang, S.J. Doong, and P.L. Cen, *AIChE Symp. Ser.*, *81*(No. 242), 84 (1985).
103.   S.J. Doong and R.T. Yang, *AIChE J.*, *32*, 397 (1986).
104.   K.T. Koonce, H.A. Deans, and R. Kobayashi, *AIChE J.*, *11*, 259 (1965).
105.   D.L. Peterson and F. Helfferich, *J. Phys. Chem.*, *69*, 1283 (1965).
106.   E. Van der Vlist and J. Van der Meijden, *J. Chromatog.*, *79*, 1 (1973).
107.   S.H. Hyun and R.P. Danner, *AIChE Symp. Ser.*, *78*(No. 219), 19 (1982).
108.   H.B. Gilmer and R. Kobayashi, *AIChE J.*, *11*, 702 (1965).
109.   R. Kobayashi, P.S. Chappelear, and H.A. Deans, *Ind. Eng. Chem.*, *59*(10), 63 (1967).
110.   P.D. Rolniak and R. Kobayashi, *AIChE J.*, *26*, 616 (1980).
111.   R.P. Danner, M.P. Nicoletti, and R.S. Al-Ameeri, *Chem. Eng. Sc.*, *35*, 2129 (1980).
112.   S.H. Hyun and R.P. Danner, *Ind. Eng. Chem. Fundam.*, *24*, 95 (1985).
113.   O. Talu and I. Zwiebel, paper presented at the Annual AIChE Meeting, Chicago, November, 1985.
114.   R.J. Grant, R.S. Joyce, and J.E. Urbanic, *Fundamentals of Adsorption* (A.L. Myers and G. Belfort, eds.) (New York: Engineering Foundation, 1984), p. 219.
115.   M. Manes, *Fundamentals of Adsorption* (A.L. Myers and G. Belfort, eds.) (New York: Engineering Foundation, 1984), p. 335.
116.   A.L. Myers, *Fundamentals of Adsorption* (A.L. Myers and G. Belfort, eds.) (New York: Engineering Foundation, 1984), p. 365.

CHAPTER 4

Rate Processes in Adsorbers

Adsorptive gas separation processes are carried out in fixed-bed adsorbers which contain porous adsorbent particles or pellets. (Past and present attempts have been made to use moving and fluidized beds, but all failed with one exception — see Chapter 6.) Mathematical models are needed to understand the dynamics of adsorbers, thereby controlling and predicting the separation results. The model yields a complete set of flow velocity (u) concentration (C), and temperature (T) as functions of time (t) and location in the bed (z). From these data, a direct and simple calculation will give all important results for the separation process — namely, product purity, product recovery and productivity. (Definitions of these terms will be given in Chapter 7.)

The model for the separation process should adequately account for the mass and heat balance as well as the equilibrium isotherm. The resistances to heat and mass transfer both inside and outside the sorbent pellet can be important. The local rate of adsorption is assumed instantaneous because it approximates the order of the collision frequency of the gas on the solid surface, which is much greater than the transport processes. The model equations are thus coupled by the equilibrium isotherm, and the continuity of fluxes at the exterior surface of the pellet.

There exists a close analogy between fixed-bed adsorbers and chemical reactors where reactions take place in porous catalyst pellets. The only major differences are that in reactor modeling the local reaction rate is finite and the reaction is usually assumed irreversible for the sake of mathematical simplicity. Under circumstances when the reaction is reversible and the reaction rate is much higher than transport rates, the models for reactors and adsorbers are identical. In fact, in the so-called chemical-kinetic models for adsorber breakthrough curves, the local rate of adsorption is treated as ion exchange between the fluid and solid phases. These models were originally derived for ion exchange in fixed beds, which include the models of Walter [1], Thomas [2], Vermeulen and Hiester [3], and so on. Because of the close analogy between adsorbers and heterogeneous reactors, a wealth of information can be drawn from studies on reactors, which have been summarized in many texts [4–13].

4.1   GOVERNING EQUATIONS FOR ADSORBERS

All models for an adsorption bed must include the following:

1.   The adsorption isotherm
2.   Mass and heat balance in the interpellet gas phase
3.   Mass and heat balance inside each pellet

All the foregoing equations are coupled. The boundary conditions are written according to the specific separation process (e.g., temperature swing and pressure swing).

The equations which follow are written for the case of uniform pressure in bed and a single adsorbate. It is straightforward to extend these equations to a multicomponent mixture.

The equilibrium isotherm is given by:

$$q = q(T_P, C^P) \tag{4.1}$$

where q is the amount adsorbed per volume of pellet, C^P is the gas-phase concentration inside the pore, and T_P is temperature inside the pore.

The mass balance within a spherical pellet is described by:

$$D_e\left(\frac{\partial^2 C^P}{\partial r^2} + \frac{2}{r}\frac{\partial C^P}{\partial r}\right) = \frac{\partial q}{\partial t} \tag{4.2}$$

where D_e is the effective diffusivity. The factor 2 in $2/r$ is replaced by 1 for cylindrical and 0 for platelet pellets. In writing this equation the adsorbate accumulation in the gas phase, $\alpha \partial C^P/\partial t$ (where α is the void fraction within the pellet), has been neglected and would otherwise appear on the right hand side. This equation applies for sorbents with a uniform pore structure, such as activated carbon, alumina, silica and molecular sieve carbon, but not zeolites. (For a bidisperse, but uniform pore structure, a single D_e is generally used.) In regard to zeolites, the pellet is composed of small crystals which are bound together by a macroporous binder. Thus two mass balance equations are needed, one for the crystal (micropores) and one for the binder (macropores), and are coupled by continuity at the exterior surface of the crystal.

The mass balance for the bulk flow in the bed, or the interpellet phase, is:

$$-D_z\frac{\partial^2 C}{\partial z^2} + \frac{\partial uC}{\partial z} + \frac{\partial C}{\partial t} + \frac{1-\varepsilon}{\varepsilon}ka(C - C_R^P) = 0 \tag{4.3}$$

where D_z = axial dispersion coefficient
$\quad\quad u$ = interstitial velocity
$\quad\quad C$ = interpellet concentration
$\quad\quad \varepsilon$ = interpellet void fraction

a = exterior surface area of pellets per volume of bed
k = average mass transfer film coefficient
C_R^P = concentration at the pellet surface (R_P = radius of pellet)
t = time
z = distance in the bed from the entrance

In this equation the concentration is assumed to be uniform in the radial direction and radial dispersion is neglected.

Equations 4.2 and 4.3 are coupled by the continuity at the pellet surface:

$$D_e\left(\frac{\partial C^P}{\partial r}\right)_{R_P} = k(C - C_R^P) \qquad (4.4)$$

The heat balance equation inside the pellet is:

$$k_e\left(\frac{\partial^2 T_P}{\partial r^2} + \frac{2}{r}\frac{\partial T_P}{\partial r}\right) = \rho_s C_{ps}\frac{\partial T_P}{\partial t} + H\frac{\partial q}{\partial t} \qquad (4.5)$$

where T_P = temperature within the pellet
k_e = effective heat conductivity of the pellet
ρ_s = density
C_{ps} = heat capacity of the solid pellet
H = heat of adsorption (being negative) or desorption

Again, the accumulation in the gas phase is neglected.

For an adiabatic bed, heat balance for the bulk gas in the bed (i.e., interpellet) yields:

$$\frac{\partial uT}{\partial z} + \frac{\partial T}{\partial t} + \frac{1-\varepsilon}{\varepsilon}\frac{ah}{\rho C_P}(T - T_{pR}) = 0 \qquad (4.6)$$

where T is the interpellet gas temperature, ρ and C_P pertain to the gas phase, and h is the average film coefficient for heat transfer. A second-order term involving axial thermal conductivity, which is analogous to axial dispersion, is usually negligible.

Equations 4.5 and 4.6 are coupled by:

$$k_e\left(\frac{\partial T_P}{\partial r}\right)_{R_P} = h(T - T_{pR}) \qquad (4.7)$$

The mass balance (eqs. 4.2, 4.3) and heat balance (eqs. 4.5, 4.6) equations are coupled through the dependence of C and C^P on T (and pressure P in a process involving pressure changes). The dependence can usually be approximated by the ideal gas law. A further link between these equations is the adsorbate concentration, q, which appears in equations 4.2 and 4.5, and is obtained from equation 4.1.

The boundary conditions for equations 4.1–4.7 are defined by the specific separation process and its operating conditions. In addition, the following parameters need to be evaluated in order to solve these equations: α, ε, ρ, ρ_s, C_p, C_{ps}, R_p, a, H, D_z, D_e, k_e, h, and k. Values of the first nine parameters are readily available or readily measurable. This is not true for the transport properties: D_z, D_e, k_e, h, and k. They are complex functions of gas flow, bed, and pore structures. However, correlations are available for evaluating these transport properties and will be summarized later.

4.2   TRANSPORT PROCESSES IN ADSORBERS

The transport processes at any given location in the adsorber or for any given sorbent particle are never at a steady state. In other words, the temperature and concentration profiles inside and outside of a given particle are continually changing until the particle is totally saturated or regenerated when the transport processes cease. Figure 4.1 shows typical temperature and concentration profiles for a particle in an adsorber during the adsorption and desorption steps. These profiles are constantly changing and are given by the solutions to equations 4.1 to 4.7. The relative magnitudes of the differentials in temperature and concentration inside and outside the particle reflect the relative importance of the resistances. The steps with smaller resistances are often neglected in modeling. The situation sketched in Figure 4.1 is realistic under conditions of practical interests. Further discussion on the relative importance of the two resistances will be given in a later section.

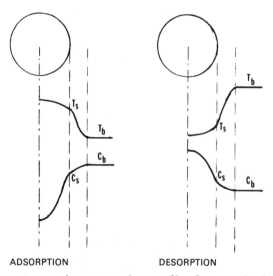

ADSORPTION   DESORPTION

Figure 4.1   Temperature and concentration profiles for an adsorbent particle in an adsorber during adsorption and desorption. Subscripts b and s denote bulk and surface, respectively.

4.2.1 External Transport Processes: Film Coefficients

The rate of heat and mass transport between a solid surface and a flowing fluid is limited by a film adjacent to the surface. This film is a laminar boundary layer that exists due to the no-slip or continuity condition at the surface. Thus the transport processes are represented by the film coefficients which are defined according to the linear laws of Fick and Fourier.

For mass transfer:

$$\text{Flux} = k(C_s - C_b)$$

or, based on per unit volume of bed:

$$\frac{dq}{dt} = ka(C_s - C_b) \tag{4.8}$$

For heat transfer, also based on per unit volume of bed:

$$\text{Rate} = ha(T_s - T_b) \tag{4.9}$$

The "film" extends from the surface to infinity for stagnant fluid surrounding a spherical particle. Integrating Fourier's conduction law from surface to infinity and comparing the result with the definition of k gives the limiting value of 2 for Nusselt number ($= 2hR_p/k_g$ where k_g is the thermal conductivity of gas). The film becomes considerably thinner and the transfer coefficient is higher for a flowing fluid. The transfer coefficients depend, in a complex manner, on the flow conditions, and actually differ from one point to another on the same particle. For example, by using boundary layer theory, Lee and Barrow [14] were able to develop correlations for different heat and mass transfer film coefficients for the front and back halves of a sphere in a flow. Similarly, the transfer coefficients are different for a single particle than for a bed of particles. In practice, however, an average value for the film coefficient is used. The average value can be calculated from an appropriate empirical correlation.

The j-Factor Correlations

A popular approach in correlating experimental data for the average film coefficients has been through the use of j-factors for mass transfer:

$$j_D = \frac{k\rho}{\mu}\left(\frac{\mu}{\rho D_m}\right)^{2/3} \tag{4.10}$$

where μ is viscosity and D_m is molecular diffusivity. The literature on experimental data has been summarized to give the following empirical correlation [15] for

Reynolds number $(2R_pG/\mu)$ greater than 10:

$$j_D = \frac{0.458}{\varepsilon}\left(\frac{2R_pG}{\mu}\right)^{-0.407} \tag{4.11}$$

where G is the superficial mass flux based on per unit cross-sectional area of empty bed.

In the absence of radiation, the correlation for heat transfer is analogous to that for mass transfer:

$$j_D = j_H = \frac{h}{C_p\mu}\left(\frac{C_p\mu}{k_g}\right)^{2/3} \tag{4.12}$$

The Ranz-Marshall Type Correlations

Much of the mass transfer data in packed beds have been correlated by the Ranz-Marshall equation [16]:

$$\frac{2kR_p}{D_m} = 2.0 + 0.6\left(\frac{\mu}{\rho D_m}\right)^{1/3}\left(\frac{2R_pG}{\mu}\right)^{1/2}$$

or

$$\mathrm{Sh} = 2.0 + 0.6\ \mathrm{Sc}^{1/3}\ \mathrm{Re}^{1/2} \tag{4.13}$$

where Sh, Sc, and Re stand for the Sherwood, Schmidt, and Reynolds numbers, respectively.

A recent correlation of this type has been made by Wakao and Funazkri [17]. Their correlation is significant because they pointed out an error made in most of the previous correlations, including that given by equations 4.10 and 4.11. In typical experiments measuring mass transfer film coefficients, effluents are analyzed from packed beds in which evaporation, sublimation, or adsorption takes place. A mass balance equation similar to equation 4.3 is solved to calculate the mass transfer coefficient. In most of the published literature, however, the axial dispersion term is neglected. Twenty sets of experimental data were reanalyzed to obtain the corrected mass transfer coefficients by including the dispersion term [17]. The resulting correlation for $3 < \mathrm{Re} < 10^4$ is:

$$\mathrm{Sh} = 2.0 + 1.1\ \mathrm{Sc}^{1/3}\ \mathrm{Re}^{0.6} \tag{4.14}$$

The Sherwood number and, consequently, the mass transfer coefficient, calculated from equation 4.14, is higher than that from equation 4.11. When axial dispersion becomes more significant, the difference between these two values grows as Reynolds number is decreased. At $\mathrm{Re} = 10$, the mass transfer coefficient obtained from equation 4.14 is approximately twice that from equation 4.11 at Sc near 1. The two values converge when Re exceeds approximately 100. Another advantage that equation 4.14 has over 4.11 is that it can possibly be used at low Reynolds numbers, when Sh correctly approaches a limiting value.

Recommended Correlation

When axial dispersion is included in modeling fixed-bed adsorbers, equation 4.14 should be used. It is important to bear in mind, however, that this equation was obtained by using an axial dispersion coefficient given by the following equation [17]:

$$\frac{\varepsilon D_z}{D_m} = 20 + 0.5 \text{ Sc Re} \tag{4.15}$$

If the dispersion term is neglected from the mass balance equation, a more realistic value for the mass transfer coefficient can be obtained from equation 4.11. With less certainty, the heat transfer coefficient may be calculated from equation 4.11 with j_H defined by equation 4.12.

Comparison of Temperature and Concentration Differences across Film

Using the correlations for k and h, the temperature difference across the film, $\Delta T = T_b - T_s$, and the concentration difference, $\Delta C = C_b - C_s$, can be compared. At steady state, an energy balance on the particle gives:

$$ka(\Delta C)H = ha\Delta T \tag{4.16}$$

Using the foregoing correlations for k and h, and noting the ratio of Schmidt number and its counterpart in heat transfer, Prandtl number, which approximates unity for gases, we have:

$$\Delta T = \frac{H}{\rho C_p} \Delta C \tag{4.17}$$

This equation applies for both adsorption and desorption at steady state. However, steady state is never reached for adsorption and desorption in a particle, and:

$$\Delta T < \frac{H}{\rho C_p} \Delta C \tag{4.18}$$

The value of $H\Delta C/(\rho C_p)$ is usually quite significant under practical conditions. An important example is illustrated by the adsorption of water vapor from air in zeolites at room temperature. The value of H/C_p for this system is nearly $-3,000°C$. Thus a decrease in concentration by 1% (by volume) across the film during adsorption (i.e., $\Delta C/\rho = 0.01$) would cause a temperature rise of up to 30°C across the film.

4.2.2   Internal (Intraparticle) Transport Processes

All sorbents possess a high surface area, and essentially the entire surface area is inside the particle or pellet. The adsorptive gases contained in an "inert" carrier gas must penetrate into the porous structure during adsorption, and penetrate out of it during desorption. A local temperature rise or drop accompanies the adsorption or desorption, respectively. The local temperature change influences the equilibrium adsorption isotherm as well as the rate of mass transfer. Fortunately, the effective thermal conductivities for the commercial sorbent pellets are relatively high, and the external heat transfer resistance dominates the heat transfer process. This is evidenced by the fact that the temperature gradient within the pellet during adsorption is small and can be neglected. Consequently, the discussion in this section will focus primarily on mass transfer.

Mass flux in a porous sorbent is given by the sum of the individual fluxes:

$$N = -D_e \nabla C + Y\left(\frac{D_e}{D_m}\right) N_t - D_s \nabla q - \frac{CB_0}{\mu} \nabla P \qquad (4.19)$$

| Flux | Gaseous diffusion | Convective flux due to diffusion | Surface flux | Viscous flow |

where Y = mole fraction
   N_t = total net flux in the direction of N
       (and = 0 for equimolal counterdiffusion)
   B_0 = Darcy permeability
   P = total pressure

Both gaseous and surface fluxes follow Fick's first law of diffusion. The viscous flow term is usually small and will therefore be neglected. The methods for evaluating the three other fluxes and the diffusion coefficients will be given next.

Gaseous Diffusion in Single Cylindrical Pores

Diffusion in the gas phase results from collisions. Collisions among the gas molecules dominate the process for diffusion in a large pore, and thus the diffusion is the same as bulk diffusion, referred to here as *molecular diffusion*. When the pore diameter becomes smaller, collisions between the molecules and the pore wall become increasingly important. In a very small pore, collisions with the wall dominate, and the diffusion process assumes an entirely different mechanism, known as *Knudsen diffusion*. The relative importance of the two different mechanisms for diffusion is determined by the ratio of the pore diameter and the mean free path of the gas molecules. As a rule of thumb, molecular diffusion prevails when the pore diameter is greater than ten times the mean free path; Knudsen diffusion may be assumed when the mean free path is greater than ten times the pore diameter.

The mean free path is determined by the ratio between the average molecular speed and the collision frequency:

$$\text{Mean free path} = \frac{1}{\sqrt{2}n\pi\sigma^2} \tag{4.20}$$

where n = gas number density in molecules/volume
σ = collision diameter

The collision diameter can be calculated from transport properties or the second virial coefficient and is available from various sources [18]. The mean free path given by equation 4.20 is 2×10^{-5} cm (0.2 μm) for air at 1 atm and 300K. This is in the range of macropore sizes.

In the Knudsen diffusion regime, the exchange of momentum from the gas molecules to the pore wall is important. The momentum given up by the colliding molecules to the wall must be balanced by the force exerted on the two ends of the pore, which is given by the pressure gradient across the pore. The diffusivity is given by [19]:

$$D_k = \frac{2r_p}{3}\left(\frac{8RT}{\pi M}\right)^{1/2} = 9.7 \times 10^3 r_p \left(\frac{T}{M}\right)^{1/2} \tag{4.21}$$

where r_p = pore radius, cm
M = molecular weight
T = temperature, K
D_k = Knudsen diffusivity, cm^2/s

Note that this equation applies only when the mean free path is much greater than the pore radius. The value of D_k should not exceed molecular diffusivity.

The molecular diffusivity for a binary gas mixture can be evaluated by the familiar Chapman-Enskog equation [18]:

$$D_m = 0.0018583 \frac{T^{3/2}(1/M_A + 1/M_B)^{1/2}}{P\sigma_{AB}^2\Omega_{AB}} \tag{4.22}$$

where D_m = molecular diffusivity between A and B, cm^2/s
T = temperature, K
M_A and M_B = molecular weights
P = total pressure, atm
$\sigma_{AB}, \varepsilon_{AB}$ = constants in the Lennard-Jones potential-energy function for the pair AB; σ_{AB} is in Å

Ω_{AB} = collision integral, a function of $k_B T/\varepsilon_{AB}$ where k_B is Boltzmann's constant

For evaluation of the collision parameters, see reference 18 or other texts.

The two mechanisms for diffusion are both important when the mean free path and pore diameter are of the same order of magnitude. In this case, as well as in the case where the mean free path is not known, the following equation is used for the diffusivity [20, 21]:

$$D = \frac{1}{(1 - \alpha Y_A)/D_{mAB} + (1/D_k)} \tag{4.23}$$

where

$$\alpha = 1 + \frac{N_B}{N_A} \tag{4.24}$$

In adsorption and desorption processes, $N_A \approx -N_B$ (the negative sign indicates that the two fluxes are in opposite directions). Thus:

$$D \approx \frac{1}{(1/D_m) + (1/D_k)} \tag{4.25}$$

This result was obtained earlier by Bosanquet [referenced in 7, p. 26], and Pollard and Present [22].

The flux for molecular diffusion should include the convective flow term, or, by substituting equation 4.23 into Fick's first law, and, assuming $D_k \to \infty$, we have:

$$N_A = -D_m \frac{dC_A}{dr} + Y_A(N_A + N_B) \tag{4.26}$$

Using the same substitution and noting that $D_m \gg D_k$, the flux in Knudsen diffusion is:

$$N_A = -D_k \frac{dC_A}{dr} \tag{4.27}$$

Gaseous Diffusion in Porous Sorbents

Equation 4.23 or 4.25 gives the diffusivity in a single cylindrical pore. The pores in a commercial sorbent, however, are interconnected void spaces. The structure is highly complex and, except in statistical terms, cannot be well defined. Because of its importance in many fields, especially reaction engineering, diffusion in porous materials has been extensively studied and reviewed in several texts [7, 10, 12, 23,

24, 25]. A model is necessary for calculating an effective diffusivity in the porous material. Several useful models have been proposed: simple empirical method, parallel-pore model, random-pore model, and dusty-gas model. The first three models will be briefly described.

In the *dusty-gas model*, flux equations are written for a pseudo mixture composed of n gases plus a dummy species (or dust) of very massive molecules ($M \rightarrow \infty$), representing the porous solid. The flux of the dust is made zero by momentum balance. In the same manner that Knudsen diffusion is treated, the resulting flux equations can describe the transition from molecular bulk diffusion to Knudsen diffusion as the dust concentration is increased. However, controversy on the physical significance of the dusty-gas model is not resolved, since the model does not contain any representation of the porosity and pore-size distribution. The reader is referred to the treatments of Jackson [24] and Mason [25] for detailed discussion and applications of this model.

Simple Empirical Method. The actual diffusion path will not equal the distance in the radial direction, but will be quite tortuous. The actual path depends on the pore structure. It is customary to define the ratio between the actual diffusion path length and the net distance in the direction of flux, or the radial distance, as *tortuosity factor*, τ. Taking into account that the volume occupied by the solid is not available for pore diffusion, the value of D for single pores can be converted to effective diffusivity:

$$D_e = \frac{\alpha D}{\tau} \tag{4.28}$$

where α is the intrapellet void fraction.

The value of τ also varies empirically with α. A log-log plot of D_e versus α for a variety of porous materials (Figure 4.2) actually shows a fairly straight line with a slope of nearly 1.5, or, approximately, $D_e = \alpha^2 D/\tau$ [27]. This relation has indeed been used in recent modeling studies of gas-solid reactions where the porosity decreases during the reaction. Equation 4.28 is used for estimating D_e for the following reasons: (1) its dependence on porosity is not important because porosity does not change during adsorption or desorption, and (2) the obtained empirical values of τ in the literature were based on this equation.

The empirical values of tortuosity factors for the commercial sorbents are summarized in Table 4.1. These values are taken from limited sources and give only approximate ranges for the tortuosity factor. The data for activated alumina and silica gel are taken from various sources summarized by Satterfield [23]. The data for activated carbon are obtained from the following two sources: (1) the diffusivity data of Costa et al. [28] on an activated carbon manufactured in Spain, which gave a range of 4–6 for τ, and (2) the data of Liu on Calgon carbons measured by a transient technique, with τ averaging 65 for three gases [29], all at near room temperature. The data for zeolites refer to diffusion in the binders. The tortuosity

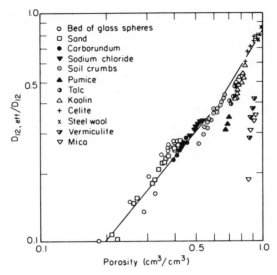

Figure 4.2   The ratio of effective pore diffusivity over molecular diffusivity for macropores in various materials. Note that the slope is nearly 1.5. Source: Currie [26]. Reprinted with permission.

Table 4.1   Approximate Values for Tortuosity Factors in Commercial Sorbents

Sorbent	τ	*Sources*
Alumina	2–6	[23]
Silica gel	2–6	[23]
Activated carbon	5–65	[28, 29]
Macropores in zeolites	1.7–4.5	[30, 31]

factors for carbons are usually high. For example, a factor as high as 100 has been measured for graphite [27] as well as for sintered pellets [32].

Parallel-Pore Model.   If the pore structure is visualized as an array of parallel cylindrical pores, the effective diffusivity can be directly calculated from D, the diffusivity in a single cylindrical pore [33]. Johnson and Stewart [34] derived a model utilizing the pore-size distribution. If $f(r)dr$ is the volume fraction for the pores with radii between r and $r + dr$, the integrated result of the fluxes gives:

$$D_e = \frac{1}{\tau} \int_0^\infty D(r)f(r)dr \tag{4.29}$$

Knowing the pore-volume distribution, D_e can be evaluated by this integral.

Random-Pore Model. This model was derived for bidisperse pore structures [35]. It is assumed that the porous material consists of repeating units, each comprising two stacked layers of microporous particles, with microporosity α_i. The void fraction between the particles is α_a. Furthermore, the sizes of the micropores and macropores are known; therefore, the values of D can be calculated from equation 4.25 to yield D_i and D_a, respectively. The effective diffusivity across such a structure, obtained by adding four possible fluxes, is:

$$D_e = D_a \alpha_a^2 + \frac{\alpha_i^2(1 + 3\alpha_a)}{1 - \alpha_a} D_i \qquad (4.30)$$

For a monodisperse pore structure, the D_e value would be either $\alpha_a^2 D_a$ or $\alpha_i^2 D_i$. However, since the α^2 factor is due to the assumption that two layers make up each repeating unit, it is meaningless to apply this model to a monodisperse material. (A trilayer repeating unit would yield a factor of α^3.)

The foregoing models can be used to give, at best, an order-of-magnitude estimate of the effective diffusivity. No clear advantage of any model has been shown. Experimental determination of the effective diffusivity should be made whenever possible.

Surface Diffusion

As a result of the concentration gradient in the pores, a surface gradient also exists on the pore wall along the gas-phase concentration gradient, assuming adsorption equilibrium is rapidly established. The surface flux associated with the surface concentration gradient is referred to as *surface diffusion*. Thus the gas-phase diffusion in pore and the surface diffusion on the pore wall proceed in parallel.

Surface diffusion can be important, and dominating, in the total flux in porous material, provided: (1) surface area is high, and (2) surface concentration is high. Both these conditions are met in adsorptive gas separation processes. The surface flux is definitely important for diffusion in the sorbents. For example, in the diffusion of methane, ethane, and ethylene in activated carbon at 20°C and pressures below 0.2 atm, the contribution of surface diffusion to the total flux ranges from approximately 40% to 80% [28]. Similarly, for propane diffusion in silica gel at below 75°C and low pressures, the contribution of surface diffusion is over 40%. A similarly important contribution has been reported for diffusion of CO_2 in alumina [36]. It may be convenient to lump surface diffusion into an effective diffusivity. The characteristics of the separation process, however, may not be correctly simulated or predicted by lumping because the surface diffusivity, as will be defined shortly, has a strong dependence on concentration, whereas the effective diffusivity is assumed constant.

It is generally accepted that surface diffusion takes place by the hopping of molecules between adsorption sites, where the molecules rest at the energy minima in the potential-energy diagram [37]. An adsorbed molecule can either desorb by overcoming the energy of desorption, or hop to an adjacent site by overcoming an energy for surface diffusion. The energy barrier for surface diffusion is lower than that for desorption to the gas phase. In a narrow pore or crevice, the temporarily detached molecule can hop to a site on the opposite wall; hence the energy barrier for surface diffusion can exceed that on a plane surface. The hopping mechanism is evidenced by the fact that surface diffusion is an activated process, having an Arrhenius temperature dependence.

By analogy to Fick's law, the surface diffusivity, D_s, may be defined in terms of surface concentration or amount adsorbed:

$$N_s = -D_s \frac{dq}{dr} \tag{4.31}$$

Dependence of D_s on q.   Extensive studies have revealed that the surface diffusivity has a strong dependence on surface concentration, or fractional surface coverage, θ. The observed dependence is [38]:

$$\frac{D_{s,\theta}}{D_{s,\theta=0}} = \frac{1}{1-\theta} \tag{4.32}$$

This dependence can be explained by the HIO model (Higashi, Ito, and Oishi) [39], based on the random walk (or hop) of molecules. It assumes that the transit time between sites is negligible relative to a residence time, Δt, at each site, given by:

$$\frac{1}{\Delta t} = v e^{-\Delta E / RT} \tag{4.33}$$

where v is the vibration frequency of the bonding that holds the molecule to the site, and ΔE is the effective bond energy — that is, the difference in energy between the states corresponding to adsorption at the ground vibrational level of the bond and the free mobility on the surface. The surface diffusivity is thus obtained by the Einstein equation:

$$D_s = \frac{\lambda^2}{2\Delta t} \tag{4.34}$$

where λ is the average distance between sites.

It is further assumed that when a molecule encounters a site already occupied by another molecule, it immediately bounces off and continues without stopping until it finds an unoccupied site at which to rest. The average number of jumps a molecule takes to find an empty site at surface coverage θ is:

$$\eta_\theta = \sum_{k=1}^{\infty} k(1-\theta)\theta^{k-1} = \frac{1}{1-\theta} \tag{4.35}$$

which takes the same length of time, Δt. Thus the relation in equation 4.32 is obtained.

The HIO model predicts values in agreement with experimental data reasonably well up to $\theta = 0.6$ or 0.7. At higher values of θ, the values predicted become greater than those measured. When $\theta = 1$, the model would give a value of infinity. This discrepancy has been circumvented by a modified model in which multilayer adsorption is allowed and a finite residence time is assigned to the second and higher-number layers [38]. To account for the second-layer adsorption, the result from the modified model gives:

$$\frac{D_s}{D_{s,\theta=0}} = \frac{1}{1 - \theta + \theta(v_1/v_2)\exp[-(\Delta E_1 - \Delta E_2)/RT]} \tag{4.36}$$

where the subscripts 1 and 2 denote first and second layers, respectively. The modified model improves data correlation from various sources and, more important, predicts a finite value at $\theta = 1$. The experimental data of Higashi et al. [39] are correlated by both models, equations 4.35 and 4.36, as shown in Figure 4.3.

Estimation of Surface Diffusivity. The temperature dependence of surface diffusivity can be expressed by:

$$D_s = D_0 e^{-E/RT} \tag{4.37}$$

where E is the activation energy for surface diffusion. Sladek et al. [40] have developed a general correlation that may be used to estimate surface diffusivity. The correlation is based on equation 4.37, and is shown in Figure 4.4 and Table 4.2.

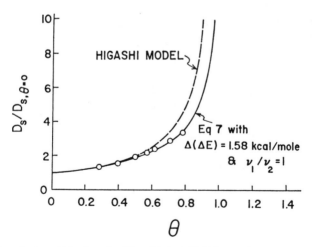

Figure 4.3 Correlation of the data by Higashi et al. [39] for surface diffusion of propane on silica glass at 35°C. Source: Yang, Fenn, and Haller [38]. Reprinted with permission.

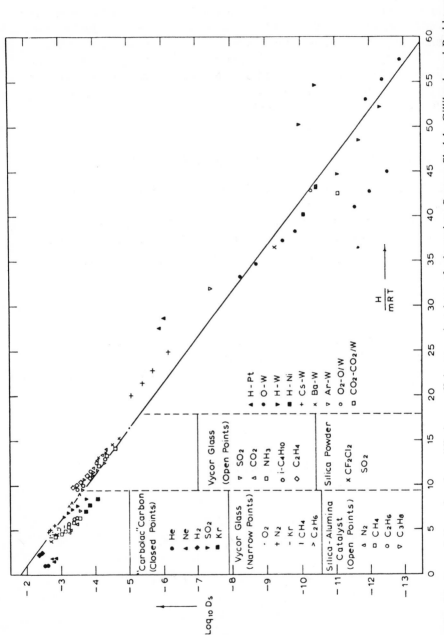

Figure 4.4 Empirical correlation of surface diffusion coefficients against heat of adsorption. Source: Sladek, Gilliland, and Baddour [40]. Reprinted with permission.

Table 4.2 Values of *m* for Use in Figure 4.4 Based on the Type of Adsorption Bonds

Bond	Solid	m	Examples of Available Surface Diffusion Data
van der Waals polar adsorbate	Conductor	2	SO_2–carbon
	Insulator	1	SO_2, NH_3–glass
Nonpolar adsorbate	Conductor	1	Ar–W, N_2–carbon
	Insulator	1	Kr, C_2H_4–glass
Ionic	Conductor	2	Cs, Ba–W
	Insulator	1	None
Covalent	Conductor	3	H-metals, O–W
	Insulator	1	None

Source: Sladek, Gilliland, and Baddour [40]. Reprinted with permission.

The correlation is made from data for both physical adsorption and chemisorption. Since surface diffusion is related to the strength of adsorption, D_s is plotted against the parameter H/mRT. Here, H is the heat of adsorption and m is an integer having a value of 1, 2, or 3, depending on the nature of the surface bond and the solid, as given by Table 4.2. Because the correlation has not been tested beyond their own work, the value obtained should be treated as an estimate.

For calculating surface diffusion flux in a porous structure, a tortuosity factor is needed. Although the tortuosity factor for surface diffusion is not necessarily equal to that for gas-phase diffusion in the same structure, the same tortuosity factor is usually assumed for both diffusion modes.

For statistical mechanical treatments of surface diffusion, which also predict the dependence of D_s on q as shown in Figure 4.3, the reader is referred to Lee and O'Connell [93, 94].

Diffusion in Molecular-Sieve Sorbents

Adsorption of gases by commercial zeolite pellets occurs almost entirely within the zeolite crystals; contribution by the macroporous binder is negligible. Since diffusion in the crystals is very slow, with a diffusion time constant, D/r_c^2 (where r_c is the radius of crystal), usually well below 10^{-4} s^{-1}, there is little doubt that intracrystalline diffusion can play an important or limiting role in adsorption and desorption.

The literature on the experimental data and theoretical interpretations on intracrystalline diffusion in zeolites has been reviewed by Walker et al. [41], Breck [42], Barrer [43], and Ruthven [44]. Most of the data have been on the small-pore (4–5 Å aperture) zeolites. The diffusivities for nonpolar and small gas molecules such as nitrogen and *n*-paraffins from methane to *n*-butane in these zeolites range from 10^{-14} to 10^{-12} cm^2/s, at 20–200°C. The studies that have been conducted on intracrystalline diffusion so far have been almost exclusively limited to single gases.

It is not clear how diffusivities of a binary or multicomponent gas mixture, as encountered in all industrial processes, are related to the single-component diffusivities. The following discussion is based on single-gas diffusion data.

The intracrystalline diffusivity is influenced by the following factors [43]:

1. Concentration of the diffusing molecules within the crystal
2. Temperature
3. Crystalline channel geometry and dimensions
4. Shape, size, and polarity of the diffusing molecules
5. Cation distributions, size, charge, and number
6. Lattice defects; structural changes caused by diffusing molecules and sample pretreatments

The first three factors collectively are responsible for the molecular-sieving properties. The effects of the individual factors on diffusivity have been discussed in detail by Barrer [43]. For a given gas-zeolite system, the diffusivity as defined by Fick's law is dependent on temperature and concentration, which are the first two factors.

Temperature Dependence.   The temperature dependence of diffusivity may be expressed by Arrhenius' law. The apparent activation energies for diffusion in the small-pore (4–5 Å) zeolites by the small nonpolar molecules range from 3 to 11 kcal/mole. The activation energy clearly is related to the relative size and shape of the diffusing molecule and the effective aperture size in the crystal. For a given zeolite, the value of the apparent activation energy for diffusion increases with the van der Waals diameter of the gas molecule. Plots of this kind (E versus diameter) have been made by Barrer [45] on several zeolites and a silica glass, as well as by Ruthven on zeolites 4A and 5A, and a molecular-sieve carbon for a variety of gases [44].

Sorbate Concentration Dependence.   This subject, though not well understood, is important in process modeling and even more so in understanding the mechanism of the diffusion process.

Diverse dependences of diffusivity on sorbate concentration have been reported in the literature. Four possible behaviors have all been shown: A–C in Figure 4.5, and one in which the diffusivity first increases with C, reaching a maximum before starting its decline. The latter behavior was reported for water diffusion in heulandite at 20°C [46]. The three types of behavior shown in Figure 4.5 represent more recent data using differential uptake curves (uptake rates using small step increments in gas pressure) [47], as well as the pulsed field gradient NMR method (by applying a pulsed magnetic gradient field to the sample, the NMR signal provides a direct measure of the mean square displacement during the known time interval between pulses, and subsequently the value of diffusivity through the Einstein equation) [48]. The ranges of variation in Figure 4.5 are: 10^{-11}–10^{-12} cm^2/s for A and B, and 10^{-5}–10^{-7} cm^2/s for C.

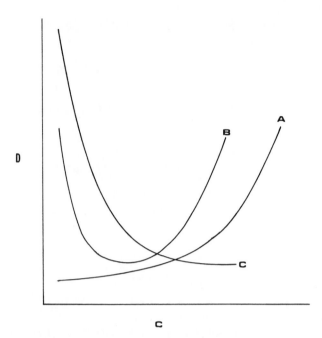

Figure 4.5 Dependences of intracrystalline diffusivities on sorbate concentration. Examples for: (*A*) CO_2 in 4A zeolite and *n*-paraffins in 5A zeolite; (*B*) Ar, Kr, Xe, N_2, and O_2 in 5A; (*C*) *n*-paraffins in 13X. Scale of diffusivities for *A* and *B*: $10^{-11} - 10^{-12}$ cm²/s, and for *C*: $10^{-5} - 10^{-7}$ cm²/s.

Two unrelated interpretations have been proposed for the increase and decline of *D* with *C*. Darken's relation has been assumed responsible by several groups for the increase of *D* with *C* [47, 49, 50]. The decline of *D* with *C* has been attributed to a decrease in the mean jump distance, since there are more frequent collisions at higher concentrations [51].

Darken's relation [52] was originally derived to explain the Kirkendall effect: When two binary alloys of different concentrations are joined together, a movement in the boundary is observed [53]. The basic thesis for the derivation is that chemical potential gradient, rather than concentration gradient, is the true driving force for diffusion. A relationship can then be derived between the true diffusion coefficient and the Fickian, or observed, diffusion coefficient. Neglecting the off-diagonal diffusion coefficients, the flux equation for species 1 is:

$$N = -M_{11}\frac{d\mu}{dx} = -D\frac{dC}{dx} \qquad (4.38)$$

where μ is chemical potential, and M_{11} is coefficient for the flux due to the gradient of the same species. The mobility of an atom, B, is given by:

$$B = \frac{v}{F}$$

(4.39)

where v is the mean velocity of the atom and F is the force acting on the atom. The flux is then:

$$N = vC = BFC = -BC\frac{d\mu}{dx}$$

(4.40)

Combining equations 4.38 and 4.40, and noting that

$$\mu = \mu_0 + RT \ln a$$

(4.41)

we have:

$$D = B\frac{d\mu}{d \ln C} = BRT\frac{d \ln a}{d \ln C}$$

(4.42)

Equation 4.42 is referred to as *Darken's relation*.

In order to find the sorbate concentration dependence of D, gas pressure, P, has been used to substitute for the activity of the adsorbed molecules, a (the reason for the substitution is "ideal gas behavior" [44]):

$$D = BRT\frac{d \ln P}{d \ln C}$$

(4.43)

and if P and C are related by the Langmuir isotherm, which is frequently the case for zeolites, we have:

$$D = \frac{BRT}{1-(q/q_s)} = \frac{BRT}{1-\theta}$$

(4.44)

where q_s is the saturated amount adsorbed and θ is the fractional saturation. Equation 4.44 closely resembles the behavior of the systems that show behavior A (in Figure 4.5).

There are lingering questions about the application of Darken's relation to the interpretation of the concentration dependence of intracrystalline diffusivity. The validity of substituting the activity of the sorbed molecules, a, by the gas-phase pressure, P, in equation 4.42 is not clear. Furthermore, perfect Arrhenius plots were obtained for D_0 ($D_0 = BRT$ in equation 4.43); see, for example, the data from various sources on zeolites 4A and 5A [54, 55]. If B has an Arrhenius dependence on temperature, then the additional linear function of T would clearly show a curvature on the Arrhenius plot for D_0. (The apparent overall activation energy is 4–7 kcal/mole, whereas the linear T dependence is equivalent to an "activation energy" of 0.6 kcal/mole at 25°C, which is clearly not negligible.) Furthermore, most of the diffusivities were calculated (incorrectly) by using an isothermal analysis of the experimental data on (nonisothermal) uptake rates.

It is entirely feasible to interpret the sorbate concentration dependence of diffusivity (eq. 4.44) as a hopping mechanism, akin to surface diffusion. Only a vacant site in the cage can accommodate a hopping molecule, hence the $(1 - \theta)^{-1}$ dependence (eq. 4.32). At still higher sorbate concentrations, the increased collision frequency with other hopping molecules results in a shorter mean hop distance and thereby a lower diffusivity. Such an effect is not expected for surface diffusion because the space for hopping is relatively unlimited.

Although there is little doubt that the diffusivity is concentration-dependent, the experimental difficulties in measuring diffusivity have resulted in diverse and inconsistent data. Different experimental techniques can yield different diffusivities. For example, widely different diffusivities were obtained from three different techniques for n-paraffins of similar sizes in ZSM-5 zeolite: 10^{-11} cm^2/s by integral gravimetric uptake curves [56], $> 10^{-9}$ cm^2/s by NMR [57], and 10^{-6} cm^2/s by a large-crystal permeation experiment [58]. Diffusivities varying by three orders of magnitude were obtained by using the same technique and the same type of zeolite from different sources and by different groups [54]. Slightly different sample pretreatment temperatures also yielded opposite dependences of diffusivity on concentration [59]. Since these inconsistencies remain unresolved, an order-of-magnitude information on the diffusivity, obtained by chromatographic methods [60, 61, 62] and by integral uptake curves [56], remains useful for practical purposes.

Intrapellet Mass Balance for Zeolites.   Because of the unique structure of the commercial zeolite pellets, equation 4.2 is not applicable. This equation is, however, applicable to all other commercial sorbents including molecular sieve carbon because of their homogeneous pore structures. A zeolite pellet consists of small crystals, usually 1–9 μm cubes, bound together by a macroporous material. The mass balance for the pellet requires two equations, one for the crystals (assumed spherical with radius r_c) and one for the binder (with radius R_p). For the crystals, the following solid-diffusion equation is usually used:

$$\frac{1}{r^2} \frac{\partial}{\partial r} \left(r^2 D_c \frac{\partial q}{\partial r} \right) = \frac{\partial q}{\partial t} \tag{4.45}$$

with B.C.:

$$\frac{\partial q}{\partial r}(0, t) = 0, \quad q(r_c, t) = \frac{k_1 C(R, t)}{1 + k_2 C(R, t)} \tag{4.46}$$

where r is the radial distance coordinate in the crystal and R is that in the pellet. Langmuir isotherm is assumed for the system. For the pellet, mass balance yields:

$$\frac{1}{R^2} \frac{\partial}{\partial R} \left(R^2 D_p \frac{\partial C}{\partial R} \right) = \frac{\partial C}{\partial t} + \left(\frac{1 - \alpha}{\alpha} \right) \frac{\partial \bar{q}}{\partial t} \tag{4.47}$$

with B.C.:

$$\frac{\partial C}{\partial R}(0, t) = 0, \qquad C(R_p, t) = C_{\text{bulk}} \tag{4.48}$$

and q averaged over crystals:

$$\bar{q}(R, t) = \frac{3}{r_c^2} \int_0^{r_c} q r^2 dr \tag{4.49}$$

With C replaced by C^P, equations 4.45–4.49 can be used in place of equation 4.2 in the model for the adsorber.

Equations 4.45 to 4.49 describe the uptake rate of a single pellet. For $C_{\text{bulk}} = C_0 = \text{const.}$, initially clean pellet, and Henry's law isotherm, Ruckenstein et al. [63] obtained an analytic solution for the uptake rate. The uptake rate is determined by two parameters: $\alpha' = (D_c/r_c^2)/(D_p/R_p^2)$ and $\beta = 3\alpha'(q_0/C_0)(1 - \alpha)/\alpha$. This solution was later extended by Ma and Lee to account for a decreasing C_0 in a finite batch volume [64].

Diffusion in Molecular-Sieve Carbon.   Molecular-sieve carbon offers unique new applications, such as production of nitrogen from air, and possibly separation of CO_2 from CH_4 and other hydrocarbons in tertiary oil recovery and methane production by fermentation. These new applications result from highly different effective diffusivities between the gases. Unfortunately, very limited information on the diffusivities has appeared in the published literature. Qualitative uptake curves for O_2 and N_2 have been reported for a molecular sieve carbon manufactured by Bergbau-Forschung GmbH in Germany [90], for O_2 and N_2, plus CO_2 and CH_4 in a carbon manufactured by Calgon Corporation in Pittsburgh [91]. The diffusion constants of 1.7×10^{-4} s^{-1} and 7.0×10^{-6} s^{-1} were reported for oxygen and nitrogen, respectively, in the Bergbau-Forschung carbon [90]. The relative O_2/N_2 uptake curves reported for the Calgon carbon were in approximate agreement with the foregoing figures. More detailed and extensive data were reported for diffusion in the carbon manufactured by Takeda Chemical Company in Japan [65, 66]. The diffusivities of small-size hydrocarbons, monotonic gases, nitrogen, and oxygen fall in the range of 10^{-8} to 10^{-6} cm^2/s at 25°C. A concentration dependence similar to that for surface diffusion, $D = D_0(1 - \theta)^{-1}$, was observed for all investigated gases. Unfortunately, the Takeda carbon has not demonstrated the desired property for kinetic separation — that is, a large difference in diffusivity between the gases to be separated. The diffusivity of oxygen in the Takeda carbon at 300K was 6.9×10^{-7} cm^2/s, compared to a value of 2.2×10^{-7} cm^2/s for nitrogen under the same conditions [66]. The ratio of diffusivities for the same gas pair in the Bergbau-Forschung carbon was nearly 30 [90], in contrast to the factor of three for the Takeda carbon. The uptake curves for CO_2 and CH_4 in the Takeda carbon were rapid and nearly identical [67]. A recent study on the diffusion constants of oxygen and nitrogen in two Bergbau-Forschung carbons [92] showed approximately the same ratio, but higher individual values, as that in reference 90.

Relative Importance of Internal and External Resistances

The relative importance of internal and external resistances to mass and heat transfer has been an important subject of study on solid-catalyzed gas reactions. Excellent reviews can be found in references 7, 8, 9, 11, and 12. These findings are directly applicable to adsorption and desorption, and pertinent results from the various studies will be given.

By equating mass flux across the film to the diffusive flux across the interface at the pellet exterior surface, we have, as given in equation 4.4:

$$k(C - C_R^P) = D_e \left(\frac{\partial C^P}{\partial r} \right)_{R_P} \tag{4.4}$$

In dimensionless form:

$$\frac{C^P}{C} = y \qquad \frac{r}{R_P} = z$$

$$\left(\frac{\partial y}{\partial z} \right)_{z=1} \bigg/ (1 - y)_{z=1} = \frac{kR_P}{D_e} = (\mathrm{Bi})_m \tag{4.50}$$

The dimensionless group, kR_P/D_e, is the Biot number for mass transfer. Similarly, for heat flux:

$$h(T - T_{PR}) = k_e \left(\frac{\partial T_p}{\partial r} \right)_{R_P} \tag{4.7}$$

$$\left(\frac{\partial (T_p/T)}{\partial z} \right)_{z=1} \bigg/ (1 - y)_{z=1} = \frac{hR_P}{k_e} = (\mathrm{Bi})_h \tag{4.51}$$

where hR_p/k_e is the Biot number for heat transfer.

The Biot number expresses the ratio between the internal and external gradients. Its magnitude suggests the relative importance of internal and external resistances. A high Biot number would indicate that the major resistance is within the pellet.

The mass and heat Biot numbers in fixed beds have been the subject of numerous correlations with many variations. Typical correlations are [9]:

$$(\mathrm{Bi})_m = \frac{a}{2\varepsilon} \frac{D_m}{D_e} \mathrm{Re}^{1+b} \mathrm{Sc}^{1/3} \tag{4.52}$$

$$(\mathrm{Bi})_h = \frac{a}{2\varepsilon} \frac{k_g}{k_e} \mathrm{Re}^{1+b} \mathrm{Pr}^{1/3} \tag{4.53}$$

For $3 < \mathrm{Re} < 2{,}000$:

$$a = 0.357, \qquad b = -0.359$$

For the gas-sorbent systems of interest in gas separation, the magnitudes of the Biot number are usually:

$$(\mathrm{Bi})_m \gg 1, \qquad (\mathrm{Bi})_h < 1$$

Assuming that the ratio between molecular diffusivity and effective pore diffusivity is 10, and that the gas conductivity over pellet conductivity (k_g/k_e) is 0.1, Aris [7] estimated that the mass Biot number for a packed bed is in the range between 5 and 500, whereas the heat Biot number ranges from 0.05 to 5. The mass Biot number for zeolites should be some six to eight orders of magnitude higher than these values. This analysis indicates that the major resistance for mass transfer is within the pellet, whereas the opposite is true for heat transfer. Exceptions do exist for solid catalyzed reactions [7, Chap. 2]. The analyses and experimental results on heat transfer in a catalyst particle [68, 69, 70] showed, however, that the major resistance for heat transfer lies in the external film. For mass transfer in adsorption, the external film resistance is clearly negligible. For heat transfer in adsorption, the situation is not so clear-cut. The theoretical analysis of Brunovska et al. [71] indicated that both resistances can be important depending on the sorbate-sorbent combination, but experimentally they showed that film resistance dominates the overall heat transfer for adsorption of *n*-heptane in a large (1 cm diameter) zeolite pellet [72]. In adsorber calculations, the heat transfer resistances have generally been neglected, and the temperature is assumed uniform in the fluid and solid phases in the radial direction in the bed.

4.2.3   Dispersion in Packed Beds

If a concentration gradient exists in a packed bed, a diffusive mass flux will occur. In addition, eddy (turbulent) diffusion due to the flow also contributes to the mass flux. The resultant flux is referred to as *mass dispersion*, which may be expressed mathematically in terms of Fick's law, where the proportionality constant is called *dispersion coefficient*. Dispersion occurs in both radial and axial directions in the bed. The radial dispersion is, however, regarded as unimportant, when the adsorbed bed diameter is far greater than the particle diameter. The dispersion coefficient is usually expressed in terms of Peclet number ($\mathrm{Pe} = 2R_p\mu/D_z\rho$), and:

$$\frac{1}{\mathrm{Pe}} = \frac{1}{(\mathrm{Pe})_m} + \frac{1}{(\mathrm{Pe})_t} \tag{4.54}$$

where D_z is the axial dispersion coefficient, whereas $(\mathrm{Pe})_m$ and $(\mathrm{Pe})_t$ are the Peclet numbers for molecular and turbulent diffusion, respectively.

The Peclet numbers are correlated with Reynolds and Schmidt numbers. One of the many empirical correlations is the following [73]:

$$\frac{1}{Pe} = \frac{0.3}{ReSc} + \frac{0.5}{1 + 3.8/(ReSc)} \tag{4.55}$$

for

$$0.008 < Re < 400 \quad \text{and} \quad 0.28 < Sc < 2.2$$

This correlation, shown in Figure 4.6, is capable of describing a peak in Pe and the asymptotic value of 2 for Pe at high Reynolds numbers.

4.3   LINEAR DRIVING FORCE AND OTHER APPROXIMATIONS FOR MASS TRANSFER RATE

As concluded from the preceding section, the overall mass transfer rate between the bulk flow and the internal surface of a sorbent particle is limited to pore diffusion (or intracrystalline diffusion) under practical conditions in gas separation. The gas film diffusion resistance will be neglected. The effect of pore diffusion on the adsorber dynamics is therefore crucially important. Qualitatively, a higher pore diffusion rate will result in a sharper or steeper concentration wavefront, consequently giving a better separation. In order to make a quantitative prediction of the behavior, the complete solution of the mass and heat balance equations given in section 4.1 must be used.

A solution of the model requires simultaneous solutions of the mass balance equation within the particle (eq. 4.2) as well as in the bed or for the bulk flow (eqs. 4.3 and 4.4). The model can be substantially simplified if the mass balance equation within the particle is eliminated. This can be done by making simplifying assumptions that result in an expression relating the overall uptake rate in a particle to the bulk flow concentration:

$$\frac{\partial \bar{q}}{\partial t} = f(q^*) \tag{4.56}$$

where $\bar{q}$ is the average or overall amount adsorbed in the particle, and q^* is the amount adsorbed in equilibrium with the bulk flow concentration C. Furthermore, it is desirable that the function in equation 4.56 does not contain the time elapsed in the uptake, t. Equation 4.56 can then be used to replace equation 4.4, and substituted in the last term on the right-hand side of equation 4.3. The particle mass balance equation is thereby eliminated from the model. Several useful approaches that have been suggested to achieve this goal will be discussed: linear driving force, nonlinear driving force, and parabolic concentration profile within the particle.

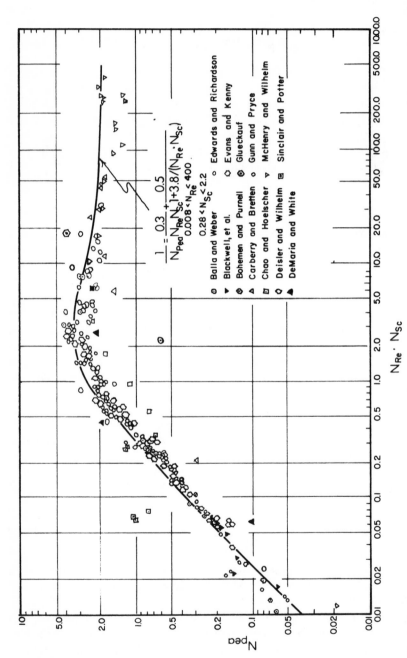

Figure 4.6 Correlation for axial dispersion Peclet number (N_{Pea}) against Reynolds (N_{Re}) and Schmidt (N_{Sc}) numbers in packed beds. Source: Wen and Fan [73]. Reprinted with permission.

Each approach can save a tremendous amount of computation time in the model.

The linear driving force (LDF) approximation was first suggested by Glueckauf and Coates [75, 76]. Consider the rate of uptake by a sorbent particle located at a certain point in the fixed-bed adsorber. When the upstream portion of the bed is saturated with the sorbate, the concentration "front" will pass through (or *elute*) the particle. If the front is extremely steep or sharp, and if a step function is assumed (which is not possible because the dispersion flux would be infinitely great), a well-known solution for the uptake rate is available [74]. Thus solving the mass balance equation for the particle (eq. 4.2), subject to the boundary condition $t = 0$, $q = 0$, $t > 0$, $q(R_p) = q_0^*$, where q_0^* is the value of q in equilibrium with the feed concentration C_0, we have:

$$\bar{q} = q_0^* \left\{ 1 - \frac{6}{\pi^2} \sum_{n=1}^{\infty} \frac{1}{n^2} \exp(-n^2 \pi^2 D_e t / R_p^2) \right\} \tag{4.57}$$

However, the concentration front is not represented by a step function. Glueckauf [75, 76] derived solutions for the uptake rate for different increases in concentration: an exponentially increasing concentration representing a steep front, and a linearly increasing concentration approximating a diffuse front. The solution for $D_e t / R_p^2 > 0.1$ is [76]:

$$\frac{\partial \bar{q}}{\partial t} = \frac{\pi^2 D_e}{R_p^2} (q^* - \bar{q}) + \left(1 - \frac{\pi^2}{15} \right) \frac{\partial q^*}{\partial t}$$
$$- \left(\frac{1}{15} - \frac{2\pi^2}{315} \right) \frac{R_p^2}{D_e} \frac{\partial^2 q^*}{\partial t^2} + \cdots \tag{4.58}$$

where q^* is in equilibrium with the bulk flow concentration C, and is continuously varying with C. The higher-derivative terms including the second derivative are negligible. If conditions are such that the interior is close enough to equilibrium (e.g., large t or D_e), we may replace $\partial q^* / \partial t$ by $\partial \bar{q} / \partial t$ and:

$$\frac{\partial \bar{q}}{\partial t} = \frac{15 D_e}{R_p^2} (q^* - \bar{q}) \tag{4.59}$$

which is nearly the same equation as they previously suggested, except for a coefficient of 14 rather than 15 [75].

Equation 4.59 is the basis for the LDF approximation. It has been widely used in adsorber and gas separation models for breakthrough curves, desorption behavior, cyclic separation processes, and so on. Often, however, it has been used without its validity being justified. First, the solution is derived for $D_e t / R_p^2 > 0.1$. The diffusion time constant (D_e / R_p^2) for activated carbon is in the order of $10^{-1}\,\mathrm{s}^{-1}$, and is $10^{-3}\,\mathrm{s}^{-1}$ for zeolite crystals, which make the application of LDF in the initial period of uptake invalid, especially for zeolite crystals. Two other factors must be considered before using the LDF equation: curvature of the adsorption isotherm, and the boundary conditions pertinent to the process. Before discussing the effects of these factors on the LDF results, some nonlinear driving force approximations will be presented.

For a step-function change in concentration, the solution for equation 4.57 is approximated by Vermeulen [77] as the following:

$$\frac{\partial \bar{q}}{\partial t} = \frac{\pi^2 D_e}{R_p^2} \frac{q^{*2} - \bar{q}^2}{2\bar{q}} \tag{4.60}$$

The boundary condition of a single-step change in bulk concentration is a good representation of the condition in an adsorber bed when the adsorption isotherm is very steep — that is, when the Langmuir constant approaches ∞ or "irreversible" isotherm. Indeed, equation 4.60 is superior to the LDF equation for a steep isotherm.

4.3.1 Applicability to Various Isotherms under Adsorber Conditions

During the passage of the concentration front, a sorbent particle in the bed experiences a continuously increasing concentration. This gives way to a continuously increasing sorbate concentration at the exterior surface of the particle, q^*. Two approximations for the dependence of q^* on t were used by Glueckauf [76].

Linear Adsorption Isotherms

The following is assumed for a diffuse front, and has been shown [76] to be a good approximation for linear isotherms (in a dilute, no-dispersion, isothermal bed):

$$q^* = q_0^* [\tfrac{1}{2} + A(y)] \tag{4.61}$$

$$y = \gamma(t - t_1); \qquad A(y) = \frac{1}{\sqrt{2\pi}} \int_0^{x=y} \exp \frac{-x^2}{2} dx$$

where q_0^* is the equilibrium sorbate concentration corresponding to the bulk concentration in the feed ($q^* \to q_0^*$ at large t), and γ and t_1 are constants characteristic of the concentration front.

Using the foregoing boundary condition (eq. 4.61), an exact solution has been obtained by Glueckauf [76] for the mass balance equation in the spherical particle (eq. 4.2). (The other boundary conditions are the usual ones at $r = 0$ and R_p.) The exact solution is then compared with the approximations:

$$\frac{\partial \bar{q}}{\partial t} = \frac{\pi^2 D_e}{R_p^2} (q^* - \bar{q}) + \left(1 - \frac{\pi}{15}\right) \frac{\partial q^*}{\partial t} \tag{A}$$

$$= \frac{15D_e}{R_p^2}(q^* - \bar{q}) \tag{B}$$

$$= \frac{\pi^2 D_e}{R_p^2} \frac{q^{*2} - \bar{q}^2}{2\bar{q}} \tag{C}$$

Equation A represents the two-term approximation of equation 4.58, B is the LDF approximation, and C is the approximation for a step change given by Vermeulen [77]. Figure 4.7 shows the comparisons of the exact solution with the three approximations for a diffuse concentration front (that is, with the boundary condition approximated by equation 4.61). The comparisons indicate that the LDF is an adequate approximation for adsorbers under conditions when linear adsorption isotherms (or Henry's law) are followed.

Langmuir Isotherms

For adsorption following the Langmuir-type isotherms, the concentration front is sharp. The reason will become clear in the next section. The sharp front can be approximated by [76]:

$$q^* = q_0^*\{1 - e^{-k(t_2 - t)}\} \tag{4.62}$$

where $q^* \rightarrow q_0^*$ when $t \rightarrow t_2$, and k is a constant characteristic of the shape of the front.

An exact solution for the mass balance equation for the spherical particle (eq. 4.2) with the foregoing boundary condition (eq. 4.62) was also obtained by Glueckauf [76], which can be compared with approximations A, B, and C.

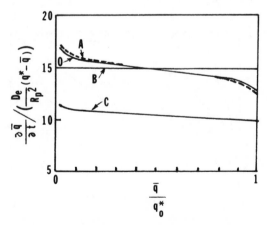

Figure 4.7 Comparison of the exact solution (curve *0*) for the uptake rate by a spherical particle with approximations *A*, *B* (LDF), and *C* (Vermeulen's), during the passage of a diffuse concentration front (for a linear adsorption isotherm). Source: Glueckauf [76]. Reprinted with permission.

The comparison depends strongly on the shape of the concentration front, or on the curvature of the adsorption isotherm. The curvature of the isotherm may be characterized by the distribution factor:

$$K_d = \frac{X(1-Y)}{Y(1-X)} \tag{4.63a}$$

where $X = q^*/q_0^*$ and $Y = C/C_0$, or:

$$K_d = \frac{q^*}{q_0^* - q^*} \frac{C_0 - C}{C} \tag{4.63b}$$

where K_d is the distribution factor that is frequently used in adsorber studies. (The equilibrium factor, β, is another frequently used parameter, where $\beta = 1/K_d$.) The curvature of a Langmuir isotherm is characterized by K_d; $K_d = 1$ for linear isotherm and $\rightarrow \infty$ for an irreversible or square isotherm. The value of K_d (or β) depends strongly on the end value C_0, or the feed concentration to the adsorber according to the following relationship for Langmuir isotherms [$q^* = q_m BC/ (1 + BC)$]:

$$K_d = 1 + BC_0 \tag{4.63c}$$

Some values of K_d are given in Figure 4.8, which increase linearly with C_0.

The comparison of the theoretical uptake rate with the approximations for A, B, and C is given in Figure 4.9. Two important conclusions can be drawn from Figure 4.9. First, the LDF (B) approximation is not a good one for highly curved isotherms, for example when $K_d > 3$, where Vermeulen's approximation (C)

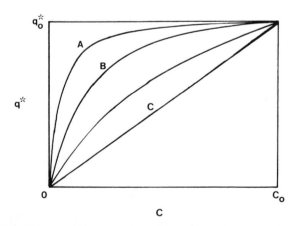

Figure 4.8 Distribution factor, K_d, or equilibrium factor, β, $\beta = 1/K_d$, for Langmuir isotherms. K_d increases linearly with the feed concentration C_0 (eq. 4.63c). At C_0, $K_d = 30$ for A, 8 for B, and 1 for C.

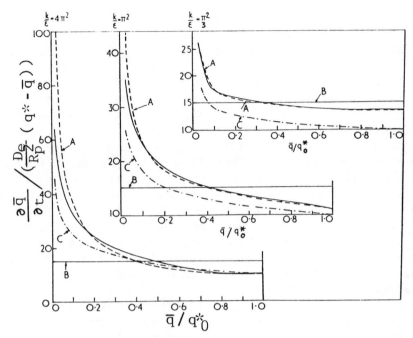

Figure 4.9 Comparison of approximations *A*, *B* (LDF), and *C* with the theoretical uptake rate (solid curve) for a spherical sorbent particle during the passage of a sharp concentration front, which is characterized by the curvature of the Langmuir isotherm, or distribution factor, K_d. From left to right, $K_d = 10$, 4.4 and 2.5. Source: Glueckauf [76]. Reprinted with permission.

becomes superior. Second, all approximations fail during the early stage of the uptake, even for small K_d. The rate of uptake predicted by the LDF approximation falls well below the true rate when the amount adsorbed in the particle is small. Approximation A is excellent under all conditions but is not convenient to use in adsorber studies.

Another nonlinear driving force approximation that is superior to the LDF at large K_d values is [78, 79]:

$$\frac{\partial \bar{q}}{\partial t} = \frac{15D_e}{R_p^2} \frac{1 - \varepsilon}{\rho_b} \left(\frac{C_0}{q_0^*} \right) \psi(K_d) \frac{q^* - \bar{q}}{\{1 - (1 - 1/K_d)\bar{q}/q_0^*\}^{1/2}} \qquad (4.64)$$

where ψ is an empirical function of K_d obtained by matching the midpoint slopes of the numerically solved concentration fronts with those using the nonlinear approximation [78, 79], with ρ_b being the mass of sorbent per volume of bed ($\psi = 0.548/[1 - 0.452\,\beta^{1/2}]$ where $\beta = 1/K_d$). This approximation is reduced to LDF when $K_d \to 1$, and to a square-root driving force approximation when $K_d \to \infty$; the latter was proposed by Acrivos [80].

4.3.2   Application of LDF to Cyclic Processes

The applicability of the LDF approximation to the pressure swing adsorption (PSA) process has been discussed by Nakao and Suzuki [81], and by Raghavan et al. [89]. An idealized two-step cycle is considered: The bulk concentration outside a spherical particle is cycled stepwise between zero and a constant value, with an equal time θ_c for each step, where $\theta_c = D_e t/R_p^2$. The particle is initially free of sorbate. The total amount adsorbed in the particle accumulates with the number of cycles until a steady level is reached, maintaining a cyclic steady state. The amount adsorbed in the particle at cyclic steady state is calculated by solving the mass balance equation (eq. 4.2) and by using the LDF approximation. The two results are then compared. As can be expected from Figures 4.7 and 4.9, the LDF with a coefficient of 15 underestimates the rate of uptake when the amount adsorbed is small, which is the case when the half-cycle time θ_c is small. Comparing the two solutions, the value of the coefficient, K (which is 15 in the LDF approximation), is given as a function of the half-cycle time, θ_c, in Figure 4.10. This figure also includes the results by Raghavan et al., who calculated the K values for the adsorbers in the PSA process [89].

From Figure 4.10, it is seen that the LDF approximation will underestimate the rate of uptake when applied to cyclic processes with a short cycle time — that is, with fast cycles. This, however, does not pose a problem with respect to the applicability of the LDF approximation because in almost all commercial cyclic gas separation processes the value of $D_e t/R_p^2$ is well above 1%. For zeolite crystals

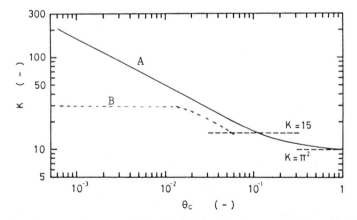

Figure 4.10   (*A*) The corrected coefficients, K, for the LDF approximation ($K = 15$ in equation 4.59) for a particle subjected to an idealized two-step concentration change simulating a PSA process. The time for each step, t, is expressed by $\theta_c = D_e t/R_p^2$; (*B*) Same as *A*, except the mass balance equation for the adsorber column (eq. 4.3) is solved for the PSA cycle, $K_d = 2$. Source (*A*): Nakao and Suzuki [81]. Reprinted with permission. (*B*): Raghavam, Hassan, and Ruthven [89]. Reprinted with permission.

with a 1 micron radius, as in commercial zeolite sorbents, the value of 1% for $D_e t / R_p^2$ corresponds to approximately a half-cycle time of 10 s. This is equivalent to the fastest pressure-swing cycle used in industry, the rapid pressure-swing adsorption process [82]. The value of $D_e t / R_p^2$ is generally greater for activated carbon and alumina and silica sorbents, and much greater for temperature-swing processes.

The limitation placed by the value of K_d on the application of the LDF approximation is also not a severe one in present commercial applications such as drying, purification, and air separation. For example, the value of K_d is less than 3 for the adsorption of nitrogen and oxygen in 5A zeolite at the ambient temperature and pressures up to 10 atm [83], for the adsorption of water vapor on alumina and silica at 20 Torr and ambient temperature [42], and for hydrocarbons in all sorbents at moderate pressures. However, the value of K_d can greatly exceed 3 for bulk separation applications; thus caution must be exercised in applying the LDF approximation. If, on the other hand, the LDF approximation is applied in model simulation where the coefficient is treated as an empirical constant, similar to a mass transfer coefficient, these factors need not be considered.

Furthermore, it is important to point out that in any PSA process, the amount adsorbed and desorbed during, respectively, the repressure and depressure steps are large. In the analyses in references 81 and 89, these steps are either excluded or frozen. The K values will be lower when these steps are properly included. A detailed discussion is given in section 8.1.3 of Chapter 8.

4.3.3 Parabolic Concentration Profile within Particle

If the concentration profile within the spherical sorbent particle is known, considerable savings in numerical computations can be achieved, because the integration along the radial distance in the particle is no longer necessary. This has been shown for modeling PSA [84] and temperature-cycling gas separation processes [85] by assuming a parabolic concentration profile, which was first used by Liaw et al. [86], and by Rice [87]. This is a reasonable assumption, since the profiles obtained by exact solutions are almost always parabolic in shape [84, 88]. By using such a profile, it has been shown that a rather simple analytic solution for the breakthrough curves is possible (for isothermal condition, both internal and external mass transfer resistances are important, and a linear isotherm is assumed) [86].

The parabolic concentration profile, perhaps more interestingly, can lead to an exact solution that is identical to Glueckauf's LDF approximation (eq. 4.59). The derivation follows [86].

Equation 4.2 is recast into:

$$\frac{\partial q}{\partial t} = \frac{D_e}{r^2} \frac{\partial}{\partial r} \left(\frac{\partial q}{\partial r} \right) \tag{4.65}$$

The rate of change of $\bar{q}$, the volume-average q, is:

$$\frac{\partial \bar{q}}{\partial t} = \frac{3}{R_p^3} \int_0^{R_p} \frac{\partial q}{\partial t} r^2 dr \tag{4.66}$$

From equations 4.65 and 4.66, we have:

$$\frac{\partial \bar{q}}{\partial t} = \frac{3D_e}{R_p} \left(\frac{\partial q}{\partial r} \right)_{\text{at } r=R_p} \tag{4.67}$$

Assuming a parabolic distribution for q:

$$q = a_0 + a_2 r^2 \tag{4.68}$$

which satisfies the requirement of $\partial q / \partial r = 0$ at $r = 0$.

$$\left(\frac{\partial q}{\partial r} \right)_{\text{at } r=R_p} = \frac{5}{R_p} (q_{R_p} - \bar{q}) \tag{4.69}$$

From equations 4.67 and 4.69, we have:

$$\frac{\partial \bar{q}}{\partial t} = \frac{15D_e}{R_p^2} (q_{R_p} - \bar{q}) \tag{4.70}$$

Equation 4.70 is identical to the LDF equation (eq. 4.59).

Although the uniqueness of equation 4.68 that leads to equation 4.70 has not been shown, it may be regarded as a good simplifying assumption.

The pore-diffusion models [84, 85] are, however, different from the LDF models. The LDF models are equivalent to using equation 4.65 combined with a parabolic concentration profile. Equation 4.65 is a "solid diffusion" equation, which does not account for the pore voids. The pore-void fraction is not negligible (e.g., 0.61 in activated carbon). The pore-diffusion models are based on a different equation, which involves the pore diffusivity and also accounts for the gases in the pore voids. A detailed discussion of the pore-diffusion model will be given in section 8.3 of Chapter 8.

Solid Diffusion versus Pore Diffusion

The complete pore-diffusion equation is:

$$D_e \left(\frac{\partial^2 C^P}{\partial r^2} + \frac{2}{r} \frac{\partial C^P}{\partial r} \right) = \frac{\partial q}{\partial t} + \alpha \frac{\partial C^P}{\partial t} \tag{4.71}$$

where q and C^P are related by the equilibrium isotherm since gas-solid equilibrium is assumed inside the pores. The foregoing equation is different from the solid diffusion equation (eq. 4.65). The term $\alpha \partial C^P / \partial t$ is the accumulation in the pore voids, which is absent from equation 4.65.

It is important to note that the diffusivity, D_e, is different in the two equations (eqs. 4.65 and 4.71). The D_e used in equation 4.71 is the effective pore diffusivity, which is based on the concentration gradient. This is the D_e that is measured experimentally — for example, by the Wicke-Kallenbach technique [8–13]. The D_e defined in equations 4.65 and 4.70 is based on the solid phase concentration gradient, which is not the experimental pore diffusivity reported in the literature, except for diffusion in zeolite crystals. In the measurement of diffusivities in zeolite crystals, equation 4.65 has been the starting equation on the basis of which the experimental data are treated [43]. In practical calculations, the choice of the diffusion equation should be consistent with that based on which D_e is determined.

NOTATION

a	outer surface area of pellets per unit bed volume; activity
B	Langmuir constant; mobility of atom
B_0	Darcy permeability
C	gas-phase concentration in bulk flow; interpellet concentration; concentration in zeolite crystal
C_0	concentration in the feed to adsorber
C^P	gas phase concentration inside pores, based on total volume of porous sorbent
C_P	heat capacity; subscripts a, b, and s denote, respectively, adsorbate, inert carrier gas, and solid phase
D_c	crystalline diffusivity in zeolites
D_e	effective diffusivity
D_k	Knudsen diffusivity
D_m	molecular diffusivity
D_P	diffusivity in pellet
D_s	surface diffusivity
D_z	axial dispersion coefficient
G	superficial mass or molar flux
h	heat transfer coefficient in the gas film
H	heat of adsorption (which is negative), or desorption (being positive); Heaviside function $= H(t)$
k	mass transfer coefficient through gas film
k_e	effective heat conductivity of pellet
k_g	thermal conductivity of gas
K	Henry's law constant
K_d	distribution factor, defined by equation 4.59
L	bed length
M	molecular weight

N	flux
N_t	total flux
P	total pressure
Pe	Peclet number $= 2R_p\mu/D_z\rho$
Pr	Prandtl number $= C_p\mu/k_g$
q	amount adsorbed (per unit volume of sorbent)
$\bar{q}$	average amount adsorbed in a pellet or particle
q^*	equilibrium amount adsorbed
q_0^*	q^* at C_0
q_s	saturated q
r	radial distance in pellet or particle
r_c	zeolite crystal radius
r_p	pore radius
R	gas constant; radical distance in pellet
Re	Reynolds number $= 2R_pG/\mu$
R_p	radius of pellet
Sc	Schmidt number $= \mu/\rho D_m$
Sh	Sherwood number $= 2kR_p/D_m$
t	time
t_B	breakthrough time
T	temperature
T_p	temperature within porous pellet
u	interstitial velocity
X	mole fraction in the adsorbed phase
Y	mole fraction in the gas phase
z	axial distance in bed from the inlet
Z	dimensionless distance in bed
α	void fraction within the pellet or intrapellet void fraction
β	equilibrium factor $= 1/K_d$
ε	interpellet void fraction (in fixed beds)
θ	fractional surface coverage
μ	chemical potential; viscosity of gas
v	vibrational frequency
ρ	gas density
ρ_b	density of inert carrier gas
τ	tortuosity factor

REFERENCES

1. J.E. Walter, *J. Chem. Phys.*, *13*, 229, 332 (1945).
2. H.C. Thomas, *Ann. N.Y. Acad. Sc.*, *49*, 161 (1948).
3. T. Vermeulen and N. Hiester, *Chem. Eng. Prog.*, *48*(10), 505 (1952).
4. E.E. Peterson, *Chemical Reaction Analysis* (Englewood Cliffs, N.J.: Prentice-Hall, 1965).
5. O. Levenspiel, *Chemical Reaction Engineering*, 2nd ed. (New York: Wiley, 1972).

6. H.S. Fogler, *The Elements of Chemical Kinetics and Reactor Calculations* (Englewood Cliffs, N.J.: Prentice-Hall, 1974).
7. R. Aris, *Mathematical Theory of Diffusion and Reaction in Permeable Catalysts*, Vol. 1. (London: Oxford University Press, 1975).
8. J.J. Carberry, *Chemical and Catalytic Reaction Engineering* (New York: McGraw-Hill, 1976).
9. J.B. Butt, *Reaction Kinetics and Reactor Design* (Englewood Cliffs, N.J.: Prentice-Hall, 1980).
10. J.M. Smith, *Chemical Engineering Kinetics*, 3rd ed. (New York: McGraw-Hill, 1981).
11. G.F. Froment and K.B. Bischoff, *Chemical Reactor Analysis and Design* (New York: Wiley, 1979).
12. H.H. Lee, *Heterogeneous Reactor Design* (Boston: Butterworth, 1985).
13. J.M. Thomas and W.J. Thomas, *Introduction to the Principles of Heterogeneous Catalysis* (New York: Academic Press, 1967).
14. K. Lee and H. Barrow, *Int. J. Heat Mass Transf.*, *11*, 1013 (1968).
15. P.N. Dwivedi and S.N. Upadhay, *Ind. Eng. Chem. Proc. Des. Dev.*, *16*, 157 (1977).
16. W.E. Ranz and W.R. Marshall, *Chem. Eng. Prog.*, *48*, 173 (1952).
17. N. Wakao and T. Funazkri, *Chem. Eng. Sci.*, *33*, 1375 (1978).
18. R.B. Bird, W.E. Stewart, and E.N. Lightfoot, *Transport Phenomena* (New York: Wiley, 1960).
19. W. Kauzmann, *Kinetic Theory of Gases* (New York: Benjamin, 1966).
20. R.B. Evans III, G.M. Watson, and E.A. Mason, *J. Chem. Phys.*, *35*, 2076 (1961).
21. D.S. Scott and F.A.L. Dullien, *AIChE J.*, *8*, 29 (1962).
22. W.G. Pollard and R.D. Present, *Phys. Rev.*, *73*, 762 (1948).
23. C.N. Satterfield, *Mass Transfer in Heterogeneous Catalysis* (Cambridge, Mass.: MIT Press, 1970).
24. R. Jackson, *Transport in Porous Catalysts* (New York: Elsevier, 1977).
25. E.A. Mason and A.P. Malinauskas, *Gas Transport in Porous Media: The Dusty-Gas Model* (New York: Elsevier, 1983).
26. J.A. Currie, *Brit. J. Appl. Phys.*, *11*, 318 (1960).
27. R.T. Yang and R.T. Liu, *Ind. Eng. Chem. Fundam.*, *21*, 262 (1982).
28. E. Costa, G. Calleja, and F. Domingo, *AIChE J.*, *31*, 982 (1985).
29. R.T. Liu, unpublished data, Calgon Corporation, Pittsburgh, Pa. (1984).
30. R.W.H. Sargent and C.J. Whitford, *Molecular Sieve Zeolites, Adv. in Chem. Ser.* (R.F. Gould, ed.), *102*, 247 (1971).
31. Y.H. Ma and S.Y. Ho, *AIChE J.*, *20*, 279 (1974).
32. J.H. Krasuk and J.M. Smith, *AIChE J.*, *18*, 506 (1972).
33. A. Wheeler, *Catalysis*, Vol. 2 (P.H. Emmett, ed.) (New York: Reinhold, 1955).
34. M.F.L. Johnson and W.E. Stewart, *J. Catalysis*, *4*, 248 (1965).
35. N. Wakao and J.M. Smith, *Chem. Eng. Sci.*, *17*, 825 (1962).
36. J.B. Rivarola and J.M. Smith, *Ind. Eng. Chem. Fundam.*, *3*, 308 (1964).
37. P.C. Carman, *Flow of Gases Through Porous Media* (New York: Academic Press, 1956).
38. R.T. Yang, J.B. Fenn, and G.L. Haller, *AIChE J.*, *19*, 1052 (1973).
39. K. Higashi, H. Ito, and J. Oishi, *J. Atomic Energy Soc. Japan*, *5*, 846 (1963).
40. K.J. Sladek, E.R. Gilliland, and R.F. Baddour, *Ind. Eng. Chem. Fundam.*, *13*, 100 (1974).
41. P.L. Walker, Jr., L.G. Austin, and S.P. Nandi, *Chemistry and Physics of Carbon*, Vol. 2 (P.L. Walker, Jr., ed.) (New York: Dekker, 1966).
42. D.W. Breck, *Zeolite Molecular Sieves*, Chap. 8 (New York: Wiley, 1973), reprinted by Krieger, Malabar, Fla. (1984).
43. R.M. Barrer, *Zeolites and Clay Minerals*, Chap. 6 (New York: Academic Press, 1978).

44. D.M. Ruthven, *Principles of Adsorption and Adsorption Processes*, Chap. 5 (New York: Wiley, 1984).
45. R.M. Barrer, *Molecular Sieve Zeolites*, *Adv. Chem. Ser.* (R.F. Gould, ed.), *102*, 1 (1971).
46. A. Tiselius, *Z. Phys. Chem.*, *169A*, 425 (1934).
47. D.M. Ruthven and K.F. Loughlin, *Chem. Eng. Sci.*, *26*, 1145 (1971).
48. J. Kärger, H. Pfeifer, M. Rauscher, and A. Walter, *J. Chem. Soc. Faraday Trans. I*, *76*, 717 (1980).
49. R. Ash and R.M. Barrer, *Surface Sci.*, *8*, 461 (1967).
50. J. Kärger, *Surf. Sci.*, *36*, 797 (1973).
51. J. Kärger and D.M. Ruthven, *J. Chem. Soc. Faraday Trans. I*, *77*, 1485 (1981).
52. L. Darken, *Trans. AIME*, *174*, 184 (1948).
53. P.G. Shewmon, *Diffusion in Solids*, Chap. 4 (New York: McGraw-Hill, 1963).
54. H. Yucel and D.M. Ruthven, *J. Chem. Soc. Faraday Trans. I*, *76*, 60 (1980).
55. H. Yucel and D.M. Ruthven, *J. Chem. Soc. Faraday Trans. I*, *76*, 71 (1980).
56. P.D. Wu and Y.H. Ma, *Proc. 6th Inter. Zeolite Conf.* (Guildford, Surrey, U.K.: Butterworths, 1984), p. 251.
57. J. Kärger, H. Pfeifer, and W. Heink, *Proc. 6th Intern. Zeolite Conf.* (Guildford, Surrey, U.K.: Butterworths, 1984), p. 184.
58. A. Paravar and D.T. Hayhurst, *Proc. 6th Intern. Zeolite Conf.* (Guildford, Surrey, U.K.: Butterworths, 1984), p. 217.
59. H.W. Habgood, *Canad. J. Chem.*, *36*, 1384 (1958).
60. Y.H. Ma and C. Mancel, *AIChE J.*, *18*, 1148 (1972).
61. L.P. Hsu and H.W. Haynes, Jr., *AIChE J.*, *27*, 81 (1981).
62. A.S. Chiang, A.G. Dixon, and Y.H. Ma, *Chem. Eng. Sci.*, *39*, 1451, 1461 (1984).
63. E. Ruckenstein, A.S. Vaidyanathan, and G.R. Youngquist, *Chem. Eng. Sci.*, *26*, 1306 (1971).
64. Y.H. Ma and T.Y. Lee, *AIChE J.*, *22*, 147 (1976).
65. K. Chihara, M. Suzuki, and K. Kawazoe, *AIChE J.*, *24*, 237 (1978).
66. K. Chihara, M. Suzuki, and K. Kawazoe, *J. Coll. Interf. Sci.*, *64*, 584 (1978).
67. P.L. Cen and R.T. Yang, unpublished results (1985).
68. J.C.M. Lee and D. Luss, *Ind. Eng. Chem. Fundam.*, *8*, 596 (1969).
69. J.J. Carberry, *Ind. Eng. Chem. Fundam.*, *14*, 129 (1975).
70. J.P.G. Kehoe and J.B. Butt, *AIChE J.*, *18*, 347 (1972).
71. A. Brunovska, V. Hlavacek, J. Ilavsky, and J. Valtyni, *Chem. Eng. Sci.*, *33*, 1385 (1978).
72. J. Ilavsky, A. Brunovska, and V. Hlavacek, *Chem. Eng. Sci.*, *35*, 2475 (1980).
73. C.Y. Wen and L.T. Fan, *Models for Flow Systems and Chemical Reactors* (New York: Dekker, 1975).
74. H.S. Carslaw and J.C. Jaeger, *Conduction of Heat in Solids*, 2nd ed. (Oxford: Oxford University Press, 1959).
75. E. Glueckauf and J.E. Coates, *J. Chem. Soc.*, 1315 (1947).
76. E. Glueckauf, *Trans. Faraday Soc.*, *51*, 1540 (1955).
77. T. Vermeulen, *Ind. Eng. Chem.*, *45*, 1664 (1953).
78. T. Vermeulen and R.E. Quilici, *Ind. Eng. Chem. Fundam.*, *9*, 179 (1970).
79. T. Vermeulen, G. Klein, and N.K. Hiester, *Chemical Engineers' Handbook* (R.H. Perry and C.H. Chilton, eds.) (New York: McGraw-Hill, 1973), Chap. 16.
80. T. Vermeulen, *Adv. in Chem. Eng.*, *2*, 147 (1958).
81. S. Nakao and M. Suzuki, *J. Chem. Eng. Japan*, *16*, 114 (1983).
82. R.L. Jones, G.E. Keller II, and R.C. Wells, U.S. Patent 4,194,892 (1980).
83. G.A. Sorial, W.H. Granville, and W.O. Daly, *Chem. Eng. Sci.*, *38*, 1517 (1983).

84. R.T. Yang and S.J. Doong, *AIChE J.*, *11*, 1829 (1985).
85. M.C. Tsai, S.S. Wang, and R.T. Yang, *Ind. Eng. Chem. Proc. Des. Dev.*, *24*, 57 (1985).
86. C.H. Liaw, J.S.P. Wang, R.A. Greenkorn, and K.C. Chao, *AIChE J.*, *25*, 376 (1979).
87. R.G. Rice, *Chem. Eng. Sci.*, *37*, 83 (1982).
88. B.F. Towler and R.G. Rice, *Chem. Eng. Sci.*, *29*, 1828 (1974).
89. N.S. Raghavan, M.M. Hassan, and D.M. Ruthven, *Chem. Eng. Sci.*, forthcoming.
90. K. Knoblauch, *Chem. Eng.*, *85*(25), 87 (1978).
91. R.V. Carrubba, J.E. Urbanic, N.J. Wagner, and R.H. Zanitsch, *AIChE Symp. Ser.*, *80*(No. 233), 76 (1984).
92. D.M. Ruthven, N.S. Raghavan, and M.M. Hassan, *Chem. Eng. Sci.*, forthcoming.
93. C.S. Lee and J.P. O'Connell, *AIChE J.*, *32*, 96 (1986).
94. C.S. Lee and J.P. O'Connell, *AIChE J.*, *32*, 107 (1986).

CHAPTER 5

Adsorber Dynamics: Bed Profiles and Breakthrough Curves

The term *breakthrough curves* refers to the response of an initially clean bed (i.e., free of adsorbate) to an influent of constant (i.e., time-independent) composition. A broader definition of the term includes a uniformly presaturated bed as well as an influent with changing concentration. A clear definition of these terms, with a particular emphasis on those used in chromatography, can be found in Chapter 2 of reference 1.

As discussed in the preceding chapter, the sorbate concentration in the flow at any given point in the bed is a function of time, resulting from the movement of the concentration front in the bed. The shape or the width of the breakthrough curve is crucially important in the design of adsorbers and cyclic separation processes. A sharp concentration front is desirable for efficient separation.

The breakthrough curve for a gas containing a single sorbate is obtained by the solution of the mass and heat balance equations for both the bed and sorbent particle, along with the equilibrium isotherm (eqs. 4.1 to 4.7). In principle, a concentration front and a temperature plateau are associated with each sorbate in the feed mixture. Analytic solutions, though desirable, are available for only a limited number of simple cases involving a single sorbate. The voluminous literature on breakthrough curves has been discussed comprehensively by Vermeulen et al. [3], Ruthven [4], Rodrigues [2]; and, with an emphasis on multicomponent mixtures, by Helfferich and Klein [1], Rhee [5], and Sweed [6]. In contrast to the extensive interest in the adsorption breakthrough curves, little attention has been paid to the desorption breakthrough curves despite its commercial importance. The important aspects of desorption breakthrough curves have been discussed for the single sorbate case by Basmadjian et al. [7, 108].

As will be shown shortly, the shape of the breakthrough curve is determined by the nature or type of the adsorption isotherm. In addition, it is influenced by the individual transport processes in the bed and in the particles: All factors tend to make the front more dispersive or less sharp. The front is dispersed by both mass and heat dispersions in the axial direction, and also by the mass and heat transfer resistances in the particle.

5.1   EQUILIBRIUM THEORY: ISOTHERMAL, SINGLE-SORBATE

5.1.1   Shapes of Isotherms

After the adsorber bed is regenerated, a feed mixture with a constant sorbate concentration is fed into the inlet. The feed is thus a step function, or a Heaviside function, with a square wavefront. As the front travels down the bed, the shape changes. This change is determined primarily by the shape of the equilibrium isotherm. The transport processes in the bed and within the particles have only a secondary effect on the wavefront.

According to the influence on the propagation of the concentration wavefront, the equilibrium isotherm

$$q^* = q^*(C) \tag{5.1}$$

may be classified into the following types, shown in Figure 5.1:

A (linear isotherm): $K_d = 1$ and $d^2q^*/dC^2 = 0$

B (favorable isotherm): $K_d > 1$ and $d^2q^*/dC^2 < 0$

C (unfavorable isotherm): $K_d < 1$ and $d^2q^*/dC^2 > 0$

D (irreversible isotherm): $K_d \to \infty$

where K_d is the distribution factor, defined by equation 4.63 in Chapter 4. Type B (favorable) isotherm is encountered in almost all commercially important gas separation processes except the system water vapor in activated carbon. Type A is a

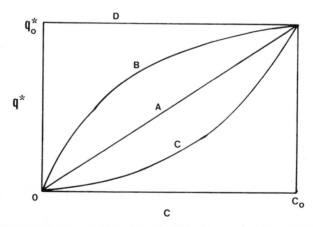

Figure 5.1   Shapes of isotherms in determining the sharpness of concentration wavefront: (*A*) linear; (*B*) favorable; (*C*) unfavorable; (*D*) irreversible.

special case of type B when the feed concentration, C_0, is small (i.e., dilute systems). The BET-type isotherm, which has an inflection point, is not included. However, the influence of this type of isotherm can be qualitatively understood from the other types.

5.1.2 Velocity of Concentration Front

The velocity of the concentration front was first derived by DeVault [8] for the case of constant fluid velocity in the bed, $u = \text{constant}$. The other assumptions in his derivation were: no dispersion (or plug flow), isothermal and equilibrium model. The term *equilibrium model* is used to refer to the case where instant equilibrium is reached in the bed between the bulk flow and the adsorbed phase. These assumptions provide a first approximation to the behavior of the adsorber.

Under these conditions, the mass balance equation is:

$$\frac{\partial C}{\partial t} + u\frac{\partial C}{\partial z} + \frac{1-\varepsilon}{\varepsilon}\frac{\partial q}{\partial t} = 0 \tag{5.2}$$

and q is given by the isotherm:

$$q = q^*(C) \tag{5.3}$$

Combining these two equations, and noting $\partial q^*/\partial t = (\partial q^*/\partial C)(\partial C/\partial t)$, we have:

$$\frac{\partial C}{\partial t} + \frac{u}{1 + \dfrac{1-\varepsilon}{\varepsilon}\left(\dfrac{dq^*}{dC}\right)}\frac{\partial C}{\partial z} = 0 \tag{5.4}$$

Substituting

$$-\left(\frac{\partial t}{\partial z}\right)_c \frac{\partial C}{\partial t} = \frac{\partial C}{\partial z}$$

the result is:

$$u_c = \left(\frac{\partial z}{\partial t}\right)_c = \frac{u}{1 + \dfrac{1-\varepsilon}{\varepsilon}\dfrac{dq^*}{dC}} \tag{5.5}$$

where dq^*/dC is the slope of the equilibrium isotherm, and u_c is the propagation velocity of the concentration front. (For a shock discontinuity, dq^*/dC is replaced by $\Delta q^*/\Delta C$, representing properties across the shock front.) The important relationship between the front velocity and the slope of the isotherm is given by equation 5.5.

For a favorable isotherm, high-concentration fronts travel faster than low-concentration fronts. The concentration front is thus of the self-sharpening type, referred to as a compressive wave (see Figure 5.2). Physically, the limit of the wave is a shock wave or discontinuity. For an unfavorable isotherm, also shown in Figure 5.2, the lower-concentration fronts travel faster and the wave becomes more dispersed. For a linear isotherm, since $dq*/dC$ is constant, no alteration of the wavefront is caused by the equilibrium relationship.

For a step-function feed — that is, a feed with constant concentration introduced at time zero into a clean bed — equation 5.5 indicates that the stepped front should propagate without change for all types of isotherms. The situations illustrated in Figure 5.2, however, always occur because of the dispersive actions by axial dispersions and resistances to transport processes.

Equation 5.5 is derived for constant flow velocity (u) in the column. For a nontrace mixture, u increases with distance because of depletion by adsorption. An expression for the propagation velocity of the concentration front can also be derived. The mass balance equation is written in terms of mole fraction, Y, assuming instant equilibrium:

$$\frac{\partial Y}{\partial t} + u\frac{\partial Y}{\partial z} + Y\frac{\partial u}{\partial z} + \frac{1}{C_t}\left(\frac{1-\varepsilon}{\varepsilon}\right)\frac{dq*}{dt} = 0 \qquad (5.6)$$

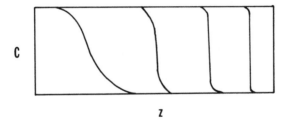

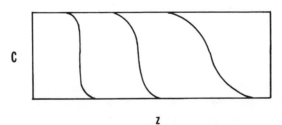

Figure 5.2 *Upper:* Compressive or self-sharpening wavefront caused by a favorable isotherm. *Lower:* Dispersive wavefront caused by an unfavorable isotherm.

where C_t is the total concentration, which is a constant for the gas mixture with negligible pressure drop in the bed.

The variation of velocity in the bed is given by the mass balance:

$$\varepsilon C_t \frac{\partial u}{\partial z} = -(1-\varepsilon)\frac{\partial q^*}{\partial t} \tag{5.7}$$

or

$$\frac{\partial u}{\partial z} = -\left(\frac{1-\varepsilon}{\varepsilon}\right)\frac{dq^*}{dC}\frac{\partial Y}{\partial t} \tag{5.8}$$

Combining equations 5.6 and 5.7 and using chain rule, an equation similar to equation 5.4 is obtained:

$$\frac{\partial C}{\partial t} + u_C \frac{\partial C}{\partial z} = 0 \tag{5.9}$$

where u_C is the wavefront propagation velocity:

$$u_C = \frac{u}{1 + \left(\dfrac{1-\varepsilon}{\varepsilon}\right)(1-Y)\dfrac{dq^*}{dC}} \tag{5.10}$$

For the simplest system of linear isotherm, $dq^*/dC = K$, the following is obtained by combining equations 5.8 and 5.9:

$$\frac{du}{dY} = \frac{K\left(\dfrac{1-\varepsilon}{\varepsilon}\right)u}{1 + K\left(\dfrac{1-\varepsilon}{\varepsilon}\right)(1-Y)} \tag{5.11}$$

Equation 5.11 may be integrated from the inlet condition, $u = u_0$ and $Y = Y_0$ (feed concentration) to u_C and Y, giving:

$$u_C = \frac{\left[1 + K\left(\dfrac{1-\varepsilon}{\varepsilon}\right)(1-Y_0)\right]u_0}{\left[1 + K\left(\dfrac{1-\varepsilon}{\varepsilon}\right)(1-Y)\right]^2} \tag{5.12}$$

The derivation of equation 5.12 has been given by Ruthven [4], except that the feed concentration (Y_0) was assumed to be zero, and a slightly different result was obtained. Equation 5.12 shows that u_C is an increasing function of Y, which indicates that the effect of varying flow velocity on the shape of the wavefront is a compressive one even for a linear adsorption isotherm. (For constant u in the bed, with a linear isotherm, the wavefront is neither compressive nor dispersive.) Thus the variation of flow velocity due to adsorption has a compressive effect on the concentration front similar to that of a favorable isotherm.

5.1.3   Breakthrough Curves

A breakthrough curve is the history of the effluent concentration from a bed subject to a stepped concentration input, $C_0 H(t)$, where $H(t) = 0$ at $t < 0$ and $H(t) = 1$ at $t \geqslant 0$.

For favorable and linear isotherms with no axial dispersion, the effluent concentration is also a step function:

$$C = C_0 H(t - t_{st}) \tag{5.13}$$

where t_{st} is the stoichiometric time given by:

$$t_{st} = \frac{L}{u_C} \tag{5.14}$$

where L is the length of the bed, and u_C is given by equation 5.5.

For unfavorable isotherms with an equilibrium factor:

$$\beta = \frac{1}{K_d} = \frac{Y(1-X)}{X(1-Y)} \tag{5.15}$$

where $X = q^*/q_0^*$, $Y = C/C_0$ and $\beta > 1$, the breakthrough curves can be derived from equation 5.5 [2, 9].

Equation 5.5 is written in dimensionless form, with $Z = z/L$ and $\theta = t/t_{st}$:

$$u_Y = \left(\frac{\partial Z}{\partial \theta}\right)_Y = \frac{1 + \dfrac{1-\varepsilon}{\varepsilon}\dfrac{q_0^*}{C_0}}{1 + \dfrac{1-\varepsilon}{\varepsilon}\dfrac{q_0^*}{C_0^*}\dfrac{dX}{dY}} = \frac{1+\xi}{1+\xi\dfrac{dX}{dY}} \tag{5.16}$$

with ξ defined in equation 5.16.

Equation 5.16 is integrated between $z = 0$ and 1 at $\theta = 0$ and θ, giving:

$$\theta = \frac{1 + \xi(dX/dY)}{1 + \xi} \tag{5.17}$$

With the isotherm equation 5.15, we have:

$$Y = \frac{\left[\dfrac{\beta}{(1+\xi)\beta - 1}\right]^{1/2} - \beta}{1 - \beta} \tag{5.18}$$

The throughput parameter, T, is defined as mass of product per unit mass of solid phase [2, 3, 9]:

$$T = \frac{C_0(V - \varepsilon v)}{q_0^*(1 - \varepsilon)v} \tag{5.19}$$

where V is the total volume of gas passing through the bed of volume v. The breakthrough curves are then expressed as [9]:

$$Y = \frac{\left(\dfrac{\beta}{T}\right)^{1/2} - \beta}{1 - \beta}, \qquad \frac{1}{\beta} \leqslant T \leqslant \beta \tag{5.20}$$

The breakthrough curves are plotted in Figure 5.3 [2], for various values of β.

For equilibrium models with unfavorable isotherms, the time required for breakthrough, t_B, can be calculated by substituting $V = ut_Bv/L$ into equation 5.20

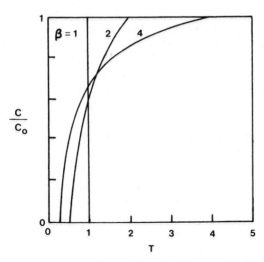

Figure 5.3 Breakthrough curves based on the equilibrium model with no axial dispersion for unfavorable isotherms. Source: Rodrigues [2]. Reprinted with permission.

and solving t_B for $Y = 0$. We then have:

$$t_B = \frac{L}{u}\left(\frac{1 + (\xi/\beta)}{1 + \xi}\right), \qquad \xi = \frac{1 - \varepsilon}{\varepsilon}\frac{q_0^*}{C_0} \tag{5.21}$$

which is smaller than the stoichiometric breakthrough time, L/u.

5.1.4   Effects of Axial Dispersion

The shape of the breakthrough curve, or the concentration front, is dispersed by both hydrodynamic (axial dispersion) and kinetic (finite transport rates) factors. The effect of axial dispersion on the breakthrough curves based on equilibrium theory and linear isotherm has been discussed by Lapidus and Amundson [10], van Deemter et al. [11], Levenspiel and Bischoff [12], and others. The solution of Levenspiel and Bischoff follows. The asymptotic solution for the mass balance equation (eq. 5.2) including a dispersion term, $-D_z \partial^2 C/\partial z^2$, for the effluent following a stepped change in the influent concentration from zero to C_0 in a long bed is:

$$\frac{C}{C_0} = \frac{1}{2}\left[1 - \text{erf}\,\frac{1 - (t/\bar{t})}{2(D_z t/uL\bar{t})^{1/2}}\right] \tag{5.22}$$

where

$$\bar{t} = \frac{L}{u}\left[1 + K\left(\frac{1 - \varepsilon}{\varepsilon}\right)\right]$$

The solution shows that the width expansion of the concentration front around the center at $\bar{t}$ is proportional to $t^{1/2}$. The expansion rate due to an unfavorable isotherm is proportional to simply t. Therefore, in the first approximation, the dispersive effect of the hydrodynamics is not as strong as that of the equilibrium isotherm.

5.2   NONEQUILIBRIUM THEORY: ISOTHERMAL, SINGLE-SORBATE

Sorbents of large pellet sizes are desirable to reduce the pressure drop across the bed and to minimize elutriation. For industrial applications the sorbent size is usually greater than 40–60 mesh, and the idealized equilibrium model is seldom accurate in predicting the breakthrough behavior. Thus mass transfer resistances are included in the nonequilibrium models.

If the adsorption isotherm is linear, analytic solutions for the concentration history/profile are possible by solving the mass balance equation and mass transfer rate equations, applying the Laplace transform method. (The difficulty lies in the inverse transform to obtain the time-domain solution [109].) For nonlinear isotherms, numerical solutions are necessary and are possible for systems involving almost any degree of complications. A good compilation of the numerical solutions is available [4].

Two different approaches have been taken in treating the mass transfer resistance within the pellet. In the diffusion models, the pellet is treated as a homogeneous phase in which diffusion takes place with a constant diffusivity. This is a good representation of the gas-porous solid system for which the effective diffusivity, D_e, may be used. The most important model of this type is that of Rosen [13, 14]. Solutions using the linear-driving-force approximation are based on the same approach. The other approach is known as the *chemical kinetic* model and was first developed by Thomas [15, 16]. This approach was developed for ion-exchange beds, assuming that the mass transfer rate is the difference between two opposing second-order reactions with different rate constants.

Results of the Rosen and Thomas model follow. In addition, an analytic solution for beds containing the increasingly important zeolite pellets will be given [17]. As discussed in Chapter 2, zeolite pellets are unique in structure and contain small (1–9 μm) crystals bound together in pellets by binders that have pores much larger than those in the crystals. Solutions for such a bidisperse sorbent are considerably more difficult.

5.2.1 The Rosen Model

The rate of transfer in adsorption by a spherical pellet is assumed to be the combined rate of external film diffusion and internal pore diffusion. Simplifying assumptions in the Rosen model are: plug flow (no axial dispersion), isothermal, linear isotherm, constant flow velocity, and constant effective diffusivity. The bed is initially clean. An exact solution was derived by Rosen [13; given in tabular form in 14] for the effluent concentration, with a stepped change in the influent concentration.

The mass balance equation in the bed is:

$$\frac{\partial C}{\partial t} + u\frac{\partial C}{\partial z} + \frac{1-\varepsilon}{\varepsilon}\frac{\partial \bar{q}}{\partial t} = 0 \qquad (5.23)$$

where $\bar{q}$ is the volume-average adsorbate concentration:

$$\bar{q} = \frac{3}{R_p^3}\int_0^{R_p} KC^p r^2 dr \qquad (5.24)$$

where C^p is the gas phase concentration inside the pores. Linear isotherm is assumed for q inside the pellet, $q = KC^p$. The concentration within the pellet is solved by the diffusion equation:

$$\frac{\partial C^p}{\partial t} = D_e \left(\frac{\partial^2 C^p}{\partial r^2} + \frac{2}{r} \frac{\partial C^p}{\partial r} \right) \tag{5.25}$$

Also, the coupling equation between equations 5.23 and 5.25 is the rate of mass transfer across the film:

$$\frac{\partial \bar{q}}{\partial t} = \frac{3k}{R_p} (C - C_{r=R_p}^p) \tag{5.26}$$

The initial and boundary conditions are:

$$C^p = 0 \quad \text{at} \quad t = 0, \qquad 0 \leqslant r \leqslant R_p, z > 0$$

$$C = C_0 H(t) \quad \text{at} \quad z = 0, t > 0 \tag{5.27}$$

The exact solution is:

$$\frac{C}{C_0} = \tfrac{1}{2} + \frac{2}{\pi} \int_0^\infty \exp[-\eta H_1^*(\lambda, v)] \sin[2\lambda^2 \tau/15 - \eta H_2^*(\lambda, v)] \frac{d\lambda}{\lambda} \tag{5.28}$$

$$\eta = \frac{15 D_e}{R_p^2} \left(\frac{KL}{u} \right) \left(\frac{1-\varepsilon}{\varepsilon} \right)$$

$$\tau = \frac{15 D_e}{R_p^2} \left(t - \frac{L}{u} \right)$$

$$H_1^*(\lambda, v) = \frac{H_1 + v(H_1^2 + H_2^2)}{(1 + vH_1)^2 + (vH_2)^2}$$

$$H_2^*(\lambda, v) = \frac{H_2}{(1 + vH_1)^2 + (vH_2)^2}$$

$$v = \frac{D_e K}{k R_p}$$

$$H_1 = \frac{\lambda[\sin h(2\lambda) + \sin(2\lambda)]}{[\cos h(2\lambda) - \cos(2\lambda)]} - 1$$

$$H_2 = \frac{\lambda[\sin h(2\lambda) - \sin(2\lambda)]}{[\cos h(2\lambda) - \cos(2\lambda)]}$$

A simpler solution is available for the case with no film diffusion resistance [13]. For a large value of L, or long beds, the asymptotic solution is [13, 14]:

$$\frac{C}{C_0} = \tfrac{1}{2} \left[1 + \text{erf} \frac{(3U/2V) - 1}{2 \left(\frac{1 + 5v}{5V} \right)^{1/2}} \right] \tag{5.29}$$

$$U = \frac{2D_e(t - L/u)}{R_p^2}$$

= dimensionless contact time parameter

$$V = \frac{3D_e K L}{u R_p^2}\left(\frac{\varepsilon}{1 - \varepsilon}\right)$$

= dimensionless bed length parameter

v = dimensionless film resistance parameter (see earlier)

The solution given by equation 5.29 is within 1% of the exact solution for large V, $V > 50$.

The infinite integral in the exact solution converges slowly, and must be solved numerically. It should be noted that a solution for the same problem, with the same assumptions except that no film diffusion resistance was considered, was given independently by Thomas [18]. The solution given by Thomas is easier to use because the integral was solved and the solution was presented in the form of an infinite series. In the solutions of both Thomas and Rosen, C/C_0 is expressed as a function of the dimensionless groups U and V, which contain R_p^2 and L. Thus, if the breakthrough curves are known for one adsorber column with spheres of radius R_p and length L, the breakthrough curves for another column with a different pellet size and column length can be deduced.

Explicit solutions for C/C_0 are not possible for cases of the Langmuir isotherm (with spherical particle) and cylindrical particle (with linear isotherm). However, expressions for $\partial(C/C_0)/\partial V$ (here V is slightly different from that defined earlier to include the Langmuir constant and particle shape) are available and may be solved by finite difference techniques [19]. The effect of nonlinearity of the isotherm can be significant. If the cylindrical pellet is treated as a sphere with a radius equal to the hydraulic radius of the cylinder, the shape has no effect on the breakthrough curves for a wide range of height-to-diameter ratios [19].

The Rosen model has been extended to include axial dispersion, given solutions that are also in the integral forms, by Rasmuson [20], and by Rasmuson and Neretnieks [21].

5.2.2   The Thomas Model

The model by Thomas was originally derived for ion exchange in aqueous systems [15]. Therefore, the diffusion steps (in both film and pores) are assumed to be instantaneous, and the surface step is rate-controlling. It is of interest for adsorption of gases because the Langmuir isotherm is assumed. The surface rate is:

$$\frac{\partial \bar{q}}{\partial t} = k_s\left\{C(q_\infty^* - \bar{q}) - \frac{1}{B}\bar{q}\right\} \tag{5.30}$$

which, at equilibrium, takes the form of the Langmuir isotherm:

$$\bar{q} = \frac{q_\infty^* BC}{1 + BC} \tag{5.31}$$

where q_∞^* is the monolayer coverage. Equation 5.30 is the form used by Hiester and Vermeulen [22], which differs slightly from that by Thomas [15]. The asymptotic solution for the breakthrough curves for equations 5.23 (mass balance in bed), 5.27 (boundary conditions), and 5.30 is [22]:

$$\begin{aligned}
\frac{C}{C_0} = 1 + &\frac{\pi^{1/2}[1 - \mathrm{erf}(\beta\tau')^{1/2} - (\eta')^{1/2}] \exp[(\beta\tau')^{1/2} - (\eta')^{1/2}]^2}{\pi^{1/2}[1 - \mathrm{erf}(\beta\eta')^{1/2} - (\tau')^{1/2}] \exp[(\beta\tau')^{1/2} - (\tau')^{1/2}]^2} \\
&\frac{- [(\beta\tau')^{1/2} + (\beta\tau'\eta')^{1/4}]^{-1}}{+ [(\tau')^{1/2} + (\beta\tau'\eta')^{1/4}]^{-1}}
\end{aligned} \tag{5.32}$$

where $\beta = $ equilibrium factor $= (1 + BC_0)^{-1}$

$$\tau' = k_s C_0 \frac{q_\infty^*}{q_0^*}\left(t - \frac{L}{u}\right)$$

$$\eta' = k_s q_\infty^* \left(\frac{L}{u}\right)\left(\frac{1-\varepsilon}{\varepsilon}\right)$$

The solution is accurate within 1% for $(\beta\tau'\eta')^{1/2} \geqslant 6$. The Hiester-Vermeulen treatment is based on the Thomas model and works fairly well for gas adsorbers. Masamune and Smith [23] showed that pore diffusion is much slower than the surface rate for the adsorption of nitrogen in Vycor glass at 77K. The model is important for liquid systems, and it clearly shows the influence of the equilibrium factor on the breakthrough behavior. Solutions for special cases of the Thomas model were obtained independently for irreversible isotherm ($\beta = 0$) [24], linear isotherm, $\beta = 1$ [25, 26] and for unfavorable isotherm, $\beta > 1$ [9].

5.2.3   Model for Zeolites

Zeolite sorbents have the unique structure of small crystals pelleted with a clay binder. Thus a pellet contains isolated crystals with a microporous or crystalline structure bound by a continuous macroporous medium. Although the diffusivity in the crystal (typically less than 10^{-8} cm²/s) is much lower than that in the binder (nearly Knudsen, or 10^{-4} cm²/s), the resistances in both phases can be important because the respective time constants (D/R^2) are comparably small. Based on the analysis of Ruckenstein et al. [27], a semiempirical criterion was suggested by Ruthven and Loughlin [28] for the relative importance of the micropore (crystalline) and macropore (binder-phase) resistances, from the magnitude of the parameter:

$$\Omega = \frac{w(1-\alpha)(D_c/R_c^2)}{\alpha(D_p/R_p^2)}\left(\frac{dq^*}{dC_c}\right)$$ (5.33)

where w is the weight fraction of crystals in pellet; α is the void fraction in the binder phase; subscripts c and p denote crystal and binder or pellet, respectively; and dq^*/dC_c is the slope of the isotherm. It was suggested that if the value of Ω is significantly less than 1, micropore resistance dominates; macropore resistance controls if $\Omega > 100$.

The solution for the breakthrough behavior in beds with zeolite pellets is considerably more difficult than that with other sorbents. It is desirable, however, because of the increasing commercial interests in zeolites for gas separation. For the case of isothermal, single, and dilute sorbate, Kawazoe and Takeuchi [29] derived a solution similar to that of Rosen (eq. 5.28). Rasmuson [30] obtained a solution, also similar to Rosen's, for the case of axial dispersion. Like Rosen's solution, both involve an integral and require a considerable amount of numerical computation in calculating the breakthrough curves. By assuming a parabolic concentration profile in both crystal and pellet, a simple approximate solution can be derived [17], the result of which follows.

The simplified model is based on the assumptions of plug flow, isothermality, constant flow velocity, and linear isotherm. The mass balance equation for the crystals, assumed spherical with radius R_c, is (the solid diffusion equation):

$$\frac{\partial q}{\partial t} = D_c\left(\frac{\partial^2 q}{\partial r^2} + \frac{2}{r}\frac{\partial q}{\partial r}\right)$$ (5.34)

$$q = KC_c$$

where K is dimensionless, with I.C. and B.C.:

$$q = 0 \quad \text{at} \quad t = 0, \quad 0 \leqslant r \leqslant R_c, 0 \leqslant z \leqslant L$$ (5.35)

$$\frac{\partial q}{\partial r} = 0 \quad \text{at} \quad r = 0, \quad t \geqslant 0$$

$$q = KC^p \quad \text{at} \quad r = R_c, \quad t \geqslant 0$$

For the pellet, we have:

$$\frac{\partial C^p}{\partial t} + \left(\frac{1-\alpha}{\alpha}\right)\frac{\partial \bar{q}}{\partial t} = D_p\left(\frac{\partial^2 C^p}{\partial R^2} + \frac{2}{R}\frac{\partial C^p}{\partial R}\right)$$ (5.36)

$$\bar{q} = \frac{3}{R_c^3}\int_0^{R_c} qr^2\,dr = K\bar{C}_c$$

where the overhead bar indicates volume-average quantities. The I.C. and B.C. are:

$$C^p = 0 \quad \text{at} \quad t = 0, \qquad 0 \leqslant R \leqslant R_p, 0 \leqslant z \leqslant L \tag{5.37}$$

$$\frac{\partial C^p}{\partial R} = 0 \quad \text{at} \quad R = 0, \qquad t > 0$$

$$D_p \left(\frac{\partial C^p}{\partial R} \right) = k(C - C^p_{R=R_p}) \quad \text{at} \quad R = R_p, \qquad t > 0$$

The mass balance equation for the bed is:

$$\frac{\partial C}{\partial t} + u \frac{\partial C}{\partial z} + \frac{1-\varepsilon}{\varepsilon} \frac{\partial \bar{q}}{\partial t} = 0 \tag{5.38}$$

$$\bar{q} = \frac{3}{R_p^3} \int_0^{R_p} \bar{q} R^2 \, dR = K \bar{C}_c$$

with I.C. and B.C.:

$$C = 0 \quad \text{at} \quad t = 0, \qquad 0 \leqslant z \leqslant L \tag{5.39}$$

$$C = C_0 \quad \text{at} \quad z = 0, \qquad t > 0$$

By assuming parabolic concentration profiles:

$$C_c = a_0 + a_2 r^2, \qquad C^p = a_1 + a_3 R^2 \tag{5.40}$$

which lead directly to Glueckauf's linear-driving-force rates for the solid diffusion equation [31], the following is derived [17]:

$$\frac{\partial^2 \bar{C}_c}{\partial t^2} + \left[1 + \frac{1-\alpha}{\alpha} K + \frac{(D_p/R_p^2)/(D_c/R_c^2)}{1 + 5D_p/(kR_p)} \right] \frac{15 D_c}{R_c^2} \frac{\partial \bar{C}_c}{\partial t}$$

$$= \frac{(15D_c/R_c^2)/(15D_p/R_p^2)}{1 + 5D_p/(kR_p)} (C - \bar{C}_c) \tag{5.41}$$

For large values of 2σ (definition follows) (i.e., $2\sigma > 1$, which is the case under practical conditions), the second derivative term in the equation is negligible, and the solution for $\tau > x$ is [17]:

$$\frac{C}{C_0} = \exp\{-\psi[\tau - x(1-\sigma)]\} \sum_{j=0}^{\infty} \frac{[\psi(\tau - x)]^j}{(j+1)!} \sum_{i=0}^{j} \frac{(\sigma\psi x)^i}{i!} \tag{5.42}$$

and for $\tau < x$, $C/C_0 = 0$, where:

$$2\sigma = \frac{15D_c}{R_c^2}\left[1 + \frac{1-\alpha}{\alpha}K + \frac{(D_p/R_p^2)/(D_c/R_c^2)}{1 + \frac{5D_p}{kR_p}}\right]\frac{L}{u}$$

$$\psi = \frac{15D_p/R_p^2}{1 + \frac{5D_p}{kR_p}}\left(\frac{L}{u}\right) \Bigg/ \left[\frac{2\sigma}{(15D_c/R_c^2)(L/u)}\right]$$

$$\tau = ut/L, \qquad x = z/L$$

The infinite series in equation 5.42 converges slowly, which may be calculated with a programmable calculator or microcomputer. Sixty to eighty terms proved adequate under a wide range of conditions [17].

A simple criterion for the relative importance of film, macropore, and micropore diffusion can be obtained from the foregoing solution. Film diffusion is not important if:

$$\frac{5D_p}{kR_p} \ll 1 \tag{5.43}$$

which is valid under usual conditions in gas separations. In addition to the condition in equation 5.43, if

$$\frac{D_p/R_p^2}{D_c/R_c^2} \ll 1 + \left(\frac{1-\alpha}{\alpha}\right)K \tag{5.44}$$

the breakthrough curves revert to those that only consider macropore diffusion. Thus conditions 5.43 and 5.44 are sufficient for macropore diffusion control. If

$$\frac{D_p/R_p^2}{D_c/R_c^2} \gg 1 + \left(\frac{1-\alpha}{\alpha}\right)K \tag{5.45}$$

and condition 5.43 holds, micropore diffusion dominates.

For the case of macropore diffusion control, excellent agreement has been shown between Rosen's solution (eq. 5.28) and the approximate solution given by equation 5.42 under a wide range of practical conditions [17]. The solution (eq. 5.42) is dependent on the following dimensionless parameters: K, M_1, M_2, and M_3, defined by:

$$M_1 = \frac{D_p/R_p^2}{D_c/R_c^2}$$

$$M_2 = \frac{15D_p}{R_p^2}\left(\frac{L}{u}\right)$$

$$M_3 = \frac{5D_p}{kR_p}$$

The effect of M_3 is negligible under practical conditions. The effects of K, M_1, and M_2, under practical conditions, are shown in Figures 5.4, 5.5a, and 5.5b. These figures again illustrate the relatively dominant importance of the equilibrium isotherm over kinetic and hydrodynamic factors in determining the breakthrough behavior.

The simplified model solution (eq. 5.42), has been tested with success by experimental data for adsorption of N_2 and CH_4, carried in helium, in 5A zeolite beds [17], as shown in Figure 5.6.

5.2.4   Other Models

The Thomas model has been extended to other "kinetic" forms. Analytic solutions for C/C_0 have been derived for "linear kinetic" rates — that is, both forward and backward rates in equation 5.30, with constant and variable feed concentrations [32, 33], as well as the case involving intraparticle diffusion resistance [33]. A solution for the case including the surface "kinetic" rate, as well as film and intraparticle diffusion steps, has also been given [34].

Besides the linear adsorption isotherm, analytic solutions for the irreversible isotherm, $q^* = $ constant at $C > 0$, are also possible. A general solution for this type of isotherm, including both film and intraparticle diffusion resistances, has been obtained [35]. Earlier solutions for simpler cases [36, 37, 38] have been summarized by Ruthven [4]. All solutions are for plug flow, constant velocity, and isothermal conditions.

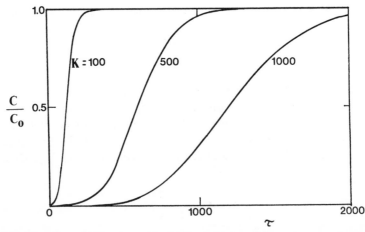

Figure 5.4   The effect of Henry's constant (K) on the breakthrough curves in zeolite beds, with $M_1 = 10$, $M_2 = 3.0$, and $M_3 = 0.1$.

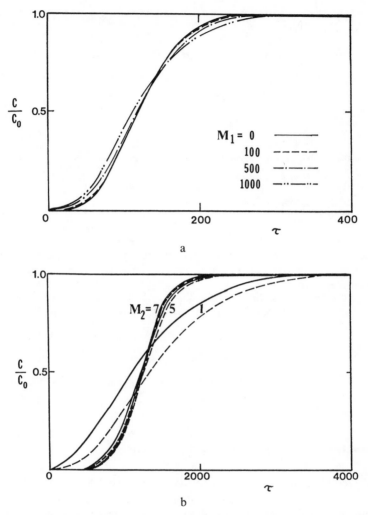

Figure 5.5 (a) The effect of $M_1[M_1 = (D_p/R_p^2)/(D_c/R_c^2)]$ on the breakthrough curves in beds of zeolites, $M_2 = 2$, $M_3 = 0$, and $K = 100$; (b) the effect of $M_2[M_2 = (15D_p/R_p^2)(L/u)]$ on the breakthrough curves in zeolite beds, $K = 1,000$, $M_1 = 10$, $M_3 = 0$. Solid curves are for the gas phase, dashed curves are for the adsorbed phase.

An alternative model, called *stage model*, treats the adsorber as a series of well-mixed tanks or stages. Within each stage, the concentration and temperature are uniform, and the effluent from the stage also has the same properties. The number of stages used in the model reflects the axial dispersion and mass transfer resistances. Analytical solutions are possible for certain special cases [2]. This approach, however, is identical to solving the governing equations numerically by using backward finite difference, where the effluent temperature and concentration are the same as those in the preceding space step [39].

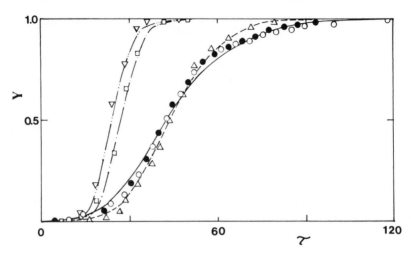

Figure 5.6 Comparison of experimental data (symbols) and predictions by equation 5.42 (curves) for breakthrough curves ($Y = C/C_0$) in 5A zeolite beds ($R_c = 1.75$ μm), at 20°C and 1 atm, in helium carrier.

Run 1 (○): N_2, $C_0 = 0.93\%$, $u = 5.55$ cm/s, $R_p = 0.794$ mm

Run 2 (●): N_2, $C_0 = 1.22\%$, $u = 5.55$ cm/s, $R_p = 0.794$ mm

Run 3 (△): N_2, $C_0 = 1.05\%$, $u = 3.23$ cm/s, $R_p = 0.794$ mm

Run 4 (□): CH_4, $C_0 = 1.30\%$, $u = 5.55$ cm/s, $R_p = 0.794$ mm

Run 5 (▽): CH_4, $C_0 = 1.30\%$, $u = 5.55$ cm/s, $R_p = 0.235$ mm

5.3   ASYMPTOTIC (CONSTANT-PATTERN) SOLUTIONS

As discussed in section 4.1, for adsorption in relatively "deep" beds of a gas with a favorable isotherm, the concentration front first expands as a result of axial dispersion and mass transfer resistances. It later ceases to expand because of the opposite influence on the front velocity by the equilibrium isotherm. Thus, a constant-pattern front, or mass transfer zone (MTZ), is developed. Conversely, for desorption or elution of a saturated bed by a relatively inert gas, a constant pattern develops for unfavorable isotherms. A mathematical proof for the existence of a constant pattern is given for both of the aforementioned cases, with and without finite axial dispersion [40].

With the constant-pattern behavior, one is interested in the concentration profile, at a given time, within the mass transfer zone. The mass balance equation in the bed for constant fluid velocity, u, as will be shown shortly, is reduced to the simple statement:

$$\frac{C}{C_0} = \frac{\bar{q}}{q_0^*} \tag{5.46}$$

Equation 5.46 may be solved in combination with the equilibrium isotherm (relating q and C) and a proper mass transfer rate equation, which is the only differential equation to be solved. The mathematics is thus considerably simplified, and more complex conditions can be handled, such as the most important Langmuir isotherm as well as nonisothermal and multicomponent situations.

The bed mass balance equation for the adsorbate is:

$$\frac{\partial C}{\partial t} + \frac{\partial (uC)}{\partial z} + \frac{1-\varepsilon}{\varepsilon}\frac{\partial q}{\partial t} = 0 \tag{5.47}$$

For constant-pattern behavior, the front velocity (u_f) is a constant:

$$u_f = -(\partial M/\partial t)_z/(\partial M/\partial z)_t = -[\partial(uC)/\partial t]/[\partial(uC)/\partial z] \tag{5.48}$$

where M can be any bed or fluid property.

The bed mass balance equation becomes:

$$\frac{\partial}{\partial t}\left(C - \frac{uC}{u_f} + \frac{1-\varepsilon}{\varepsilon}q\right) = 0$$

or

$$C - \frac{uC}{u_f} + \frac{1-\varepsilon}{\varepsilon}q = \text{constant} \tag{5.49}$$

The constant-pattern profiles are illustrated in Figure 5.7. The concentration of the inert carrier is $C_t - C$, where C_t is the total concentration. The continuity equations for the sorbate and carrier, respectively, in zones I (saturated), II (MTZ),

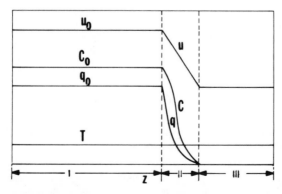

Figure 5.7   Constant-pattern behavior for isothermal, single-adsorbate adsorption. Zone I: saturated; zone II: MTZ; zone III: clean.

and III (clean), are given by [41]:

$$C_0 - \frac{u_0 C_0}{u_f} + \frac{1-\varepsilon}{\varepsilon} q_0 = C - \frac{uC}{u_f} + \frac{1-\varepsilon}{\varepsilon} q = 0 \qquad (5.50)$$

$$C_t - C_0 - \frac{u_0 C_t}{u_f} + \frac{u_0 C_0}{u_f} = C_t - C - \frac{uC_t}{u_f} + \frac{uC}{u_f} = C_t - \frac{u_3 C_t}{u_f} \qquad (5.51)$$

Equations 5.50 and 5.51 can be combined to get [41]:

$$\frac{q}{q_0} = \frac{C}{C_0} \left(\frac{C_t - C_0}{C_t - C} \right) \qquad (5.52)$$

Equation 5.52 reduces to equation 5.46 for dilute sorbate mixtures, where u is approximately constant. Equation 5.52 is the mass balance equation in the bed for concentrated mixtures with varying fluid velocity.

For the important Langmuir isotherm, analytic solutions are available for, under isothermal conditions, mass transfer rates that are controlled by gas-film and solid phase and approximated by the linear-driving-force equation. The Langmuir isotherm is:

$$q^* = \frac{q_s BC}{1 + BC} \qquad (5.53)$$

With the LDF approximation:

$$\frac{dq}{dt} = k(q^* - q) \qquad (5.54)$$

Equations 5.46, 5.53, and 5.54 can be combined and integrated to give the concentration in the MTZ [41]:

$$k(t_2 - t_1)\left(\frac{1+B}{B}\right) = \frac{1}{1 - (q_0/q_s)} \ln \frac{\phi_2(1 - \phi_1)}{\phi_1(1 - \phi_2)} + \ln \frac{\phi_1}{\phi_2} \qquad (5.55)$$

where

$$\phi_1 = C_1/C_0, \qquad \phi_2 = C_2/C_0$$

An error was pointed out by Sircar and Kumar [41] in the earlier solution by Hall et al. [42] where factor $(1 + B)/B$ was left out. (The same error exists in the solutions given in references 43 and 44.) A similar solution is given by Michaels [43] for the case of film diffusion control. For concentrated mixtures (with a varying u), solutions similar to that of Michaels and equation 5.55 have been obtained by using equation 5.52 [41]. No analytic solution is available for the case of pore-diffusion control, where q in equation 5.46 is written as $\bar{q}$, which was obtained from the solution of the diffusion equations as the volume-averaged q in the particle. However, solutions in tabulated and graphical forms are available [43, 44]. Constant-pattern solutions for the linear isotherm of the form $q^* = k_1 + k_2 C$ have been derived [45, 46]. A summary of the solutions for more complex cases are given in reference 41.

5.4 NONISOTHERMAL OR ADIABATIC ADSORPTION

Because of the exothermic heat of adsorption, true isothermality never exists in fixed-bed adsorbers. The situation worsens for bulk separation — that is, for high-concentration feeds. The heat of adsorption combined with the gas flow forms a temperature wave that propagates along with the concentration wave. The relative velocities of the two waves are determined by the thermal, adsorptive, and transport properties as well as the carrier gas flow rate. Depending on the relative magnitude of these properties, different shapes and combinations of concentration and temperature waves as well as their transfer zones (both front and back) are possible.

For a single adsorbate, detailed solutions of the coupled nonlinear heat and mass balance equations plus the equilibrium isotherm equation can readily be obtained by standard numerical methods [e.g., 106, 107]. Without recourse to numerical solutions, however, important features of the nonisothermal adsorber behavior have been obtained by both the constant-pattern and equilibrium approaches (i.e., negligible heat and mass transfer resistance), using the method of characteristics and wave theory. The constant-pattern approach has been adopted by a number of authors for solving adiabatic or nearly adiabatic adsorption [47–50]. The adiabatic equilibrium theory was analyzed by Amundson et al. [51], Rhee et al. [83, 84], and by Pan and Basmadjian [52]. With simplifying assumptions, analytic solutions are possible for the special case of irreversible isotherm [53, 54]. Leavitt proposed and experimentally observed the "middle zone," as shown in Figure 5.8 [47]. Among the results given by Amundson et al., it was shown that it is possible to have a "pure temperature wave." This is a temperature wave that completely precedes and leads the concentration wave [51], with the thermal wave being propelled by the gas flow rate. Some important features for adiabatic, single-component adsorption have been given by Pan and Basmadjian [49], using constant-pattern analysis and will be summarized. These features were also realized by Rhee et al. [83, 84].

The constant-pattern, combined temperature and concentration profiles, are illustrated in Figure 5.8 along with the notations of the three distinct zones in the bed. By combining the mass and heat balances between the middle zone and the exit and inlet zones, the following equations are obtained [48]:

$$\frac{G_b}{\rho_b u_C} = \frac{q_2 - q_3}{Y_2 - Y_3} = \left(\frac{\bar{C}_{ps}}{\bar{C}_{pb}}\right)_3 + \frac{(qH)_2 - (qH)_3}{\bar{C}_{pb3}(T_2 - T_3)} \tag{5.56}$$

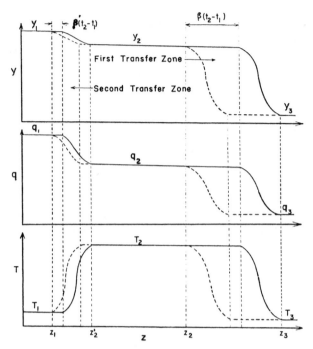

Figure 5.8   Adiabatic adsorption with a nondilute feed: constant-pattern concentration and temperature profiles. - - - - - - profiles at time t_1. ———— profiles at $t_2 > t_1$. Two transfer zones separate the three constant zones: (1) feed conditions, (2) equilibrium middle zone, and (3) initial bed conditions. Source: Pan and Basmadjian [48]. Reprinted with permission.

$$\frac{G_b}{\rho_b u_C'} = \frac{q_1 - q_2}{Y_1 - Y_2} = \left(\frac{\bar{C}_{ps}}{\bar{C}_{pb}}\right)_1 + \frac{(qH)_1 - (qH)_2}{\bar{C}_{pb1}(T_1 - T_2)} \tag{5.57}$$

where G_b is the molar flux of the carrier gas; ρ_b is adsorbent density; u_C and u_C', respectively, are the velocities of the first and second concentration fronts; C_p is the heat capacity with a second subscript a, b, and s, respectively, denoting adsorbate, carrier gas, and solid sorbent. The overhead bar indicates summed values: $\bar{C}_{ps} = C_{ps} + qC_{pa}$, $\bar{C}_{pb} = C_{pb} + YC_{pa}$. Equations 5.56 and 5.57 can be solved along with the equilibrium isotherm, $q_2 = q^*(Y_2, T_2)$, for the values of u_C, u_C' and the plateau (zone 2) parameters $(q, Y, T)_2$.

Before pursuing this analysis, it may be noted that a differential form of equations 5.56 and 5.57 may be readily derived using the coherence condition for concentration and temperature [1]; that is, the concentration velocity (u_C) and temperature velocity (u_T) are equal. The temperature velocity may be derived from the heat balance:

$$u\frac{\partial T}{\partial z} + \frac{\partial T}{\partial t} + \left(\frac{1-\varepsilon}{\varepsilon}\right)\frac{C_{ps}}{C_{pb}}\frac{\partial T}{\partial t} = \left(\frac{1-\varepsilon}{\varepsilon}\right)\left(\frac{-H}{C_{pb}}\right)\frac{\partial q}{\partial t} \tag{5.57a}$$

where thermal and concentration equilibrium is assumed. Upon rearranging:

$$\frac{\partial T}{\partial z} + \frac{1}{u}\left[1 + \left(\frac{1-\varepsilon}{\varepsilon}\right)\frac{C_{ps}}{C_{pb}} - \left(\frac{1-\varepsilon}{\varepsilon}\right)\left(\frac{-H}{C_{pb}}\right)\frac{dq}{dT}\right]\frac{\partial T}{\partial t} = 0 \qquad (5.57b)$$

This is an analog of equation 5.4 for concentration, which is a wave equation with the wave propagation velocity given by:

$$u_T \equiv \left(\frac{\partial z}{\partial t}\right)_T = \frac{u}{1 + \left(\frac{1-\varepsilon}{\varepsilon}\right)\frac{C_{ps}}{C_{pb}} - \left(\frac{1-\varepsilon}{\varepsilon}\right)\left(\frac{-H}{C_{pb}}\right)\frac{dq}{dT}} \qquad (5.57c)$$

If $u_C = u_T$, we have:

$$\frac{dq}{dC} = \frac{C_{ps}}{C_{pb}} + \left(\frac{H}{C_{pb}}\right)\frac{dq}{dT} \qquad (5.57d)$$

Equation 5.57d is the differential form of equations 5.56 and 5.57.

The approximate energy balance for a pure thermal wave, assuming $T_s = T_{\text{gas}}$, is:

$$G_b C_{pb}\frac{\partial T}{\partial z} + \rho_b C_{ps}\frac{\partial T}{\partial t} = 0 \qquad (5.58)$$

The velocity of the pure thermal wave is:

$$u_T \equiv \left(\frac{\partial z}{\partial t}\right)_T = \frac{G_b C_{pb}}{\rho_b C_{ps}} \qquad (5.59)$$

For isothermal adsorption, the velocity of the concentration wave is given by equation 5.56, letting $q_3 = Y_3 = 0$ and replacing subscript 2 by 1:

$$(u_C)_{\text{iso}} = \frac{G_b Y_1}{\rho_b q_1} \qquad (5.60)$$

Since any temperature rise will enhance u_C, $u_C > (u_C)_{\text{iso}}$. Comparing equations 5.59 and 5.60, whenever

$$\frac{C_{ps}}{C_{pb}} > \left(\frac{q}{Y}\right)_1 \qquad (5.61)$$

we have

$$u_C > (u_C)_{\text{iso}} > u_T \qquad (5.62)$$

This condition states that the thermal wave cannot pull ahead of the mass transfer zone whenever the solid/gas heat capacity ratio exceeds the inlet equilibrium ratio of $(q/Y)_1$.

The maximum temperature for the plateau zone is:

$$T_{2\,max} = T_1 + \frac{-(qH)_1}{C_{pb}(q/Y)_1 - C_{ps}} \tag{5.63}$$

Thus, the condition for the existence of combined T and C wave fronts is:

$$\frac{C_{ps}}{C_{pb}} > \frac{q^*(T_{2\,max}, Y_1)}{Y_1} \tag{5.64}$$

The condition for a pure thermal wave (preceding the concentration front) is:

$$\frac{C_{ps}}{C_{pb}} < \frac{q^*(T_{2\,max}, Y_1)}{Y_1} \tag{5.65}$$

In deriving condition 5.65, the slower movement of the rear front of the T plateau (which is less sharp than the leading front) has not been considered. Based on the result of Furnas [55], which showed the velocity of the trailing temperature edge to be about two-thirds the mean value of the temperature front, Pan and Basmadjian gave a "conservative" condition for the existence of a pure temperature wave:

$$\frac{3C_{ps}}{2C_{pb}} < \frac{q^*(T_{2\,max}, Y_1)}{Y_1} \tag{5.66}$$

The foregoing condition is easily satisfied by a number of adsorption systems of industrial importance, such as water vapor on zeolites, silica gel, and alumina, where a separate pure thermal wave was indeed observed in these systems [49]. Equation 5.66 further indicates that the formation of pure thermal waves is favored by either increasing the pressure or decreasing the feed concentration. Equation 5.63 also provides an important implication for practical application. Since the plateau temperature of the pure thermal wave is independent of the initial bed temperature, but only dependent on feed conditions (in zone 1), the breakthrough time of the adsorbate is consequently independent of the initial bed temperature. This suggests that if condition 5.66 is satisfied, it is not necessary to cool the bed after regeneration, which is usually done in thermal swing cycles in industry [49].

The distinct zones and sharp transition fronts shown in Figure 5.8 are obscured or smoothed out by the dispersive factors: axial mass and thermal dispersions, resistances to mass and thermal transfer, and the diffuse trailing edges of the waves. The temperature and concentration profiles in a nearly adiabatic bed of activated carbon for the adsorption of a 50/50 H_2/CH_4 mixture are shown in Figure 5.9.

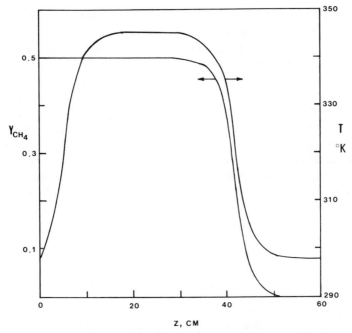

Figure 5.9 Nearly asymptotic concentration and temperature profiles in an activated carbon bed with a feed of a 50/50 H_2/CH_4 into a bed initially filled with H_2.

The aforementioned adiabatic equilibrium theory is based on the method of characteristics, which also requires numerical calculation or integration along the characteristic lines. Complete profiles and breakthrough curves can be constructed on the basis of the theory. Interesting and important features can be discerned from the characteristic curves for adsorption of multicomponent mixtures [1, 51, 56, 57]; single adsorbate systems [52, 58–60]; and desorption by a purge gas [39, 52, 58, 60, 61]. For adiabatic adsorption, an interesting temperature, referred to as reversal temperature, exists when the two sides in 5.64 or 5.65 are equal as Y_1 approaches zero. At this temperature a small concentration perturbation in the feed will travel at the same velocity as a temperature perturbation [59, 60]. To exploit this temperature, a separation technique has been suggested where a warm feed that has saturated the bed is suddenly cooled, resulting in a section of bed that is free of adsorbate [60]. Such an effect was referred to as the *guillotine* effect.

5.5   DESORPTION

Industrial adsorbers are regenerated by hot purge — hence the name *thermal swing*. (Depressurization accomplishes the same purpose in pressure-swing processes.) The purge gas is usually a fraction of the cleaned product from the adsorber, any nonadsorbing inexpensive gas, or heated feed. The desorption step is often the cost-determining factor in the separation process. However, very few studies on desorption have appeared in the published literature.

Isothermal desorption has been studied by a number of researchers [62–64], but results are only applicable to the nearly thermally neutral displacement desorption. For adiabatic desorption of a single sorbate, the system is governed by two coupled partial differential equations for heat and mass balance, as well as the equilibrium isotherm, for the simplest case of the equilibrium model. Numerical solutions can be obtained, even with the addition of the rate equations for heat and mass transfer, by standard finite difference methods. Several studies have been made on desorption in this fashion, including the stage model [39, 65–67]. Solutions of the equilibrium model by using the method of characteristics, however, have revealed the most significant results in desorption [39, 52, 58, 60, 61, 68]. The following results are those by Basmadjian and co-workers [52, 58, 68, 108].

The governing equations for an adiabatic, equilibrium, single-adsorbate system are:

$$G_b \frac{\partial Y}{\partial z} + \rho_b \frac{\partial q}{\partial t} = 0 \tag{5.67}$$

$$G_b \frac{\partial}{\partial z}\left[(1+Y)\frac{\bar{C}_{pb}T}{1+Y}\right] + \rho_b \frac{\partial}{\partial t}(\bar{C}_{ps}T + qH) = 0 \tag{5.68}$$

$$q = q^*(T, Y) \tag{5.69}$$

The same symbols are used in section 5.5.4. The gas phase energy and adsorbate accumulation rates are insignificant compared to those in the solid phase and hence are neglected in equations 5.67 and 5.68. By using the method of characteristics these two partial differential equations are reduced to four ordinary differential equations which are then combined to give the following two characteristic equations [52, 58]:

$$\left(\frac{\partial q}{\partial Y}\right)_{\mathrm{I}} = \frac{\bar{C}_{ps}}{\bar{C}_{pb}}\left(1 - \frac{H}{\lambda_-}\right) = \frac{G_b}{\rho_b u_{\mathrm{CI}}} \tag{5.70}$$

$$\left(\frac{\partial q}{\partial Y}\right)_{\mathrm{II}} = \frac{\bar{C}_{ps}}{\bar{C}_{pb}}\left(1 - \frac{H}{\lambda_+}\right) = \frac{G_b}{\rho_b u_{\mathrm{CII}}} \tag{5.71}$$

where

$$\lambda_\pm = -\frac{1}{2(\partial q/\partial T)}(\bar{C}_{ps} - \bar{C}_{pb}\partial q/\partial Y - H\partial q/\partial T)$$

$$\mp \frac{1}{2\partial q/\partial T}[(\bar{C}_{ps} - \bar{C}_{pb}\partial q/\partial Y - H\partial q/\partial T)^2$$

$$+ 4\bar{C}_{ps}H\partial q/\partial T]^{1/2} \tag{5.72}$$

The subscripts I and II, respectively, denote the characteristics along the leading and rear zone, which are both separated by a plateau, as shown in Figure 5.10. The front movement velocities, u_{CI} and u_{CII}, can also be calculated from the foregoing equations. These two equations are solved with the isotherm equation, 5.69. The boundary conditions are the (constant) state of the (inlet) purge gas for the I characteristic, and the (uniform) initial bed condition for the II characteristic. When either of these coincides with the origin, a singularity occurs in equation 5.72. Also, boundary condition is given since the slopes of the characteristics are equal to the isotherm slopes at the origin. When the analysis indicates that a particular transfer zone is a shock (i.e., stable), the ODE is replaced by the following algebraic shock equations for conservation across the shock discontinuity:

$$\frac{q - q_j}{Y - Y_j} = \left(\frac{\bar{C}_{ps}}{\bar{C}_{pb}}\right)_j + \frac{qH - (qH)_j}{(\bar{C}_{pb})_j(T - T_j)} = \frac{G_b}{\rho_b u_{Cs}} \qquad (5.73)$$

The subscript j refers to initial bed or feed conditions.

For any desorption (or adsorption) system, the set of characteristic equations can be solved numerically (e.g., Runge-Kutta), resulting in the q–Y diagram (or *hodograph*; others use a C-T diagram) shown in Figure 5.11. The isotherms may be superimposed on the q–Y diagram; thus each point on the diagram represents a unique set of q–Y–T values at a particular time and location in the bed. The propagation velocity, u_C, can also be calculated from these equations. The complete

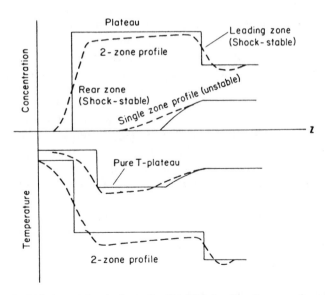

Figure 5.10 Typical desorption bed profiles for high loading (two-zone) and low loading (single zone). Equilibrium theory (———), actual profiles (- - - - - -). Source: Basmadjian, Ha, and Pan [58]. Reprinted with permission.

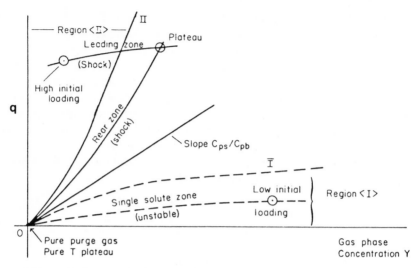

Figure 5.11 q–Y diagram (hodograph) for desorption profiles. Source: Basmadjian, Ha, and Pan [58]. Reprinted with permission.

concentration and temperature profiles at any given time, t, or the breakthrough curves at z, can therefore be constructed from the q–Y–T diagram. The q–Y diagram is composed of two families of curves representing, respectively, I and II characteristics. The curves in the II family run approximately parallel to each other. Starting from the initial loading point on Figure 5.11, a I characteristic is drawn and represents the leading transfer zone profile (in Figure 5.10). A II characteristic is drawn through the feed (purge) gas point, in this case the origin, which represents the rear transfer zone. The intersecting point represents the plateau conditions. Combined with the values of u_C, the profiles on Figure 5.10 are obtained, at time t (starting from the initial bed conditions). (Two paths on the q–Y diagram are possible, but only one is realistic judging from the actual temperature increase or decrease along the front [52].) Whenever the values of u_C on a given front (calculated from equations 5.70 or 5.71) lead to the physically unacceptable profiles of the "overhanging" type (e.g., an inverted S shape for the leading front), the relevant portion of the profile is replaced by a shock discontinuity and equation 5.73 is used.

The q–Y diagram contains two regions designated $\langle I \rangle$ and $\langle II \rangle$ (Figure 5.11). They are bounded by the coordinate axes and the limiting characteristics $\bar{I}$ and $\bar{II}$, whose slope at the origin is equal to the heat capacity ratio C_{ps}/C_{pb}.

Examples of desorption breakthrough curves constructed by the method described earlier are shown in Figure 5.12. Experimental data are also shown, which compare well with the equilibrium theory. The good agreement, indicating the lack of mass and heat transfer resistances, is due to the low flowrate and hence the slow breakthrough.

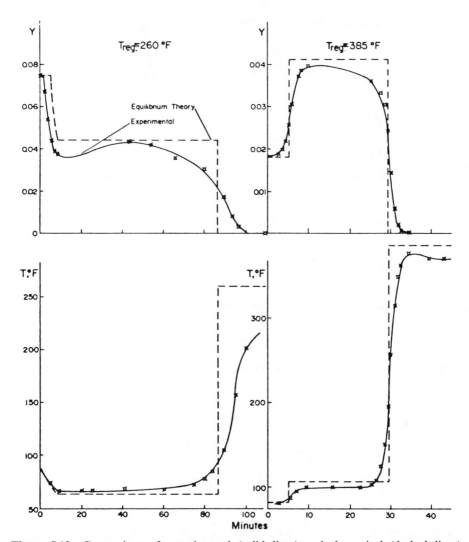

Figure 5.12 Comparison of experimental (solid lines) and theoretical (dashed lines) breakthrough curves for desorption. The theoretical curves are constructed from the q–Y diagram, the CO_2 isotherms, and the values of u_C. The one-foot bed of 5A zeolite is presaturated and then purged with N_2. *Left:* presaturated with 7.5% CO_2 in N_2, purged with N_2 at $G_b = 2.13$ lb-mol/hr/ft^2. *Right:* presaturated with 1.8% mol CO_2 in N_2, and purged with N_2 at $G_b = 4.46$ lb-mol/hr/ft^2. Source: Basmadjian, Ha, and Proulx [68]. Reprinted with permission.

The primary quantities of interest in bed regeneration are the desorption time, t_{des}, and the purge gas consumption, $(G_b)_{des}$, for a given purge gas temperature. Desorption time is given by the bed height, Z, divided by propagation velocity of the rear zone, u_{CII}, at the purge gas state. From equation 5.71:

$$t_{des} = \frac{Z}{(u_{CII})_{feed}} = \frac{Z\rho_b}{G_b}\left(\frac{\partial q}{\partial Y}\right)_{II\,feed} = \frac{\text{Bed weight } W \times \text{Slope } S_{des}}{\text{Purge gas flowrate } (G'_b)_{des}} \qquad (5.74)$$

where $S_{des} = \dfrac{\Delta q}{\Delta Y}$ (for shock rear zone)

$\qquad = \left(\dfrac{dq}{dY}\right)_{II\,feed}$ (for unstable rear zone)

$\qquad = \left(\dfrac{\Delta q}{\Delta Y}\right)_{tangent\ thru\ feed\ to\ shock}$

> (for shock at feed point and sectionally unstable at higher concentrations)

The specific purge gas consumption follows:

$$(\bar{G}_b)_{des} = S_{des} \qquad (5.75)$$

and the relative purge/feed consumption is R_G:

$$R_G = \frac{(\bar{G}_b)_{des}}{(\bar{G}_b)_{ads}} = \frac{S_{des}}{S_{ads}} \qquad (5.76)$$

Similarly, the relative purge/feed time, R_t, is:

$$R_t = \frac{t_{des}}{t_{ads}} = \frac{(G'_b)_{des}S_{des}}{(G'_b)_{ads}S_{ads}} \qquad (5.77)$$

Both S_{des} and S_{ads} can be calculated from the q–Y diagram.

By studying the q–Y diagram, a number of important features on desorption were recognized by Basmadjian and co-workers [58, 68], as will be summarized.

5.5.1   Conditions for Regeneration with Cold Purge

It can be shown that the origin of the q–Y diagram can be reached only by the II characteristics that lie entirely in region $\langle II\rangle$ and by the I characteristics that lie entirely in region $\langle I\rangle$. All other characteristics will stop short of the coordinate axes at some limiting high or low temperature isotherm [52]. It then follows that if the initial bed loading is located in region $\langle I\rangle$ and pure regenerant is used, the II characteristic will be represented by the origin. The desorption profile will consist of a single temperature and concentration zone traced out by the I characteristic, followed by a pure thermal wave when the origin is reached. Any other combination of initial loading and regenerant results in two-zone C and T profiles. Examples of both types of profiles are shown in Figure 5.10. When the initial bed loading is within region $\langle I \rangle$, the front concentration and temperature profiles, as well as the following pure thermal wave, will be independent of the inlet gas temperature. Thus the resulting desorption time and purge gas consumption are also independent of the purge inlet temperature. This leads to the important conclusion that a cold purge gas should be used under this condition, and preheating the purge will not improve the regeneration. A less obvious point under this condition is that a cold adsorber feed mixture can also be used without affecting the results because the leading desorption zone will be the same as using a pure regenerant [58]. Some practical difficulties, however, may be encountered in exploiting these attractive features [58].

5.5.2   Characteristic Purge Gas Temperature

A watershed point occurs at the purge gas temperature of the limiting characteristic $\overline{\text{II}}$ (Figure 5.11). At this point the slope at the origin has reached the minimum value of C_{ps}/C_{pb}. Beyond this point (above this temperature) no II characteristic can emanate from the origin because, as directly deduced from equation 5.70 and 5.71:

$$\left(\frac{dq}{dY}\right)_{\text{I}} \leqslant \frac{\overline{C}_{ps}}{\overline{C}_{pb}} \leqslant \left(\frac{dq}{dY}\right)_{\text{II}} \tag{5.78}$$

The shock curve (eq. 5.73) must then be used, and the rear desorption zone will then be at least a partial shock front. This is a desirable feature for desorption, as the rear front determines the degree of completion for regeneration. The temperature at which this transition occurs is termed *characteristic* or *reversal temperature*, T_0. It is equal to the temperature of the isotherm with a slope of C_{ps}/C_{pb} at the origin,

Table 5.1   Characteristic Temperatures, T_0, for Various Systems at 1 atm

System	T_0, °F
CO_2/CH_4/5A zeolite	~230
H_2O/air/5A zeolite	>600
H_2O/air/Silica gel	~250
H_2S/CH_4/5A zeolite	~400
Acetone/air/activated carbon	~300

Source: Basmadjian, Ha, and Proulx [68]. Reprinted with permission.
Values are accurate within $\pm 10\%$, because of uncertain values for K,
$\quad C_{ps}$ and C_{pb}.

or, since Henry's law is approached:

$$(K)_{T_0} = \frac{C_{ps}}{C_{pb}}(= B_{T_0}) \tag{5.79}$$

where K is the limiting slope of the isotherm at zero concentration. Some values of T_0 are given in Table 5.1. Efficient regeneration is accomplished at temperatures above T_0.

5.5.3   Minimum Desorption Time and Gas Consumption

Although low desorption time and purge gas consumption are attained at the characteristic temperature, these quantities will continue to decrease at still higher temperatures. The theoretical minimum values are calculated for purge gas temperature equaling infinity. At this temperature, the rear front is a shock and equation 5.73 yields:

$$\left(\frac{\Delta q}{\Delta Y}\right)_{min} = \frac{\bar{C}_{ps}}{\bar{C}_{pb}} \simeq \frac{C_{ps}}{C_{pb}} \tag{5.80}$$

Table 5.2   Results of Equilibrium Analysis of the Desorption Process, with N_2 Assumed to Be an Inert Carrier

Regeneration Temperature, °F	Plateau Concentration, mol of CO_2/mol of Purge	Specific Purge Gas Consumption, lb-mol of Purge/lb of Bed	Purge Gas Consumption, % of Feed Treated, R_G
Adsorber Feed: $Y = 0.01$ mol of CO_2/mol of N_2; $T = 80°F = T_{bed}$ (5A molecular sieves)			
$P = 1$ atm; purge with N_2			
50	0.0026	0.80	615%
116.7	0.010	0.17	130
205.3	0.020	0.074	57
400	0.035	0.045	36
600	0.043	0.039	30
∞	0.06	0.028	22
$P = 20$ atm; purge with N_2			
110°F	0.01	2.0	560%
205.3	0.029	0.22	61
400	0.062	0.072	20
600	0.084	0.050	14
∞	0.15	0.028	7.8

Source: Basmadjian, Ha, and Proulx [68]. Reprinted with permission.

where the minimum R_G and R_t values are calculated from equations 5.74, 5.75, 5.76, and 5.77. For the system $CO_2/N_2/5A$ zeolite, $(R_G)_{min} = 22\%$. More results for this system at 1 and 20 atm pressures are given in Table 5.2. The choice of a proper purge temperature depends on the relative costs of gas to energy.

The procedure described in the preceding has been more recently extended by Basmadjian to include all mass transfer steps and axial dispersion. A rapid two-step graphical procedure was developed, which can be used for both adsorption and desorption [71, 72], by using a modified application of the Hiester-Vermeulen graphical solution [22].

5.6 MULTICOMPONENT ADSORPTION AND DESORPTION

When the gas or fluid mixture contains more than one adsorbable species (i.e., it is a multicomponent mixture), the concentrations of various species shift relative to one another as the fluid travels. The shifts, however, soon stabilize to form the concentration fronts (other terms are *transitions, boundaries, mass transfer zones,* and *wavefronts*) that we observe (and which we can mathematically describe). These stable fronts are called coherent fronts [1, 73, 74, 75]. A coherent front consists of traveling loci of constant compositions, or in a coherent front (1):

$$u_{Ci} = u_{Cj} = u \qquad \text{for all } i \text{ and } j \tag{5.81}$$

These stable fronts may be either abrupt (shock) or gradual. In an isothermal, *n*-component mixture, (including the "inert" carrier) there are generally $n - 1$ concentration fronts, separated by n plateau zones (or constant-state zones). In a nonisothermal or adiabatic adsorber, the number of concentration fronts can, in principle, at least double because each temperature front can generate at least one additional concentration front. The additional concentration fronts may have considerable overlapping, which in combination with the dispersive forces (i.e., axial dispersion and resistances to the transport processes) result in smoothed profiles or breakthrough curves.

Figure 5.13 illustrates the typical multicomponent adsorption process with dilute adsorbates. In this example, the mixture contains four components. Thus four plateau zones are formed, which are separated by three transition zones. The widely known phenomenon of *roll-up* or *roll-over* in multicomponent adsorption is also illustrated in this figure and refers to the humps on the CO_2 and H_2S breakthrough curves, where the concentration exceeds the feed condition. These roll-up humps correspond to the plateau zones. Roll-up is caused by the displacement of a weaker adsorbate by a stronger one. (Different pore diffusivities may also contribute to this phenomenon.) All transition and plateau zones, or breakthrough curves and bed profiles, can readily be calculated by assuming certain idealized conditions.

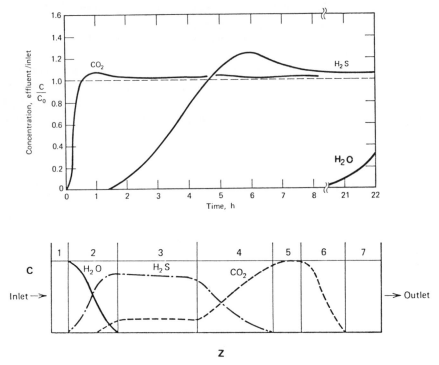

Figure 5.13 Breakthrough curves (above, experimental) and mole fraction profiles in bed (below). The 5A-zeolite bed, initially clean, is subjected to a constant feed of "commercial-grade" methane containing $\sim 3\%$ (vol.) H_2O, 1.14% CO_2, and 730 ppm H_2S. The process is nearly isothermal at 23°C. Four plateau zones in the bed are separated by three coherent fronts. Source: Chi and Lee [76]. Reprinted with permission.

Calculations of multicomponent adsorption/desorption responses are highly complicated. No analytic solution exists. The governing equations can be solved numerically with modern high-speed computers. Our present understanding of the multicomponent system, however, has been achieved without recourse to numerical methods. The major advances in the theory of multicomponent adsorption (or, more broadly, adsorption, ion exchange, and chromatography) were made during two periods of time: the late 1940s and approximately two decades later. The theory is based on equilibrium assumption; that is, no rate processes and axial dispersion are considered. Furthermore, the fluid velocity is assumed constant. Other assumptions, although they can be relaxed, include: isothermal process, constant separation factors (to be defined) or Langmuir isotherms, and constant (and uniform) boundary conditions.

Under these idealized conditions, the basic equations and some qualitative conclusions were set forth by DeVault [8]. Walter obtained explicit solutions for certain ion-exchange systems in which the equilibrium is governed by constant separation factors [9]. A rigorous analysis for adsorption/desorption involving two adsorbates following the Langmuir isotherm was made by Glueckauf in 1949 [56]. Results similar to Glueckauf's were obtained independently by Sillen [77] using the ψ-condition. These early theories were critically reviewed (and Glueckauf's results were extended to more than two adsorbates) by Bayle and Klinkenberg [78]. Some two decades later, Klein et al. published a thorough analysis of a multicomponent ion-exchange system, assuming uniform bed presaturation and constant feed composition but allowing variable separation factors [79]. Their analysis, expressed in terms of throughput parameter (T), provided complete predictions of bed profiles and breakthrough curves. Tondeur and Klein [80] completed the constant separation factor analysis made by Walter for a multicomponent mixture. At the same time, Helfferich advanced the concept of coherence for the fronts and devised the mathematical tool of *H-function* (hyperplane function) [73, 74]. Using the H-function, the equilibrium composition diagram can readily be transformed into the orthogonalized diagram, where h_i are the new dependent variables. Solutions for more general multicomponent systems with relaxed conditions can be conveniently calculated by Helfferich's method. A detailed discussion of the method and its applications is contained in the seminal work of Helfferich and Klein [1]. Independently, a general theory was published by Rhee, Aris, and Amundson [57, 81]. The theories, or calculation methods, of Helfferich and of Rhee et al. are basically identical [57, 82]. The Ω-transformation used by Rhee et al. [57, 81] is the same as Helfferich's H-transformation, with the values of ω_i (in the Ω space) related to h_i through Langmuir constants [75]. By mathematically treating temperature as an additional adsorbate in the system, Rhee et al. [83, 84] extended their calculations to adiabatic systems, as did Sweed [85]. Here, the coherence of enthalpy (with concentration) is assumed. Sweed also qualitatively discussed the effects of dispersion and the deviation of "real" systems from the idealized equilibrium system. All discussions by Rhee, Amundson, and co-workers were made based on the Langmuir isotherm. The following summary is taken from the derivation of Rhee, Aris, and Amundson [57]. (Glueckauf's paper [56] provides a good reading for beginners.)

5.6.1 Isothermal Equilibrium Theory

Under the assumption of the idealized conditions of isothermality, constant fluid velocity, local equilibrium for temperature and concentration between the two phases, and no dispersion, the mass balance equation for species i is:

$$\frac{\partial C_i}{\partial \bar{z}} + \frac{\partial C_i}{\partial \bar{t}} + v\frac{\partial q_i^*}{\partial \bar{t}} = 0 \tag{5.82}$$

$$q_i^* = f_i(C_1, C_2, \ldots, C_m) \tag{5.83}$$

where $\bar{z} = z/L$
$\bar{t} = ut/L$
$v = (1 - \varepsilon)/\varepsilon$
$i = 1, 2, \ldots, m$

The derivative of the isotherm can be expressed as:

$$\frac{\partial q_i^*}{\partial \bar{t}} = \frac{\partial f_i}{\partial C_1}\frac{\partial C_1}{\partial \bar{t}} + \frac{\partial f_i}{\partial C_2}\frac{\partial C_2}{\partial \bar{t}} + \cdots + \frac{\partial f_i}{\partial C_m}\frac{\partial C_m}{\partial \bar{t}} \tag{5.84}$$

Substituting into equation 5.82, we have:

$$\frac{\partial C_i}{\partial \bar{z}} + \frac{\partial C_i}{\partial \bar{t}} + v\sum_{j=1}^{m}\frac{\partial f_i}{\partial C_j}\frac{\partial C_j}{\partial \bar{t}} = 0, \qquad i = 1, 2, \ldots, m \tag{5.85}$$

If the bed presaturation is uniform and the feed composition is constant, we have constant initial and boundary (entry) conditions; then equation 5.85 forms a Riemann's problem. It has been proved that, if it is unique, the solution of a Riemann's problem is a function of only $\bar{z}/\bar{t}$ [77, 86]. Thus the solution is:

$$C_i = C_i(\bar{z}/\bar{t}), \qquad i = 1, 2, \ldots, m \tag{5.86}$$

and C_j is a unique function of C_i. Thus,

$$\frac{\partial C_j}{\partial \bar{t}} = \frac{dC_j}{dC_i}\frac{\partial C_i}{\partial \bar{t}} \tag{5.87}$$

Combining equations 5.85 and 5.87,

$$\frac{\partial C_i}{\partial \bar{z}} + \frac{\partial C_i}{\partial \bar{t}}\left(1 + v\sum_{j=1}^{m}\frac{\partial f_i}{\partial C_j}\frac{dC_j}{dC_i}\right) = 0, \qquad i = 1, 2, \ldots, m \tag{5.88}$$

Defining

$$\frac{Df_i}{DC_i} = \sum_{j=1}^{m}\frac{\partial f_i}{\partial C_j}\frac{dC_j}{dC_i} \tag{5.89}$$

which is the directional derivative of the unique solution — that is, a single curve (curve Γ) in the m-dimensional concentration space — we have:

$$\frac{\partial C_i}{\partial \bar{z}} + \frac{\partial C_i}{\partial \bar{t}}\left(1 + v\frac{Df_i}{DC_i}\right) = 0 \tag{5.90}$$

It follows that the concentration velocity (u_C) is given by:

$$\frac{1}{u_{C_i}} = \frac{d\bar{t}}{d\bar{z}} = 1 + v\frac{Df_i}{DC_i} \tag{5.91}$$

Since u_C must be the same for all species, or all C_i (which is Helfferich's coherence condition, equation 5.81), we have:

$$\frac{Df_1}{DC_1} = \frac{Df_2}{DC_2} = \cdots = \frac{Df_m}{DC_m} \tag{5.92}$$

Equation 5.92 is the "fundamental differential equation" for multicomponent adsorption.

For a binary solute (adsorbate) system, Glueckauf solved equation 5.92 for both the Freundlich isotherm [87] and the Langmuir isotherm [56]. Using a ternary solute system as an example, Davison showed that Glueckauf's solution could be extended to more than two solutes [88]. For illustration purposes, Glueckauf's solution for binary solute is briefly summarized here.

Partial differentiation of equation 5.92 for a binary solute system leads to [56]:

$$\left(\frac{dC_1}{dC_2}\right)^2 + \frac{(\partial f_2/\partial C_2) - (\partial f_1/\partial C_1)}{\partial f_2/\partial C_1}\left(\frac{\partial C_1}{\partial C_2}\right) - \frac{\partial f_1/\partial C_2}{\partial f_2/\partial C_1} = 0 \tag{5.93}$$

Equation 5.93 is an algebraic quadratic equation which gives two roots for dC_1/dC_2; both are real, one being positive and the other negative. These two roots represent two first-order ODEs. Figure 5.14 shows that the solutions of the two ODEs can be mapped out on a $C_1 - C_2$ hodograph, with one family of curves having positive slopes and the other showing negative slopes. The Langmuir isotherm (extended to two adsorbates; see Chapter 3) is used for the f_1 and f_2 functions. The propagation velocities at any given point on the $C_1 - C_2$ map can be calculated directly from equation 5.91, again assuming the extended Langmuir isotherm. Given the initial bed composition and feed concentration, represented respectively by points A and C in Figure 5.14, the bed profiles at any given time can be constructed. The intersection (B) of characteristic curves AB and BC represents

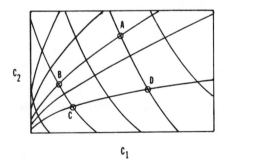
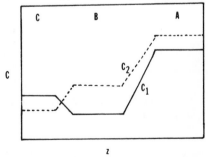

Figure 5.14 Adsorption and desorption for two solutes. The equilibrium C_1–C_2 hodograph based on arbitrary isotherms is shown in the left figure. Using the concentration propagation velocities, the bed profiles can be constructed for any given initial bed (point A) and feed (point C) conditions (right figure). Note that a Langmuir system will result in straight lines in the hodograph.

the middle plateau zone, whereas AB and BC represents the two transitions. Path ADC is not used because it would result in physically impossible concentration profiles as well as unreasonable propagation velocities. (Conditions will be given later for determining whether the transitions are shock or gradual.)

For an m-solute system, we let ω be a parameter running along the curve Γ, which is the desired solution in the m-dimension concentration space. We may express:

$$\frac{Df_i}{DC_i} = \frac{Df_i/D\omega}{DC_i/D\omega} = \sum_{j=1}^{m} f_{ij}\frac{DC_j/D\omega}{DC_i/D\omega} \tag{5.94}$$

Substituting into equation 5.91:

$$vf_{i1}\frac{DC_1}{D\omega} + \cdots + (1 + vf_{ii} - u_{C_i}^{-1})\frac{DC_i}{D\omega} + \cdots$$

$$+ vf_{im}\frac{DC_m}{D\omega} = 0, \qquad (i = 1, 2, \ldots, m) \tag{5.95}$$

Assume the extended Langmuir isotherm for equation 5.83,

$$q_i^* = \frac{q_{si}K_iC_i}{1 + \sum\limits_{j=1}^{m} K_jC_j}, \qquad i = 1, 2, \ldots, m \tag{5.96}$$

which is arranged in the sequence with increasing adsorption strength:

$$q_{s1}K_1 < q_{s2}K_2 < \cdots < q_{sm}K_m \tag{5.97}$$

The following dimensionless variables are introduced:

$$\bar{X}_i = K_iC_i, \qquad i = 1, 2, \ldots, m \tag{5.98a}$$

$$E = 1 + \sum_{i=1}^{m} \bar{X}_i \tag{5.98b}$$

From equation 5.86 and the definition of ω, C_i is a unique function of ω, and consequently:

$$\bar{X}_i = \bar{X}_i(E), \qquad (i = 1, 2, \ldots, m) \tag{5.99}$$

Using the new dimensionless variables, Rhee et al. [57] expressed:

$$\frac{Df_i}{DC_i} = q_{si}K_i\frac{E - \bar{X}_i/(D\bar{X}_i/DE)}{E^2}, \qquad i = 1, 2, \ldots, m \tag{5.100}$$

Equation 5.100 is then substituted into the fundamental differential equation, 5.92. The only possible solution is shown to be [57]:

$$\frac{D^2 \bar{X}_i}{DE^2} = 0, \qquad i = 1, 2, \dots, m \qquad (5.101)$$

which can be integrated to give:

$$\bar{X}_i - \bar{X}_{i0} = J_i(E - E_0), \qquad i = 1, 2, \dots, m \qquad (5.102)$$

where J_i is the integration constant. By summing the m equations, we get:

$$\sum_{i=1}^{m} J_i = 1 \qquad (5.103)$$

From equation 5.100 and the fundamental equation we get [57]:

$$K_1\left(q_{s1} - \frac{q_1^*}{J_1}\right) = K_2\left(q_{s2} - \frac{q_2^*}{J_2}\right) = \cdots = K_m\left(q_{sm} - \frac{q_m^*}{J_m}\right) \equiv \omega \qquad (5.104)$$

From equations 5.103 and 5.104,

$$\sum_{i=1}^{m} \frac{K_i q_i^*}{q_{si} K_i - \omega} = 1 \qquad (5.105)$$

There are m real and positive roots for equation 5.105, which may be arranged as:

$$0 \leqslant \omega_{(1)} \leqslant q_{s1} K_1 \leqslant \omega_{(2)} \leqslant q_{s2} K_2 \leqslant \omega_{(3)} \leqslant \cdots \leqslant q_{sm} K_m \qquad (5.106)$$

Equation 5.105 represents a one-to-one continuous mapping of the m-dimensional space onto the orthogonalized Ω- space. The inverse mapping is also continuous and given by [57]:

$$\bar{X}_i = \left(\frac{q_{si} K_i}{\omega_{(i)}} - 1\right) \prod_{\substack{j=1 \\ j \neq i}}^{m} \frac{(q_{si} K_i/\omega_{(i)}) - 1}{K_i/K_j - 1}, \qquad i = 1, 2, \dots, m \qquad (5.107)$$

Equation 5.91 defines the direction of the characteristic on the $\bar{z}-\bar{t}$ plane, making it obvious that M different directions exist. We shall denote the kth characteristic as C^k, with its direction given by:

$$\sigma_{(k)} = (d\bar{t}/d\bar{z})_{\omega_{(k)}} = 1 + v\frac{\omega_{(k)}}{E} \qquad (5.108)$$

The last term is obtained from equation 5.104, $Df_i/DC_i = \omega/E$. Following equation 5.106, we have for the order of propagation velocities:

$$1 < \sigma_{(1)} < \sigma_{(2)} < \cdots < \sigma_{(m-1)} < \sigma_m \qquad (5.109)$$

where $\sigma_{(k)}$ represents the reciprocal of the concentration velocity. Equation 5.109 indicates that there are m transitions or waves, moving in the sequence such that the wave corresponding to the strongest adsorbate moves the slowest, while all move slower than the flow velocity.

In the $\bar{z}-\bar{t}$ plane, the C^k characteristic is necessarily a straight line because $\sigma_{(k)}$ remains constant for every k. This is equivalent to the coherence condition discussed by Helfferich [73].

If the following occurs:

$$\frac{\partial \sigma_{(k)}}{\partial \bar{z}} > 0 \qquad (5.110)$$

then the C^k and other characteristics would overlap on the $\bar{z}-\bar{t}$ plane and the solution could not be determined uniquely. This can be resolved by allowing discontinuities in the solution. Equation 5.110 thus sets the condition for a shock transition.

For a shock transition, the reciprocal of velocity is:

$$\sigma^s = (d\bar{t}/d\bar{z})^s = 1 + v\Delta f_i/\Delta C_i \qquad (5.111)$$

where Δ denotes the jump across the discontinuity. The mass balance equation is then:

$$\frac{\Delta f_1}{\Delta C_1} = \frac{\Delta f_2}{\Delta C_2} = \cdots = \frac{\Delta f_m}{\Delta C_m} \qquad (5.112)$$

There exist m different sets of J_i (J_i is related to ω by equation 5.104), each of which corresponds to a different Γ. The kth one is denoted as Γ^k. A shock wave, if its image lies on a Γ^k, is called a k-shock, and its propagation path is denoted S^k as shown in Figure 5.15. The continuous waves, labeled C^2, C^{k-1}, ..., C^m are also shown in Figure 5.15. These waves, the Ss and Cs, separate regions of constant state, or the plateau regions. These plateau regions are denoted as $\bar{X}_i^k$ in Figure 5.15. Thus $\bar{X}_i^k$ is the concentration of i species between the k and $k+1$ wave regions. Also shown in Figure 5.15 are $\bar{X}_i^I$ and $\bar{X}_i^F$, representing the concentrations in the initial and feed (final) conditions, respectively. The concentrations in the plateau regions can be determined by equation 5.107. An alternative and more convenient equation for replacing equation 5.107 is also given by using a recurrence formula [57]:

$$\bar{X}_i^k = \bar{X}_i^I \prod_{j=1}^{k} (1 - q_{is}K_i/\omega_j^F)/(1 - q_{is}K_i/\omega_j^I)$$

$$= \bar{X}_i^F \prod_{j=k+1}^{m} (1 - q_{is}K_i/\omega_j^I)/(1 - q_{is}K_i/\omega_j^F) \qquad (5.113)$$

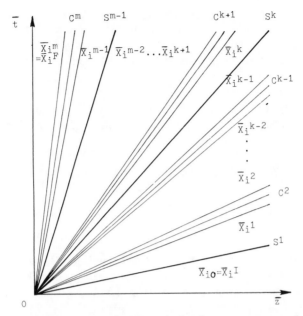

Figure 5.15 Characteristic lines (Cs) and the solution for *m*-component adsorption system in the $\bar{z}$–$\bar{t}$ plane. The thick lines labeled *S* are shock discontinuities. Source: Rhee [82]. Reprinted with permission.

Once every plateau zone composition is determined, it is straightforward to construct the solutions for bed profiles by the following procedure:

1. If $\omega_k^F > \omega_k^I$, the k transition is continuous. We then apply equation 5.108 to calculate the propagation velocities and draw as many straight characteristics, C^k, as desired. The constant values of $\bar{X}_i$ along each C^k are determined from equation 5.102, or:

$$\bar{X}_i = \bar{X}_i^k - J_i^k(E - E^k), \qquad i = 1, 2, \ldots, m \tag{5.114}$$

where

$$J_i^k = K_i q_i^k / (q_{is} K_i - \omega_k^F) \tag{5.115}$$

2. If $\omega_k^F = \omega_k^I$, the k transition does not appear in the solution.
3. If $\omega_k^F < \omega_k^I$, the k transition is a shock discontinuity, and:

$$\sigma_k^s = 1 + v\omega_k^I / E^k = 1 + v\omega_k^F / D^{k-1} \tag{5.116}$$

From the foregoing conditions, it is apparent that for the adsorption process— that is, saturation of an initially clean bed—all transitions are shock discontinuities, or the self-sharpening type (by a favorable isotherm as discussed for the adsorption of single solute systems). All transitions are continuous or have a proportionate pattern type for desorption or elution of a presaturated bed, also discussed for single-sorbate systems. However, the picture is not as clear for mixed cases, which must be determined by the foregoing conditions.

Three numerical examples will be given here, starting with a mixed adsorption/desorption problem. In all examples, the values of q_{is} are identical, in accordance with the requirement for thermodynamic consistency for the extended Langmuir isotherm (Chapter 3, section 3.1.1).

$$q_{is} = 1.0 \text{ mole/liter for all } i$$

$$\varepsilon = 0.4 \quad \text{or} \quad \upsilon = 1.5$$

Example 1

Mixed adsorption/desorption. The initial bed condition (I) and the feed composition, or the final bed condition, (F) follow. The corresponding values of ω will also be shown, as calculated from equation 5.105. The units of Cs are moles/liter, and units of K are the reciprocals of C.

i	1	2	3
K_i	5.0	7.5	10.0
C_i^F	0.150	0.060	0.020
C_i^I	0.032	0.114	0.075
ω_i^F	2.445	6.667	9.586
ω_i^I	2.797	5.409	8.974

For the given example, three transitions are expected since all values for ω are different. The first one is a shock wave because $\omega_1^F < \omega_1^I$. The second and third are both diffuse (or proportionate pattern type) because $\omega_2^F > \omega_2^I$ and $\omega_3^F > \omega_3^I$. Between the three waves there are two plateau zones. The first one is characterized by (ω_1^F, ω_2^I, and ω_3^I) and the second by (ω_1^F, ω_2^F, and ω_3^I). The plateau compositions can be readily calculated from equation 5.113. For example:

$$\bar{X}_3^1 = \bar{X}_3^I(1 - q_{s3}K_3/\omega_1^F)/(1 - q_{s3}K_3/\omega_1^I) = 0.90$$
$$\bar{X}_3^2 = \bar{X}_3^F(1 - q_{s3}K_3/\omega_3^I)/(1 - q_{s3}K_3/\omega_3^F) = 0.53$$

Once the concentrations are determined, the $\bar{z}/\bar{t}$ plane can be readily constructed as shown in Figure 5.16. The concentration profiles can then be constructed for any given time from the $\bar{z}/\bar{t}$ plane as shown for $\bar{t} = 4$ in Figure 5.16. The solution, Γ, in the concentration space (three-dimensional) is also known. The projections of the Γ image on the two-dimensional ($\bar{X}_1$, $\bar{X}_3$) and ($\bar{X}_2$, $\bar{X}_3$) planes, from the feed to the initial states, are also shown in Figure 5.15.

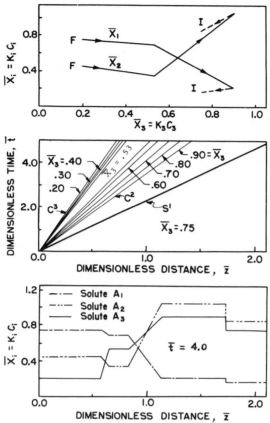

Figure 5.16 Solution of example 1. Two-dimensional projections of the solution paths (upper), the $\bar{z}-\bar{t}$ plane and the characteristics (middle), and the concentration profiles at $\bar{t}=4$ (lower). Source: Rhee [82]. Reprinted with permission.

Example 2

Adsorption by a clean bed with the initial and feed conditions:

i	1	2	3
K_i	5.0	10.0	15.0
C_i^F	0.05	0.05	0.05
C_i^I	0	0	0
ω_i^F	3.387	7.050	12.563
ω_i^I	5.0	10.0	15.0

Since all ω values increase from the feed to initial states, there are three shock waves, which are shown as S^3, S^2, and S^1 in Figure 5.17. The two-plateau state,

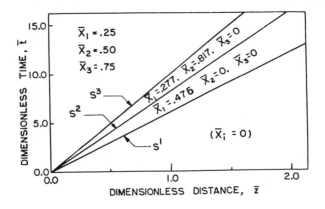

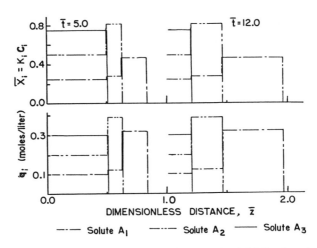

Figure 5.17 Adsorption of a three-adsorbate mixture in an initially clean bed, solution for example 2. The $\bar{z}$–$\bar{t}$ plane (upper) and bed profiles at $\bar{t} = 5$ and 12 (lower). Source: Rhee [82]. Reprinted with permission.

bound by S^2 and S^3, is characterized by $(\omega_1^F, \omega_2^F,$ and $\omega_3^I)$. Since $\omega_3^I = 15.0$, $\bar{X}_3^2 = 0$ (from eq. 5.113), which indicates that A_3 will be exhausted across S^3. From the relation $\omega_3^F < \omega_3^I$ it is obvious that $\bar{X}_1$ and $\bar{X}_2$ will increase across S^3. Similar predictions can be made for the one-plateau, which is determined by $(\omega_1^F, \omega_2^F,$ and $\omega_3^I)$. The $\bar{z}$–$\bar{t}$ plane and the concentration profiles at $\bar{t} = 5$ and 12 are shown in Figure 5.17.

Example 3

Desorption of a uniformly presaturated bed. The initial and feed conditions are given next along with the corresponding values of ω:

i	1	2	3
K_i	5.0	10.0	15.0
C_i^F	0	0	0
C_i^I	0.05	0.05	0.05
ω_i^F	5.0	10.0	15.0
ω_i^I	3.387	7.050	12.562

Since all ω values decrease from the feed state to the initial bed state, three transitions of a diffuse or proportionate-pattern type are expected. One solute will emerge through each transition. The three families of characteristics as well as the bed profiles are shown in Figure 5.18.

A basically identical solution to the problem of multicomponent ion exchange was given by Helfferich [73]. The solution was expressed in terms of

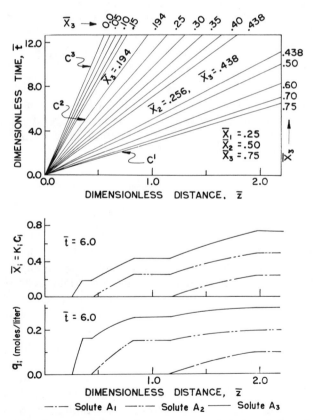

Figure 5.18 Desorption or elution of a presaturated bed, solution for example 3. Characteristics in the $\bar{z}–\bar{t}$ plane (upper) and bed profiles at $\bar{t} = 6$ (lower). Source: Rhee [82]. Reprinted with permission.

constant separation factors (α_{ij}), defined by:

$$\alpha_{ij} = \frac{X_i/Y_i}{X_j/Y_j} = \frac{q_i^*/C_i}{q_j^*/C_j} \qquad (5.117)$$

The constant separation factor is a direct consequence of the extended Langmuir isotherm (Chapter 3, section 3.1.1) where:

$$\alpha_{ij} = \frac{q_{si}K_i}{q_{sj}K_j}\left(=\frac{K_i}{K_j}\right) \qquad (5.118)$$

The second equality arises in accordance with thermodynamic consistency. In practical calculations, however, the saturated adsorbed amounts are not equal.

The H-transformation used by Helfferich is similar to the Ω-transformation used by Rhee et al. [57, 81], both transforming the concentration space into the orthogonalized H or Ω space. The transformation variables, h_i, can be obtained from the composition, Y_i, and are the roots if h or the H-function [73, 75]:

$$\sum_{i=1}^{m} \frac{Y_i}{h - \alpha_{1i}} = 0 \qquad (5.119)$$

A similar procedure for constructing the bed profiles and predicting the breakthrough curves using the H-transformation for multicomponent adsorption/desorption was outlined in reference 73 and discussed in detail in reference 1. The ω roots are related to the h roots by reference 75:

$$\omega_i = \frac{q_{sm}K_m}{h_{m+1-i}} \qquad (5.120)$$

where m denotes the species with the smallest separation factor.

The equilibrium model, using either H or Ω transformation, can yield solutions for systems with any number of adsorbates. The simplifying assumptions of uniform bed presaturation, constant feed, and a constant separation factor can be relaxed, but with considerable complications as discussed by Helfferich and Klein [1].

5.6.2   Adiabatic Equilibrium Theory

The solution in the preceding section has been extended to adiabatic systems by Rhee and Amundson [83], and Rhee, Heerdt, and Amundson [69, 84]. This has been described in a series of three papers, which will be summarized.

Assume thermal and mass transfer equilibrium — that is, T, C_i and $q_i(=q_i^*)$ are uniform at any given distance z in the bed. The system contains m species: 1, 2,

..., $(m-1)$ are the adsorbates and the mth species is the temperature. The concentration of the mth species may be regarded as *energy concentration*.

The mass balance equations for the $m-1$ adsorbates are [83]:

$$u\left[\frac{\partial C_i}{\partial z} - \frac{1-\varepsilon}{\varepsilon}(u_{C_i}/u)\frac{\partial q_i}{\partial z}\right] + \varepsilon\left(\frac{\partial C_i}{\partial t} + \frac{1-\varepsilon}{\varepsilon}\frac{\partial q_i}{\partial t}\right) = 0,$$

$$i = 1, 2, \ldots, (m-1) \tag{5.121}$$

The energy balance equation is:

$$u\left[\frac{\partial T}{\partial z} - \frac{1-\varepsilon}{\varepsilon}(u_C/u)\frac{\partial}{\partial z}\left(\frac{C_{ps}}{C_{pf}}T - \sum_{i=1}^{m-1}\frac{-H_i}{C_{pf}}q_i\right)\right]$$

$$+ \varepsilon\left[\frac{\partial T}{\partial t} + \frac{1-\varepsilon}{\varepsilon}\frac{\partial}{\partial t}\left(\frac{C_{ps}}{C_{pf}}T - \sum_{i=1}^{m-1}\frac{-H_i}{C_{pf}}q_i\right)\right] = 0 \tag{5.122}$$

These m equations can be reduced to a simple form by expressing the following for the mth species:

$$C_{pf}C_m = C_{pf}T = \text{energy concentration in fluid} \tag{5.123}$$

$$C_{pf}q_m = C_{ps}T - \sum_{i=1}^{m-1}(-H_i)q_i$$

$$= \text{energy concentration in solid phase} \tag{5.124}$$

and letting

$$v = (1-\varepsilon)/\varepsilon; \qquad \bar{z} = z/L; \qquad \bar{t} = ut/L$$

and

$$\mu = \frac{1-\varepsilon}{\varepsilon}(u_C/u) \quad \text{for all } m \text{ species} \tag{5.125}$$

Equation 5.125 is based on the coherence condition for both concentration and temperature.

Equations 5.121 and 5.122 are reduced to:

$$\frac{\partial}{\partial t}(C_i - \mu q_i) + \frac{\partial}{\partial t}(C_i + v q_i) = 0 \tag{5.126}$$

or

$$\frac{\partial}{\partial t}(C_i - \mu f_i) + \frac{\partial}{\partial t}(C_i + v f_i) = 0 \tag{5.127}$$

where f_i is the equilibrium isotherm function:

$$q_i = f_i(C_1, C_2, \ldots, C_m), \qquad i = 1, 2, \ldots, m-1 \tag{5.128}$$

Suppose the initial bed and feed mixture are at constant states of concentrations and temperature, with a jump discontinuity at $\bar{z} = 0$. This problem is a Riemann's problem, as discussed in section 5.6.1. Again, if the solution is unique, a one-parameter solution exists:

$$C_i = C_i(\omega), \qquad i = 1, 2, \ldots, m \tag{5.129}$$

where ω is an independent parameter. As in equation 5.94, the following directional derivative is introduced:

$$\frac{Df_i}{DC_i} = \frac{df_i/d\omega}{dC_i/d\omega} = \sum_{j=1}^{m} f_{ij} \frac{dC_j/d\omega}{dC_i/d\omega}, \qquad i = 1, 2, \ldots, m \tag{5.130}$$

The conservation equation, equation 5.127, may be reduced to the form:

$$\sigma \equiv \left(\frac{d\bar{t}}{d\bar{z}}\right)_\omega = \frac{1 + v(Df_i/DC_i)}{1 - \mu(Df_i/DC_i)} \tag{5.131}$$

Since equation 5.131 is independent of the choice of i, we have:

$$\frac{Df_1}{DC_1} = \frac{Df_2}{DC_2} = \cdots = \frac{Df_m}{DC_m} \tag{5.132}$$

which is the fundamental differential equation. Equation 5.131 may be rearranged to:

$$\sigma' \equiv \frac{\sigma - 1}{\sigma\mu + v} = \frac{Df_i}{DC_i} \tag{5.133}$$

Combining equations 5.130 and 5.133, we get:

$$f_{i1}\frac{dC_1}{d\omega} + \cdots + f_{i(i-1)}\frac{dC_{i-1}}{d\omega} + (f_{ii} - \sigma')\frac{dC_i}{d\omega}$$

$$+ f_{i(i+1)}\frac{dC_{i+1}}{d\omega} + \cdots + f_{im}\frac{dC_m}{d\omega} = 0 \tag{5.134}$$

Upon combining with equation 5.132, we have a system of m linear equations for $dC_i/d\omega$, which may be given in the matrix form:

$$(\nabla \mathbf{f} - \sigma'\mathbf{I})\frac{d\mathbf{C}}{d\omega} = 0 \tag{5.135}$$

or

$$|\nabla \mathbf{f} - \sigma' \mathbf{I}| = 0 \tag{5.136}$$

where $dC/d\omega$ is not zero since there is a nontrivial solution.

In equation 5.129, we may replace ω by C_m (or temperature) as the key variable and delete the last equation of the system (eq. 5.135). A linear system results from equation 5.135:

$$f_{i1}\frac{dC_1}{dT} + \cdots + f_{i(i-1)}\frac{dC_{i-1}}{dT} + (f_{ii} - \sigma')\frac{dC_i}{dT} + f_{i(i+1)}\frac{dC_{i+1}}{dT} + \cdots$$

$$+ f_{i(m-1)}\frac{dC_{m-1}}{dT} = -f_{im}, \qquad i = 1, 2, \ldots, (m-1) \tag{5.137}$$

This system of $(m-1)$ equations may be solved for the value of $(dC_i/dT)^{m-1}$. The value of σ' is calculated from equation 5.136 if the equilibrium isotherms are known.

Equations 5.136 and 5.137 may thus be used to construct the bed profiles for the adsorption system with the known isotherms and the σ values from equation 5.133. The hodographs to be used are the $C-T$ graphs which are constructed by integrating the solutions of dC_i/dT obtained from equation 5.137. Along the path on the $C-T$ hodographs, starting from feed condition, the transition (wave) is a continuous one if the propagation speed continues to increase (from the trailing to the leading edge). The portion of the transition in which this is not obeyed is a shock discontinuity.

The preceding analysis can be applied to adiabatic adsorption systems with an arbitrary number of adsorbates. The solution for a two-sorbate system was given by Rhee, Heerdt, and Amundson as an illustration [84].

From equation 5.136, we have the following for $m = 3$:

$$(\sigma')^3 - P_2(\sigma')^2 + P_1\sigma' - P_0 = 0 \tag{5.138}$$

$$\text{where } P_2 = f_{11} + f_{22} + \frac{C_{ps}}{C_{pf}} - \frac{-H_1}{C_{pf}}f_{13} - \frac{-H_2}{C_{pf}}f_{23} \tag{5.139}$$

$$P_1 = f_{11}f_{22} - f_{12}f_{21} + \frac{C_{ps}}{C_{pf}}(f_{11} + f_{22})$$

$$+ \frac{-H_1}{C_{pf}}(f_{12}f_{23} - f_{22}f_{13})$$

$$+ \frac{-H_2}{C_{pf}}(f_{21}f_{13} - f_{11}f_{23}) \tag{5.140}$$

$$P_0 = |\nabla \mathbf{f}|$$

With the Langmuir isotherm:

$$f_{ii} = \frac{q_{si}K_i(1 + K_iC_i)}{E^2} \tag{5.141}$$

$$f_{ij} = \frac{-q_{si}K_iK_jC_i}{E^2} \tag{5.142}$$

$$f_{i3} = \frac{q_{si}K_iC_i}{E^2}\left(\frac{d\ln K_i}{dT}\right)\left[1 + K_jC_j\left(1 - \frac{d\ln K_j}{d\ln K_i}\right)\right] \tag{5.143}$$

$$\frac{d\ln K_i}{dT} = -\frac{1}{T}\left(\frac{-H_i}{RT} - \tfrac{1}{2}\right) \tag{5.144}$$

for $i, j = 1, 2$ $(i \neq j)$, and

$$P_0 = C_{ps}q_{1s}q_{2s}K_1K_2/(C_{pf}E^3) \tag{5.145}$$

The C–T hodographs can be constructed from the solutions for equation 5.137:

$$\frac{dC_i}{dT} = \frac{f_{i3}(f_{jj} - \sigma') - f_{ij}f_{j3}}{(f_{11} - \sigma')(f_{22} - \sigma') - f_{12}f_{21}} \tag{5.146}$$

for $i, j = 1$, and 2 $(i \neq j)$. Equation 5.146 allows the construction of the $C_1 - T$ and $C_2 - T$ hodographs.

As is clear from equation 5.138, the value of σ' is independent of parameter μ. Therefore, equations 5.131 and 5.133 can be combined to yield

$$\sigma = 1 + v\sigma' \tag{5.147}$$

Numerical examples were given by Rhee et al. [84] on the adiabatic adsorption of cyclohexane (1) and benzene (2), which are carried by inert nitrogen in a charcoal bed. Two cases are given here.

Example 1

Desorption by pure nitrogen. All concentrations, gas-phase and adsorbed-phase, are given in moles/l, and T in °K. The initial bed condition is denoted by A, where $C_1 = 5$, $C_2 = 10$, $T = 380$, $q_1 = 1.029$, and $q_2 = 3.514$. The qs are the equilibrium adsorption calculated from the extended Langmuir isotherm for mixture (Chapter 3, section 3.1.1). The state of the constant feed is $C_1 = 0$, $C_2 = 0$, $T = 350$, and $q_1 = q_2 = 0$. Equation 5.146 is used with the σ' values from equation 5.138 to construct the C_1–T and C_2–T hodographs, shown in Figure 5.19. In Figure 5.19, as one passes in the direction of flow starting from the feed mixture B, the state varies successively along BD, DE, and EA, which are the three transition states or waves. The points D and E represent the two plateau zones. By testing the variation of σ' along the transitions, we find the transitions to be the proportionate pattern type. Also, no shock portions should exist. In the first plateau zone (point D): $C_1 = 0$, C_2

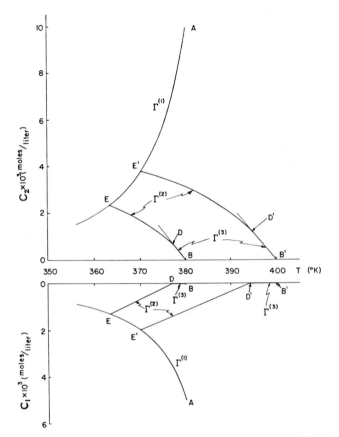

Figure 5.19 The $C-T$ hodograph planes for example 1. Source: Rhee, Heerdt, and Amundson [84]. Reprinted with permission.

$= 0.699$, $T = 377$, $q_1 = 0$, and $q_2 = 1.973$. In the second plateau zone (point E): $C_1 = 1.305$, $C_2 = 2.355$, $T = 363.2$, $q_1 = 0.885$, and $q_2 = 3.197$. The $\bar{z}-\bar{t}$ plane can be constructed from the solutions of equations 5.138 and 5.147, shown in Figure 5.20. The propagation velocity, in $d\bar{z}/d\bar{t}$, is given in the $\bar{z}-\bar{t}$ plane. For example, the speed at the head of the first wave is 4.94×10^{-2}, which continues to decrease to that at the tail of 1.17×10^{-2}. The bed profiles of C, q, and T are also given in Figure 5.20 for $\bar{t} = 20$. From the bed profiles, it is seen that the first wave propagating in the front carries away the major portions of the desorbed gases (73.9% of the cyclohexane and 76.4% of the benzene) and cools the column by 16.8K. The bed is completely desorbed at $\bar{t} = 3{,}985.2$.

Example 2

Adsorption in a clean bed. The initial bed, point B, is at $T = 380$K, $C_1 = C_2 = q_1 = q_2 = 0$. The feed mixture, point A, is at $T = 380$K, $C_1 = 5$, $C_2 = 10$, $q_1 = 1.029$,

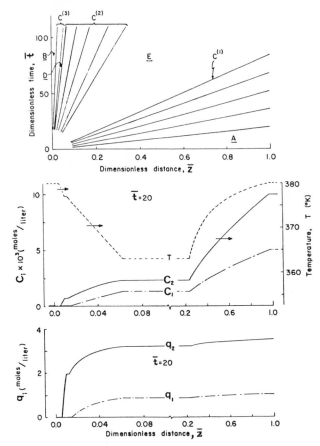

Figure 5.20 The $\bar{z}-\bar{t}$ plane solution for example 1, showing three transitions and four plateau zones (upper). Bed concentration (gas-phase, middle, solid-phase, lower) profiles at $\bar{t} = 20$. Source: Rhee, Heerdt, and Amundson [84]. Reprinted with permission.

and $q_2 = 3.514$. The sample procedure used in example 1 is followed. The C–T hodographs are shown in Figure 5.21. Along the path AG, σ' increases from A to I and then decreases from I to G. Thus the transition AG is not entirely a continuous transition, but is a combined continuous/shock wave. The combined wave has been discussed by Amundson, Aris, and Swanson [51] and by Rhee and Amundson [83]. Similarly, along path GH, σ' increases from G to I' and then decreases from I' to H. This wave is also a combined one. The path $H'B$ represents a pure thermal wave, which leads the concentration waves. The pure thermal wave forms a "contact discontinuity" [84]. The points G and H' represent the two plateau states. The $\bar{z}-\bar{t}$ plane representing the three waves and the four plateau states (A, G, H', and B) are shown in Figure 5.22. Figure 5.22 also shows the bed profiles and temperature distribution at $\bar{t} = 140$. The third wave, which is near the feed side, achieves the complete adsorption of benzene while passing the cyclohexane to the front and

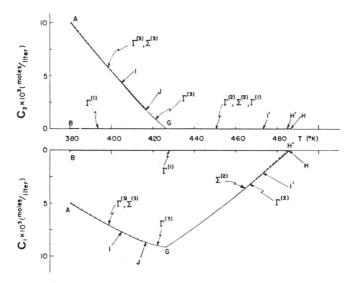

Figure 5.21 $C-T$ hodographs for example 2. Source: Rhee, Heerdt, and Amundson [84]. Reprinted with permission.

keeping the heat evolved in the front. The cyclohexane is completely adsorbed across the second wave while the contact discontinuity carries away the heat of adsorption. The complete saturation of the bed, or complete breakthrough, is accomplished at $\bar{t} = 355$.

5.6.3 Nonequilibrium Systems and Conclusions

Factors Governing Adsorber Response

As discussed in this chapter, the equilibrium isotherm is a major factor in determining the response in a fixed-bed adsorber. The other factors are: resistances to heat and mass transfer between the bulk flow and the interior of the sorbent particles, axial heat and mass dispersions, and radial dispersions. (Little or no attention has been paid to the effects of heat and radial dispersions on adsorption, although it is known that their effects can be significant in fixed-bed reactors.) All transport and dispersion factors cause the transitions or waves to spread or broaden, and may thus be referred to as "dispersive forces" after Basmadjian et al. Still another factor, to which little attention has been paid for the sake of mathematical simplicity, is the variation of flow velocity in the bed. The velocity has been assumed constant in all theoretical treatments except numerical computation models, which have not yet been discussed.

For bulk separation (i.e., separation of concentrated mixtures) the variation of flow velocity is large, and consequently its influence on the bed response (or separation) can become overwhelming when compared to all other factors,

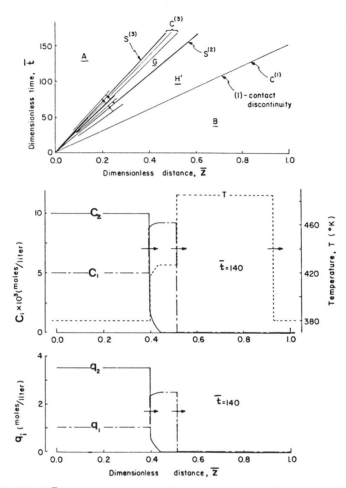

Figure 5.22 The $\bar{z}$–$\bar{t}$ plane and the bed profiles for the solution of example 2. Source: Rhee, Heerdt, and Amundson [84]. Reprinted with permission.

including the equilibrium isotherm. The flow variation is a direct consequence of the mass continuity, $\partial(\rho u A)/\partial z = 0$. For example, with a feed containing 50% adsorbate, the flow velocity will be doubled in the zone beyond complete adsorption. Qualitatively, the effect that increasing flowrate during adsorption brings is the sharpening of the transitions or wavefronts, whereas broadening occurs during desorption. The sharpening effect due to the variation of flow velocity in adsorption has been shown quantitatively in section 5.1.2 for the case of isothermal adsorption with linear isotherms. In terms of separation results, the variation of flow velocity is desirable for collecting the light species and undesirable for recovering the adsorbates (by purge).

Based on this principle, the width of the mass transfer zone or length of the unused bed (LUB) can be shortened, and thereby the separation improved, by applying a continually increasing feed rate to the adsorber. A slow flow during the initial period helps the approach to mass transfer equilibrium. The optimal feed rate/time relationship can only be determined through numerical modeling for the specific adsorption system. The reverse holds for desorption — that is, using a continually decreasing purge rate. Such an application apparently has not been exploited.

Constant-Pattern Behavior and Dispersion

These subjects have already been discussed in the preceding sections and reviewed fully elsewhere [1, 3, 4, 85]. The constant-pattern analysis has a limited value because the constant-pattern wave can develop only at a shock discontinuity predicted by the equilibrium theory. For adiabatic adsorption with favorable isotherms, all waves are not shocks, as shown in section 5.6.2. The constant-pattern wave is the result of the dispersive forces acting on the discontinuity. The constant-pattern waves are coherent. It is important, however, that the diffuse or proportionate-pattern waves are also coherent, as stressed by Helfferich and Klein [1].

Numerical Models

Treatments of nonequilibrium problems must resort to numerical methods. For an *n*-component mixture, the numerical model would involve the solution of at least $(3n + 1)$ coupled partial differential equations: *n* mass balance equations, 1 heat balance equation, *n* mass transfer rate equations, and *n* equilibrium isotherms. More equations are required for zeolite sorbents because of the bidisperse pore structure. These equations can be solved numerically, in principle, without difficulty for systems involving a relatively high number of components — for example, five-component systems, as shown in Chapter 6.

An increasing number of numerical solutions or simulations for multicomponent adsorption have appeared in the literature, with increasing sophistication and complexity. All are based on an adiabatic assumption. Recent examples include: the bidisperse pore model by Morbidelli et al. [89], the constant-pattern model of Sircar and Kumar [41], desorption of binary mixtures [67], adsorption of binary mixture [90], and others [91–101]. Some of the last references cited dealt with aqueous systems and were hence isothermal.

Basically three types of numerical methods have been used for solving nonequilibrium adsorber problems: the method of characteristics, the method of orthogonal collocation, and finite-difference methods [102]. Using the method of characteristics, it is possible to replace the first-order hyperbolic PDE by a set of equivalent first-order ordinary differential equations, which are then integrated along a specified "characteristic" curve. For complex situations, such as systems with the Langmuir isotherms, this method must be combined with numerical integration techniques such as the Newton-Raphson method [91, 96]. By using the method of orthogonal collocation, second-order PDEs, both linear and nonlinear, are transformed into first-order ODEs [103, 104]. The ODEs are then solved by any standard numerical integration routine such as Newton-Raphson or Runge-

Kutta [92, 99]. The methods of characteristics and orthogonal collocation have been mostly applied to solving adsorption and desorption problems with uniform initial conditions. For cyclic processes with varying boundary and initial conditions, it is more convenient to use finite-difference methods, which can be categorized into explicit and implicit methods. Although no iteration is needed for the explicit method, it is less accurate and often requires more computation time because of the limiting stability. The implicit method gives high accuracies and is stable for all ratios of $\Delta t/\Delta x^2$ [102, 105]. The finite-difference method has been the most extensively used in solving adsorber problems. The computation time, which increases with sharpness of the fronts since smaller time steps are necessary, is generally the longest for the finite-difference methods.

The equilibrium theory discussed in sections 5.6.1 and 5.6.2 nonetheless predicts the maximum number of transitions and plateau zones. It also provides a relatively easy calculation for predicting the approximate separation results as well as the effects of the operating conditions on these results.

NOTATION

a	outer surface area of pellets per unit bed volume
A	cross-sectional area of bed
B	Langmuir constant
C	gas-phase concentration in bulk flow; interpellet concentration; concentration in zeolite crystal
C^k	kth characteristic on the z/t plane
C_0	concentration in the feed to adsorber
C^p	gas-phase concentration inside pores, based on total volume of porous sorbent
C_p	heat capacity, with subscripts a, b, f, and s respectively, denoting adsorbate, inert carrier gas, fluid phase, and solid phase.
D_c	crystalline diffusivity in zeolites
D_e	effective diffusivity
D_k	Knudsen diffusivity
D_m	molecular diffusivity
D_p	diffusivity in pellet or binder macropores
D_s	surface diffusivity
D_z	axial dispersion coefficient
E	equilibrium isotherm parameter, dimensionless (eq. 5.97b)
f	isotherm function
G	superficial mass or molar flux
G_b	molar flux of the carrier gas
h	heat transfer coefficient in the gas film, roots of the H-function
H	heat of adsorption (which is negative), or desorption (being positive), Heaviside function $= H(t)$
k	mass transfer coefficient through gas film

k_e	effective heat conductivity of pellet
k_g	thermal conductivity of gas
K	Henry's law constant; Langmuir constant
K_d	distribution factor, $K_d = (q^*/C)(C_0 - C)/(q_0^* - q^*)$
L	bed length
M	molecular weight
N	flux
N_t	total flux
P	total pressure
Pe	Peclet Number $= 2R_p\mu/D_z\rho$
P_r	Prandtl number $= C_p\mu/kg$
q	amount adsorbed (per unit volume of sorbent pellet)
$\bar{q}$	average amount adsorbed in a pellet or particle
q^*	equilibrium amount adsorbed
q_0^*	q^* at C_0
q_s	saturated value of q (or monolayer value of q)
r	radial distance in pellet or particle
r_c	zeolite crystal radius
r_p	pore radius
R	gas constant
Re	Reynolds number $= 2R_pG/\mu$
R_p	radius of pellet
Sc	Schmidt number $= \mu/\rho D_m$
Sh	Sherwood number $= 2kR_p/D_m$
t	time
t_B	breakthrough time
t_{st}	stoichiometric time
$\bar{t}$	dimensionless time $= ut/L$
T	temperature; throughput parameter in equation 5.19
T_p	temperature within porous pellet
u	interstitial (not superficial) velocity
u_C	propagation velocity of concentration front or concentration velocity, defined by $u_C = (\partial z/\partial t)_C$
u_T	propagation velocity of temperature front or temperature velocity, defined by $u_T = (\partial z/\partial t)_T$
X	mole fraction in the adsorbed phase
$\bar{X}$	dimensional gas-phase concentration, $\bar{X}_i = K_i C_i$
Y	mole fraction in the gas phase
z	axial distance in bed from the inlet
$\bar{z}$	dimensionless distance in bed $= z/L$
Z	same as $\bar{z}$
α	void fraction within the pellet or intrapellet void fraction
α_{ij}	separation factor, defined by equation 5.116
β	equilibrium factor $= 1/K_d$
ε	interpellet void fraction (in fixed beds)

θ fractional surface coverage, dimensionless time $= t/t_{st}$
μ viscosity of gas
υ $(1 - \varepsilon)/\varepsilon$
ρ gas density
ρ_b density of inert carrier gas
σ $(\partial \bar{t}/\partial \bar{z})_c$, reciprocal of concentration velocity, dimensionless (eq. 5.107)
τ tortuosity factor

REFERENCES

1. F. Helfferich and G. Klein, *Multicomponent Chromatography: Theory of Interference* (New York: Marcel Dekker, 1970). University Microfilms No. 2050382, Ann Arbor, Mich. (1979).
2. A.E. Rodrigues, *Percolation Processes: Theory and Applications* (A.E. Rodrigues and D. Tondeur, eds.) (Alphen aan den Rijn, The Netherlands and Rockville, Md.: Sijthoff and Noordhoff, 1981), pp. 31–82.
3. T. Vermeulen, G. Klein, and N.K. Hiester, *Chemical Engineers' Handbook* (R.H. Perry and C.H. Chilton, eds.) (New York: McGraw-Hill, 1973), Chap. 16.
4. D.M. Ruthven, *Principles of Adsorption and Adsorption Processes* (New York: Wiley, 1984), Chaps. 8, 9.
5. H.K. Rhee, in Rodrigues and Tondeur, *Percolation Processes* [2], pp. 285–328.
6. N.H. Sweed, in Rodrigues and Tondeur, *Percolation Processes* [2], pp. 329–362.
7. D. Basmadjian, K.D. Ha, and C.Y. Pan, *Ind. Eng. Chem. Proc. Des. Dev.*, *14*, 328 (1975).
8. D. DeVault, *J. Am. Chem. Soc.*, *65*, 532 (1943).
9. J.E. Walter, *J. Chem. Phys.*, *13*, 229 (1945).
10. L. Lapidus and N.R. Amundson, *J. Phys. Chem.*, *56*, 984 (1952).
11. J.J. van Deemter, F.J. Zuiderweg, and A. Klinkenberg, *Chem. Eng. Sc.*, *5*, 271 (1956).
12. O. Levenspiel and K. B. Bischoff, *Adv. in Chem. Eng.*, *4*, 95 (1963).
13. J.B. Rosen, *J. Chem. Phys.*, *20*, 387 (1952).
14. J.B. Rosen, *Ind. Eng. Chem.*, *46*, 1590 (1954).
15. H.C. Thomas, *J. Am. Chem. Soc.*, *66*, 1664 (1944).
16   H.C. Thomas, *Ann. N.Y. Acad. Sc.*, *49*, 161 (1948).
17. P.L. Cen and R.T. Yang, *AIChE J.*, in press (1986).
18. H.C. Thomas, *J. Chem. Phys.*, *19*, 1213 (1951).
19. C.R. Antonson and J.S. Dranoff, *CEP Symp. Ser.*, *65*(No. 96), 20 (1969).
20. A. Rasmuson, *AIChE J.*, *27*, 1032 (1981).
21. A. Rasmuson and I. Neretnieks, *AIChE J.*, *26*, 686 (1980).
22. N.K. Hiester and T. Vermeulen, *Chem. Eng. Prog.*, *48*, 505 (1952).
23. S. Masamune and J.M. Smith, *AIChE J.*, *10*, 246 (1964).
24. G. Bohart and E. Adams, *J. Am. Chem. Soc.*, *42*, 523 (1920).
25. J.E. Walter, *J. Chem. Phys.*, *13*, 332 (1945).
26. A. Klinkenberg, *Ind. Eng. Chem.*, *40*, 1992 (1948).
27. E. Ruckenstein, A.S. Vaidyanathan, and G.R. Youngquist, *Chem. Eng. Sc.*, *26*, 1306 (1971).
28. D.M. Ruthven and K.F. Loughlin, *Can. J. Chem. Eng.*, *50*, 550 (1972).
29. K. Kawazoe and Y. Takeuchi, *J. Chem. Eng. Japan*, *7*, 431 (1974).

30. A. Rasmuson, *Chem. Eng. Sc.*, *37*, 787 (1982).
31. C. H. Liaw, J.S.P. Wang, R.A. Greenkorn, and K.C. Chao, *AIChE J.*, *25*, 376 (1979).
32. N.R. Amundson, *J. Phys. Coll. Chem.*, *54*, 812 (1950).
33. F.J. Edeskuty and N.R. Amundson, *J. Phys. Chem.*, *56*, 148 (1952).
34. S. Masamune and J.M. Smith, *AIChE J.*, *11*, 34 (1965).
35. H. Yoshida, T. Kataoka, and D.M. Ruthven, *Chem. Eng. Sc.*, *39*, 1489 (1984).
36. R.S. Cooper, *Ind. Eng. Chem. Fundam.*, *4*, 308 (1965).
37. R.S. Cooper and D.A. Liberman, *Ind. Eng. Chem. Fundam.*, *9*, 620 (1970).
38. T.W. Weber and R.K. Chakravorti, *AIChE J.*, *20*, 228 (1974).
39. M.D. LeVan and D.K. Friday, *Fundamentals of Adsorption* (A.L. Myers and G. Belfort, eds.) (New York: Engineering Foundation, 1984), p. 295.
40. D.O. Cooney and E.N. Lightfoot, *Ind. Eng. Chem. Fundam.*, *4*, 233 (1965).
41. S. Sircar and R. Kumar, *Ind. Eng. Chem. Proc. Des. Dev.*, *22*, 271 (1983).
42. K.R. Hall, L.C. Eagleton, A. Acrivos, and T. Vermeulen, *Ind. Eng. Chem. Fundam.*, *5*, 212 (1966).
43. A.S. Michaels, *Ind. Eng. Chem.*, *44*, 1922 (1952).
44. D.R. Garg and D.M. Ruthven, *Chem. Eng. Sc.*, *28*, 791 (1973).
45. C. Tien and G. Thodos, *AIChE J.*, *6*, 364 (1960).
46. C. Tien and G. Thodos, *AIChE J.*, *11*, 845 (1965).
47. F.W. Leavitt, *Chem. Eng. Prog.*, *58*, 54 (1962).
48. C.Y. Pan and D. Basmadjian, *Chem. Eng. Sc.*, *22*, 285 (1967).
49. C.Y. Pan and D. Basmadjian, *Chem. Eng. Sc.*, *25*, 1563 (1970).
50. D.M. Ruthven, D.R. Garg, and R.M. Crawford, *Chem. Eng. Sc.*, *30*, 803 (1975).
51. N.R. Amundson, R. Aris, and R. Swanson, *Proc. Roy. Soc.*, *A286*, 129 (1965).
52. C.Y. Pan and D. Basmadjian, *Chem. Eng. Sc.*, *26*, 45 (1971).
53. P. Ozil and L. Bonnetain, *Chem. Eng. Sc.*, *33*, 1233 (1978).
54. H. Yoshida and D.M. Ruthven, *Chem. Eng. Sc.*, *38*, 877 (1983).
55. C.C. Furnas, *Trans. Inst. Chem. Eng.*, *24*, 142 (1930).
56. E. Glueckauf, *Dis. Faraday Soc.*, *7*, 12 (1949).
57. H.K. Rhee, R. Aris, and N.R. Amundson, *Phil. Trans. Roy. Soc. London*, *267A*, 419 (1970).
58. D. Basmadjian, K.D. Ha, and C.Y. Pan, *Ind. Eng. Chem. Proc. Des. Dev.*, *14*, 328 (1975).
59. P. Jacob and D. Tondeur, *Chem. Eng. J.*, *22*, 187 (1981).
60. P. Jacob and D. Tondeur, *Chem. Eng. J.*, *26*, 41 (1983).
61. D.K. Friday and M.D. LeVan, *AIChE J.*, *31*, 1322 (1985).
62. E. Kehat and M. Heineman, *Ind. Eng. Chem. Proc. Des. Dev.*, *9*, 72 (1970).
63. I. Zwiebel, R.L. Gariepy, and J.J. Schnitzer, *AIChE J.*, *18*, 1139 (1972).
64. D.R. Garg and D.M. Ruthven, *Adv. Chem. Ser.*, *121*, 345 (1973).
65. A. Rodrigues and D. Tondeur, *J. Chim. Phys.*, *72*, 785 (1975).
66. D.K. Friday and M.D. LeVan, *AIChE J.*, *28*, 86 (1982).
67. S. Sircar and R. Kumar, *Ind. Eng. Chem. Proc. Des. Dev.*, *24*, 358 (1985).
68. D. Basmadjian, D.K. Ha, and D.P. Proulx, *Ind. Eng. Chem. Proc. Des. Dev.*, *14*, 340 (1975).
69. H.K. Rhee, E.D. Heerdt, and N.R. Amundson, *Chem. Eng. J.*, *1*, 279 (1970).
70. H.K. Rhee and N.R. Amundson, *Chem. Eng. J.*, *3*, 121 (1972).
71. D. Basmadjian, *Ind. Eng. Chem. Proc. Des. Dev.*, *19*, 129 (1980).
72. D. Basmadjian, *Ind. Eng. Chem. Proc. Des. Dev.*, *19*, 137 (1980).
73. F.G. Helfferich, *Ind. Eng. Chem. Fundam.*, *6*, 362 (1967).

74. F.G. Helfferich, *Adv. Chem. Ser.*, *79*, 30 (1968).
75. F.G. Helfferich, *AIChE Symp. Ser.*, *80*(233), 1 (1984).
76. C.W. Chi and H. Lee, *AIChE Symp. Ser.*, *69*(134), 95 (1973).
77. L.G. Sillen, *Arkiv. Kemi Miner. Geol.*, *2*, 477 (1950).
78. G.G. Bayle and A. Klinkenberg, *Recl. Trav. Chim.*, *73*, 1037 (1954).
79. G. Klein, D. Tondeur, and T. Vermeulen, *Ind. Eng. Chem. Fundam.*, *6*, 339 (1967).
80. D. Tondeur and G. Klein, *Ind. Eng. Chem. Fundam.*, *6*, 351 (1967).
81. H.K. Rhee, Ph.D. Thesis, University of Minnesota (1968).
82. H.K. Rhee, *Percolation Processes: Theory and Applications* (A.E. Rodrigues and D. Tondeur, eds.) (Rockville, Md.: Sijthoff and Noordhoff, 1981), pp. 285–328.
83. H.K. Rhee and N.R. Amundson, *Chem. Eng. J.*, *1*, 241 (1970).
84. H.K. Rhee, E.D. Heerdt, and N.R. Amundson, *Chem. Eng. J.*, *3*, 22 (1972).
85. N.H. Sweed, *Percolation Processes: Theory and Applications* (A.E. Rodrigues and D. Tondeur, eds.) (Rockville, Md.: Sijthoff and Noordhoff, 1981), pp. 329–362.
86. P.D. Lax, *Communs. Pure Appl. Math.*, *10*, 537 (1957).
87. E. Glueckauf, *J. Chem. Soc.*, 1321 (1947).
88. B. Davison, *Disc. Faraday Soc.*, *7*, 45 (1949).
89. M. Morbidelli, E. Santacesaria, G. Storti, and S. Carra, *Ind. Eng. Chem. Proc. Des. Dev.*, *24*, 83 (1985).
90. A.I. Liapis and O.K. Crosser, *Chem. Eng. Sc.*, *37*, 958 (1982).
91. J.H. Harwell, A.I. Liapis, R. Litchfield, and D.T. Hanson, *Chem. Eng. Sc.*, *35*, 2287 (1980).
92. N.S. Raghavan and D.M. Ruthven, *Chem. Eng. Sc.*, *39*, 1201 (1984).
93. Y. Takeuchi and E. Furuya, *Fundamentals of Adsorption* (A.L. Myers and G. Belfort, eds.) (New York: Engineering Foundation, 1984), p. 629.
94. C. Tien, *Fundamentals of Adsorption* (A.L. Myers and G. Belfort, eds.) (New York: Engineering Foundation, 1984), p. 647.
95. W.J. Weber, Jr., *Fundamentals of Adsorption* (A.L. Myers and G. Belfort, eds.) (New York: Engineering Foundation, 1984), p. 679.
96. J.S.C. Hsieh, R.M. Turian, and C. Tien, *AIChE J.*, *23*, 363 (1977).
97. S.C. Wang and C. Tien, *AIChE J.*, *28*, 565 (1982).
98. L. Marcussen, *Chem. Eng. Sc.*, *37*, 299 (1982).
99. A.I. Liapis and D.W.T. Rippin, *Chem. Eng. Sc.*, *33*, 593 (1978).
100. J.W. Carter and H. Husain, *Chem. Eng. Sc.*, *29*, 267 (1974).
101. D.O. Cooney, *Ind. Eng. Chem. Proc. Des. Dev.*, *13*, 368 (1974).
102. C.D. Holland and A.I. Liapis, *Computer Methods for Solving Dynamic Separation Problems* (New York: McGraw-Hill, 1983).
103. J.V. Villadsen, *Selected Approximation Methods for Chemical Engineering Problems* (Lyngsby: Demarks Tekniske Hojskile, 1970).
104. B.A. Finlayson, *The Method of Weighted Residuals and Variational Principles* (New York: Academic Press, 1972).
105. R.D. Richtmyer and K.W. Morton, *Difference Methods for Initial Value Problems*, 2nd ed. (New York: Interscience Publishers, 1967).
106. O.A. Meyer and T.W. Weber, *AIChE J.*, *13*, 457 (1967).
107. J.W. Carter, *Trans. Inst. Chem. Eng.*, *44*, T253 (1966).
108. D. Basmadjian, *The Adsorption Drying of Gases and Liquids*, in *Advance in Drying*, Vol. 3 (A.S. Mujumdar, ed.) (New York: Hemisphere, 1984).
109. H.W. Haynes, Jr., *Chem. Eng. Sc.*, *30*, 955 (1975).

CHAPTER 6

Cyclic Gas Separation Processes

Adsorptive gas separation processes can be divided into two types: *bulk separation* and *purification*. The former involves adsorption of a significant fraction, 10% by weight or more according to Keller's definition [1], from a gas stream, whereas in purification less than 10% by weight of a gas stream to be adsorbed. Such a differentiation is useful because, in general, different process cycles are used for different types of separation.

The major commercial gas separation processes and sorbents have been discussed in Chapter 2. Purification includes: drying (or dehydration) of air, natural gas, olefin-containing cracked gas, synthesis gas, and other industrial gases; hydrogen purification; sweetening (removal of acid gases) of natural gas and plant-recycle gases; solvent removal; and air purification processes. The major bulk separation processes are the production of oxygen and nitrogen from air, separation of *n*-paraffins from iso-paraffins and aromatics, and hydrogen from industrial gases. Molecular-sieve zeolites and activated carbon are the major sorbents used. However, the molecular-sieving property is not used in most of the commercial processes where zeolites are used. The separation is based on differences in equilibrium isotherms, and the slow intracrystalline diffusion is actually detrimental to separation. The molecular-sieving property is used in only three known commercial processes:

1. *n*- and iso-paraffin separation using 5A zeolite
2. Drying of various gas streams using zeolites
3. Nitrogen production from air using molecular-sieve carbon

The two former separations are accomplished based on selective molecular exclusion, whereas the latter is the only process using differences in pore diffusivity.

Fixed-bed adsorbers are used in almost all known commercial processes with the exception of the Purasiv HR process [1]. For continuous feed and products, dual-bed or multibed systems are used in which each bed goes through adsorption/regeneration cycles. Although the operation of each bed is batchwise, the system as a whole is a continuous one that is operated in a cyclic steady state. Based on the method of sorbent regeneration and the mechanical arrangement, a number of process cycles and combinations of cycles have been developed. They are:

1.   *Thermal-swing adsorption:* In this process cycle, the bed is regenerated by raising the temperature. The most convenient way of raising the temperature is by purging the bed with a preheated gas. This is the oldest and most completely developed adsorption cycle. Because heating is a slow and often rate-limiting step, the length of each cycle usually ranges from several hours to over a day. In order to make the time length of the adsorption step comparable to that of regeneration, the cycle is used only for purification purposes.

2.   *Pressure-swing adsorption:* In this cycle the bed regeneration is accomplished by reducing the total pressure. The cycle time is short, usually in minutes or even seconds, due to the possibility of rapid pressure reduction. Though ideally suited for bulk separations, this cycle can be used for purifications as well. An increasing number of purification processes are being switched from temperature swing to this cycle, and an increasing number of bulk separation processes are being developed using this cycle. This is the youngest basic cycle and also the most flexible one in terms of process modification. Unlike the temperature-swing and other cycles, many new applications are possible with the pressure-swing cycle. This cycle is also the most difficult and complex to model. For these reasons, two separate chapters will be devoted to a detailed discussion of this cycle.

3.   *Inert purge:* This cycle is similar to the temperature-swing cycle except that preheating of the purge gas is not required. Usually a fraction of the light product (raffinate) is used as the inert purge gas. This cycle will be discussed in conjunction with the temperature-swing cycle.

4.   *Gas chromatography:* The laboratory analytical chromatography has been an appealing tool for large-scale separation for many years. Only recently have commercial attempts appeared successful.

5.   *Parametric pumping and cycling-zone adsorption:* These two processes, as will be described, have yet to find a commercial application. Nevertheless, there are still ongoing research activities, and future applications are not out of the question. For this as well as scientific reasons, these processes are included for discussion.

6.   *Moving-bed and simulated moving-bed processes:* In these processes the gas mixture and solid sorbent are contacted in a countercurrent movement. Thus, unlike the temperature- and pressure-swing processes, the process is truly steady state in that the flowrates and compositions of all streams entering and leaving the adsorbent bed are constant. Besides the process simplicity, a further advantage of the moving-bed process is in minimizing the required inventory of adsorbent.

6.1   SORBENT REGENERATION

Four methods are used for sorbent regeneration; all involve measures to lower the equilibrium adsorbed amount. As illustrated in Figure 6.1, this can be done either by reducing the partial pressure of the adsorbate or by raising the temperature.

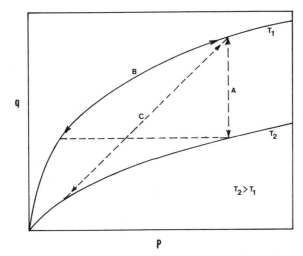

Figure 6.1 Schematic representation of equilibrium isotherms showing methods for sorbent regeneration: (*A*) temperature swing, (*B*) pressure swing or inert gas purge, and (*C*) hot inert purge.

    1.   The thermal swing (or temperature swing) is most efficiently accomplished by purging the bed with a preheated gas. A number of gases can be used, including adsorber feed mixture, a fraction of the light (raffinate) product from the adsorption step, air, steam, and so on. When gases other than the adsorber feed mixture are used, the driving force for desorption is enhanced by the concurrent reduction of the partial pressure.

    2.   The pressure swing is accomplished by reducing the total pressure in the adsorber at essentially constant temperature.

    3.   Inert purge stripping removes the adsorbate without changing the temperature or pressure. The void in the bed is filled with the inert gas upon completion of regeneration. The raffinate product becomes slightly contaminated by the inert gas during the next adsorption step unless the raffinate is used as the inert purge gas.

    4.   Displacement gas purge differs from inert purge in that a gas or vapor that adsorbs about as strongly as the adsorbate is used as the purge gas. Regeneration is thus facilitated both by adsorbate partial-pressure reduction and by competitive adsorption of the displacement medium.

    The use of a displacement agent, however, results in additional separation steps. Since the displacement agent is actually adsorbed, it is present in the void as well as on the surface when the next adsorption step begins. The desorption of the displacement agent during this step results in a diffuse or proportionate-type concentration front that severely contaminates the raffinate product (assuming the isotherm for the displacement agent is the favorable type). Figure 6.2 shows a displacement-purge cycle. As shown in the figure, the displacement agent is

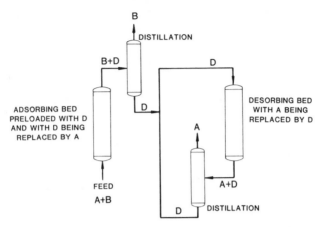

Figure 6.2 Displacement-purge cycle: (*A*) adsorbate, (*B*) less-adsorbed component (or raffinate), and (*D*) displacement agent. Source: Keller [1]. Reprinted with permission.

recycled, at the expense of an additional distillation step. The easy separation of $A + D$ and $B + D$ is thus a primary factor in choosing the displacement agent. This cycle is employed only in circumstances where the adsorbate is very strongly bonded to the sorbent.

6.2   TEMPERATURE-SWING ADSORPTION AND INERT PURGE CYCLE

Temperature- or thermal-swing adsorption (TSA) is the oldest cyclic adsorber process. Dual-bed systems are most commonly used. Limited examples of the dual-bed arrangements are shown in Figure 6.3, in which no external source of regenerant (e.g., air, steam, or other available gases) is used. A three-bed design has also been used for systems with a long length of unused bed (LUB, which is approximately one-half of the mass transfer zone or the span of the concentration front). In the three-bed system, a *guard bed* is located between the adsorber and that being regenerated [3]. When the concentration of the adsorber effluent reaches nearly that of the feed stream, the beds are switched. The loaded primary adsorber goes to regeneration, the former guard bed assumes the primary position and the freshly activated bed becomes the guard. By this rotation, the LUB section is always contained in the guard bed, and the primary adsorber is always fully loaded to its capacity when regeneration begins. Thus both a high-purity product and an economic regeneration are achieved. The cost of the additional bed, however, may outweigh its benefits for many common purification processes.

The extensive literature on adsorber analysis is presented in Chapter 5. This chapter also includes the relatively scarce theoretical analyses on regeneration/desorption. The theoretical analyses resort to equilibrium theory; that is, mass

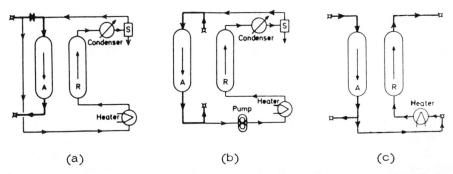

Figure 6.3 Dual-bed temperature-swing adsorption processes: (a) regeneration with feed at the same pressure for adsorption; (b) regeneration with product at the same pressure for adsorption; (c) regeneration with product at a reduced pressure. Source: Carter [2]. Reprinted with permission.

and heat transfer rates are assumed to be instantaneous. Since the adsorption and desorption steps in TSA are operated slowly, each spanning for hours, the equilibrium theories are indeed good. Often, quantitative agreements are obtained between theory and experiment (see Chapter 5). Mass and heat transfer are considered *dispersive forces*, which have a dispersive or smearing effect on the concentration and temperature fronts. The detailed bed profiles and breakthrough curves can be calculated only by the numerical solution of the mass and heat balance equations (section 4.1), coupled with the equations for equilibrium adsorption from mixture.

Experimental and theoretical results on the TSA process are limited to the first cycle of adsorption, followed by regeneration using hot purge [4–8]. No cyclic results on TSA have been reported. Since the bed regenerated by hot purge is usually very clean, the cyclic steady state is approached in the first cycle. This fact is implied but not clearly stated in several studies where the cyclic experiments were performed but only the first-cycle results were reported [2, 3, 7]. This is in contrast with the inert (cold) purge cycles, where several cycles are needed to approach a cyclic steady state [9–12]. The difference is caused by the fact that cold purge is relatively ineffective and the TSA cycle requires the times for adsorption and regeneration to be equal in length.

The numerical solution of the complete heat and mass balance equations requires accurate data on the transport processes. Since the data and accurate predictions of these properties as well as equilibrium adsorption from mixtures are not available, simple and semiempirical procedures have been reported for engineering design [3, 8, 13–16].

The regeneration step in the TSA cycle requires time to heat, desorb, and cool the bed. It is often the time-limiting step in the TSA cycle and is also the most complex and least understood one. The following discussion on TSA will be focused on the regeneration step.

6.2.1   Equilibrium-Theory Calculations

The discussion will be based on the equilibrium theory of Basmadjian et al. [5, 6], which is presented in detail in section 5.5 of Chapter 5.

Purge Temperature

As shown in section 5.5, efficient desorption is accomplished at temperatures above the "characteristic temperature," T_0. The characteristic temperature is equal to the temperature at which the slope of the adsorption isotherm at the origin is equal to C_{ps}/C_{pb}, the ratio of the heat capacities of the solid phase and the inert carrier gas. For a Langmuir isotherm:

$$q = \frac{K(T)P}{1 + B(T)P} \tag{6.1}$$

T_0 is determined by:

$$K(T_0) = \frac{C_{ps}}{C_{pb}} \tag{6.2}$$

where q is the amount adsorbed; P is pressure; and C_{ps} and C_{pb} are, respectively, the heat capacities for the solid phase (sorbent plus adsorbate) and inert carrier gas. The values for some systems are given in Table 5.1. As the temperature is increased beyond the characteristic temperature, however, the energy cost increases accordingly without a significant gain in desorption. Thus the characteristic temperature is actually the optimal temperature for desorption.

Materials problems must also be considered in selecting the regeneration temperature. In the presence of hydrocarbons, coke deposition occurs on zeolites as a result of the catalytic decomposition at temperatures as low as 100°C, depending on the hydrocarbon compound, its partial pressure, and other factors. Severe oxidation takes place in activated carbon at above about 100°C in the presence of trace amounts of oxygen.

Purge Time by Gases with Various Concentrations

Once the temperature has been selected, the desorption time can easily be estimated from equilibrium theory for various concentrations of the purge gas. The needed equations are given in section 5.5. A summary of the relevant equations follows.

$$\frac{G_b}{\rho_b u_{CII}} = \frac{\overline{C_{ps}}}{C_{pb}}\left(1 - \frac{H}{\lambda}\right) \tag{6.3}$$

$$\lambda = -\frac{1}{2(\partial q/\partial T)}(\overline{C_{ps}} - \overline{C_{pb}}\partial q/\partial y - H\partial q/\partial T)$$

$$-\frac{1}{2\partial q/\partial T}[(\overline{C_{ps}} - \overline{C_{pb}}\partial q/\partial y - H\partial q/\partial T)^2 + 4\overline{C_{ps}}H\partial q/\partial T]^{1/2} \qquad (6.4)$$

$$\text{Desorption time } t_{des} = \frac{\text{Bed height}}{u_{CII}} \qquad (6.5)$$

where q is the equilibrium adsorption, given by equation 6.1; u_{CII} is the propagation velocity of the trailing edge of the concentration front; G_b is the molar flux of the carrier gas; Y is the mole fraction of the adsorbate in the gas phase; H is the heat of adsorption; and the overbar denotes average values. The desorption time can be calculated directly from equations 6.1, 6.3, 6.4, and 6.5.

The foregoing results are derived for a uniformly loaded bed prior to regeneration. Experimental results, compared to this analysis, showed a relative insensitivity of bed desorption behavior to the initial loading uniformity [6].

6.2.2 Nonequilibrium Models

The equilibrium theory is based on the assumption that the bed is uniformly saturated. In practice, uniform distribution throughout the bed is not obtained because the feed is stopped at the breakthrough or "break" point. Thus a high loading will be found at the inlet end and will approach zero at the outlet end. Under these conditions, the flow direction of the purge, whether cocurrent with the adsorber feed or countercurrent, will affect the desorption behavior. Such an effect can only be modeled by the numerical solution of the mass and heat balance equations. Carter [7, 17, 18] uses one of these numerical models in which a linear isotherm is assumed.

The numerical simulation of a TSA cycle for the drying of air by activated alumina is shown in Figures 6.4, 6.5, 6.6, and 6.7. The curves shown in Figure 6.4 reflect an inert purge cycle, which agreed well with experimental data [18]. The inert purge regeneration is clearly very inefficient: the peak concentration reached only 50% of the feed concentration, and the time for regeneration is excessively long. Purge at a higher temperature, 93.3°C, is clearly much more efficient (Figure 6.5). It is interesting to note that this temperature is close to the characteristic temperature (T_0) of the system. The direction of the purge of a fully saturated bed does not influence the desorption behavior. For a partially saturated bed with adsorption stopped at the break point, approximately 1.1 hour in Figure 6.4, the direction of the purge is important. The cocurrent and countercurrent purge results are compared in Figures 6.6 and 6.7. The amount desorbed is higher at any given time for the countercurrent purge. The temperature peak for the cocurrent purge is real as a result of the readsorption of water vapor near the end of the partially saturated bed. This temperature peak has been routinely observed experimentally in both TSA [1, 7] and pressure-swing cycles [19]. The latter readsorption, near the outlet, takes place during cocurrent depressurization.

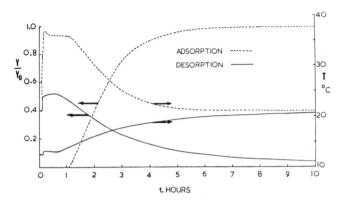

Figure 6.4   Numerical solutions for the concentration and temperature of the effluent during adsorption and purge of a fully saturated bed of activated alumina. The feed is air containing 0.0048 g H_2O/g at 0.258 kg/m^2/s, and the regenerant is dry air at the same flowrate, both at 21.1°C. Sources: Carter [7, 18]. Reprinted with permission.

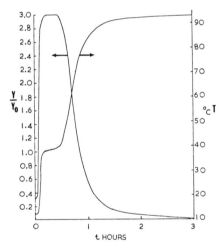

Figure 6.5   Desorption of a fully saturated bed with dry air at an inlet temperature of 93.3°C. Other conditions are the same as in Figure 6.4. Source: Carter [7]. Reprinted with permission.

6.2.3   Empirical Heat Transfer Model for Regeneration

It is clear from Figure 6.4 through Figure 6.7 that the adsorbed water is practically all removed from the bed when the effluent temperature starts to approach the inlet purge gas temperature. This point is further illustrated in Figure 6.8, which shows pilot plant data of the regeneration half-cycle of a 4A zeolite drier [8].

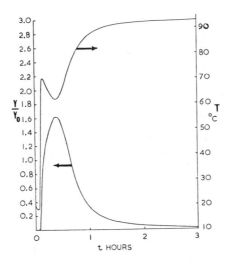

Figure 6.6 Desorption purge of a partially saturated bed (saturated at the break point in Figure 6.4) with an inlet temperature of 93.3°C in the same direction as adsorption. Source: Carter [7]. Reprinted with permission.

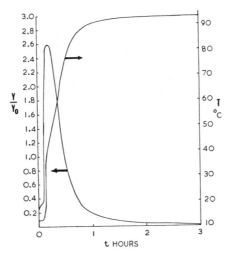

Figure 6.7 Desorption of a partially saturated bed (same as in Figure 6.6) with a 93.3°C inlet temperature in the reverse direction to adsorption. Source: Carter [7]. Reprinted with permission.

A design method was suggested [8] based on the criterion that the bed is considered regenerated and switched to the next cycle when the effluent temperature reaches 90% of the inlet temperature. If heat transfer rate is assumed to be the controlling step, without considering heat balance or mass transfer rate, the transient temperature response at the outlet can be calculated by using the well

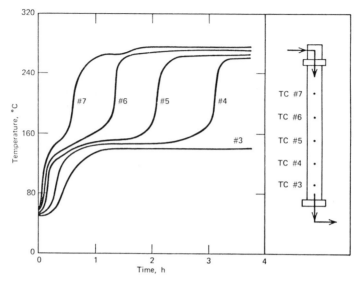

Figure 6.8   Temperature history in the bed during the regeneration half-cycle of a 4A zeolite air dryer. Hot air is used as the regenerant. Source: Chi [8]. Reprinted with permission.

known analytical solution of Anzelius [20]. The heat transfer rate in Anzelius's model is controlled by the film coefficient. The theoretical solution for the outlet temperature reaching 90% of the inlet temperature is shown in Figure 6.9, the required dimensionless time versus dimensionless height, using the *j*-factor calculated from equations 4.11 and 4.12. Compared with the regeneration data in

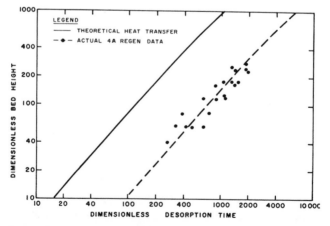

Figure 6.9   Comparison of pilot plant regeneration data of a 4A zeolite air drier with theoretical solution assuming that film heat transfer between gas and particles is the controlling step. Source: Chi [8]. Reprinted with permission.

Figure 6.9, the actual regeneration time is about six times that of theoretical heat transfer. The dashed line in Figure 6.9 was used for regeneration design [8].

The heat balance requires that the sensible heat carried by the hot regenerant be used mainly to raise the temperature of the sorbent plus sorbate and the heat of desorption. A small fraction of the sensible heat is also required for heating the vessel and the heat loss to the surroundings. In the pilot plant experiments shown in Figure 6.9, about 30% of the sensible heat was supplied each for desorption and heating the sorbent plus sorbate. The other 40% was used to heat the vessel and was attributed to heat loss since a four-inch inside-diameter bed was used [8].

The comparison shown in Figure 6.9 clearly indicates that the heat transfer rate is not the controlling step. The rate of regeneration is actually controlled by other factors—heat balance and perhaps also mass transfer. This result simply reinforces the commonly used assumption that heat transfer resistance is negligible in adsorber calculations. Although the dashed line in Figure 6.9 can be used for design purposes, this line would have to be measured for each specific system at the specific size. Thus this method has very limited use.

6.2.4   Isothermal Inert Purge Cycle

Under conditions discussed in section 5.5.1 of Chapter 5, a cold purge is preferred over a hot purge because they both result in the same desorption time and gas consumption. The adsorption/regeneration cycle can then run in an essentially isothermal manner.

Model simulation of the isothermal inert purge cycle has been performed by Bunke et al. [9, 10] and by Chao and Ruthven [11, 12]. In both models, constant

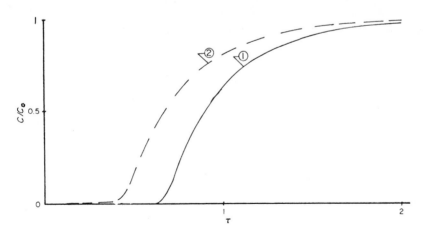

Figure 6.10   Breakthrough curves in the isothermal inert purge cycles with countercurrent purge: (1) first cycle; (2) cyclic steady state. $\tau_{ads} = \tau_{des} = 2$, where τ is the actual time divided by the stoichiometric saturation time. Source: Bunke and Gelbin [9]. Reprinted with permission.

flow velocity and the Langmuir isotherm are assumed. The mass transfer rate is assumed from monodisperse pore diffusion by Bunke et al., and by the linear driving force approximation by Chao and Ruthven. The two models differ by the length of the adsorption half-cycle: A fixed time during the breakthrough is used by the former, whereas the latter terminates the adsorption half-cycle just before the breakthrough, or at the break point. The results of the two models, however, are similar. In both models it is shown that several cycles are needed before a cyclic steady state is reached, starting from the first cycle with a thoroughly regenerated bed. The difference in the results between the first cycle and the cyclic steady state is quite substantial, as shown in Figure 6.10. The bed profiles at the end of desorption, expressed as the amount of remaining adsorbate divided by the equilibrium saturated amount at the feed condition, are shown in Figure 6.11. This figure shows that the flow direction of the purge gas is important and, furthermore, that the fraction of the unused bed capacity is substantial.

6.3   CHROMATOGRAPHY

The interest in upscaling gas chromatography throughput dates almost from the inception of the technique. This interest, however, has been concentrated on laboratory-scale separations, referred to as *preparative chromatography*. Despite numerous attempts for the scale-up to production or plant scale, only recently has the effort apparently been successful. Elf Aquitaine Development and the Société de Récherches Techniques et Industrielles (SRTI) have announced a process for separating mixtures that are difficult to separate by distillation [21–23]. The Elf-SRTI process is presently separating up to 100 metric tons per year of perfume ingredients commercially. A plant capable of separating 100,000 metric tons of C_4–C_{10} normal and iso-paraffins per year has also been announced [23]. A schematic diagram of the process is shown in Figure 6.12.

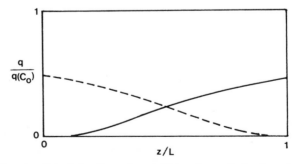

Figure 6.11 Fractional bed loading, $\theta = q/q(C_0)$, where C_0 is the adsorber feed concentration, following desorption in cyclic steady state as a function of a bed height, z/L. Cocurrent desorption (solid curve); countercurrent desorption (dashed curve). Source: Bunke and Gelbin [9]. Reprinted with permission.

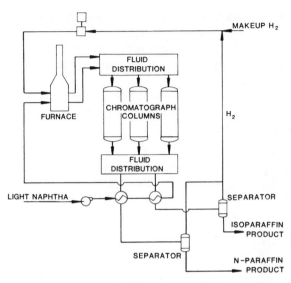

Figure 6.12 Elf Aquitaine chromatographic separator for separating *n*- and iso-paraffin from a light naphtha feed. Source: Keller [1]. Reprinted with permission.

Since all products are contaminated by the carrier gas, a noncondensable and nonadsorbing gas such as hydrogen or helium is used. This gas can easily be separated from the products and recycled.

The high separating efficiency of chromatography as compared to adsorption processes [24] is caused by the continuous contact and equilibration between the gas and sorbent phases. Each contact is equivalent to an equilibrium stage or theoretical plate. Usually several hundred to several thousand such equilibrium stages can be achieved in a short column [24]. Thus chromatography should be most useful in cases of difficult and impractical separations — for example, mixtures with relative volatilities too low for distillation and separation factors too low for cyclic adsorption processes.

A major obstacle to production-scale chromatographic separation is the great difficulty encountered in achieving a homogeneous column packing. The problem worsens for larger size columns. Nonhomogeneous packing results in a nonideal flow such as channeling, and in short-circuit passages, all of which lower the separation efficiency. In addition, with large columns it is desirable to have high radial dispersion; at the same time, the axial dispersion should be low. The use of corrective devices such as internal baffles can improve the separation efficiency [25–28]. The successful development of the Elf Aquitaine–SRTI process is the result of the development of a proprietary packing technique that effects a high column efficiency. Improved large zeolite column-packing methods have also been announced by Asahi Company for plant-scale chromatographic separation of *p*-xylene and ethylbenzene in the liquid phase [29, 30].

Despite its fundamental drawbacks, the theoretical plate concept still remains the most useful way of discussing the separation efficiency of chromatographic columns. In the plate theory, the column is thought to consist of a finite number of hypothetical stages, and equilibrium is attained in each stage. The separation efficiency is indicated by the equivalent height of each stage: A high separation efficiency is achieved by a small equivalent height. The equivalent height, or height equivalent to a theoretical plate (HETP), is given by the van Deemter equation for linear adsorption isotherms [31]:

$$\mathrm{HETP} = \frac{A}{u} + B + Cu \qquad (6.6)$$

where $A = 2D_m/\tau$
$\qquad B = 4R_p/\mathrm{Pe}$
$\qquad C \approx 2\varepsilon/[kK(1 - \varepsilon)]$

Here u is the interstitial velocity, D_m is the molecular diffusivity, τ is the axial tortuosity, R_p is the particle radius, Pe is the Peclet number, ε is the interparticle void fraction, k is the mass transfer coefficient used in the linear driving force equation, and K is Henry's constant for the linear isotherm.

The dependence of HETP on u is illustrated in Figure 6.13, showing the three contributions to the HETP. The optimum velocity which yields the minimum HETP is:

$$u_{\mathrm{opt}} = \left(\frac{B}{C}\right)^{1/2} \qquad (6.7)$$

Below u_{opt}, peaks are broadened mainly by molecular diffusion. Above u_{opt}, the mass transfer resistance is the main cause for broadening. Equation 6.6 is the simplest form of the van Deemter equation. Many other effects can be taken into account leading to more complex equations. The number of equivalent theoretical

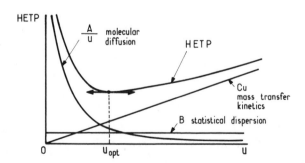

Figure 6.13 The dependence of HETP, which is the indicator of the inefficiency of separation on the flow velocity. Source: Villermaux [32]. Reprinted with permission.

plates (NETP), to which the column is equivalent, is given by the following equation for a pulse injection (referred to as *elution chromatography*):

$$\text{NETP} = \frac{t_R^2}{\sigma^2} = \frac{16t_R^2}{d^2} \tag{6.8}$$

where t_R is the retention time and σ is the half width. The quantities t_R, σ, and d are illustrated in Figure 6.14. The resolution between two Gaussian elution bands is defined by the parameter:

$$R_{AB} = \frac{t_{RA} - t_{RB}}{4\sigma_{AB}} \tag{6.9}$$

where

$$\sigma_{AB} = \frac{\sigma_A + \sigma_B}{2}$$

Complete resolution requires $R_{AB} \geqslant 1.5$. The NETP needed to achieve the resolution R_{AB} for two Gaussian bands is:

$$\text{NETP(Pulse Injections)} = 4R_{AB}^2 \left(\frac{\alpha + 1}{\alpha - 1} \right)^2 \tag{6.10}$$

where

$$\alpha = \frac{t_{RA}}{t_{RB}} \tag{6.11}$$

Thus, for pulse or small injections, the column height required for complete

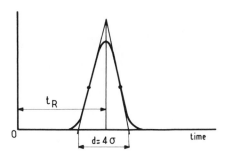

Figure 6.14 Illustration of a Gaussian elution band from a pulse injection. Source: Villermaux [32]. Reprinted with permission.

resolution is obtained directly as the product of HETP (eq. 6.6) and NETP (eq. 6.10).

In plant-scale processes, long injections with a duration of generally 10–30 seconds are required for the desired throughput. The injections are rectangular shaped (referred to as *eluto-frontal chromatography*). Figure 6.15 shows the resolution of two rectangular injections, *A* and *B*. For such injections it can be shown that the NETP required for a resolution equivalent to $R_{AB} \geq 1.5$ is [33]:

$$\text{NETP (Rec. Inj.)} = \text{NETP (P. Inj.)} \left(1 + \frac{\sigma_i}{\sigma_{AB} R_{AB}}\right)^2 \qquad (6.12)$$

The value of σ_i is obtained from the duration ($= 4\sigma_i$) of the injection, as shown in Figure 6.15. The value of NETP (P. Inj.) is calculated from equation 6.10. The ratio σ_i/σ_{AB} in practice is much greater than unity, which means the NETP required for rectangular injections is much greater than that for pulse injections. Further column design equations are given by LeGoff and Midoux [33].

A wealth of information exists in the literature on the theory, design and costs of plant-scale chromatography [24, 28, 32–35]. Although all of the published theories and designs are based on isothermal conditions, the successful scale-up of several processes [1, 12] implies that the temperature excursions, which are detrimental to separation, have been dealt with successfully. Such effects are negligible in laboratory-scale chromatography.

6.4   MOVING-BED AND SIMULATED MOVING-BED PROCESSES

An ideal moving-bed adsorption process can have several major advantages over both the cyclic fixed-bed and the chromatographic processes. In the cyclic fixed-

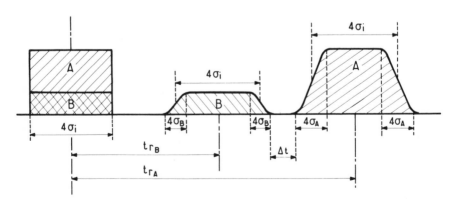

Figure 6.15 Resolution of two rectangular injections. Source: LeGoff and Midoux [33]. Reprinted with permission.

bed processes, the heavy (more strongly adsorbed) products vary continuously in composition and flowrate. This makes the integration of the cyclic process with downstream processing difficult. In the chromatographic process, the sorbent is not used efficiently. Certain parts of the bed at certain times are not performing a useful function. These deficiencies could be circumvented by a moving-bed process in which a continuous steady state is achieved by countercurrent fluid-solid contact. In addition, if a desorbent or carrier is used, the process would be similar to a chromatographic process. Thus a high separating power is achieved, which is equivalent to having a large number of separation stages.

Several recent reviews have been published on the early development and the present status of moving-bed processes [36–38]. Currently there are no moving-bed processes in commercial operation. The simulated moving-bed processes, under the general name of Sorbex, are restricted to liquids and apparently are not competitive with the pressure-swing adsorption process for gas-phase applications (e.g., for the separation of normal/iso-paraffins). In principle, however, the Sorbex process can be applied to gas-phase separations, where it can be competitive for difficult separations (with separation factors near unity) and situations suitable for process integration.

An exception is the Purasiv HR process, which is a combined fluidized-bed/moving-bed process [1]. The process utilizes an attrition-resistant carbon called bead activated carbon. Its main uses are for solvent removal from air, with large units in operation in the United States and Japan.

6.4.1   Hypersorption

The earliest attempt at commercialization of the moving-bed process has been Hypersorption. A comprehensive review of the process was given by Szirmay [39], and its details were discussed in a series of papers by Berg [40, 41; see also references in 41].

The earliest patent on the process was obtained by Soddy in 1922 [42]. The renaissance of Soddy's process came around 1946, when Berg, working for the Union Oil Company in California, published results on a moving charcoal bed and named the process Hypersorption [40]. Six large plants were built by Foster and Wheeler Corporation between 1947 and 1949 [39], with capacities ranging up to 16,000,000 SCF/day [41].

Continuous operation was achieved by the countercurrent contacting of an upflowing gas against a downflowing bed of activated carbon. Four applications were carried out in the plants [41]. A typical one was the recovery of ethylene from a cracked gas primarily containing H_2/CH_4. A schematic of the process is shown in Figure 6.16. The column represents a fractionating tower. A lift line outside the column recirculates the activated carbon pellets to the top. Inside the column the solid is transported downward as a suspension in the gas flow. An important aspect of the design is the temperature gradient imposed on the column. There are two heat-exchanger sections, a cooler at the top, and a heated stripper section at the

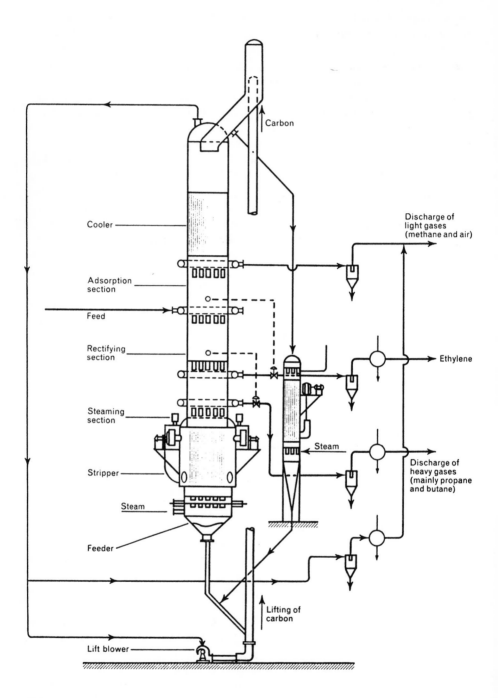

Figure 6.16 Schematic of the Hypersorption process. Source: Berg [41]. Reprinted with permission.

bottom. Dowtherm is used for heating. There are four trays between the cooler and the stripper. The feed is introduced through a distribution tray near the middle of the column; passes countercurrent to the moving carbon sorbent; and is disengaged as lean overhead product through a tray immediately below the cooling section, at the top of the column. The adsorbates are recovered as two streams: The disengaging tray immediately below the feed point releases the intermediate ethylene product, whereas the disengaging tray near the bottom of the column disengages the more strongly adsorbed propylene as well as the carrier steam. A number of heavy products can be taken below the feed point.

A typical Hypersorption tower, as designed in the early 1950s, was 4.5 feet in diameter and 85 feet tall. It was designed to process, typically, 1,800,000 SCF/day of feed gas at 75 psig pressure. The maximum carbon circulation rate in such a unit was about 32,000 lb/hr. The temperatures for the stripping section and cooling section were, respectively, 510°F and 410°F.

The Hypersorption column bears some resemblance to a temperature-programmed gas/solid chromatography, with steam being used as a carrier gas. However, the countercurrent operation has converted the transient concentration and temperature pulses of the chromatography into steady-state temperature and composition profiles in the column, which allows continuous and steady feed and products [37].

No data have been released on the operation of the six commercial Hypersorption plants built in the late 1940s. No information was released on their shutdown, nor have new plants since been announced. The major problem involved in Hypersorption is the handling of large amounts of solids, which causes the attrition, elutriation, and other difficult problems.

More recent attempts on rejuvenating the Hypersorption process include the proposals for separating ethane and ethylene by Szirmay [39, 43], and the separation of hydrogen and methane by the U.S. Bureau of Mines, now the Department of Energy [44, 45]. Both have used activated carbon and showed favorable cost analyses.

6.4.2   Simulated Moving-Bed Process: Sorbex

Sorbex is the general name for a family of processes all using the same mechanical device and the same principle [36–38]. Examples of Sorbex separations are: normal from branched and cycloparaffins (Molex process), olefins from olefin-paraffin mixtures (Olex), p-xylene from other C_8 hydrocarbons (Parex), p-diethylbenzene from mixed diethylbenzene isomers (p-DED), mixed C_8 aromatics (Ebex), and fructose from corn syrup (Sarex).

Sorbex employs a vertical fixed bed but simulates the continuous counter-current moving-bed operation. The ingenious design is based on the use of (1) a desorbent and (2) a rotary valve for switching and directing the flows. Thus Sorbex retains the advantages of continuous countercurrent operation while avoiding the problem of solid handling associated with moving beds.

A desorbent (*D*) must be used in Sorbex, which adsorbs approximately as strongly as the most strongly adsorbed component in the feed mixture but can easily be separated by distillation from the mixture components. Using the desorbent, the principle of Sorbex is illustrated by a moving bed in Figure 6.17. The feed here is a binary mixture of *A* and *B*. The order of the strengths for adsorption in this example is: $D > A > B$. The raffinate contains $B + D$, which is further separated by distillation to yield the *B* product. A portion of the raffinate stream is recycled to the top of the bed. Distillation of extract product $A + D$ yields the *A* product. The bed shown in Figure 6.17 is functionally divided into four zones. The primary function of zone I is to adsorb *A* from the mixture. In zone II, the major change is the displacement of *B* from the sorbent. By proper regulation of the fluid flow rate in zone II, *B* can be completely desorbed from the sorbent while *A* is not completely desorbed. The primary function of zone III is to desorb *A*, which is displaced by *D*. A portion of the fluid leaving the bottom of zone III is withdrawn as extract; the remainder flows downward into zone II to function as reflux. The purpose of zone VI is to reduce the required circulation rate of the fresh desorbent. This is desirable in order to reduce the load on the fractionators that separate the desorbent from products *A* and *B*. These functions are clearly illustrated by the composition profile in the bed, also shown in Figure 6.17. More detailed explanations of the actions taking place in the zones are available elsewhere [37].

All the aforementioned functions in the moving bed can be achieved in the design, shown in Figure 6.18 [46–48; patents granted to Universal Oil Products,

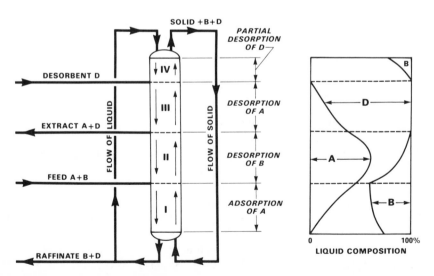

Figure 6.17   The principle of Sorbex. The composition profile is shown for the components following the order of adsorption strengths: $D > A > B$. Source: de Rosset, Neuzil, and Broughton [37]. Reprinted with permission.

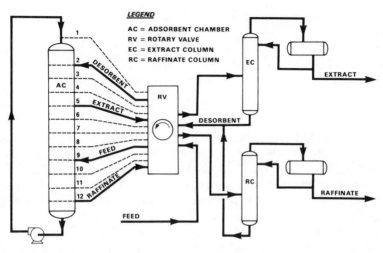

Figure 6.18 Sorbex: simulated moving bed for adsorptive separation. Source: de Rosset, Neuzil, and Broughton [37]. Reprinted with permission.

Inc.]. This design is equivalent to moving the two feed lines and two withdrawal lines continually around a stationary circular bed. The key to the Sorbex design is the use of the fluid-directing device, rotary valve. Through the rotary valve, the multiple access lines to the fixed bed are periodically switched and connected to the four lines shown on the right-hand face of the valve. At any particular moment only four of the access lines are open. Figure 6.18 shows the flows at the time when lines 2, 5, 9, and 12 are active. The lines are then switched to the adjacent positions. Functionally, the bed has no top or bottom. A more detailed explanation of the operation of the system, as well as a simplified mathematical model for the process, is available elsewhere [37].

Although Sorbex could in principle be used for gas- or vapor-phase separations, it has been limited to liquid-phase applications since its commercialization in 1963. The vapor-phase separation of *n*- and iso-paraffins is carried out by pressure-swing adsorption, which is also done by Molex for liquid-phase separation. Apparently, Sorbex is not yet competitive for gas-phase separations. As Sorbex is presently designed, axial dispersion could pose a problem in its application to vapor-phase separations.

6.5 PARAMETRIC PUMPING AND CYCLING ZONE ADSORPTION

These processes are briefly discussed here because of their theoretical importance as well as future possibilities for commercial application.

6.5.1   Thermal Parametric Pumping

Parametric pumping systems have been extensively studied since the original invention by Wilhelm around 1962 [54]. Comprehensive reviews on the theoretical and experimental results are available in the literature [49–53].

Direct Mode

As an introduction to parametric pumping, the batch, direct thermal mode system [55] will be considered, as shown in Figure 6.19. In this configuration, the fixed-bed sorbent is heated or cooled directly by the flowing media in the surrounding jacket. The mixture to be separated is moved cyclically up and down through the column by the reciprocating motion of the pistons at the two ends. At the same time as the flow direction changes, the column temperature is also changed. For example, Figure 6.19 shows that the flow upward passes a hot column, whereas the downward flow is through a cold column. By this cyclic process, the adsorbed component or solute is gradually concentrated in the top reservoir. This batch direct mode parametric pump produced separation factors exceeding 10^5 by cycling the temperature between 4°C and 70°C for a liquid mixture of toluene and heptane in a bed of silica gel [55]. (*Separation factor* is generally defined as the ratio between the concentration in the feed and that in the purified product. The separation factor referred to here is the ratio of the concentration in the top reservoir to that in the bottom reservoir.)

Recuperative Mode

The configuration shown in Figure 6.19 is called direct mode. However, it was the recuperative mode, shown in Figure 6.20, which was first studied [56]. This mode

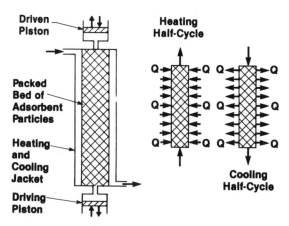

Figure 6.19 Batch, direct thermal mode parametric pumping. Source: Sweed [49]. Reprinted with permission.

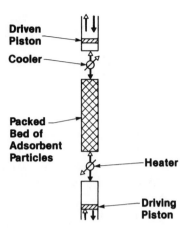

Figure 6.20 Batch, recuperative thermal mode parametric pumping. Source: Sweed [49]. Reprinted with permission.

differs from the direct mode in that the entering fluid outside the column is preheated and precooled. The recuperative thermal mode was studied extensively but with disappointing separation results because the volume of displacement per half-cycle was limited to a low range. High separation factors were obtained only years later when the volume of displacement was extended to a higher value [49]. The high separation factor achieved with the direct mode [55], in the meantime, stimulated intense interest and research in the following years. The research that followed in many different laboratories took several distinct paths: theoretical modeling, making the batch process continuous, extending to other binary and multicomponent mixtures, and using equilibrium variables other than temperature (such as pH). Nearly a hundred papers and dissertations on the subject of parametric pumping have been covered in the aforementioned reviews [49–53].

The theoretical models on parametric pumping fall into two categories. The first involves the numerical solution of the coupled mass balance equation, equilibrium isotherm, and a linear mass transfer rate equation [57]. The other one is the equilibrium-theory approach [58]. In both studies it is assumed that temperature is uniform and the flow velocity is constant. Furthermore, a linear isotherm must be assumed in the equilibrium theory so that analytic results on the separation factor can be derived using the method of characteristics.

A clear picture on the origin of the separation is given by the equilibrium theory of Pigford et al. [58], and was later extended by Aris [59]. The propagation velocity of the concentration front in the adsorber column is given by equation 5.5 in Chapter 5:

$$u_C = \left(\frac{\partial z}{\partial t}\right)_c = \frac{u}{1 + \frac{1-\varepsilon}{\varepsilon}\frac{dq^*}{dC}}$$

(6.13)

where u is the interstitial fluid velocity, ε is the bed porosity, and q^* is the equilibrium amount adsorbed which is given by the isotherm:

$$q^* = q^*(C) \tag{6.14}$$

Since for any isotherm,

$$\frac{dq^*}{dC}(\text{cold}) > \frac{dq^*}{dC}(\text{hot}) \tag{6.15}$$

because adsorption is stronger at lower temperatures, it follows:

$$u_C(\text{hot}) > u_C(\text{cold}) \tag{6.16}$$

As depicted in Figure 6.21, each cold-hot cycle results in an upward net movement of adsorbable solute toward the top of the column. In the limit of a large number of cycles, essentially all of the solute will be "pumped" from the lower to the top reservoir. When the temperature and flow direction changes are out of phase by 90° — that is, the switching times of the two differ by one-quarter of the total cycle time — a diagram similar to Figure 6.21 will show that there is no net movement during each cycle, and hence no separation [58].

Parametric pumping, both thermal and pH modes, has been studied primarily for separating liquid mixtures. The thermal mode has also been used with some success for separating gas mixtures, including the separation of propane/ethane on activated carbon [60], and of air/CO_2 on silica gel [61]. However, there are difficulties with the thermal mode for gas separation. In a constant-volume system, the gas pressure increases during the hot half-cycle, defeating the purpose of this half-cycle when desorption is intended.

No parametric pumping process has been commercialized. A promising parametric pumping process for gas separation has only recently been disclosed [62] and will be discussed separately.

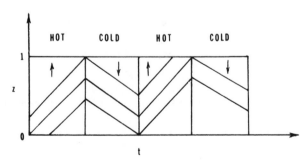

Figure 6.21 Schematic of paths in thermal parametric pumping, illustrating the origin of separation.

6.5.2 Pressure Parametric Pumping: Molecular Gate

This process or the equipment, referred to by Keller as "molecular gate" [63], is akin to the thermal parametric pump except that a cyclic pressure variation replaces the temperature variation [62]. A schematic of the equipment is shown in Figure 6.22. Simultaneous pressure and flow variations are effected by the two pistons at the ends of the bed. The two pistons (numbered 10 and 10′ in the figure), having the same diameter, are operated with different stroke lengths. If the stroke of the bottom piston is longer, and the two pistons are operated in phase, an upward flow is created in a high-pressure bed, while a lower pressure accompanies the downward flow. During downflow in the low-pressure column, the adsorbate desorbs and is carried downward. During upflow in the high-pressure column the same component is adsorbed, but at a lower position in the column than at the start of the previous cycle. Thus the strongly adsorbed component is concentrated toward the lower end while the less strongly adsorbed component moves upward. This is, however, a simplified picture of the process. The actual flow and pressure variations in the column (as well as temperature variations due to heats of adsorption and desorption) are far more complicated than the foregoing description.

The total bed volume in the experimental unit shown in Figure 6.22 is approximately 9 cubic inches [62]. The bed is packed with sorbent particles. The volume in each piston is up to 50 cubic inches, which is much larger than the bed voids. The valves (numbered 12 and 12′) are opened slightly to release a small fraction of the gas in each stroke. (From the data given in reference 62, less than 10% of the gas contained in the piston is released as the product.) A binary gas

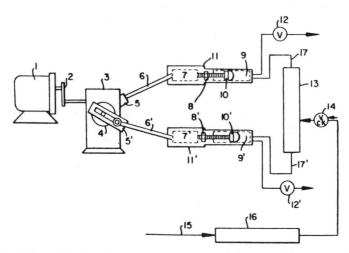

Figure 6.22 Schematic of molecular gate-pressure parametric pump. Source: Keller and Kuo [62].

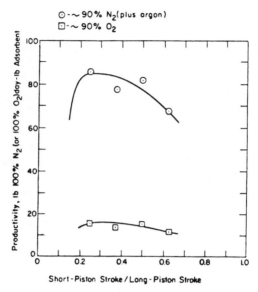

Figure 6.23 Separation of air with 13X zeolite by molecular gate. The effect of relative cyclic volume displacement on adsorption column productivity. Source: Keller and Kuo [62].

mixture is continually fed, at about 2 atm pressure, to the bed at a position indicated in Figure 6.22. Two high-purity products are released in the ends.

The experimental results [62] for separating air in a 13X zeolite bed are shown in Figure 6.23. The experimental details are shown in Table 6.1. The bed contained 93 grams of 13X zeolite. The diameters of the pistons were 4 inches. The separation results can be further improved when the two pistons are operated slightly out of phase. The best results for the air separation example were obtained at approximately 45°, as shown in Figure 6.24.

Table 6.1 Separation of Air by Zeolite 13X by Molecular Gate

Piston Stroke Length, in.		Flowrate, std. liters/hr			Product Purity, mol % O_2		Productivity, lb 100% Gas/lb Sorbent/Day	
Long	Short	Total	Long Piston	Short Piston	Long Piston	Short Piston	N_2	O_2
4	0	22.6	18.9	3.7	9.7	77.7	5.5	1.1
4	1.0	340.0	292.7	47.3	9.8	90.0	85.2	15.7
4	1.5	305.1	264.5	40.6	9.7	90.5	77.1	13.6
4	2.0	324.9	278.6	46.3	9.4	89.4	81.5	15.3
4	2.5	269.0	232.5	36.5	9.9	89.5	67.6	12.0

Source: Keller and Kuo [62].

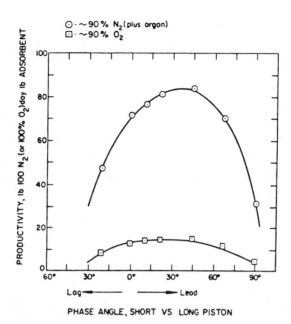

Figure 6.24 Separation of air by molecular gate. The effect of piston phase angle variations on adsorption column productivity. Source: Keller and Kuo [62].

The product purities can be increased at the expense of sorbent productivity, as shown in Table 6.2. The process has also been used to separate a 50/50 mixture of H_2/CH_4 using activated carbon [62]. The results are shown in Table 6.3.

This process is a promising one for small-scale binary gas separations where the recovery of both components is desired. High-purity products of both components can be simultaneously obtained. The commercial status of the process has not been reported.

Table 6.2 Separation of Air with 13X Zeolite by Molecular Gate

Flow Rate, std. liters/hr			Product Purity, %		Productivity, lb/lb Adsorbent-Day		Recovery, %	
Total	Long Piston	Short Piston	Long Piston N_2	Short Piston O_2	N_2	O_2	N_2	O_2
15.57	12.15	3.42	99.9	95.0	4.42	1.35	98.5	99.8
18.36	14.61	3.75	97.8	94.0	5.20	1.47	98.4	91.9
24.99	20.75	4.24	95.7	89.2	7.23	1.57	100.4	72.4
30.14	25.07	5.07	92.0	82.0	8.40	1.75	96.7	65.9
38.29	32.12	6.17	89.0	70.2	10.40	1.80	94.4	54.2

Source: Keller and Kuo [62].

Table 6.3   Separation of 50/50 Mixture of H_2/CH_4 with Activated Carbon by Molecular Gate

Flow Rate, std. liters/hr			Product Purity, %		Productivity, lb/lb Adsorbent-Day		Recovery, %	
Total	Long Piston	Short Piston	Long Piston CH_4	Short Piston H_2	CH_4	H_2	CH_4	H_2
15.01	7.26	7.75	100.0	99.0	2.44	0.33	96.7	100.2
21.28	10.51	10.77	98.0	96.1	3.46	0.44	96.8	97.4
28.54	14.24	14.30	94.1	92.2	4.51	0.56	93.9	92.4

Source: Keller and Kuo [62].

6.5.3   Thermal Cycling Zone Adsorption

Cycling-zone adsorption (CZA) is similar to parametric pumping except that in CZA the flow direction is steady and does not alternate. This process, invented by Pigford and co-workers [64, 65], is shown in Figure 6.25 in the single-zone version with temperature used as the cycling variable. As in parametric pumping, there are two modes of operation, direct and traveling-wave, shown in Figure 6.25. In the direct mode, heat is alternately supplied and removed through the walls. In the traveling-wave mode, the feed mixture is alternately heated or cooled before entering the column, analogous to the recuperative mode in parametric pumping. The product stream is collected separately during the two half-cycles. Thermodynamic parameters other than temperature, such as pH, have also been used as the cycling variables. The thermal and pH CZA processes are more suited for liquid-phase separations. For gas-phase separations, the pressure version of CZA appears

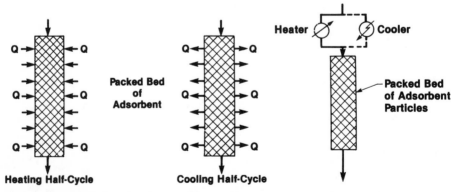

Figure 6.25   Thermal cycling-zone adsorber: direct (or standing-wave) mode (left), and traveling-wave mode (right). Source: Sweed [49]. Reprinted with permission.

to be more suitable. Modeling results of pressure CZA have been reported recently [66] and will be discussed separately following this section.

The number of studies carried out on CZA is relatively small, as compared to parametric pumping. The subject has been reviewed extensively by Wankat et al. [50, 67] and briefly by Sweed [49]. The studies on CZA have predominantly focused on liquids. Only a brief summary, with an emphasis on the origin of separation, will be given here.

The single-zone CZA process, shown in Figure 6.25, is identical to thermal-swing adsorption (TSA) with cocurrent regeneration using the feed gas as regenerant. Thus products rich and lean in the solute (adsorbate) are alternately obtained during, respectively, the hot and cold half-cycles. The novelty of the process, however, is in the use of a series of multiple zones (beds) to amplify the separation [64]. Figure 6.26 illustrates the direct mode CZA with four beds in a series. The temperature changes in adjacent beds are totally (180°) out of phase. A recuperative mode operation is also possible with heat exchangers placed at the inlet of each bed. Theoretically, based on equilibrium theory with a linear isotherm, an n-zone CZA process produces the same separation factor as parametric pumping after n cycles. The CZA process, however, has the advantage of not having to alternate the flow. The theoretical limit is not, in reality, reached as a result of the dispersive forces (heat and mass transfer resistances, dispersion) and nonlinear isotherm. The reason for the enhanced separation by multiple beds is illustrated in Figure 6.27 [50]. As shown in section 6.5.1 of this chapter (eq. 6.16), the

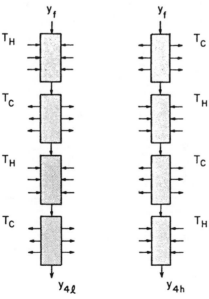

First half-cycle   Second half-cycle

Figure 6.26 Multiple-zone, directing heating (T_H) and cooling (T_C) operation of cycling-zone adsorber. Source: Pigford, Baker, and Blum [64]. Reprinted with permission.

concentration wave propagates faster in a hot bed than in a cold bed. By following lines AA', BB', and DD', in Figure 6.27, the solute fed to the first zone during time period AB exits the second zone during period $A'B'$. The effluent is diluted because period $A'B'$ is longer than period AB. Additional beds will further dilute the product exiting a cold bed. Likewise, the feed during period BD is concentrated into $B'D'$ from a hot bed. Quantitative descriptions of the process have been given by equilibrium [65, 68–70] and nonequilibrium theory [71].

Frey [73] proposed the use of layered beds of two sorbents that display opposite dependence of separation factor on temperature, resulting in sharpened wavefronts and separation.

The only study on gas mixture separation using thermal CZA with a multiple zone is by van der Vlist [72]. Air was separated by zeolite in two-bed direct thermal mode CZA, with temperature cycling between 10°C and 40°C. The separation was not effective, however, as the peak separation factor during each cycle was approximately 5.

6.5.4 Pressure Cycling Zone Adsorption

A pressure CZA process recently suggested by Platt and Lavie appears to be more efficient than thermal CZA in separating gas mixtures.

The process consists of n beds in series. The gas flow through the beds is controlled by a sequence of control valves, as shown in Figure 6.28. The gas mixture is fed into the high source pressure, P_{N+1}, at one end and discharged from the other end at low pressure, P_0. The pressure drop across each bed is assumed negligible; thus it is uniform in each bed.

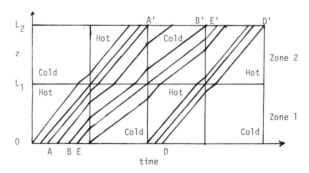

Figure 6.27 Constant-concentration lines in a two-zone direct mode CZA, showing the lines are diluted at the outlet (L_2) when zone 2 is cold and concentrated when heated. Source: Wankat [50]. Reprinted with permission.

Figure 6.28 A pressure cycling-zone adsorption process.

The pressure within each bed is varied continuously in a sine-wave fashion. The variation is generated by the programmed control valves. The pressure variation with time is given by the following equation for the kth bed:

$$P_k(t) = F_k + a_k \cos(k\pi - \omega t), \qquad k = 1, 2, \ldots, N \qquad (6.17)$$

Thus the pressure in the kth bed, P_k, oscillates at frequency ω with amplitude a_k around an average value, F_k. The pressure variation in the adjacent bed downstream lags in phase by 180°. Since the flow is never reversed, the following constraint applies:

$$F_k - a_k > F_{k-1} + a_{k-1}, \qquad k = 2, 3, \ldots, N \qquad (6.18)$$

Since two adjacent beds are run out of phase by 180°, the highest pressure in the downstream bed is reached when the pressure in the upstream bed reaches its minimum. Equation 6.18 simply indicates the constraint for a positive flow.

No experiments were conducted on this process. The separation of ethylene from a dilute (1%) ethylene/nitrogen mixture with activated carbon was studied using a theoretical model [66]. In the model, assumptions were made for instantaneous equilibrium, isothermality, and the linear isotherm. The model results for a single bed ($n = 1$) are shown in Figure 6.29. The highest separation factor, defined as high concentration/low concentration, is nearly 90. Calculations were also made for multiple beds, but the results were not as good as that with one bed, because of the constraint shown in equation 6.18. Also, the same total pressure

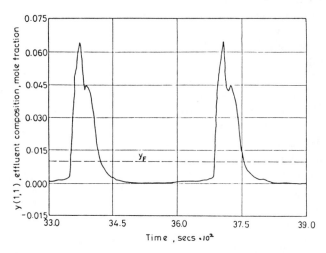

Figure 6.29 The theoretical effluent concentration of ethylene from a carbon bed in which the pressure is varied in a sine-wave: $P(t) = 20.26 + 18.23 \cos(\pi - 2t)$ bar. The bed is isothermal at 298K. The cycle time is approximately 300 seconds. Source: Platt and Lavie [66]. Reprinted with permission.

drop between the feed and discharge was used. With two beds, the maximum separation factor was approximately one-half of the value obtained with a single bed.

The process described in the foregoing may be considered a constrained pressure-swing adsorption (PSA) process. It is very similar to PSA except that there are more degrees of freedom to operate in PSA. As a result, the PSA is much more efficient in separation and is also simpler to operate because only stepped changes in pressure are required.

NOTATION

a	amplitude of oscillation
B	Langmuir constant
C	gas-phase concentration
C_0	feed concentration
C_p	heat capacity, with subscripts a, b, f, and s, respectively, denoting adsorbate, inert carrier gas, fluid phase, and solid phase
D_m	molecular diffusivity
D_z	axial dispersion coefficient
F	mean value of oscillation
G	superficial molar or mass flux
G_b	molar flux of the carrier gas
H	heat of adsorption
HETP	height equivalent to a theoretical plate
k	mass transfer coefficient
K	Henry's law constant; Langmuir constant
L	bed length
NETP	number of equivalent theoretical plates
P	total pressure
Pe	Peclet number $= 2R_p \mu / D_z \rho$
q	amount or equilibrium amount adsorbed
q^*	equilibrium amount adsorbed
R	resolution parameter
R_p	radius of pellet
t	time
t_R	resolution time
t_{st}	stoichiometric time = time for breakthrough assuming a square wave front
T	temperature
T_0	characteristic temperature, defined in equation 6.2
u	interstitial velocity
u_C	propagation velocity of concentration front
Y	mole fraction in the gas phase
z	axial distance in bed from the inlet

α	separation factor, defined by equation 6.11
ε	interpellet void fraction in fixed bed
μ	viscosity of gas
ρ	gas density
ρ_b	density of inert carrier gas
σ	band half-width
σ_i	one-quarter of the duration of a rectangular injection
τ	tortuosity factor, or dimensionless time $= t/t_{st}$
ω	pressure oscillation frequency

REFERENCES

1. G.E. Keller II, "Gas-Adsorption Processes: State of the Art," in *Industrial Gas Separations* (T.E. Whyte, Jr., C.M. Yon, and E.H. Wagener, eds.), ACS Symp. Ser. 223 (Washington, D.C.: American Chemical Society, 1983).
2. J.W. Carter, "The Adsorption Separation Process," in *Properties and Applications of Zeolites* (R.P. Townsend, ed.), Special Publ. No. 33 (London: Chemical Society, 1979).
3. C.W. Chi and W.P. Cummings, "Adsorptive Separation Processes: Gases," in *Kirk-Othmer Encyclopedia of Chemical Technology*, 3rd ed., Vol. 1 (New York: Wiley-Interscience, 1978).
4. C.Y. Pan and D. Basmadjian, *Chem. Eng. Sc.*, *25*, 1653 (1970).
5. D. Basmadjian, K.D. Ha, and C.Y. Pan, *Ind. Eng. Chem. Proc. Des. Dev.*, *14*, 328 (1975).
6. D. Basmadjian, K.D. Ha, and D.P. Proulx, *Ind. Eng. Chem. Proc. Des. Dev.*, *14*, 340 (1975).
7. J.W. Carter, *AIChE J.*, *21*, 380 (1975).
8. C.W. Chi, *AIChE Symp. Ser.*, *74*(No. 179), 42 (1978).
9. G. Bunke and D. Gelbin, *Chem. Eng. Sc.*, *33*, 101 (1978).
10. D. Gelbin, G. Bunke, H. Wolff, and J. Neinass, *Chem. Eng. Sc.*, *38*, 1993 (1983).
11. J. Chao, Ph.D. Thesis, University of New Brunswick, Fredericton, N.B., Canada (1981), results presented in reference 12.
12. D.M. Ruthven, *Principles of Adsorption and Adsorption Processes* (New York: Wiley, 1984).
13. T. Vermeulen, G. Klein, and N.K. Hiester, "Adsorption and Ion Exchange," in *Chemical Engineer's Handbook* (R.H. Perry and C.H. Chilton, eds.), 5th ed. (New York: McGraw-Hill, 1973), section 16.
14. J.J. Collins, *CEP Symp. Ser.*, *63*(No. 74), 31 (1967).
15. H. Lee and W.P. Cummings, *CEP Symp. Ser.*, *63*(No. 74), 42 (1967).
16. C.W. Chi and H. Lee, *AIChE Symp. Ser.*, *69*(No. 134), 96 (1973).
17. J.W. Carter, *Trans. Inst. Chem. Eng.*, *44*, T253 (1966).
18. J.W. Carter, *Trans. Inst. Chem. Eng.*, *46*, T213 (1968).
19. R.T. Yang and S.J. Doong, *AIChE J.*, *11*, 1829 (1985).
20. A. Anzelius, *Z. Angew. Math. Mech.*, *6*, 291 (1926).
21. R.G. Bonmati, G. Chapelet-Letourneux, and J.R. Margulis, *Chem. Eng.*, March 24, 70 (1980).
22. Anon., *Anal. Chem.*, *52*, 481A (1980).
23. J.R. Bernard, J.P. Gourlia, and M.J. Guttierrez, *Chem. Eng.*, May 18, 92 (1981).
24. P. Valentin, "Design and Optimization of Preparative Chromatographic Separations,"

in *Percolation Processes: Theory and Applications* (A.E. Rodrigues and D. Tondeur, eds.) (Rockville, Md.: Sijthoff and Noordhoff, 1981).

25. R.F. Baddour, U.S. Patent 3,250,058 (1966).
26. A.B. Carel and G. Perkins, Jr., *Anal. Chim. Acta., 34*, 83 (1966).
27. J.C. Giddings, *J. Gas Chrom., 1*(1), 12 (1963).
28. J.M. Ryan, R.S. Timmins, and J.F. O'Donnell, *Chem. Eng. Prog., 64*(8), 53 (1968).
29. M. Seko, T. Miyaki, and K. Inada, *Ind. Eng. Chem. Prod. Res. Dev., 18*, 263 (1979).
30. M. Seko, H. Takeuchi, and T. Inada, *Ind. Eng. Chem. Prod. Res. Dev., 21*, 656 (1982).
31. J.J. van Deemter, F.J. Zuiderweg, and A. Klinkenberg, *Chem. Eng. Sc., 5*, 271 (1956).
32. J. Villermaux, "Theory of Linear Chromatography," in *Percolation Processes: Theory and Applications* (A.E. Rodrigues and D. Tondeur, eds.) (Rockville, Md.: Sijthoff and Noordhoff, 1981).
33. P. LeGoff and N. Midoux, "Energy and Cost Optimization of Preparative Chromatography Columns," in Rodrigues and Tondeur, *Percolation Processes: Theory and Applications.*
34. J.R. Conder and J.H. Purnell, *CEP Symp. Ser., 65*(No. 91), 1 (1969).
35. J.R. Conder, "Production Scale Chromatography," in *New Developments in Gas Chromatography* (J. Purnell, ed.) (New York: Wiley, 1973).
36. D.B. Broughton and S.A. Gembicki, *AIChE Symp. Ser., 80*(No. 233), 62 (1984).
37. A.J. de Rosset, R.W. Neuzil, and D.B. Broughton, "Industrial Applications of Preparative Chromatography," in *Percolation Processes: Theory and Applications* (A.E. Rodrigues and D. Tondeur, eds.) (Rockville, Md.: Sijthoff and Noordhoff, 1981).
38. D.B. Broughton, "Adsorptive Separation Processes: Liquids," in *Kirk-Othmer Encyclopedia of Chemical Technology*, 3rd ed., Vol. 1 (New York: Wiley, 1978).
39. L.V. Szirmay, *AIChE Symp. Ser., 71*(No. 152), 104 (1975).
40. C. Berg, *Trans. Inst. Chem. Eng., 42*, 665 (1946).
41. C. Berg, *Chem. Eng. Prog., 47*(11), 585 (1951).
42. F.D. Soddy, U.S. Patent 1,422,007–008 (1922).
43. L.V. Szirmay, *AIChE Symp. Ser., 68*(No. 120), 110 (1972).
44. J.W. Mulvihill, W.P. Haynes, S. Katell, and G.B. Taylor, "Cost Estimates of Processes for Separating Mixtures of Methane and Hydrogen," Bu Mines Report of Investigation 6530, Dept. of Interior (1964).
45. J.W. Mulvihill, W.P. Haynes, R.J. Haren, and J.H. Field, *ACS Div. Fuel Chem. Preprints*, Vol. 10 (Washington, D.C.: American Chemical Society, 1965), p. 132.
46. D.B. Broughton and C.G. Gerhold, U.S. Patent 2,985,589 (1961).
47. D.B. Carson, U.S. Patent 3,040,777 (1962).
48. C.G. Gerhold and D.B. Broughton, U.S. Patent 3,192,954 (1965).
49. N.H. Sweed, *AIChE Symp. Ser., 80*(No. 233), 44 (1984).
50. P.C. Wankat, "Cyclic Separation Techniques," in *Percolation Processes: Theory and Applications* (A.E. Rodrigues and D. Tondeur, eds.) (Rockville, Md.: Sijthoff and Noordhoff, 1981).
51. H.T. Chen, "Parametric Pumping," in *Handbook of Separation Techniques for Chemical Engineers* (P.A. Schweitzer, ed.) (New York: McGraw-Hill, 1979).
52. R.G. Rice, *Sep. Purif. Methods, 5*, 139 (1976).
53. N.H. Sweed, *Progress in Separation Purification*, Vol. 4 (E.S. Perry and C.J. van Oss, eds.) (New York: Wiley-Interscience, 1971), p. 171.
54. N.H. Sweed and R.H. Wilhelm, *Ind. Eng. Chem. Fundam., 8*, 221 (1968).
55. R.H. Wilhelm and N.H. Sweed, *Science, 159*, 522 (1968).
56. R.H. Wilhelm, A.W. Rice, and A.R. Bendelius, *Ind. Eng. Chem. Fundam., 5*, 141 (1966).

57. R.H. Wilhelm, A.W. Rice, R.W. Rolke, and N.H. Sweed, *Ind. Eng. Chem. Fundam.*, 7, 337 (1968).
58. R.L. Pigford, B. Baker III, and D.E. Blum, *Ind. Eng. Chem. Fundam.*, 8, 144 (1969).
59. R. Aris, *Ind. Eng. Chem. Fundam.*, 8, 603 (1969).
60. T.J. Jencziewski and A.L. Myers, *Ind. Eng. Chem. Fundam.*, 9, 316 (1970).
61. R.R. Patrick, J.T. Schrodt, and K.J. Kermode, *Sep. Sc.*, 7, 331 (1972).
62. G.E. Keller II and C.H.A. Kuo, U.S. Patent 4,354,859 (1982).
63. G.E. Keller II, private communication (1984).
64. R.L. Pigford, B. Baker III, and D.E. Blum, *Ind. Eng. Chem. Fundam.*, 8, 848 (1969).
65. B. Baker III and R.L. Pigford, *Ind. Eng. Chem. Fundam.*, 10, 283 (1971).
66. D. Platt and R. Lavie, *Chem. Eng. Sc.*, 40, 733 (1985).
67. P.C. Wankat, J.C. Dore, and W.C. Nelson, *Separat. Purif. Methods*, 4, 215 (1975).
68. R. Gupta and N.H. Sweed, *Ind. Eng. Chem. Fundam.*, 10, 280 (1971).
69. D. Meir and R. Lavie, *Chem. Eng. Sc.*, 29, 113 (1974).
70. W.C. Nelson, D.F. Silarski, and P.C. Wankat, *Ind. Eng. Chem. Fundam.*, 17, 32 (1978).
71. K.S. Knaebel and R.L. Pigford, *Ind. Eng. Chem. Fundam.*, 22, 336 (1983).
72. E. van der Vlist, *Separat. Sc.*, 6, 727 (1971).
73. D.D. Frey, *Separat. Sc. Tech.*, 17, 1485 (1983).

CHAPTER 7

Pressure-Swing Adsorption: Principles and Processes

The cryogenic separation of air involves liquefaction followed by distillation. Because of the complexity of the process, a very large production scale is required for it to be economical. The finding that nitrogen (as a result of its higher quadruple moment) is preferentially adsorbed over oxygen on zeolites by Barrer [1, 2], and the successful development of synthetic zeolites [3, 4] stimulated the search for a method to separate air by adsorption in the 1950s and 1960s.

The original idea of using pressure swing to separate air was disclosed in a patent by Skarstrom [5] and independently, in a different version, by Guerin de Montgareuil and Domine [6], both filed in 1958. (The French patent by the latter, No. 1,223,261, was actually filed in 1957.) The basic difference between the two is that in the Skarstrom cycle the saturated bed is purged at a low pressure by a fraction of the light product, whereas in the Guerin-Domine cycle, vacuum desorption is used. These pressure-swing cycles, however, only yielded modest separations of oxygen and nitrogen [5, 6] due to the low separation factor between the two gases, which is approximately between 2 and 3 on zeolites. Meanwhile, Skarstrom found a very high efficiency in air drying by his cycle [5].

Thus, without major modification, the Skarstrom PSA cycle was immediately accepted for commercial use in air drying as well as other purification processes [7]. The PSA process is at least as efficient and perhaps more so than the TSA process for drying of air and industrial gases [7]. No data are available on the relative market share that these two processes possess. However, it was estimated in 1979 that one-half of the air driers were of the Skarstrom type [66]. Unlike air drying, the product recovery also has importance, as does product purity in other purification processes, such as hydrogen purification and the removal of normal paraffins. Many process improvements have subsequently been developed based on the Skarstrom cycle, which enable the rapidly growing commercial use of PSA for hydrogen purification, hydrogen production, n-paraffin separation, air separation, and an increasing number of other applications.

7.1 BASIC CONCEPTS AND DEVELOPMENTS

A multitude of sophisticated PSA processes and designs have been implemented for various separations. However, there are not many basic ideas on which these designs are made. These ideas can be combined and synthesized, with minor modifications, to accomplish the desired separations.

To facilitate the discussions that follow, some terminologies will first be defined. The performance of the separation process is measured by three parameters: (1) *product purity*, (2) *product recovery*, and (3) *adsorbent productivity*. If more than one of the constituents are to be recovered, (1) and (2) apply to all products. The product purity is a volume-averaged quantity since the effluent concentration and flowrate from a PSA process, without the use of surge or mixing tanks, vary with time. Product recovery measures the amount of component that is contained in the product stream divided by the amount of the same component in the feed mixture. Adsorbent productivity is measured by the amount of product or feed mixture processed per unit amount of sorbent per unit time. For a given separation, the product purity is predetermined, the energy requirement is usually proportional to the recovery, and the size of the sorbent bed is inversely proportional to the sorbent productivity. It is important to bear in mind that these three parameters are interrelated for any given PSA process, and the interrelationship can only be determined through a model for the process. In addition to these parameters, the term *strong adsorptive* will be used to refer to the strongly adsorbable gas, whereas weak adsorptive will be used for the weakly adsorbable gas. The product mostly containing the weak adsorptive may also be called loosely *light product* or *raffinate*, the latter in analogy to liquid-liquid extraction.

The major developments contributing to the commercial PSA processes are listed next.

7.1.1 Skarstrom Cycle and Guerin-Domine Cycle

The Skarstrom cycle, originally referred to as *heatless adsorption*, uses a two-bed apparatus as shown in Figure 7.1. The original patent, filed in 1958, was assigned to Esso Research and Engineering Company [5]. After the adsorption step, the first bed is depressurized to atmospheric pressure. At the same time the compressed feed mixture is switched to the second bed to repressurize it. It then starts the adsorption step at the feed pressure. A fraction of the purified effluent from the second bed is passed through the first bed, countercurrent to the feed direction, to purge the bed at atmospheric pressure. After the purge, the unit is ready for the next cycle. Thus each bed undergoes two half-cycles, the times of which are equal. For a purification process, steady and continuous flows of both feed and purified product are achieved.

For air drying, an interesting experiment was performed by Skarstrom to give "proof that a real drying process is involved" [5, 7]. Two beds containing Mobil beads (silica gel pellets) were saturated by a wet air with 3,800 ppm water vapor.

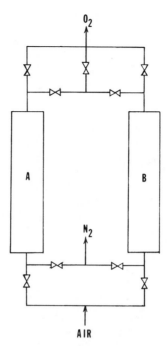

Figure 7.1   The Skarstrom cycle. Two steps are involved in the cycle for each bed: (1) repressurization followed by feed in *A*, while O_2 is withdrawn, and (2) blowdown and purge with O_2 (both downward) of *A* while N_2 is withdrawn. The functions of *A* and *B* are reversed in the next cycle. Note that this is not used commercially for air separation.

With the wet air feed, the PSA process was turned on. The effluent product from the adsorption step steadily declined while the low-pressure regeneration half-cycle gradually dried out the beds. The results are shown in Figure 7.2. From the flow data shown in the figure, one-half of the dried air was used as the purge gas in reaching the desired product purity of 1 ppm.

Two useful ideas were also described by Skarstrom in his invention. First, short cycles and low throughput per cycle should be maintained in order to "conserve the heat of adsorption." This idea was derived from the observation that long cycles and high throughputs would result in hot beds during adsorption and cold beds during regeneration, both detrimental to separation. The other idea was that the volume of both purge and feed, at their respective pressures, should be at least equal to ensure complete purge, or displacement, during regeneration. These two basic ideas have been found to be very useful in later developments.

The Skarstrom cycle has been widely used for air drying. For oxygen production from air, however, the oxygen recovery was too low and hence the energy requirement too high to be economical.

The Guerin-Domine patent [6], filed about the same time as Skarstrom's patent, was assigned to L'Air Liquide. The cycle is a versatile one. Depending on the nature of the mixture to be separated, it can vary in the number of beds, the

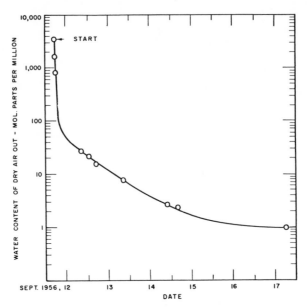

Figure 7.2 Performance of the Skarstrom cycle with two initially wet beds. Sorbent: Mobil beads (silica gel) desiccant, 1 lb each bed. Cycle time: 3 min each half-cycle. Flows: feed = 1 SCFM at 40 psig and 3,800 ppm H_2O; dried air = 0.5 SCFM at 40 psig. Source: Skarstrom [5]. Reprinted with permission.

interconnections, and the scheme of operation. Designs of one to six beds have been proposed [6]. A two-bed version is shown in Figure 7.3. As shown in the figure, each bed goes through three steps: pressurization (with only the feed end open), depressurization through the other bed(s), both in a cocurrent direction with the feed when oxygen is formed, and evacuation from the midpoint of the bed when nitrogen is withdrawn.

Using 5A zeolite in the Guerin-Domine cycle, excellent results were obtained (considering it was about three decades ago) on air separation [6]. The separation results with a two-bed system shown in Figure 7.3 and a source pressure of 2.6 atm were: 98% O_2 (argon-free basis) purity at 51% recovery and 96.3% N_2 at 58% recovery. These results were substantially better than Skarstrom's in both product purities and recoveries. Because of the low adsorption selectivity between O_2 and N_2, a good separation was obtained with this cycle by the use of the evacuation step (0.5 to 1 Torr) to desorb the bed, and the use of an additional clean bed to elute O_2. The short cycle time of operation apparently helped keep the temperature from excessive fluctuation.

With improvements in the cycle, a vacuum-swing adsorption process has been successfully commercialized by Air Products since the late 1970s for simultaneous nitrogen/oxygen generation, as will be discussed.

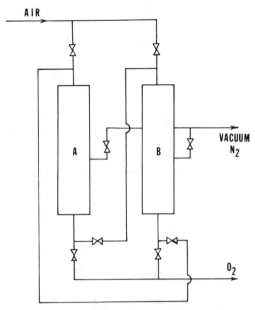

Figure 7.3 The Guerin-Domine cycle. Three steps are involved in the cycle for each bed: (1) pressurization of *A* with air (while *B* is being evacuated), (2) blowdown of *A* through *B* (both downward) to collect O_2, and (3) evacuation of *A*. The functions of *A* and *B* are reversed in the next cycle.

7.1.2 Cocurrent Depressurization

The first major process improvement after the invention of the Skarstrom and the Guerin-Domine cycles was the introduction of the cocurrent depressurization step. To incorporate this step into the Skarstrom cycle, the adsorption step is cut short well before the break point; that is, the concentration front is far from reaching the outlet of the bed. The adsorption step is immediately followed by cocurrent depressurization before the bed is desorbed by further blowdown and purge, as required in the Skarstrom cycle.

The large void space in the adsorber plays a limiting role in the recovery of the strong adsorptive. The void fraction ranges from approximately 67% for silica and alumina to 74% for zeolites and 78% for activated carbon. The composition of the gas contained in the voids in the saturated bed is the same as the feed mixture. At the feed pressure, the amount of gas in the voids can be equal to or greater than the amount adsorbed on the sorbent surface. The total concentration of the strong adsorptive in the bed (in the voids plus the adsorbate) is not high. This is the gas that is desorbed under the best regeneration conditions in the Skarstrom and Guerin-Domine cycles. The major function of the cocurrent depressurization step is to increase the concentration of the strong adsorptive in the bed. This is done by lowering the pressure in the voids which enhances the concentration of the strong adsorptive in both phases.

The net result of the incorporation of the cocurrent depressurization (CD) step in the Skarstrom cycle is the product purity enhancement of the strong adsorptive, which in turn increases the product recovery of the weak adsorptive.

The CD step was first used by Union Carbide in the IsoSiv process in a Texas PSA plant in 1961 [8–10]. The process, shown in Figure 7.4, separated 1,000 barrels per day of "natural gasoline" feed into *n*-paraffins and branched/cyclic hydrocarbons. The feed contained 54.4% *n*-paraffins and 45.6% branched/cyclic hydrocarbons [53]. The *n*-paraffin (strong adsorptive) product purity was 95–98%, whereas the purity of the "isomer" was 98–99% [53]. Additional and larger IsoSiv plants have been built since 1961.

The CD step was mentioned, as a part of more complex PSA processes, in several patents that were all filed later than its first commercial practice in 1961 [11, 12].

The function of the CD step has been explained in detail [13, 14], as shown in Figures 7.5 and 7.6. Figure 7.5 reveals that the strong adsorptive, carbon monoxide, desorbs in order to increase the gas-phase concentration during CD. The desorbed CO is further readsorbed downstream. Both actions increase the amount of CO in the bed. The total amount of CO in the bed, relative

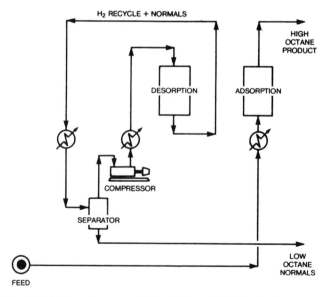

Figure 7.4 Simplified flow diagram of the Union Carbide IsoSiv process. The cycle sequence is:

Step 1: Adsorption (bed 1)
         Cocurrent depressurization + vacuum desorption + repressurization (bed 2).

Step 2: Reverse beds 1 and 2.

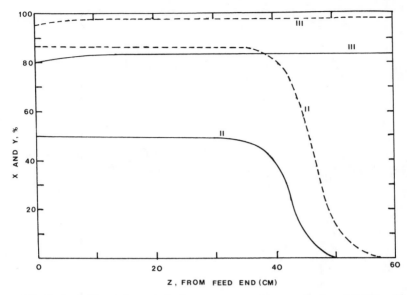

Figure 7.5 Bed profiles before and after cocurrent depressurization (CD) for H_2/CO (50/50) separation with activated carbon. Gas-phase mole fraction in voids (solid curve) at the end of adsorption (II) and end of CD (III). Dashed lines are for adsorbed phase. Adsorption pressure = 35 atm. End pressure of CD = 9.2 atm. Source: Cen and Yang [14]. Reprinted with permission.

to that of hydrogen, is shown in Figure 7.6. Thus the function of the CD step is to shift the product concentration of the strong adsorptive from approximately 80% to 95%. The product recovery of H_2 is also increased, as a result of the higher CO product purity.

7.1.3   Pressure Equalization

The term *pressure equalization* (PE) refers to the action by which the pressures in two interconnected beds are equalized. The main purpose of the PE step is to conserve the mechanical energy that is contained in the gas of the high-pressure bed. With the PE steps, the pressure in a regenerated bed is increased in a sequence of steps by the gases admitted from other beds, which are in various stages of depressurization. The energy reduction, as well as other improvements resulting from the PE steps (to be discussed later in this section), made large-scale PSA separations economically feasible.

The idea of pressure equalization was first suggested in a patent granted to Marsh et al. in 1964 [15]. The process described in the patent required an empty tank in addition to the two beds in the Skarstrom cycle. The tank was used to store a portion of the compressed gas from a saturated bed, and the gas was used to purge the same bed later. The primary objective was to recover the components

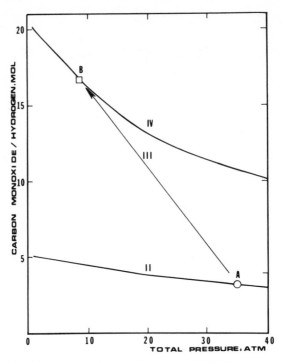

Figure 7.6 Total bed loading analysis. The ratio of CO/H_2 remaining in bed before cocurrent depressurization (*A*) and after CD (*B*). Points *A* and *B* set the limits for the concentration of the strong adsorptive product. Source: Cen and Yang [14]. Reprinted with permission.

contained in the compressed gas. The pressure equalization step, as it is currently used in commercial processes, was disclosed in the patents to Berlin [16] and Wagner [12]. Four- to five-bed arrangements were given in the Wagner patent. Figures 7.7 and 7.8 show the four-bed process and its cycle sequence, respectively. No empty tanks are required in this process. This process arrangement is ideally suited for purification processes. As shown in Figure 7.7, each bed undergoes the four steps in the sequence: A, C, B, and D. The four steps are:

A: High-pressure adsorption, with a portion of the product used to repressurize D

C: Cocurrent depressurization and equalizing the pressure with D, followed by further depressurization with the effluent used to purge B

B: Countercurrent blowdown and purge

D: Repressurization by two equalization steps

   Besides energy conservation and increased product recovery, the flow of the strong adsorptive product is "smoothed" by the pressure equalization steps. The four-bed process has been subsequently developed into the Polybed process,

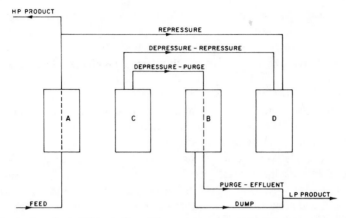

Figure 7.7 A four-bed PSA cycle with two pressure-equalization steps, marked as "repressure" and "depressure-repressure." Source: Doshi, Katira, and Stewart [17]. Reprinted with permission.

VESSEL
NUMBER

1	ADSORPTION		EQ1 ▲	C D ▲	EQ2 ▲	C D ▼	PURGE ▼	EQ2 ▼	EQ1 ▼	R ▼							
2	C D ▼	PURGE ▼	EQ2 ▼	EQ1 ▼	R ▼	ADSORPTION			EQ1 ▲	C D ▲	EQ2 ▲						
3	EQ1 ▲	C D ▲	EQ2 ▲	C D ▼	PURGE ▼	EQ2 ▼	EQ1 ▼	R ▼	ADSORPTION								
4	EQ1 ▼	R ▼	ADSORPTION		EQ1 ▲	C D ▲	EQ2 ▲	C D ▼	PURGE ▼	EQ2 ▼							

EQ - EQUALIZATION   ▲——— COCURRENT FLOW
C D ▲ - COCURRENT DEPRESSURIZATION   ▼— COUNTERCURRENT FLOW
C D ▼ - COUNTERCURRENT DEPRESSURIZATION
R - REPRESSURIZATION

Figure 7.8 Cycle sequence chart of the four-bed PSA process. Source: Cassidy and Holmes [8]. Reprinted with permission.

consisting of nine to ten beds, which is successfully used for large-scale production of high-purity hydrogen.

7.1.4 Pretreatment Beds

Water vapor and carbon dioxide, both very strongly adsorbed on zeolites, created a major problem in the separations of air as well as other mixtures when zeolites were used. These gases are not easily desorbed and hence tend to accumulate in the bed, leading to a stoppage in operation. The problem can be solved by using a separate pretreatment bed outside the PSA system, which must be regenerated separately from the PSA. For process simplicity, it is desirable to include the pretreatment bed(s) within the PSA system so the integrated system can be regenerated as a whole.

The idea of integrating the pretreatment beds into the PSA system was first suggested by Heinze [18], as shown in Figure 7.9. The Heinze process is essentially identical to the Guerin-Domine cycle with the exception of the added pretreatment beds. Heinze's process was slightly improved by Tamura [19], mainly by allowing a flow in the adsorption step. The sorbent in the pretreatment bed should be different from that in the main bed since a relatively inefficient sorbent is used in the former, unlike the efficient sorbent used in the main bed. Although both of the afore-mentioned processes were commercialized for oxygen production [20], a more efficient process was later developed by Sircar and Zondlo [21]. In the latter process, a desiccant such as silica gel or alumina is placed in the pretreatment bed, while the main bed contains a zeolite. By this arrangement, water vapor and carbon dioxide are adsorbed in the pretreatment beds, which are easily regenerated along with the main beds by pressure swing. An additional advantage of using small pretreatment beds is that the temperature fluctuations in the smaller beds are less severe.

The idea of integrating the pretreatment beds in PSA has also been used in hydrogen purification, in which an inefficient sorbent in the pretreatment beds adsorbs pentane and heavier compounds, whereas the main beds adsorb methane, ethane, and propane [22]. This idea should be useful in many multicomponent separations.

The pretreatment bed can be combined with the main bed; that is, two sorbents are packed in the same bed with the desiccant (alumina or silica gel)

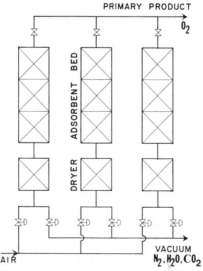

Figure 7.9 The integration of pretreatment beds in the PSA system for process simplifi-cation. The main beds contain zeolites, whereas the pretreatment beds contain a desiccant for easy regeneration.

placed near the feed end followed by the zeolite bed. This arrangement is widely used in the production of oxygen from air [66], as well as other separations.

7.1.5 Purge by Strong Adsorptive

As discussed in section 7.1.2, the feed gas stored in the void space of the saturated bed severely limits the separation performance, especially for the product purity of the strong adsorptive. The cocurrent depressurization step can improve the separation. An illustrative example was given for the separation of a 50/50 hydrogen/methane mixture on activated carbon [23]. Using the Skarstrom cycle, the highest product purities were approximately 99% for hydrogen and 80% for methane. With the addition of the cocurrent depressurization step in the cycle, the methane product purity was increased to approximately 90%. A more drastic modification of the cycle must be made in order to increase further the methane product purity.

A more effective method is to purge out the void spaces, after adsorption, by using the strong adsorptive gas. The idea was first suggested in a patent to Tamura [24]. In this cycle, a high-pressure purge step in which the strong adsorptive gas is used follows the high-pressure adsorption step in the Skarstrom cycle. The purge is conducted cocurrent to the feed direction.

For the example of hydrogen/methane separation, product purities over 99% can be simultaneously achieved for both products by using a methane purge step in the Skarstrom cycle [25]. A comparison of the separation performance of two PSA cycles, one with cocurrent depressurization and the other using methane purge, is given in Table 7.1.

There are two concentration wavefronts during cocurrent purge by the strong adsorptive: a zone filled with the pure strong adsorptive near the feed end, and a

Table 7.1 Comparison of Separation of a 50/50 H_2/CH_4 Mixture with Activated Carbon Using Two PSA Cycles

	A^a	B^b
H_2 product purity, %	97.8	99.3
Recovery, %	90.0	94.9
CH_4 product purity, %	90.0	98.0
Recovery, %	89.8	86.0
P_{HI}/P_{LO} (psig)^c	120/35	200/33
Sorbent productivity, lSTP/min/kg	6.5	6.5

[a]Repressurization — adsorption — cocurrent depressurization — countercurrent blowdown and purge. Source: Yang and Doong [23].
[b]Repressurization — adsorption — CH_4 purge — countercurrent blowdown and purge. Source: Cen and Yang [25].
[c]The effect of pressure ratio on separation is not significant in the range of this comparison.

displaced zone, which was the zone saturated with the feed mixture prior to purge. Owing to the favored isotherm of the strong adsorptive, the two wavefronts are both the self-sharpening type, which results in good separation.

A disadvantage of this PSA cycle is that compression is required for the strong adsorptive gas, which is available from the PSA process at a low pressure. There is, however, room for optimization between the cocurrent depressurization and strong adsorptive purge steps. An optimal operation should exist in which the purge is performed after some cocurrent depressurization. During cocurrent depressurization, the weak adsorptive is eluted from the saturated zone [13, 23], and the bed is enriched in the strong adsorptive. With the CD step, more important, the bed pressure is reduced and hence the energy requirement for compressing the purge gas is lowered. Apparently such a combination of these two steps has not been used.

Tamura's process was aimed at recovering high-purity nitrogen (which is the strong adsorptive on zeolites) from air [24]. Not until recently was this process commercialized by Toray Industries, Inc., as shown in Figure 7.10 [9, 26]. The nitrogen purge step is also used in the so-called vacuum-swing process [21]. The strong adsorptive purge step can also be used to increase the purity of a certain component in a multicomponent separation, by purge with the same component [27]. This component is not necessarily the strongest adsorptive in the mixture.

7.1.6   Temperature Equalization and Other Developments

Local temperature fluctuations in the bed due to the exothermic heat of adsorption and the endothermic heat of desorption have been recognized from the beginning

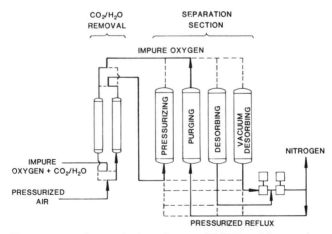

Figure 7.10   Toray process for producing nitrogen (99.9%) and low-purity oxygen (33%) with zeolite beds by using a high-pressure nitrogen purge step in the cycle. Source: Keller [9]. Reprinted with permission.

of PSA development [7]. The local temperature rise during adsorption and local temperature drop during desorption are both detrimental to the separation process. The best separation is accomplished when the beds are operated under nearly isothermal conditions. A nearly isothermal operation can be realized with short cycles and low throughput per cycle. The smallest temperature fluctuation in commercial PSA processes is observed in air drying, where the fluctuation in a PSA cycle is less than 10°C [28]. The problem becomes worse for bulk separation — separation of concentrated mixtures — because of the large amount of adsorptive that must be processed by the bed. Furthermore, a truly adiabatic operation is approached in large beds, resulting in the largest possible temperature fluctuation.

Several methods have been suggested to achieve a nearly isothermal operation and thereby improve the separation. Extremely short cycles are used in the commercially successful process for small-scale oxygen generation using a single bed of zeolites [29–31]. Short cycles are not feasible for a multibed process with Skarstrom-type cycles. The single-bed process was originally suggested by Kadlec and co-workers [32, 33] for bulk separation. The difference between the processes used by the two groups, as well as the details of the single-bed process,

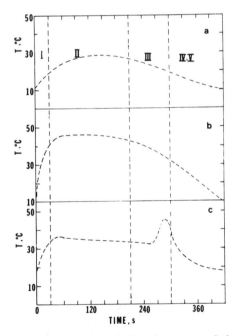

Figure 7.11 Experimental temperature variations in space and time in a carbon bed for H_2/CH_4 (50/50) separation. The letters *a*, *b*, and *c* indicate upper, middle, and lower positions in the bed with downward feed. The seven-minute cycle consists of: pressurization, adsorption, cocurrent depressurization, and countercurrent blowdown plus purge (divided by the vertical lines). Source: Yang and Doong [23]. Reprinted with permission.

Table 7.2 Cyclic Steady-State PSA Separations of 50/50 H_2/CH_4 with Iron Particle Additives (weight-percent) in Carbon Beds

Step[a]	% Additive	Adiabatic 0	Adiabatic 5	Adiabatic 10	Adiabatic 20	Isothermal 0
I	Input H_2, 1[b]	9.27	10.16	11.04	12.52	13.82
II	Output, 1	22.29	22.27	22.26	22.32	21.76
	H_2, %	99.68	99.64	99.64	99.72	99.98
III	Output, 1	9.86	9.45	8.87	8.10	9.21
	H_2, %	51.62	62.49	75.57	97.44	99.90
IV + V	Output, 1	13.38	14.73	16.17	18.29	19.03
	CH_4, %	92.96	93.30	93.63	93.34	89.21
	H_2 Recovery, %	95.04	94.78	94.54	93.54	94.08
	CH_4 Recovery, %	71.98	79.13	87.09	98.44	99.75

Source: Yang and Cen [34]. Reprinted with permission.
[a] Cycle steps: Pressurization (I), adsorption (II), cocurrent depressurization (III), countercurrent blowdown (IV), and purge (V).
[b] All volumes are at STP. Amount of carbon = 420 g.

will be given later in the chapter. Both groups used cycles of less than 30 seconds. With the short time, a nearly isothermal condition is achieved.

In a Skarstrom-type cycle, the temperature varies with time as well as position in the bed. An example for the temperature variations is given in Figure 7.11 for the separation of a 50/50 mixture of H_2/CH_4 with activated carbon. As shown in Table 7.2, the separation is substantially better for the isothermal condition than for the adiabatic condition. All data shown in this table are simulations by a model that has been verified against experimental data under widely varying conditions [13, 14]. The table also shows that iron particle additives can improve the separation. The purpose of using an inert (nonadsorbent) additive with a high heat capacity, such as iron, is to increase the heat capacity of the bed, thereby smoothing the temperature variations. An optimal amount for the inerts should be determined since the bed size will be increased by the additives. The sorbent productivity, however, is not decreased by the inerts.

For bulk PSA separations in industrial-scale beds, nearly constant temperature profiles that do not vary much with time have been observed [35, 36]. Such profiles were measured in air separation where multibeds of 5A zeolite underwent

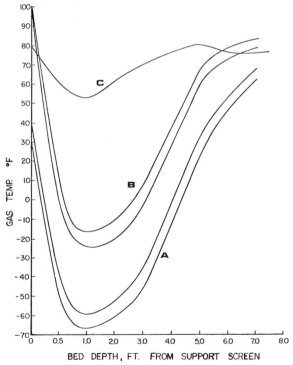

Figure 7.12 Temperature profiles in an industrial-scale zeolite bed for PSA air separation. The temperature depression near the feed end is caused by the depressurization steps and purge. (*A*) feed air at 30 and 40°F; (*B*) feed preheated to 100°F; (*C*) with heating elements inserted in the beds near the inlet. Source: Collins [36].

the same PSA cycle steps as described in Table 7.2. The beds were 2 feet in diameter and 8 feet high, and the cycle time was 2 minutes. With the feed air at 30° and 40°F, the steady-state temperature profiles are shown in Figure 7.12. The "permanent" temperature depression near the feed end was caused mainly by the countercurrent blowdown step. Apparently, the poor thermal conductivity also contributed to the local cooling. The large temperature depression of nearly 100°F severely limited the separation. Preheating the feed did not eliminate the large depression (curves B in the figure). Collins suggested the use of heaters inserted inside the beds [36], with the resulting temperature shown as curve C in Figure 7.12. By this measure, both oxygen purity and recovery were substantially enhanced. In the same figure, for curve A, the O_2 product purity was 66% at 26.7% recovery; for B, O_2 was 88% at 29.3% recovery; and for C, O_2 was 93.4% purity at 31% recovery [36]. The use of an inert additive with high heat capacity as well as high conductivity should also alleviate the aforementioned problem.

Many other innovative ideas on PSA have been suggested, a large number of them being obscured in the patent literature. A few of them will be discussed here.

To obtain a high-purity light product, the beds are repressurized by the same light product. The repressurization step thus requires a large amount of light product gas, which consequently lowers the product recovery. Repressurization by the feed mixture, on the other hand, will lower the product purity of the light product. A compromise measure between the two was suggested by Batta [37]. A bed in the PSA system is first partially repressurized to an intermediate pressure by a simultaneous introduction of compressed feed mixture from the inlet end, and a portion of the high-pressure light product from the discharge end. The light product is drawn from another bed in the system. The introduction of the light product is then stopped while the feed mixture continues to pressurize the bed to the operating pressure. By this operation, the zone near the outlet end of the bed is kept clean, and a high-purity product is still obtained. Meanwhile, the consumption of the light product in repressurization is minimized. The Lindox process is based on Batta's process using a three-bed system. A large number of plants have been built for generating 90% oxygen [38].

The sharpness of the concentration wavefront is the most important factor in the separation. The fronts are usually not sharp because of the dispersive forces (Chapter 5). A technique to increase the sharpness of the fronts has been suggested by McCombs [39]. The cycle starts with a partially repressurized bed. The feed mixture is then introduced to the bed at rates such that the bed pressure continually increases. This is done by restricting the discharge flowrate. Improved separations of air have been achieved by this technique [39]. If, however, a cocurrent depressurization step follows the feed step, the sharpened front will be destroyed. Therefore, McCombs's technique could ideally be combined with the step described in section 7.1.5. A high-pressure, cocurrent purge with the strong adsorptive will conserve the sharp wavefront and hence result in a high purity for both products.

It is well known that mixed sorbents are used in industry. The purpose of using mixed sorbents in the same bed is to achieve the combined results of the sorbents' different affinities toward different gases. Mixed sorbents, either in separate columns or in the same column, are also widely used in chromatography and ion exchange [40, 41]. In hydrogen purification [22] and the so-called vacuum-swing adsorption process [21], two beds containing different sorbents are used to take advantage of their different adsorption selectivities. More recently, schemes involving interconnected beds packed with two different sorbents were suggested for difficult separations, and theoretical analyses were performed on such systems [41, 42]. The use of a desiccant (alumina or silica gel) placed at the feed end of the zeolite bed is discussed in section 7.1.4.

Still another PSA process is the one based on *kinetic separation* — separation caused not by equilibrium selectivity but by different pore diffusivities. This is not a new idea, but the commercial reality was achieved only recently upon the successful development of molecular-sieve carbon. This and other processes will be discussed in the following section.

7.2   COMMERCIAL PROCESSES

Since the invention of the Skarstrom cycle in 1960, PSA has been rapidly developed into a major technology for air drying, hydrogen purification, *n*-paraffin removal, and small- to medium-scale air fractionation. Still, many more applications are being developed in various laboratories. The history of PSA commercialization is given in Table 7.3.

7.2.1   Air Drying

Dry compressed air is widely used in industry. Since the line pressure is usually sufficient for operating PSA, and the PSA can achieve the same or lower dew points as compared with TSA, the process was almost instantly accepted for air drying. The original two-step Skarstrom cycle has been used for this purpose with almost

Table 7.3   PSA Commercial Development Highlights

1960	Skarstrom cycle and Guerin-Domine cycle
1960	Drying of air and other gases
1961	*n*-Paraffin removal
1966	Hydrogen purification
1970	Oxygen production from air
1976	Nitrogen from air using molecular-sieve carbon
1977	Nitrogen (and oxygen) from air by "vacuum-swing adsorption" using zeolite
1977	"Polybed" systems for large-scale hydrogen production
1980	Single-bed PSA for medical oxygen
1983	Nitrogen from air by zeolite PSA

Source: Revised from Cassidy and Holmes [8].

no process modification [7, 43]. The original two-bed unit is shown in Figure 7.13. Each bed undergoes two steps in a cycle: repressurization and adsorption, followed by countercurrent blowdown and purge. The cycle time is usually between 1 and 10 minutes, equally divided between the two steps. The preferred sorbents are silica gel and activated alumina, although zeolites are also used.

Skarstrom's rules for this PSA cycle are summarized as follows:

1.   Short cycle and low throughput per cycle should be used to conserve the heat of adsorption, thereby maintaining an isothermal operation.

2.   Obey the 1:1 volume rule for the purge/feed ratio. The volume ratio is measured at their respective pressures. Thus the 1:1 ratio ensures complete displacement. The purge/feed ratio is a key parameter in determining the product purity. It is usually between 1.1 and 2.0 in practice.

3.   For a pure product, the absolute pressure ratio between the high and low pressures should be greater than the reciprocal of the mole fraction of the product contained in the feed (assuming purge/feed = 1):

$$P_{HI}/P_{LO} > 1/\text{mole fraction of product in feed}$$

This is essentially a condition for total reflux based on a purge/feed ratio of 1. The value of P_{HI} ranges from 15 to 3,500 psig when P_{LO} is atmospheric.

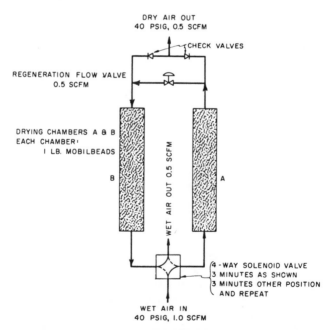

Figure 7.13 Skarstrom's experimental air drying unit. Source: Skarstrom [7]. Reprinted with permission.

4. The general rules for sizing the beds are 15 to 30 actual v/v of feed per bed per cycle when the actual purge/feed ratio is 1.1. One actual v/v of feed represents its amount at the feed pressure in the empty bed. The feed throughput can be increased substantially if a high purge/feed ratio is employed.

These rules are useful. Following these rules, the bed temperature varies within several degrees during each cycle. Recent experimental data of the process showed a temperature range of approximately 6°C under wide operating conditions [44]. The sorbent utilization is inefficient, however, since the loading is only a very small fraction of the total bed during each cycle.

The use of the carbon canister, now standard equipment in automobiles, was directly derived from the Skarstrom process, with the exception that no pressure variation is required [45]. Escaping gasoline vapors from the gas tank are adsorbed into the activated carbon bed. Whenever the automobile is operating, ambient air is drawn through the carbon bed to purge or regenerate the bed.

7.2.2 Hydrogen Purification

Hydrogen purification is a necessary step in the production of hydrogen, which at present is done by catalytic steam reforming of natural gas, naphtha, or refinery gases. It is also used to recover hydrogen from catalytic reformer effluent gas, ethylene plant effluent gas, and ammonia plant purge gas, in addition to a number of other sources [46, 47].

Since the first commercial PSA hydrogen purification unit was installed, in conjunction with a steam reformer in Toronto [46] around 1966, the technology has grown rapidly, with the collective installed hydrogen capacity of PSA systems exceeding 1 billion SCF/day worldwide [8]. It is currently the largest use of PSA in terms of both cumulative capacity and the number of installed units.

The compositions of the three major gas mixture sources for PSA hydrogen purification are:

1. Steam reformer effluent (after water gas shift): 70–75% (by volume) hydrogen. The major impurity is CO_2, with smaller amounts of CO, CH_4, and sometimes N_2.
2. Catalytic reformer effluent: 65–85% hydrogen. The primary impurity is methane, with lesser amounts of C_2–C_5 hydrocarbons.
3. Ethylene plant effluent: 70–90% hydrogen, with methane as the main impurity.

The success of PSA hydrogen purification is largely due to the high selectivities of the impurity gases over hydrogen. (Impurities with extremely high selectivities, such as H_2S and NH_3, are not desirable because a pretreatment bed or vacuum desorption would be required in the PSA cycle.) Although all commercial sorbents can be used as a result of the high selectivities, a combination of activated carbon and zeolites is used in practice. For example, in the four-bed Union Carbide process that will be discussed later, each bed is packed with activated carbon near the inlet in the first section, whereas 5A zeolite is packed in the second section [48]. Presumably, the carbon section acts as a guard bed, mainly adsorbing and desorbing water vapor and carbon dioxide.

Two PSA processes are currently used, depending on the plant capacity or size. For capacities below 13–15 million standard cubic feet (MMSCF/D) of hydrogen product per day, the three- or four-bed configuration based on Batta's patent [49] is employed. For larger sizes, Union Carbide's Polybed process, based on the patent of Fuderer and Rudelstorfer [48], has proved more economical. The Polybed process has a single-train capacity of up to 50 MMSCF/D [50–52]. Both processes yield hydrogen at purities higher than 99.999%. The product recovery for the three- to four-bed process is 70–75%, whereas an improvement to 80–85% is achieved by the Polybed process.

In both processes, the cycle steps are (1) adsorption, (2) cocurrent depressurization, (3) countercurrent blowdown, (4) purge, and (5) repressurization. The effluent gas from one bed is used to purge and repressurize other beds, the latter being referred to as *pressure equalization* (section 7.1.3). The difference in these processes lies

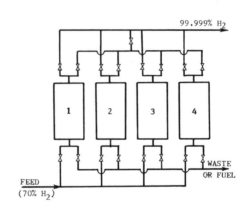

Vessel Number												
1	Adsorption			EQ1 ↑	CD ↑	EQ2 ↑	CD ↓	Purge ↓	EQ2 ↓	EQ1 ↓	R ↓	
2	CD ↓	Purge ↓	EQ2 ↓	EQ1 ↓	R ↓		Adsorption			EQ1 ↑	CD ↑	EQ2 ↑
3	EQ1 ↑	CD ↑	EQ2 ↑	CD ↓	Purge ↓	EQ2 ↓	EQ1 ↓	R ↓		Adsorption		
4	EQ1 ↓	R ↓		Adsorption			EQ1 ↑	CD ↑	EQ2 ↑	CD ↓	Purge ↓	EQ2 ↓

EQ—Equalization
CD —Cocurrent depressurization
CD —Countercurrent depressurization
R—Repressurization

↑—Cocurrent flow
↓—Countercurrent flow

Figure 7.14 Union Carbide four-bed PSA system and cycle sequence chart.

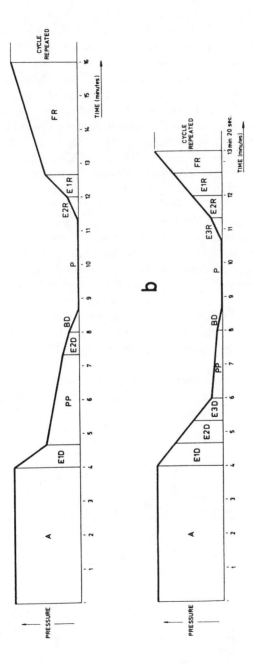

Figure 7.15 Pressure history in each bed in (a) the four-bed and (b) the ten-bed Polybed process. The cycle steps are: adsorption (A), first equalization–depressurization (E1D), similarly for E2D and E3D, cocurrent depressurization (used for purge and product) (PP), countercurrent blowdown (BD), purge (P), third equalization-repressurization (E3R), similarly for E2R and E1R, final repressurization (FR). Source: Fuderer and Rudelstorfer [48].

in the number and sequence of pressure equalization steps, which yield significant differences in separation results.

The four-bed process is illustrated in Figure 7.14. The pressure history in a cycle is illustrated in Figure 7.15a. The four-bed Batta process is an improvement from that of Wagner [12], where only one pressure equalization step is used.

During the high-pressure adsorption step, a substantial fraction of the bed is not covered by the deepest-reaching wavefront. Although the wavefronts are sharp, the uncovered portion of the bed is not clean in a cyclic steady state because of the accumulated impurities. For example, in separating a steam reformer effluent at 284 psia, the CO impurity level in the effluent from each bed increases steadily from 39 to 48, 59, and 84 ppm at pressures of 284, 236, 192, and 160 psia, respectively, during cocurrent depressurization [48]. To achieve the best separation, the following general principle should be followed: When a gas discharged from one bed has a varying impurity level and is used to purge and repressurize other beds, the most impure gas should be introduced to the other beds at the lowest pressure (for repressurization), and the purest discharge gas should be introduced at the highest intermediate pressure (for repressurization and purge).

With a limited number of beds, as in the four-bed process, only two pressure equalization steps are possible. The purge step is completed with the discharge gas from another bed undergoing the PP (middle cocurrent depressurization for purge and product) step. The final repressurization is performed by the pure high-pressure product gas from another bed. Because of the limited number of pressure equalization steps and large amount of product gas required for final repressurization, the product recovery can reach only 70–75%, at 99.999% to 99.9999% purity, in the four-bed process.

As the number of beds is further increased, more pressure equalization steps can be adapted and the beds become cleaner at a cyclic steady state. Consequently,

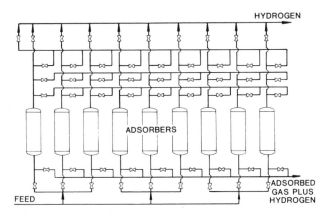

Figure 7.16 Union Carbide Polybed process for hydrogen purification. Source: Keller [9]. Reprinted with permission.

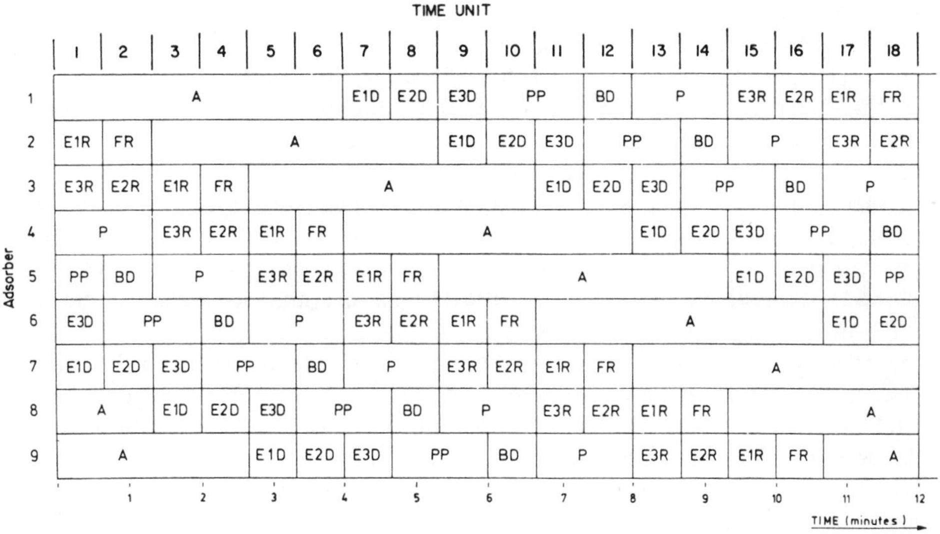

TIME UNIT

Adsorber	1	2	3	4	5	6	7	8	9	10	11	12	13	14	15	16	17	18
1	A	A	A	A	A	A	E1D	E2D	E3D	PP	PP	BD	P	P	E3R	E2R	E1R	FR
2	E1R	FR	A	A	A	A	A	A	E1D	E2D	E3D	PP	PP	BD	P	P	E3R	E2R
3	E3R	E2R	E1R	FR	A	A	A	A	A	A	E1D	E2D	E3D	PP	PP	BD	P	P
4	P	P	E3R	E2R	E1R	FR	A	A	A	A	A	A	E1D	E2D	E3D	PP	PP	BD
5	PP	BD	P	P	E3R	E2R	E1R	FR	A	A	A	A	A	A	E1D	E2D	E3D	PP
6	E3D	PP	PP	BD	P	P	E3R	E2R	E1R	FR	A	A	A	A	A	A	E1D	E2D
7	E1D	E2D	E3D	PP	PP	BD	P	P	E3R	E2R	E1R	FR	A	A	A	A	A	A
8	A	A	E1D	E2D	E3D	PP	PP	BD	P	P	E3R	E2R	E1R	FR	A	A	A	A
9	A	A	A	E1D	E2D	E3D	PP	PP	BD	P	P	E3R	E2R	E1R	FR	A	A	A

TIME (minutes): 1 · 2 · 3 · 4 · 5 · 6 · 7 · 8 · 9 · 10 · 11 · 12

Figure 7.17 Cycle sequence chart for the nine-bed Polybed process. Source: Fuderer and Rudelstorfer [48].

Figure 7.17a Union Carbide Polybed PSA system for hydrogen purification at Saber Refining, Corpus Christi, Texas. Source: kindly supplied by Mason Sze of Union Carbide Corporation.

the product gas required for final repressurization is also reduced. The net result is a higher product recovery at the same product purity.

The successful development of the Polybed process made large-scale, 13–50 MMSCF/D, high-purity hydrogen production economically feasible. The Polybed process contains seven to ten beds, with at least three pressure equalization steps and at least two receiving the feed gas during the entire cycle. Figure 7.16 illustrates a typical nine-bed system. The cycle sequence of the nine-bed system is shown in Figure 7.17. As shown in Figure 7.17, three of the nine beds are undergoing an adsorption step (and are producing) at any given time. The pressure history of a ten-bed system, which is essentially identical to that of a nine-bed system, is shown in Figure 7.15b. Comparing the four-bed and nine-bed systems in Figure 7.15, the final repressurization (FR) step is found to be much shorter in the Polybed system. These figures clearly show why the Polybed process is capable of achieving a high product recovery as well as a higher sorbent productivity. The Polybed system has also solved an engineering problem that was one of the original motivations for its development [48]. When plant capacity is increased, the size of the beds is usually increased in the vertical direction, which is, however, limited by the sorbent-pellet crushing strength. A commercial Polybed PSA system is shown in Figure 7.17a.

The economics of both the four-bed [22, 46] and Polybed process [50] are well established. The unit hydrogen product cost for the PSA-based hydrogen plants is 5–7% lower than the conventional cryogenic [46] and scrubbing [50] processes. The PSA processes are designed for feed gases containing over 60% hydrogen, at 70–100°F and 200–500 psig.

For high-purity hydrogen (99.999–99.9999%) production, 5A zeolite is used as the sorbent. Activated carbon is not used because its selectivity for impurity/hydrogen is not high enough. It is also helpful to use a surge tank for the hydrogen product to ensure the purity because the instantaneous purity during the PP step (Figure 7.15) can be less than that required.

Research activities are underway to study the more difficult separations: ammonia plant purge gas, hydrodealkylation plant purge gas, cryogenic plant-recycle gas, refinery fuel gas, and coal gasification products.

7.2.3 Bulk Separation of Normal Paraffins

The separation of *n*-paraffins (10–60%) from mixtures with branched-chain isomers and cyclic hydrocarbons cannot be easily performed by distillation because of their close relative volatilities. Zeolite 5A (the calcium form) can readily adsorb *n*-paraffins while excluding the isomers. Thus adsorption by 5A zeolite is ideally suited for this separation.

Depending on the molecular weights of the *n*-paraffins, two types of adsorption processes are used commercially. A PSA cycle including a vacuum desorption step is used to recover *n*-paraffins with carbon number approximately below 10. For *n*-paraffins with carbon number between 10 and 18, a constant-pressure cycle involving a displacement/desorption step is employed.

There are three commercial applications, also depending on the molecular weights: (1) solvent production, (2) the production of C_{10}–C_{18} *n*-paraffins for manufacturing biodegradable detergents and plasticizers, and (3) octane improvement [8]. For the first application, PSA is used for low-molecular-weight *n*-paraffin recovery. The third application entails the removal of C_5–C_9 *n*-paraffins from petroleum fractions in order to increase the octane number.

Solvent Production: IsoSiv Process

The first IsoSiv unit was installed by Union Carbide in 1961 for the recovery of high-purity *n*-paraffin solvents from a naphtha feedstock [8]. By 1980 nine more IsoSiv plants had been installed worldwide, with the largest one processing 35,000 barrels of C_5–C_6 mixtures per day [53].

Figure 7.18 illustrates the IsoSiv process. The feed mixture typically contains C_5–C_9 hydrocarbons, with nearly 50% *n*-paraffins. During the adsorption step of the PSA cycle, the wavefront of the *n*-paraffin is allowed to penetrate into about 75% of the bed. The repressurization step is achieved by the isomer raffinate. The *n*-paraffin product purity is over 95%, and the raffinate contains less than 2% of the *n*-paraffins. The economics of the IsoSiv process have recently been given [53].

High-Molecular-Weight n-Paraffin Recovery

The major commercial processes include: UOP Molex, BP, Shell, Texaco Selective Finishing (TSF), Exxon Ensorb, Union Carbide IsoSiv, and VEB Leuna Werke's

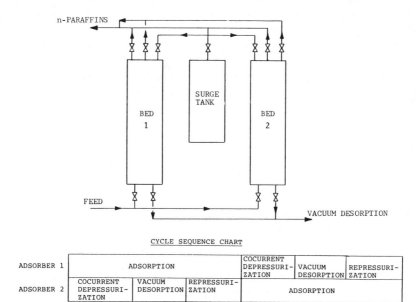

Figure 7.18   Union Carbide IsoSiv PSA process for low-molecular-weight solvent production. Source: Cassidy and Holmes, original manuscript [8].

process [54]. With the exception of the liquid phase Molex process (section 6.4.2 of Chapter 6), these processes are similar, and all are designed to recover *n*-paraffins from kerosene containing less than 25% $C_{10}-C_{18}$ *n*-paraffins.

Because of the high molecular weights of the adsorbates, efficient desorption can only be accomplished by displacement purge employing another adsorptive gas. Thus these processes employ a constant-pressure operation at a temperature in the 600–800°F range and pressure in the 30–75 psia range. Three or more beds are used, each undergoing a three-step cycle: adsorption, cocurrent purge, and countercurrent displacement/desorption. A short cocurrent purge is employed after desorption to remove the vapor mixture remaining in the void space. Thus a high-purity desorbed *n*-paraffin product can be obtained.

The only difference in the aforementioned process is in the desorbent used. It should be less strongly adsorbed than the *n*-paraffins so the *n*-paraffins can readily displace the desorbent during the adsorption step. Since the desorbent contaminates both products (raffinate and *n*-paraffins), however, it must be separated from both streams by distillation. Therefore, desorbent selection is based on high relative volatility. In most of the aforementioned processes, a low-molecular-weight *n*-paraffin such as *n*-hexane, which is available from the same system, is used as the desorbent [55]. In the Exxon Ensorb process, ammonia is used as the desorbent [56]. Both desorbents meet the required properties. Since the desorption step is the slowest in the cycle, the throughput is limited by the desorption time. Figure 7.19 shows the dependence of desorption time on the light *n*-paraffin that is used as a desorbent [55]. The desorption rate alone, however, is not the sole reason for choosing the desorbent. A large difference in carbon numbers is desirable for desorbent separation from the two product streams by distillation. A carbon number difference between two and four seems to be a reasonable compromise.

The kerosene version of the IsoSiv process has also been combined with a paraffin-isomerization process to produce a completely iso-paraffin product from a normal or mixed paraffin feed [8, 9, 53]. This combined process is used to increase the octane number of the isomerization product. Since the molecular weights of the *n*-paraffins are low and hydrogen is used in the isomerization reactor, hydrogen is employed as the purge gas to desorb the *n*-paraffins.

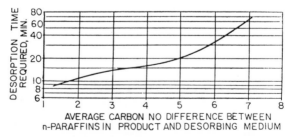

Figure 7.19 Effect of the desorbent (desorbing medium, a process-derived light *n*-paraffin) carbon number on desorption rate. Source: Cooper et al. [55]. Reprinted with permission.

7.2.4   Air Separation: Oxygen Generation

Cryogenic processes, which can produce ultrapure oxygen as well as nitrogen and inert gases, remain the most economical processes for large-scale production. For many applications of oxygen, however, a high purity is not required and the daily requirement is not large. Under these circumstances, PSA processes have proved more economical than cryogenic processes. Some of the applications requiring low-grade oxygen (below 95%) are biological treatment of wastewater, feed to ozonator for wastewater treatment, basic oxygen furnace in steel making, nonferrous metals smelting, paper and pulp industry, medical applications, and various partial oxidation processes.

The goal of research in the 1950s and 1960s, as well as the original invention of the PSA process, was oxygen generation from air. The commercialization of the oxygen process was realized in 1970. Because of the low adsorption selectivity of N_2/O_2, air separation is considerably more difficult than air drying, hydrogen purification, and *n*-paraffin removal. As shown in Figure 7.20, the selectivity ratio of N_2/O_2 on 5A zeolite is between two and three, which is in the pressure range of practical operation. (It is nearly unity on other commercial sorbents.) As seen from Figure 7.20, argon is also obtained as the raffinate product along with oxygen. Thus the limiting purity for the oxygen product is approximately 96%, since air contains approximately 1% argon. Other zeolites beside 5A also selectively adsorb nitrogen. The sorbents commercially used are 5A, 13X, and mordenite.

Medium-Size Industrial Oxygen and
Small-Size Medical Oxygen Generators

PSA-based oxygen systems are competitive with cryogenic processes at oxygen capacities approximately below 40 metric tons per day (TPD). In 1983 there were

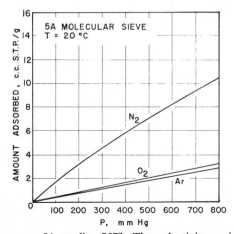

Figure 7.20 Isotherms on 5A zeolite [57]. The selectivity ratio for N_2/O_2 declines gradually to slightly less than 2 as the pressure is increased to 8 atm [58]. Source: Lee and Stahl [20]. Reprinted with permission.

200 PSA oxygen systems installed worldwide in the 1–36 TPD size range. There were also approximately 40,000 small units installed per year with capacities between 2 and 4 liters per minute, for use by patients with chronic pulmonary dysfunction (e.g., emphysema) [8].

The large systems, with oxygen capacities of 1–36 TPD, are based on the Batta patent [49], with the exception that vacuum desorption is used in some systems. Three to four beds are generally employed. The four-bed system is identical to that used for hydrogen purification, shown in Figure 7.14. These systems generate 90–95% pure oxygen at 30–60% product recovery [8]. The feed air is compressed to 20–80 psig. The compressed air is cooled to about 80–120°F, and liquid water is removed before feeding into the adsorbers. Systems employing pretreatment beds (section 7.1.4) and Batta's opposing-end pressurization technique (section 7.1.6) have also been reported [38, 59].

The small units for medical oxygen were commercialized in the mid-1970s. They are two-bed systems, each containing 1–2 pounds of zeolite, which basically

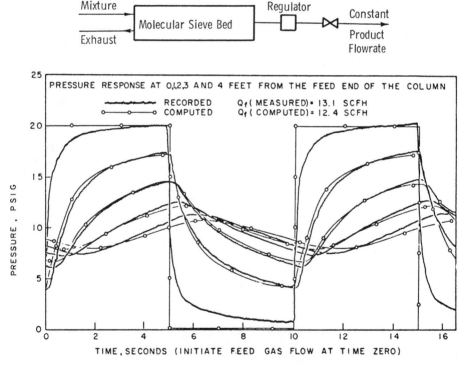

Figure 7.21 (*Upper*) The single-bed two-step cycle: high-pressure feed and low-pressure exhaust. Source: Kowler and Kadlec [33]. Reprinted with permission. (*Lower*) Steady-state pressure variation for separating 28.6% N_2 in CH_4 at 24°C. Other conditions: feed at 20 psig and exhaust at 0 psig, product flow = 1.8 SCFH, feed flow (Q_f) as marked. Source: Turnock and Kadlec [32]. Reprinted with permission.

operate on the original Skarstrom cycle [7]. The product purity is 85–95% at only 10–30% oxygen recovery [8]. The energy requirement for such systems is "about the power equivalent of four or five light bulbs" [8].

Single-Bed Rapid PSA

Because of its highly unusual nature, this process will be described in detail. It may be considered a hybrid between the Skarstrom cycle and parametric pumping (with pressure being the thermodynamic parameter). Compared with the other PSA systems, this process has the following unique advantages:

1. It is nearly isothermal as a result of the rapid cycling.
2. The use of a single-bed provides process simplicity.
3. It can yield higher sorbent productivity at equal purity and recovery.

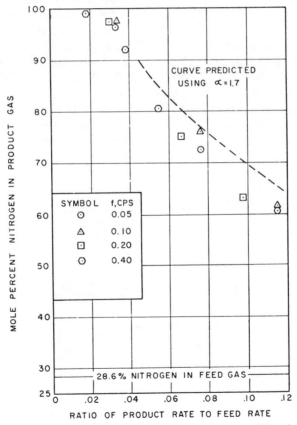

Figure 7.22 Product purity versus product recovery (expressed by the flow ratio) for separating 28.6% N_2 in CH_4 with 42–60 mesh 5A zeolite at 24°C by the Turnock/Kadlec process. Other conditions: α = selectivity ratio of CH_4/N_2, f = frequency in cycle per second. Source: Turnock and Kadlec [32]. Reprinted with permission.

The single-bed process, originally invented by Kadlec and co-workers [32, 33], is shown in Figure 7.21. The cycle consists of two steps with equal lengths in time: feed/pressurization, followed by exhaust. Feed and exhaust take place at the same end. In the meantime, a steady flow of raffinate product is withdrawn from the opposite end. The cycle time is extremely short (below 20 seconds). In addition, sorbent particles of fine sizes (42–60 mesh, as compared with 1/16 inch pellets in normal PSA cycles) are used to provide a high-pressure gradient in the bed. The high-pressure gradient is central to the success of the process. The process was studied for the separation of a N_2/CH_4 mixture (with 28.4% N_2) with 5A zeolite. The pressure history and profile are also shown in Figure 7.21. The separation is not an easy one because of the low adsorption selectivity ratio, $CH_4/N_2 = 1.7$–1.9 at 24°C. Nonetheless, excellent separations were obtained. Typical results are shown in Figure 7.22. It is seen that an N_2 product as pure as 99% can be achieved. The product recovery, however, decreases to below 10%.

Because of the low product recovery, which results in high energy consumption, this process was not used commercially for oxygen production until substantial refinements were made by Keller et al. [29–31]. In this later process, a short feed and a long exhaust were used. In addition, a short delay step was employed, with both feed and exhaust valves closed. The cycle steps are: high-pressure feed pulse (less than 1 second), delay (0.5–3 seconds) and exhaust to a low pressure (5–20 seconds). In some cases, still another short delay step, generally less than 1 second, follows the exhaust step. Two- and three-bed systems are also possible where the beds are sequenced such that the compressed feed is always flowing to the system [60]. The one-bed and three-bed systems are shown in Figure 7.23.

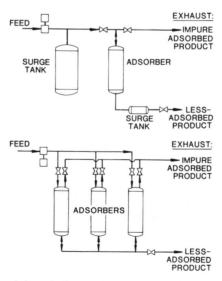

Figure 7.23   One-bed and three-bed PSA/parametric pumping systems. Source: Keller [9]. Reprinted with permission.

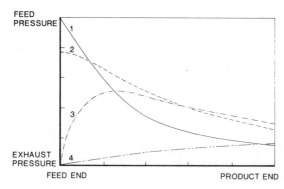

Figure 7.24   Pressure profiles in a fine zeolite bed in the one-bed process: 1: middle of feed; 2: middle of delay; 3: early in exhaust; 4: late in exhaust. Source: Keller [9]. Reprinted with permission.

Table 7.4   Comparison of Two Commercial Processes for Oxygen Production

	PSA	PSA/Parametric Pumping
Number of adsorbent beds	3	1
Supply pressure, psig	45	50
Adsorbent bed length, ft	6–10	3–4
Adsorbent particle size	1/16 inch pellets	40–80 mesh granules
Pressure cycle length	3–4 minutes	18.5 seconds
Exhaust pressure, psig	0	0
Product pressure, psig	2–5	2–5
Product purity, mol % oxygen	90	90
Oxygen recovery, %	40	38
Adsorbent productivity, ton 100% oxygen/ton adsorbent	0.5	2.3

Source: Keller and Jones [30]. Reprinted with permission.

The dynamics of the system are extremely complex. It can, however, be visualized by the changing pressure profiles in the bed, as shown in Figure 7.24. It should be noted that in the process optimization study by Kowler and Kadlec [33], the effects of unequal feed-exhaust time steps as well as the inclusion of a short delay step were investigated. But the aforementioned conditions were not identified.

With the aforementioned process modifications, oxygen recovery is substantially increased. The modified single-bed process was commercialized in 1980.

By way of summary, Table 7.4 compares the process characteristics and performance of two oxygen-generation processes: medium-size PSA and single-bed PSA/parametric pumping.

7.2.5   Air Separation: Nitrogen Generation

Cryogenic distillation continues to be the process used for large-scale generation of ultrapure nitrogen for industrial use. Much like oxygen, PSA is more economical for small- to medium-scale production of nitrogen at purities approximately below 99.7%. Such a market exists in inert-gas generating needs, such as purging, inert blanketing of fuel tanks, and N_2-based controlled atmospheres in food, metallurgical, and other industries. A more recent use of nitrogen is in enhanced oil recovery. There are at present two proven commercial processes operating on different sorbents and principles, both commercialized around 1977.

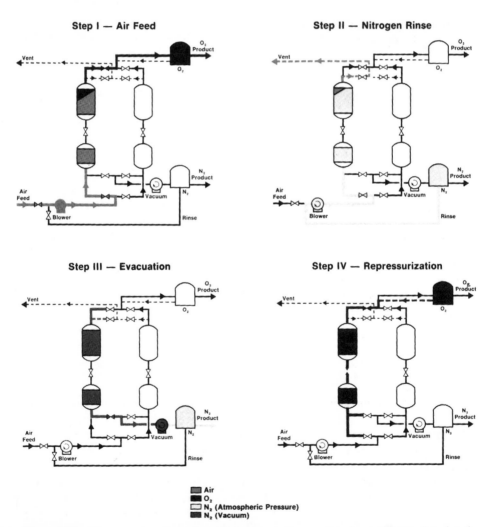

Figure 7.25   The vacuum-swing adsorption process. Source: Brochure 522-301. Reprinted with permission from Air Products and Chemicals, Inc.

Zeolite Process: Vacuum-Swing Adsorption

This process is based on the patent of Sircar and Zondlo [21]. It is similar to the Guerin-Domine cycle (section 7.1.1) but embodies substantial modifications. The cycle also employs desiccant pretreatment beds (section 7.1.4) and purge by strong adsorptive, N_2 (section 7.1.5).

Figure 7.25 illustrates the VSA cycle in which a two-bed system is employed. The main beds are packed with a zeolite sorbent. The sorbent in the pretreatment bed is a desiccant, which adsorbs and easily desorbs water vapor and carbon dioxide. The cycle is operated between a pressure slightly above 1 atm and a mechanical-pump vacuum. The cycle steps are: (1) adsorption, (2) cocurrent N_2 purge, (3) countercurrent evacuation, and (4) countercurrent O_2 repressurization. The cycle time is in the neighborhood of 6 minutes.

The purity of the N_2 product from VSA is in the range between 98 and 99.7%, containing O_2 that reaches a low concentration below 10 ppm, with a dew point below $-40°C$ $(-40°F)$. The high purity of nitrogen is achieved since argon is contained in the oxygen stream. The nitrogen recovery is approximately 50%. As shown in Figure 7.26, the VSA process competes favorably with cryogenic distillation in the range of 10,000–30,000 SCF/hr, which is a similar range for favorable O_2 production by PSA. The VSA also generates a 90% purity oxygen stream as a byproduct.

The Toray process (Figure 7.10) is similar to the VSA process, with the exception that the feed is pressurized and does not include pretreatment beds in the pressure-swing system. Its commercial status is not known.

Molecular-Sieve Carbon Process: Kinetic Separation

The molecular-sieving properties of carbons have long been known [61]. Successful control of the highly irregular structure of a coal-based molecular-sieve carbon

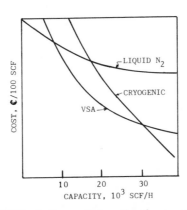

Figure 7.26 Economics (1983) of nitrogen generation from vacuum-swing adsorption and cryogenic processes. Source: Brochure 522-301. Reprinted with permission from Air Products and Chemicals, Inc.

(MSC) was accomplished in the mid-1970s by Walker and co-workers [62] and by Jüntgen [63]. Because of the different kinetic diameters of nitrogen and oxygen molecules, oxygen diffuses more rapidly in the MSC than nitrogen. The equilibrium isotherms of oxygen and nitrogen, shown in Figure 7.27, are nearly equal. The diffusion rates are very different, however. As shown in the fractional uptake curves, Figure 7.28, the oxygen molecule diffuses through the narrow gaps in the pore structure much more rapidly because of its smaller kinetic diameter. The diffusion constants (D/r^2) calculated from this figure yielded values of 1.7×10^{-4} s^{-1} for oxygen and 7.0×10^{-6} s^{-1} for nitrogen, where D is the micropore diffusity and r is the microparticle radius. A recent study showed higher diffusion constants (by

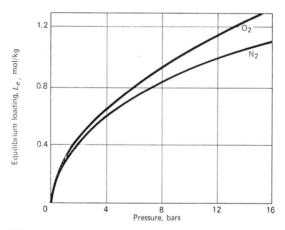

Figure 7.27   Equilibrium isotherms of O_2 and N_2 on a molecular-sieve carbon at room temperature. Source: Knoblauch [64]. Reprinted with permission.

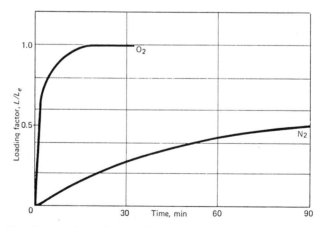

Figure 7.28   Uptake rates in molecular-sieve carbon expressed by the fraction of equilibrium amount adsorbed. Source: Knoblauch [64]. Reprinted with permission.

nearly an order of magnitude) for both gases, but approximately the same ratio [67]. Water and CO_2 molecules diffuse just as quickly as oxygen, whereas argon diffuses slowly. Consequently, the effluent from a MSC bed with air feed contains nitrogen and argon. The limiting nitrogen product purity from the adsorber is 98.7% with the balance being argon.

The PSA process developed by Bergbau-Forschung GmbH is shown in Figure 7.29, using the carbon described in reference 63. It is operated on a simple two-step cycle: adsorption and countercurrent evacuation, each step lasting 1 minute [64]. The optimal pressure for the adsorption step is 3–5 atm, and the desorption pressure is approximately 70 Torr. The nitrogen product contains 95–99.9% $N_2 + Ar$, and the nitrogen recovery is approximately 50%. The desorption product stream contains 35% O_2 and 65% N_2, CO_2, and H_2O. With an intermediate O_2 purge step, the cycle can produce an 80–90% O_2 [63]. The economical size of the process is below 35,000 SCF/hr, which again is in the same range as the PSA oxygen and VSA nitrogen processes.

A possible new application for the MSC PSA process is the separation of the effluent gas in enhanced oil recovery using CO_2 flooding, which currently employs membrane separation. The gas mixture that is to be separated contains approximately 80% CO_2, with the balance being CH_4 and higher hydrocarbons. The separation requires a CO_2 and hydrocarbon product. Using zeolite or activated carbon as the sorbent, the PSA process will separate CH_4 from the other gases since it is the most weakly adsorbed gas. Successful separation can be accomplished by membrane permeation because CO_2 is the fastest permeant. As shown in Figure 7.30, CO_2 also diffuses at a substantially higher rate than the hydrocarbons in molecular-sieve carbon [65]. Thus the PSA using MSC should readily separate CO_2 from the hydrocarbons. The separation of CO_2 and CH_4 by PSA can also find use in landfill gas application, which contains almost equal amounts of the two gases.

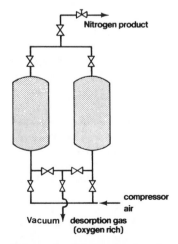

Figure 7.29 Schematic of the molecular-sieve carbon PSA.

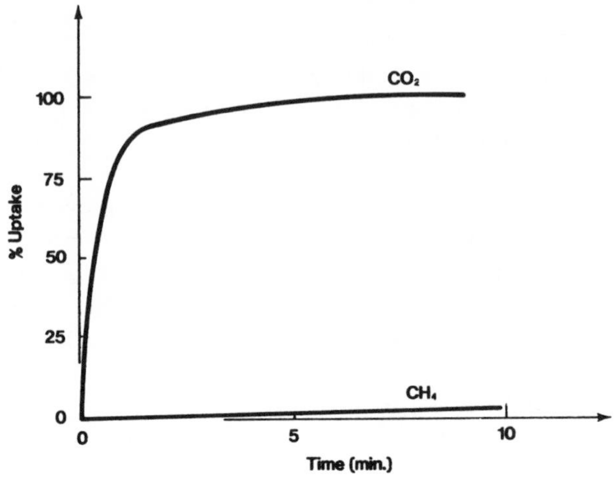

Figure 7.30   Uptake rates of CO_2 and CH_4 in molecular-sieve carbon. Source: Carrubba et al. [65]. Reprinted with permission.

REFERENCES

1. R.M. Barrer, *Proc. Roy. Soc. (London)*, *A167*, 392 (1938).
2. R.M. Barrer, *Trans. Faraday Soc.*, *40*, 555 (1944).
3. R.M. Milton, U.S. Patent 2,882,243 (1959), to Union Carbide Corporation.
4. R.M. Milton, U.S. Patent 2,882,244 (1959), to Union Carbide Corporation.
5. C.W. Skarstrom, U.S. Patent 2,944,627 (1960), to Esso Research and Engineering Company.
6. P. Guerin de Montgareuil and D. Domine, U.S. Patent 3,155,468 (1964), to Société L'Air Liquide, Paris.
7. C.W. Skarstrom, "Heatless Fractionation of Gases over Solid Sorbents," in *Recent Developments in Separation Science* (N.N. Li, ed.) Vol. 2 (Cleveland: CRC Press, 1972).
8. R.T. Cassidy and E.S. Holmes, *AIChE Symp. Ser.*, *80*(No. 233), 68 (1984).
9. G.E. Keller II, "Gas Adsorption Processes: State of the Art," in "Industrial Gas Separations," *ACS Symp. Ser. No. 223*, Amer. Chem. Soc., Washington, D.C. (1983).
10. W.F. Avery and M.N.Y. Lee, *Oil and Gas J.*, June, 121 (1962).
11. K. Kiyonaga, U.S. Patent 3,176,444 (1965), to Union Carbide Corporation.
12. J.L. Wagner, U.S. Patent 3,430,418 (1969), to Union Carbide Corporation.
13. R.T. Yang, S.J. Doong, and P.L. Cen, *AIChE Symp. Ser.*, *81*(No. 242), 84 (1985).
14. P.L. Cen and R.T. Yang, *Ind. Eng. Chem. Fundam.*, in press (1986).
15. W.D. Marsh, F.S. Pramuk, R.C. Hoke, and C.W. Skarstrom, U.S. Patent 3,142,547 (1964), to Esso Research and Engineering Company.
16. N.H. Berlin, U.S. Patent 3,280,536 (1966), to Esso Research and Engineering Company.
17. K.J. Doshi, C.H. Katira, and H.A. Stewart, *AIChE Symp. Ser.*, *67*(No. 117), 90 (1971).
18. G. Heinze, Belgian Patent 613,267 (1962), to Farbenfabriken Bayer A.G.
19. T. Tamura, French Patent 1,502,458 (1967); Ger. Offen. 1,817,004 (1969); U.S. Patent 3,533,221 (1970), to T. Tamura of Tokyo, Japan.

20. H. Lee and D.E. Stahl, *AIChE Symp. Ser.*, *69*(No. 134), 1 (1973).
21. S. Sircar and J.W. Zondlo, U.S. Patent 4,013,429 (1977), to Air Products and Chemicals, Inc.
22. R.W. Alexis, *Chem. Eng. Prog.*, *63*(5), 69 (1967).
23. R.T. Yang and S.J. Doong, *AIChE J.*, *11*, 1829 (1985).
24. T. Tamura, U.S. Patent 3,797,201 (1974), to T. Tamura, Tokyo, Japan.
25. P.L. Cen and R.T. Yang, *Separation Sc. Tech.*, in press (1986).
26. K. Miwa and T. Inoue, *Chem. Econ. and Eng. Rev.*, *12*(11), 40 (1980).
27. S. Sircar, U.S. Patents 4,171,206–207 (1979), to Air Products and Chemicals, Inc.
28. K. Chihara and M. Suzuki, *J. Chem. Eng. Japan*, *16*, 293 (1983).
29. R.L. Jones, G.E. Keller II, and R.C. Wells, U.S. Patent 4,194,892 (1980), to Union Carbide Corporation.
30. G.E. Keller II and R.L. Jones, *ACS Symp. Ser.*, *135*, 275 (1980).
31. R.L. Jones and G.E. Keller II, *J. Separ. Proc. Tech.*, *2*(3), 17 (1981).
32. P.H. Turnock and R.H. Kadlec, *AIChE J.*, *17*, 335 (1971).
33. D.E. Kowler and R.H. Kadlec, *AIChE J.*, *18*, 1207; 1212 (1972).
34. R.T. Yang and P.L. Cen, *Ind. Eng. Chem. Proc. Des. Dev.*, *25*, 54 (1986).
35. J.J. Collins, U.S. Patent 3,973,931 (1976), to Union Carbide Corporation.
36. J.J. Collins, U.S. Patent 4,026,680 (1977), to Union Carbide Corporation.
37. L.B. Batta, U.S. Patent 3,636,679 (1972), to Union Carbide Corporation.
38. J.C. Davis, *Chem. Eng.*, Oct. 16 (1972), p. 88.
39. N.R. McCombs, U.S. Patent 3,738,087 (1973), to Union Carbide Corporation.
40. G. Klein, "Design and Development of Cyclic Operations," in *Percolation Processes: Theory and Applications* (A.E. Rodrigues and D. Tondeur, eds.) (Rockville, Md.: Sijthoff and Noordhoff, 1981).
41. P.C. Wankat and D. Tondeur, *AIChE Symp. Ser.*, *81*(No. 242), 74 (1985).
42. K.S. Knaebel, "Analysis of Complementary Pressure Swing Adsorption," in *Fundamentals of Adsorption* (A.L. Myers and G. Belfort, eds.) (New York: Engineering Foundation, 1984).
43. J.P. Ausikaitis, *Am. Chem. Soc. Symp. Ser.*, *40*, 681 (1977).
44. K. Chihara and M. Suzuki, *J. Chem. Eng. Japan*, *16*, 293 (1983).
45. P.J. Clarke, J.E. Gerard, C.W. Skarstrom, J. Vardi, and D.T. Wade, *SAE Trans.*, *76*, 824 (1968).
46. H.A. Stewart and J.L. Heck, *Chem. Eng. Prog.*, *65*(9), 78 (1969).
47. H.B. Jones, Jr., paper presented at Compressed Gas Assoc. Mtg., Sarasota, FL, March 1980, Howe-Baker Engineers, Inc.
48. A. Fuderer and E. Rudelstorfer, U.S. Patent 3,986,849 (1976), to Union Carbide Corporation.
49. L.B. Batta, U.S. Patent 3,564,816 (1971), to Union Carbide Corporation.
50. J.L. Heck and T. Johansen, *Hydrocarbon Processing*, 175, January (1978).
51. F. Corr, F. Dropp, and E. Rudelstorfer, *Hydrocarbon Processing*, 119, March (1979).
52. Anon., *Chem. Eng.*, 90, December 3 (1979).
53. M.F. Symoniak, *Hydrocarbon Processing*, 110, May (1980).
54. C.W. Chi and W.P. Cummings, in *Kirk-Othmer Encyclopedia of Chemical Technology*, 3rd ed. (New York: Wiley, 1978), p. 544.
55. D.E. Cooper, H.E. Griswold, R.M. Lewis, and R.W. Stokeld, *Chem. Eng. Prog.*, *62*(4), 69 (1966).
56. W.J. Asher, M.L. Campbell, W.R. Epperly, and J.L. Robertson, *Hydrocarbon Processing*, *48*, 134, January (1969).

57. D. Domine and L. Hay, in *Molecular Sieves*, 204, *Soc. Chem. Ind., London* (1968).
58. G.A. Sorial, W.H. Granville, and W.O. Daly, *Chem. Eng. Sci.*, *38*, 1517 (1983).
59. Anon., *Chem. Eng.*, *54*, Oct. 5 (1970).
60. D.E. Earls and G.N. Long, U.S. Patent 4,194,891 (1980).
61. S.P. Nandi and P.L. Walker, Jr., *Fuel*, *43*, 385 (1964).
62. R.L. Patel, S.P. Nandi, and P.L. Walker, Jr., *Fuel*, *51*, 47 (1972).
63. H. Juntgen, *Carbon*, *15*, 273 (1977).
64. K. Knoblauch, *Chem. Eng.*, *87*, Nov. 6 (1978).
65. R.V. Carrubba, J.E. Urbanic, N.J. Wagner, and R.H. Zanitsch, *AIChE Symp. Ser.*, *80*(No. 233), 76 (1984).
66. J.W. Armond, in *Properties and Applications on Zeolites* (R.P. Townsend, ed.), Special Publ. No. 33, Chemical Society, London (1979), p. 92.
67. D.M. Ruthven, N.S. Raghavan, and M.M. Hassan, *Chem. Eng. Sc.*, forthcoming (1987).

CHAPTER 8

Pressure-Swing Adsorption: Models and Experiments

Despite the rapidly growing application of pressure-swing adsorption (PSA) since the 1960s, the list of published theoretical studies on the process is short. Nonetheless, a good deal is already understood about the process, although much more is needed.

Analytic solutions are possible for relatively simple PSA cycles (such as the Skarstrom cycle) only under the following idealized conditions:

1. Dilute mixture in a relatively inert carrier (so linear isotherms and constant flow velocity are realized)
2. Short cycle time and low throughput per cycle (for isothermality)
3. Instantaneous gas-solid equilibrium

These solutions can provide some insight into the process. Because of the cyclic nature of the process, however, the cumulative errors are large, even when compared with experiments designed specifically to meet the foregoing conditions. Numerical solutions, with the flexibility of incorporating the nonideal conditions, can simulate highly complex PSA processes with good accuracy.

The major commercial applications of PSA were discussed in Chapter 7. The aforementioned assumptions are nearly met in only one application, air drying, which is carried out with the original Skarstrom cycle. Therefore, analytical solutions will be given for the Skarstrom cycle under the aforementioned idealized conditions. Substantial deviations from these conditions are found in all other applications, including hydrogen purification. These applications also employ PSA cycles more complex than the Skarstrom cycle. Analytic solutions for these complex cycles, though possible using the idealized conditions, would be neither applicable nor meaningful. Modeling of these processes must resort to numerical solutions.

8.1   MODELS FOR SKARSTROM CYCLE

Both analytic and numerical models have been published for the Skarstrom cycle for purification purposes.

8.1.1   Analytic Model

Figure 8.1 shows the two-bed Skarstrom cycle, with two combined steps: bed pressurization and adsorption with feed introduction, and countercurrent blow-down and purge. In actual operation, four distinct steps are used, as shown in the figure. Each step introduces a concentration wavefront into the bed. Under the idealized assumptions, with linear isotherm being the key assumption, all wave-fronts retain their shapes while traveling along and eventually elute the column. This is true for the linear isotherm for both adsorption and desorption. The velocities of all wavefronts can be calculated by the method of characteristics, and by assuming ideal gas behavior (for the pressure-change steps). The compositions and average compositions of the gas mixtures contained in the segments between the wavefronts can also be calculated. The effluent gas exiting during each step in the cycle consists of one (or a fraction of one) or more of these segments. The effluent gas concentration can thus be calculated as the weighted sum of the segments. The problem of constructing a solution is therefore reduced to the geometrical problem of locating the characteristics in the distance-time plane and counting the number of changes in slope that each characteristic experiences. This procedure was first used by Pigford et al. [1] to obtain an analytic solution for thermal parametric pumping (in the direct mode). A similar analysis for other versions of parametric pumping immediately followed [2]. The same procedure was used by Shendalman and Mitchell [3] to construct a solution for the

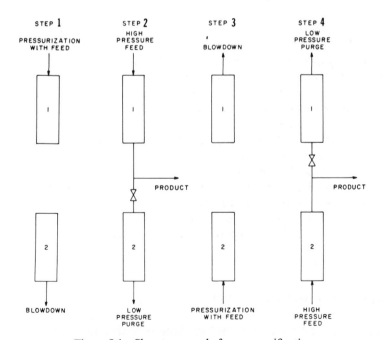

Figure 8.1   Skarstrom cycle for gas purification.

Skarstrom cycle separating a dilute adsorptive gas in an inert carrier. Chan et al. [4] extended the solution to binary mixtures with two adsorptive gases, and also obtained a more detailed solution for effluent products from all steps. The solution by Chan et al. reduces to that of Shendalman and Mitchell when Henry's constant for the carrier is zero. The solution of Chan et al. will be summarized.

The assumptions for the model are:

1. Linear isotherms are followed by both components A and B. The strong adsorptive, A, is at a trace level. The two isotherms are noninterfering.
2. The cycle is isothermal.
3. The interstitial flow velocity, u, is constant during the adsorption and purge steps.
4. Heat and mass transfer are instantaneous.
5. Plug flow is assumed, with no axial or radial dispersion.
6. Ideal gas law is obeyed.
7. Pressure gradient across the bed is negligible.

The mass balance yields, for A,

$$\varepsilon\left[\frac{\partial C_A}{\partial t} + \frac{\partial (uC_A)}{\partial z}\right] + (1-\varepsilon)\frac{\partial q_A}{\partial t} = 0 \qquad (8.1)$$

and for B:

$$\varepsilon\left[\frac{\partial C_B}{\partial t} + \frac{\partial (uC_B)}{\partial z}\right] + (1-\varepsilon)\frac{\partial q_B}{\partial t} = 0 \qquad (8.2)$$

where C is gas-phase concentration, q is the adsorbed amount per volume of pellet, t is time, z is distance, ε is the interstitial (or interpellet) void fraction and u is the interstitial velocity.

Both components adsorb independently:

$$q_A = B_A C_A; \qquad q_B = B_B C_B \qquad (8.3)$$

where B is Henry's constant and $B_A > B_B$.

Substituting equation 8.3 into equations 8.1 and 8.2, applying ideal gas law, and assuming the gas mole fraction $Y_B = 1$, we have:

$$\varepsilon\left[\frac{\partial (PY)}{\partial t} + \frac{\partial (uPY)}{\partial z}\right] + (1-\varepsilon)B_A\frac{\partial (PY)}{\partial t} = 0 \qquad (8.4)$$

$$\varepsilon\left[\frac{\partial P}{\partial t} + \frac{\partial (uP)}{\partial z}\right] + (1-\varepsilon)B_B\frac{\partial P}{\partial t} = 0 \qquad (8.5)$$

Here, P is the total pressure, and Y is the mole fraction of A where the subscript A

278 Gas Separation by Adsorption Processes

has been omitted. Since $\partial P/\partial z = 0$, equations 8.4 and 8.5 can be combined into:

$$[\varepsilon + (1-\varepsilon)B_A]\frac{\partial Y}{\partial t} + \varepsilon u \frac{\partial Y}{\partial z} + (1-\varepsilon)(B_A - B_B)Y\frac{\partial \ln P}{\partial t} = 0 \qquad (8.6)$$

From this equation, by the method of characteristics, two ordinary differential equations are obtained:

$$\frac{dt}{\varepsilon + (1-\varepsilon)B_A} = \frac{dz}{\varepsilon u} = \frac{-d\ln Y}{(1-\varepsilon)(B_A - B_B)\partial \ln P/\partial t} \qquad (8.7)$$

from which the characteristic equations are:

$$\frac{dz}{dt} = \beta_A u \qquad (8.8)$$

$$\frac{d\ln Y}{dt} = \left(\frac{\beta_A}{\beta_B} - 1\right)\frac{d\ln P}{dt} \qquad (8.9)$$

where β indicates the ratio of gas-phase capacity to the total capacity of the sorbent:

$$\beta_A = \frac{\varepsilon}{\varepsilon + (1-\varepsilon)B_A}; \qquad \beta_B = \frac{\varepsilon}{\varepsilon + (1-\varepsilon)B_B} \qquad (8.10)$$

and $\beta_A < \beta_B$.

The velocity, u, is constant during steps 2 and 4, and changing in steps 1 and 3, as described by equation 8.9.

Equation 8.8 gives the propagation velocity of the concentration front during the constant pressure steps. The penetration distances Z during these steps are:

$$Z_H = B_A u_H \Delta t \qquad (8.11)$$

$$Z_L = B_A u_L \Delta t \qquad (8.12)$$

where subscripts L and H denote the low (purge) and high (adsorption) pressure steps, with equal time length, Δt.

The changes in characteristic position and in mole fraction accompanying steps 1 and 3 (the pressure-change steps) are found as follows. Equation 8.5, with $\partial P/\partial z = 0$, yields:

$$\frac{\partial u}{\partial z} = -\left(\frac{1}{\beta_B}\right)\frac{\partial \ln P}{\partial t} \qquad (8.13)$$

which can be integrated with respect to z from the closed end where $u = 0$ at $z = 0$:

$$u = - \left(\frac{1}{\beta_B} \right) \left(\frac{\partial \ln P}{\partial t} \right) z \qquad (8.14)$$

On substituting equation 8.14 into equation 8.8, we have:

$$\frac{\partial \ln z}{\partial t} = -\beta \frac{\partial \ln P}{\partial t}; \qquad \beta = \frac{\beta_A}{\beta_B} < 1 \qquad (8.15)$$

The change in position of characteristics over a pressure-change step can be obtained by integrating the above equation to give:

$$z_H/z_L = (P_H/P_L)^{-\beta} \qquad (8.16)$$

The corresponding change in the mole fraction of A is obtained by integrating equation 8.9:

$$Y_H/Y_L = (P_H/P_L)^{\beta - 1} \qquad (8.17)$$

Through the use of equation 8.16 and the penetration distances given by equations 8.11 and 8.12, the net displacement of a concentration wavefront during a complete cycle is:

$$\Delta Z = Z_L - (P_H/P_L)^{\beta} Z_H \qquad (8.18)$$

or, from equations 8.11 and 8.12,

$$\Delta Z = \beta_A \Delta t \left[u_L - \left(\frac{P_H}{P_L} \right)^{\beta} u_H \right] \qquad (8.19)$$

The important parameter for separation, purge/feed ratio, should be defined here. Two definitions for this ratio have been used in the literature. The first one, as originally defined by Skarstrom [5], is simply the ratio of the velocities at their respective pressures:

$$\gamma = u_{\text{purge}}/u_{\text{feed}} = u_L/u_H \qquad (8.20)$$

This definition is meaningful only when the purge and feed steps have an equal length of time. A more general and useful definition is given as:

$$\frac{\text{Purge}}{\text{Feed}} \text{ ratio} = G(\text{or } \gamma) = \frac{\text{Amount of light component in purge}}{\text{Amount of light component in feed}} \qquad (8.21)$$

Under the assumed conditions in this case, they are related by:

$$\gamma = G\left(\frac{P_H}{P_L}\right)(1 - Y_f) \tag{8.22}$$

where Y_f is the mole fraction of the adsorbate in the feed.

For complete purification — that is, complete removal of A in the high-pressure product stream at steady-state operation — the following two conditions must be satisfied:

1. Breakthrough of feed into the high-pressure product stream does not occur, or

$$L(P_H/P_L)^{-\beta} \geqslant Z_H \tag{8.23}$$

where L is the total bed length.

2. Purge/feed ratio must be greater than a critical value such that ΔZ (given by equation 8.19) is positive. The critical ratio is obtained by setting $\Delta Z = 0$ in equation 8.19:

$$G_{crit} = \gamma_{crit}\left(\frac{P_L}{P_H}\right) = \left(\frac{u_L}{u_H}\right)_{crit}\left(\frac{P_L}{P_H}\right) = \left(\frac{P_H}{P_L}\right)^{\beta-1} \tag{8.24}$$

Under these two conditions, the high-pressure product in the nth cycle comes from the $n - 1/2$ cycle and experiences a low-to-high pressure change, namely [3]:

$$Y_n = Y_{n-1/2}(P_L/P_H)^{1-\beta} \tag{8.25}$$

where Y_n is the mole fraction of the effluent from the feed step.

Equation 8.25 predicts that the mole fraction in the high-pressure product steadily decreases by a constant factor $(P_L/P_H)^{1-\beta}$. This prediction, in fact, is a major deficiency of the analytic equilibrium theory. This is so because if the sorbent bed is regenerated before the startup of the first PSA cycle, we would have

$$Y_n = Y_{n-1/2} = 0 \qquad \text{with precleaned bed}$$

which contradicts experimental observations.

To circumvent this problem, Shendalman and Mitchell [3] mimicked Skarstrom's experiment (Figure 7.2, Chapter 7) and initiated the PSA cycles with a saturated sorbent bed. Thus the initial condition for equation 8.25 is:

$$Y_{\text{zeroth cycle}} = Y_f \qquad \text{with presaturated bed}$$

The mole fraction in the nth cycle is:

$$Y_n = Y_f(P_H/P_L)^{2n(\beta-1)} \tag{8.26}$$

Equation 8.26 indicates that the mole fraction of A in the high-pressure product continues to decrease indefinitely with the cycle number in order to achieve complete purification (this is not achieved in experiments and in numerical results, as will be shown later). The other process performance parameters, to be shown, are all based on steady-state operation — that is, $n \to \infty$.

The product recovery for A can be calculated by mass balance [4]:

$$\rho_\infty = (N_{feed} - N_{purge})/(N_{blowdown} + N_{feed})$$
$$= \frac{(P_H/P_L)^{1-\beta} - 1}{(P_H/P_L)^{1-\beta}(\beta L/Z_L)(P_H - P_L)/P_L} \tag{8.27}$$

where ρ_∞ is the product recovery and N is the number of moles entering or leaving the bed per half-cycle. A similar mass balance gives the overall enrichment (E_∞) in the combined blowdown and purge steps [4]:

$$E_\infty = \frac{(\beta L/Z_L)(P_H - P_L)/P_L + (P_H/P_L)^{1-\beta}}{(\beta L/Z_L)(P_H - P_L)/P_L + 1} \tag{8.28}$$

The foregoing results describe the cyclic steady-state performance of the Skarstrom cycle. The concentrations and flowrates of the effluents from all steps can be calculated by tracing the characteristics with time and summing the weighted effluent fractions [4].

As described by equations 8.23 to 8.28, four dimensionless parameters

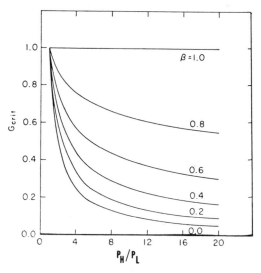

Figure 8.2 Critical purge-to-feed ratio for complete purification, varying with the pressure ratio and β where β is nearly equal to the reciprocal of the separation factor. Source: Chan, Hill, and Wong [4]. Reprinted with permission.

determine the performance of the Skarstrom cycle: β, P_H/P_L, G, and L/Z_L. The critical purge/feed ratio required for "complete cleanup" is given by equation 8.24 and shown in Figure 8.2. The product recovery of the light component (eq. 8.27) is graphically shown in Figure 8.3. In both figures, it is clearly seen that the pressure ratio beyond three or four, depending on the value of the separation factor (which is approximately $1/\beta$), does not improve the separation.

Shendalman and Mitchell [3] have tested the analytic solution against experimental data for the purification of CO_2 (1.09%) in helium with a silica gel bed using the Skarstrom cycle. As mentioned, the bed was presaturated, as in Skarstrom's experiment [5]. The result is shown in Figure 8.4. Since helium is not adsorbed in this case, $\beta_B = 1$ and $\beta = \beta_{CO_2}$. As shown in Figure 8.4, the comparison is poor and was attributed to the slow mass transfer rates [3]. The analytic solution nonetheless provides a clear picture of the qualitative dependence of the separation on the process parameters.

A major extension of the analytic theory was made by Knaebel and Hill [6] to allow for high concentration of the strongly adsorbed component, which results in a varying velocity (u) during adsorption and purge. Again, an analytic solution is possible only for linear isotherms. The characteristic equations corresponding to equations 8.8 and 8.9 are:

$$\frac{dz}{dt} = \frac{\beta_A u}{1 + (\beta - 1)Y} \tag{8.29}$$

$$\frac{d \ln Y}{dt} = \frac{(\beta - 1)(1 - Y)}{1 + (\beta - 1)Y} \frac{d \ln P}{dt} \tag{8.30}$$

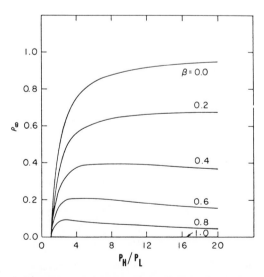

Figure 8.3 Steady-state product recovery of the light component in Skarstrom cycle. Source: Chan, Hill, and Wong [4]. Reprinted with permission.

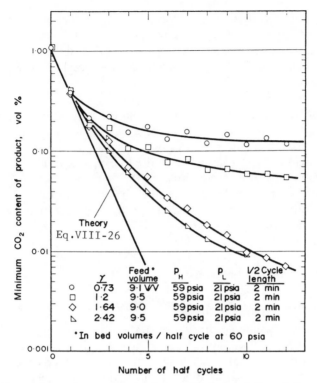

Figure 8.4 Comparison of experimental data with the analytic solution (eq. 8.26) for purification of helium containing 1.09% CO_2 by the Skarstrom cycle with silica gel. The bed was presaturated with the feed before startup. Source: Shendalman and Mitchell [3]. Reprinted with permission.

Equation 8.29 is the concentration front velocity, already derived as equation 5.10, which allows for varying interstitial velocity due to adsorption and desorption. Equation 8.30 gives the change in composition associated with the pressure-change steps. A further extension was made to compare the performance by two cases: repressurization with the feed and with the light product [6]. The critical purge-to-feed ratio for complete cleanup in the case of feed repressurization is:

$$G_{crit} = \frac{1}{[1 + (\beta - 1)Y_f]\beta_A u_H \Delta t(P_H/P_L)} \tag{8.31}$$

This equation reduces to equation 8.24 for small Y_f (feed composition) and the minimum sorbent used for complete purification [4, 6]. The critical purge-to-feed ratio for the case of repressurization with the light product is, including the gas used for repressurization in the purge amount:

$$G_{crit} = \frac{1 + \beta(P_H/P_L - 1)}{(P_H/P_L)[1 + (\beta - 1)Y_f]} \tag{8.32}$$

The critical purge/feed ratio is dependent on Y_f, β, and pressure ratio. For the same Y_f and pressure ratio, G_{crit} given by equation 8.32 is always greater than that given by equation 8.31. The difference increases as the value of β increases — that is, for lower separation factors [6]. Other separation performance parameters — light-product recovery under complete cleanup conditions, heavy-product enhancement, and so on — have also been derived [6].

An unexpected prediction by Knaebel and Hill indicates that under complete cleanup conditions pressurization with pure light product leads to higher light product recoveries than does pressurization with feed, as shown in Figure 8.5. The difference in light product recoveries is indeed large, as shown in this figure for β = 0.9 (i.e., small separation factor between the two components). The difference, however, decreases for smaller β values (i.e., for greater separation factors). This model has recently been tested satisfactorily for air separation by using linear isotherms for both oxygen and nitrogen [58].

8.1.2 Numerical Models: Isothermal

Numerical Methods for PSA Models

The PSA or any dynamic adsorption separation process is governed by a set of mass balance, heat balance, mass transfer rate (if a linear rate is assumed), and equilibrium isotherm equations. These form a set of coupled differential and algebraic equations. The partial differential equations are either hyperbolic (with no dispersion terms, which are second-order) or parabolic (with dispersion terms).

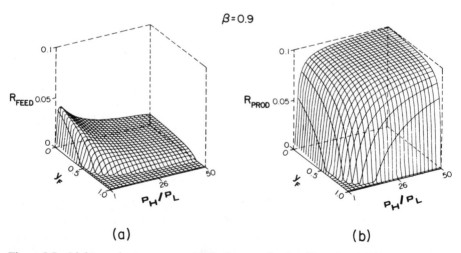

(a)   (b)

Figure 8.5   Light-product recovery with feed pressurization (R_{FEED}) and with light-product pressurization (R_{PROD}) using the Skarstrom cycle, predicted by equilibrium theory with linear isotherms, as functions of feed mole fraction (Y_F) and pressure ratio (P_H/P_L). Source: Knaebel and Hill [6]. Reprinted with permission.

This set of equations can be solved by a number of finite difference methods (e.g., Runge-Kutta, Gear's algorithm, Crank-Nicolson); orthogonal collocation; and the method of characteristics. These methods are discussed in detail in a number of texts [7–13]. The implicit backward finite difference method is generally preferred because it is relatively easy to use and, more important, is unconditionally stable for solving the hyperbolic equations (see, for example, reference 7, p. 354, and reference 13, p. 233). The Crank-Nicolson method is useful for solving parabolic equations — that is, mass and heat balance equations with dispersion terms. All the aforementioned methods have been used for solving the coupled PSA equations.

The equations to be numerically solved are often converted into a dimensionless form in which all dependent as well as independent variables are expressed in terms of dimensionless groups. There are two advantages to doing this. First, a better understanding of the parametric effects on the process can be gained. There is, however, the risk of obscuring or misunderstanding the effects if wrong dimensionless groups are formed. Second, by expressing all variables in the same scale of 0–1, the compounded truncation error caused in computation is minimized.

Isothermal PSA Models

The first published numerical model for the Skarstrom cycle was performed by Mitchell and Shendalman [14] in an attempt to reconcile the large difference between the experimental data and the equilibrium theory, as shown in Figure 8.4. The major deviation from the idealized assumptions (section 8.1.1) that caused the difference was thought to be a finite mass transfer rate in the experiments. Inclusion of the mass transfer rate in the mass balance equation would require a numerical solution. The method of characteristics in conjunction with finite difference was used in the solution.

The problem being considered is, again, the purification of a helium feed containing 1.09% CO_2 by the Skarstrom cycle. The high and low pressures of the cycle are, respectively, 4 and 1.33 atm. In the following formulation, all simplifying assumptions listed in section 8.1.1 are retained, except that a finite mass transfer rate is allowed. The mass balance equation for CO_2 is:

$$\varepsilon \left[\frac{\partial C}{\partial t} + \frac{\partial(uC)}{\partial z} \right] + (1 - \varepsilon)\frac{\partial q}{\partial t} = 0 \tag{8.33}$$

Neglecting CO_2, the overall equation of continuity is:

$$\frac{\partial P}{\partial t} + \frac{\partial(uP)}{\partial z} = 0 \tag{8.34}$$

A linear mass transfer rate for CO_2 is assumed:

$$\frac{\partial q}{\partial t} = k\left(\frac{KPY}{RT} - q \right) \tag{8.35}$$

Equations 8.33 through 8.35 can be combined to yield:

$$\frac{\varepsilon Pu}{RT}\frac{\partial Y}{\partial z} + \frac{\varepsilon P}{RT}\frac{\partial Y}{\partial t} = -(1-\varepsilon)k\left(\frac{KPY}{RT} - q\right)$$

(8.36)

Equations 8.35 and 8.36 are the governing equations for the PSA process. They may be solved for the four steps in the cycle (referring to Figure 8.1): two pressure-changing steps (steps I and III) and two constant-pressure steps (steps II and IV). Mitchell and Shendalman chose, however, not to follow through with the two pressure-changing steps because of the complexity involved. Instead, two limiting cases were considered for the two pressure-change steps:

1.   No gas-solid exchange (adsorption and desorption) is allowed to take place because the pressure changes are rapid. The solid phase is thus assumed frozen. The position of the gas phase characteristics moves according to: $z_1/z_2 = P_2/P_1$.
2.   Instant gas-solid equilibrium is assumed. This can be done by forcing an equilibrium at the end of step II (adsorption) and step IV (purge) and using the analytic equilibrium solution developed in section 8.1.1 for the two steps.

For the constant-pressure steps, the governing equations are solved as follows, with the following characteristic equations obtained by the method of characteristics from equations 8.35 and 8.36:

$$\frac{dz}{dt} = u$$

(8.37)

$$\frac{dY}{dz} = -(1-\varepsilon)k\left(\frac{KPY}{RT} - q\right)\frac{RT}{\varepsilon Pu}$$

(8.38)

$$\frac{dq}{dt} = k\left(\frac{KPY}{RT} - q\right)$$

(8.39)

The three ordinary differential equations can then be solved by any finite difference scheme.

The mass transfer coefficient, k, was measured through a breakthrough curve at 4 atm pressure [14], which was the high pressure in the PSA cycle. Also, its value was assumed to be constant and independent of pressure. The numerical solutions in the two extreme cases assumed for the pressure-changing steps are shown in Figure 8.6, along with experimental data obtained under the same operating conditions. The figure also includes the actual data of the effluent product concentration obtained from the two beds operated in tandem. The upturn at the end of each half-cycle results from CO_2 being compressed to a location not far from the product end of the bed during the repress step. The impurity is eluted from the bed at the end of the half-cycle. The experimental data shown in the right-hand

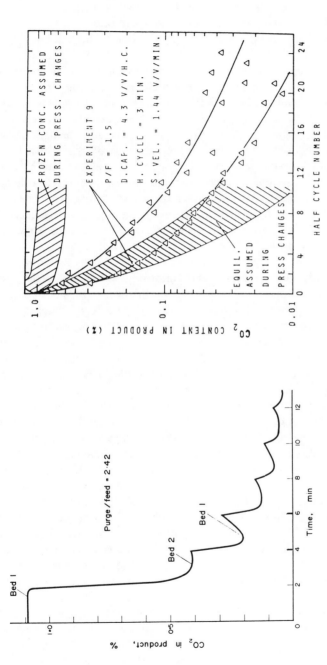

Figure 8.6 (*Left*) Typical experimental data for cleanup of 1.09% CO_2 in He by a two-bed Skarstrom cycle. Both beds are presaturated with the feed. Half-cycle time = 2 minutes. The 12 minute point corresponds to the end of the sixth half-cycle. Source Shendalman and Mitchell [3]. Reprinted with permission. (*Right*) Comparison of experimental data with two extreme cases of numerical solution. Source: Mitchell and Shendalman [14]. Reprinted with permission.

side of Figure 8.6 are the high and low points of the actual curve. The product purity is the flow-average of the curve. The dynamic capacity (d. cap.) in Figure 8.6 is simply the product of the half-cycle time and space velocity.

It is clearly shown in Figure 8.6 that the "frozen" solid assumption for the pressure-changing steps predicts much less separation than is actually achieved, whereas the equilibrium assumption predicts more separation. The prediction by the equilibrium assumption is, however, much closer to the experiment.

The numerical computation and the experimental measurement of Mitchell and Shendalman, as shown in Figure 8.6, have not been carried out to reach a cyclic steady state. The results should level off to constant values when such a state is reached. The steady-state results should be the same regardless of whether the beds are presaturated or initially clean. As mentioned, the analytic solution (given in section 8.1.1) is not capable of predicting the steady-state result because the product purity monotonically decreases with the half-cycle number. Consequently, the analytic solution cannot be used for PSA with initially clean beds. With one exception [15], initially clean beds are used in all subsequent research, and the results can be predicted by the numerical models.

An algebraic model based on the assumption of instantaneous gas-solid equilibrium was proposed by Weaver and Hamrin [15]. For this model, the total volumes of the gas streams leaving and entering the beds in all steps are assumed given (including the volumes of blowdown and purge gases). These volumes are also assumed to be independent of the cycle number. The only unknowns are the concentrations in these streams. A mass balance equation is then written around each bed at the end of each step. These are simple algebraic equations. Thus four equations are available for two beds in each half-cycle. There are, however, five unknown concentrations. The additional equation is obtained by using Skarstrom's empirical observation that at purge/feed (P/F) ratio = 1, complete cleanup is achieved and the product concentration does not decrease further with half-cycle number. The set of algebraic equations is solved starting from the first cycle. The computation was performed in a computer. Their experiment involved the difficult separation of hydrogen/deuterium (5.5% of the latter) using the Skarstrom cycle with beds containing pellets of palladium supported on alumina. Presaturated beds were used. With high P/F ratios and short cycle times, the best enrichment for deuterium was 17.5%. The experimental results agreed to within 20–30% of the model. The model is of limited value, however, because of the oversimplifications and the required knowledge of the gas stream volumes in all steps. Furthermore, this model cannot be used for PSA with initially clean beds.

Air drying by the Skarstrom cycle using silica gel was studied by Carter and Wyszynski [16]. The numerical model was similar to that of Mitchell and Shendalman [14]. Isothermal condition was assumed. The adsorption isotherm, independently measured, contained two linear segments. The linear-driving-force (LDF) equation was used for the mass transfer rate (see eq. 4.55, Chapter 4). The frozen concentration assumption was assumed for the two pressure-changing steps; that is, the concentration and distribution in the adsorbed phase were frozen. The implicit backward finite difference method was the numerical method used. The experiment involved the drying of air, saturated at 48.9°C, by cycling the pressure between 1 and 5.45 atm in beds maintained at 50.5°C. The beds were clean before the first cycle. Excellent agreement was obtained between experiment and model prediction. The results are shown in Figure 8.7. It was shown that a large number of cycles were needed for the process to reach a cyclic steady state.

8.1.3 Adsorption and Desorption during Pressure-Changing Steps

In a typical operation of the Skarstrom cycle for gas purification, the time lengths for the pressure-changing steps (repressurization and blowdown) are relatively short compared to the total cycle time. In addition, these steps present considerable difficulties when modeling the cycle. As a result, two opposite assumptions, as already discussed and shown in Figure 8.6, have been used by various groups in modeling these steps. With the frozen solid assumption no adsorption or desorption is allowed for, whereas instant gas-solid equilibrium is established according to the equilibrium assumption. Ideally, the mass transfer rates should be accounted for during these steps, as will be shown later in this chapter. In this section, the literature data regarding these two pressure-changing steps are analyzed, with an assessment given regarding whether the mass transfer rates are negligible in these short steps.

Frozen Solid-Phase Assumption

Despite the early work of Mitchell and Shendalman [14] showing a great discrepancy between experiment and theory based on the frozen solid assumption (Figure 8.6), the same assumption has been used (successfully) by all groups studying the Skarstrom cycle [16–19].

The fit between experiment and theory (with frozen solid assumption) by Carter and Wyszynski is shown in Figure 8.7. The drying of air was also studied by Chihara and Suzuki [17, 18] using activated alumina and silica gel, with a cycle time of 9 minutes and pressure cycled between 1 and 5 atm. Heat transfer was also accounted for in their model. (Their nonisothermal model will be discussed in the next section.) It suffices to say at this point that the mass transfer rates were independently measured, and that their experimental data fit well with the model based on the frozen solid assumption for the two pressure-changing steps.

The effects of the mass transfer coefficient and axial dispersion on the Skarstrom cycle performance have been examined by Ruthven and co-workers using an isothermal model [19]. The model was similar to that by Mitchell and Shendalman, discussed in section 8.1.2, except that a dispersion term was included in the mass balance equation (eq. 8.33) and the mass transfer coefficient, k in equation 8.35, was allowed to vary with pressure, via

$$k \propto 1/P \qquad (8.40)$$

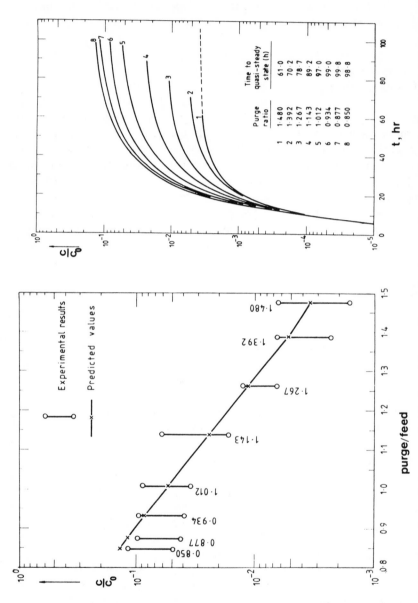

Figure 8.7 (*Left*) Comparison of theory and experiment for cyclic steady-state product concentration as a function of purge/feed ratio. (*Right*) Predicted water vapor concentration in product versus time from startup with initially dry beds. Source: Carter and Wyszynski [16]. Reprinted with permission.

The numerical model also included the frozen solid assumption. Thus two values of k were used, one for adsorption and one for purge. The effects of dispersion and mass transfer coefficient on the drying of air, using the data of Chihara and Suzuki, are shown in Table 8.1. As expected, a lower dispersion coefficient and higher mass transfer coefficient will result in a better separation. The combined effects of the two parameters, however, can be seen only by the model as shown in Table 8.1. Under practical conditions the value of the Peclet number is greater than 100. It is seen that the effects of k become increasingly important at higher Pe values, whereas a further increase in Pe has little effect on separation.

The model of Ruthven et al. [19] was also applied to the data by Mitchell and Shendalman [14] for the purification of helium containing 1.09% CO_2 by cycling the pressure between 1.33 and 4 atm. The mass transfer coefficient (k) was measured at 4 atm, and it was assumed constant and equal for both high- and low-pressure steps by Mitchell and Shendalman [14]. However, the value of k should be inversely proportional to P if either film or pore diffusion in the molecular diffusion regime is the controlling step. Consequently, the value of k was taken as three times the 4 atm value for the purge step (at 1.33 atm) in the model of Ruthven et al. By this adjustment, an excellent agreement between theory and experiment was achieved. An example of the agreement is shown in Figure 8.8. The Peclet number was taken as 140 to obtain curve B in the figure. (The Pe value for the other curves in this figure may be taken as ∞, as no dispersion is considered.) However, the effect of Pe is insignificant in the operation range. Comparing curves A and B, it is seen that a huge difference in separation can be brought about by simply changing the mass transfer coefficient in the purge step. Figure 8.8 also illustrates the steady improvement in separation when the mass transfer resistance is increasingly relaxed.

It is obvious that, by the proper choice of mass transfer rates, an agreement can be reached between theory and experiment.

Table 8.1 Effects of Dispersion (D_z) and Mass Transfer Coefficient (k) on the Steady-State High-Pressure Product Purity (C/C_0)

	C/C_0	
$Pe = uL/D_z$	$k = constant = k_1$	$k = k_1$ and $5k_1$[a]
10	0.1087	0.0838
100	0.0515	0.0281
1,000	—	0.0266

Note: Predictions by an isothermal model with frozen solid assumption during blowdown and repressure. Process conditions: Air drying with alumina; purge/feed = 2.0; $P_H = 5$ atm; $P_L = 1$ atm; $L = 0.5$ meters; half-cycle time = 4.5 min; $T = 303$K.
[a] $k = k_1$ during adsorption and $5k_1$ during purge.

Repressurization Step

Significant experimental results were obtained by Fernandez and Kenney [20] in a study of the pressurization step. This experiment involved the rapid pressurization of dry air in a 1.08-meter-long bed of 5A zeolite (1–2 mm spheres). Predried air was introduced into the bed to raise the bed pressure from 1 atm to about 6 atm in a time duration ranging from 4 to 60 seconds, depending on the final pressure. Gas samples were rapidly drawn from five sampling taps for analysis. The total delay in the gas concentration analysis varied between 0.2 and 0.7 seconds. The experimental data are shown in Figure 8.9. Also shown in this figure are the predictions by the equilibrium theory.

The equilibrium theory is essentially the same as that presented in section 8.1.1. Linear isotherms are assumed for both oxygen and nitrogen. However, the assumption regarding trace concentration of A (i.e., $Y_B = 1$) is relaxed, and thus the ensuing results are applicable to bulk separation. An analytic solution is not possible in this case.

Equations 8.1–8.3 are the governing equations. Equations 8.1 and 8.2 are

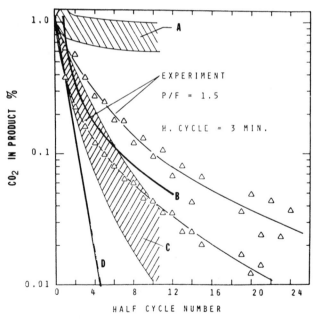

Figure 8.8 Modeling of the purification of helium, containing 1.09% CO_2, by the Skarstrom cycle [14] (see Figure 8.6). Sensitivity of separation to mass transfer rates. A: frozen solid assumed in repressure (step I) and blowdown (step III), k (mass transfer coefficient) $= k_1$ in adsorption (step II) and purge (step IV); B: frozen solid in I and III, $k = k_1$ in II, $k = 3k_1$ in IV [19]; C: equilibrium in I and III, $k = k_1$ in II and IV; D: equilibrium in I, III, II, and IV [3].

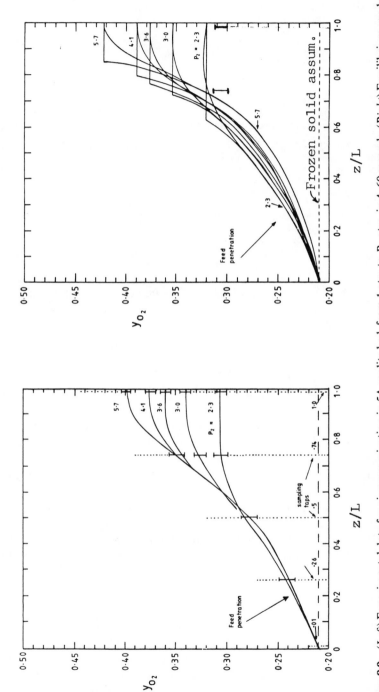

Figure 8.9 (*Left*) Experimental data for air pressurization in 5A zeolite bed, from 1 atm to P_2 atm, in 4–60 seconds. (*Right*) Equilibrium model predictions. Curves with discontinuity are "exact" solutions, and smooth curves are approximate solutions. Note the equilibrium theory slightly overpredicts the separation, whereas the frozen solid assumption fails entirely. Source: Fernandez and Kenney [20]. Reprinted with permission.

recast into [20]:

$$A\frac{\partial(uC)}{\partial z} + a_2\frac{\partial P}{\partial t} + a_3\frac{\partial P_A}{\partial t} = 0 \tag{8.41}$$

$$A\frac{\partial(uCY_A)}{\partial z} + a_1\frac{\partial P_A}{\partial t} = 0 \tag{8.42}$$

where A is the cross-sectional area of the bed, and the constant coefficients are:

$$a_1 = \frac{\varepsilon}{RT}\left(\frac{1}{\beta_A}\right) \tag{8.42a}$$

$$a_2 = \frac{\varepsilon}{RT}\left(\frac{1}{\beta_B}\right) \tag{8.42b}$$

$$a_3 = a_1 - a_2 = \frac{\varepsilon}{RT}\left(\frac{1}{\beta_A} - \frac{1}{\beta_B}\right) \tag{8.42c}$$

Equations 8.41 and 8.42 are solved with the following boundary conditions:

$$C_A(t = 0, z) = C_{A0}\text{(uniform initial concentration)} \tag{8.43}$$

$$u(t, z = L) = 0\text{(no flow at the closed end)} \tag{8.44a}$$

$$C_A(t, z = 0) = C_{Af}\text{(constant feed concentration)} \tag{8.44b}$$

$$P = P(t)\text{(measured pressure history)} \tag{8.44c}$$

The set of seven equations (eqs. 8.41–8.44) were solved numerically [20] by the method of characteristics (referred to in Figure 8.9 as *exact* solution) and cell model (*approximate* solution). In both methods, first-order ordinary differential equations were derived and were then integrated in conjunction with algebraic equations. Thus the numerical computation was simplified [20].

The comparison given in Figure 8.9 shows that gas-solid equilibrium is nearly reached during the rapid pressurization of the zeolite bed. A great amount of nitrogen and oxygen is rapidly uptaken into the solid phase. The failure of the frozen solid assumption during bed pressurization is clearly demonstrated by the experimental data of Fernandez and Kenney.

Blowdown Step

The blowdown or depressurization step follows the adsorption step in all PSA cycles. This step has been the subject of an experimental and theoretical study by Richter et al. in their development of hydrogen separation/purification processes with molecular-sieve carbon [21]. A series of blowdown experiments were conducted with molecular-sieve carbon beds initially fully or partially saturated with mixtures of hydrogen (70 to over 90%) with methane or nitrogen. The bed pressure was lowered from 30 atm to ambient by releasing the gas through a throttle valve at a constant opening. During the initial period, the pressure dropped rapidly to 10 atm in approximately 1 minute. In all experiments the amount of gas released was in close agreement with equilibrium theory. The model assumed that the Langmuir isotherm was instantaneously reached for methane or nitrogen (adsorption of hydrogen was neglected). A typical comparison between experiment and equilibrium model is shown in Figure 8.10.

For purification processes where the linear isotherm may be assumed for the blowdown step, an analytic solution for the total amount of gas discharged during blowdown is directly available from the solution given in section 8.1.1 of this chapter. The number of moles of the discharged inert carrier gas is:

$$\text{Discharged carrier} = \frac{\varepsilon V}{RT}(P_H - P_L)(1 - Y_f) \qquad (8.45)$$

where V is the total bed volume, and the number of moles of discharged adsorbate is (3):

$$\text{Discharged adsorbate} = \frac{\varepsilon V}{RT} P_H Y_f \left[\frac{\varepsilon + (1 - \varepsilon)B}{\varepsilon} \right] \left[1 - \left(\frac{P_L}{P_H} \right)^{\frac{\varepsilon}{\varepsilon + (1 - \varepsilon)B}} \right] \qquad (8.46)$$

where Y_f is the feed gas mole fraction (with which the bed is presaturated) and B is Henry's constant.

The ratio between the discharged adsorbate and discharged carrier is approximately BY_f. The value of B for water vapor on activated alumina at 303K is 9,084 [17, 19], and that for CO_2 on silica gel is 52 at 298K [14]. The ratio is not small even for a small feed concentration, Y_f.

In conclusion, an agreement between the frozen solid model and experimental data can be reached, as evidenced in the literature, as long as proper mass transfer coefficients are used in the model. The sensitivity of the PSA performance

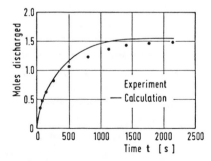
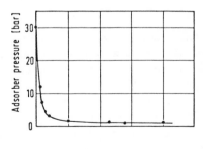

Figure 8.10 Blowdown of a molecular-sieve carbon bed presaturated with a gas mixture of H_2 and CH_4 (13.5%) at 30.3 bar. The calculation is based on instant gas-solid equilibrium. Source: Richter et al. [21]. Reprinted with permission.

to the mass transfer coefficient is clearly shown by Raghavan et al. [19]. In contrast, direct experimental results on bed pressurization by Fernandez and Kenney [20] and on bed blowdown by Richter et al. [21] have clearly demonstrated that equilibrium exchange between the gas and adsorbed phases is nearly reached in these steps. The frozen solid-phase assumption for these steps could only be used for the purpose of simplified design provided the operating ranges are well covered. The experimental results on these steps [20, 21] are too overwhelming to be ignored. Adsorption and desorption in these steps should be accounted for in order to understand the PSA process.

Linear Driving Force Rate Approximation

As seen from the foregoing discussion, the mass transfer rate is an important parameter in modeling the PSA process. A linear expression for the rate is desirable for mathematical simplificity. As in the modeling of adsorbers, the linear driving force (LDF) approximation is widely used for the mass transfer rate. A detailed discussion on the LDF is given in Chapter 4. The LDF equation approximates the rate of sorption by a spherical particle that is subject to varying increases in the ambient fluid concentration (an exponentially increasing concentration and a linearly increasing concentration). The approximation, as given by Glueckauf and Coates [22, 23], reads:

$$\frac{\partial \bar{q}}{\partial t} = \frac{15 D_e}{R_p^2} (q^* - \bar{q}) \tag{8.47}$$

where D_e is the effective pore diffusivity; R_p is the radius; and $\bar{q}$ and q^* are the average and equilibrium values of q, respectively.

Nakao and Suzuki have examined the accuracy of equation 8.47 as applied to the Skarstrom cycle [24]. However, the frozen solid assumption was assumed. Their comparison was made by numerically solving the diffusion equation

$$\frac{\partial q}{\partial t} = D_e \left(\frac{\partial^2 q}{\partial r^2} + \frac{2}{r} \frac{\partial q}{\partial r} \right) \tag{8.48}$$

through the two-step adsorption-desorption cycles by varying the ambient concentration between a constant value and zero. The result was compared with that from a linear mass transfer equation with the same form as equation 8.47. The numerical coefficient for this linear equation, which was required to yield an agreement between the two sets of results, was found to be higher than 15. The coefficient (K) has been shown in Figure 4.10. The K values given in Figure 4.10 are, however, not applicable to the Skarstrom cycle or any other PSA processes since no mass transfer is allowed during the pressure-changing steps. The K values given in Figure 4.10 will be lower and hence closer to 15 if the mass transfer rate is allowed during the pressure-changing steps. Further work is needed to establish the K values for the PSA cycle, including all cycle steps.

The analysis of Nakao and Suzuki was made for a single particle. The analysis was recently extended to adsorbers, which included the interparticle void fraction [56]. The results are also shown in Figure 4.10.

8.1.4 Other Numerical Models

Nonisothermal Model

The most important guidelines originally given by Skarstrom [5] in operating the Skarstrom cycle was to use short cycles and minimize the amount of sorbate throughput per cycle. The purpose is to "conserve" energy so an isothermal condition is achieved. The nonisothermal model [17, 25] and the air drying experiment [18] by Chihara and Suzuki have demonstrated that a small temperature swing always exists in the cycle and that such a small temperature swing has a significant effect on the separation result. A summary of their model follows.

All assumptions stated in section 8.1.1 are retained except that (1) a nonisothermal condition is allowed, and (2) mass transfer rates are finite. However, two new restrictions are added: (1) The frozen solid phase assumption is used for the pressure-changing steps, and (2) bed repressurization is not accomplished by the feed; the pressure is increased while the gas-phase concentration remains unchanged. Under these assumptions, the equations to be solved are:

$$u\frac{\partial C}{\partial z} + \frac{\partial C}{\partial t} + \frac{1-\varepsilon}{\varepsilon}\frac{\partial q}{\partial t} = 0 \tag{8.49}$$

$$\frac{\partial q}{\partial t} = k(q^* - q) \tag{8.50}$$

$$q^* = BC, \qquad \ln\frac{B}{B_0} = \frac{H}{R}\left(\frac{1}{T} - \frac{1}{T_0}\right) \tag{8.51}$$

$$k_{ez}\frac{\partial^2 T}{\partial z^2} - \varepsilon u \rho_g C_{pg}\frac{\partial T}{\partial z} + \frac{2h}{R_b}(T_0 - T) - [\varepsilon\rho_g C_{pg} + (1-\varepsilon)\rho_s C_{ps}]\frac{\partial T}{\partial t} + H\frac{\partial q}{\partial t} = 0 \tag{8.52}$$

where T_0 is the ambient temperature, k_{ez} is the axial heat dispersion, ρ is density, C_p is heat capacity, R_b is bed radius, h is the overall heat transfer coefficient through the wall, H is heat of adsorption, and ρ_g is allowed to change with temperature. Thermal equilibrium between gas and solid is assumed. These four coupled equations are solved for the two constant-pressure steps where:

$$u = u_H \qquad \text{for adsorption}$$

$$u = u_L \qquad \text{for purge}$$

The boundary conditions for the feed step are:

$$C = C_0, q = q_0^*, T = T_0 \qquad \text{at } z = 0 \tag{8.53}$$

and for the purge step:

$$C(L, t) = \frac{P_L}{P_H} C(L, t - \Delta t),$$

$$T(L, t) = T_0 \qquad \text{at } z = L \tag{8.54}$$

where Δt is the half-cycle time. Equations 8.53 and 8.54 indicate that the purge is countercurrent while the purge gas is drawn from the product gas.

Equations 8.49–8.54 can be solved by a number of numerical methods. Chihara and Suzuki transformed these equations into dimensionless form and solved them by the Crank-Nicolson implicit method. The case being studied was air drying with activated alumina. The feed air contained 0.79 gmol/m^3 water vapor. The purge/feed ratio was 2 ($u_H = 0.25$ m/s and $u_L = 0.5$ m/s). The pressure was cycled between 5 and 1 atm, with an equal half-cycle time of 9 minutes. The bed height was 1 meter. Depending on the conditions, approximately 40 cycles were needed before the process reached a cyclic steady state. The steady-state results are summarized in Table 8.2. The nonisothermal model results were essentially confirmed by experiments in a separate study [18]. In the latter study the sorbent was silica gel, and the properties were changed accordingly. The mass transfer coefficient was assumed to be inversely proportional to P. Thus two values were used. To fit the experimental data with the nonisothermal model, the mass transfer coefficients must be two to three times higher than that given by the linear driving force approximation, $15D_e/R_p^2$. The higher artificial mass transfer coefficients were clearly due in part, if not entirely, to the frozen solid assumption. The comparison shown in Table 8.2 is, however, valid. It is seen that the isothermal assumption predicts a substantially better separation than is actually achieved. The adiabatic

Table 8.2 Air Drying with Activated Alumina by Skarstrom Cycle Predicted by a Nonisothermal Model

Operation	Product concentration, C/C_0
Nonisothermal[a]	1.34×10^{-3}
Isothermal	7.50×10^{-4}
Adiabatic	3.38×10^{-3}
Nonisothermal, $L = 0.5$ m	3.18×10^{-2}
Nonisothermal, $\Delta t = 2.25$ min	4.18×10^{-4}
Nonisothermal, $P/F = 1$	5.75×10^{-3}

Source: Chihara and Suzuki [17]. Reprinted with permission.
[a] Conditions: $L = 1$ m, $\Delta t = 4.5$ min, $P/F = 2$. See text for others. The maximum temperature fluctuation of 5°C occurred near the feed end.

condition, which is nearly approached in industrial large-size dryers, results in the worst separation.

From the foregoing discussion, it is clear that both isothermality and the frozen solid phase (for the pressure-changing steps) are hypothetical assumptions used in modeling. The two assumptions both have strong but opposite effects on the model results. The isothermal assumption indicates a better separation than will actually be achieved, whereas the frozen solid assumption predicts a much weaker separation. No study has been made to examine how these two factors may offset each other. However, an interesting comparison may be made between the two modeling studies in references 16 and 17. In reference 16, both assumptions were made, and the separation was predicted well by the model using mass transfer coefficients that were measured independently. In reference 17, only a frozen solid assumption was used. In this case the separation results could be fitted only with mass transfer coefficients two to three times higher than those measured independently. Both studies employed the LDF equation for mass transfer.

For purification processes, a large number of cycles and consequently a long transient time are required to reach a steady state. (This is not true for bulk separation, as will be discussed later in this chapter.) The long startup has been shown for air drying by Carter and Wyszynski (Figure 8.7) and by Chihara and Suzuki. In the dynamic steady state, the bed is partially loaded with the loading concentrated toward the feed end. A practical measure to shorten the transient time is to preload the bed partially with sorbate. This method has been suggested and studied by Nakao and Suzuki [26] and Knaebel and Hill [27].

Steady Countercurrent-Flow Approximation

An interesting approximation for the Skarstrom cycle has been proposed by Suzuki [28]. The approximation is illustrated in Figure 8.11. In Figure 8.11a, the bed profile for the amount adsorbed (q_i) was found to oscillate by a small amplitude from the numerical simulation results [17]. This is true when the throughput per cycle is extremely small. The limiting situation, with the assumption of frozen solid phase during repressure and blowdown, is shown in Figure 8.11b. The bed profile for q_i, in the extreme case, may then be assumed time-invariant. The performance of the Skarstrom cycle may therefore be estimated by a hypothetical steady-state countercurrent-flow contactor, shown in Figure 8.11c. The computation for the performance of this contactor is less than that for the Skarstrom cycle. Furthermore, the isothermal condition must be assumed for this approximation.

In the steady-state contactor approximation, the mass transfer rate from $q_i^*(P_{iH})$ to q_i is equal to that from q_i to $q_i^*(P_{iL})$ at any given location in the bed (see Figure 8.11b), where q_i^* is the equilibrium amount of i adsorbed. The mass transfer rate can be alternatively expressed in terms of the difference between P_{iH} and $P_i^*(q_i)$ for the high-pressure side, where P_i^* is the partial pressure in equilibrium with q_i. The choice between the two driving forces depends entirely on the way the mass transfer coefficient is measured and expressed. The latter one will be used here.

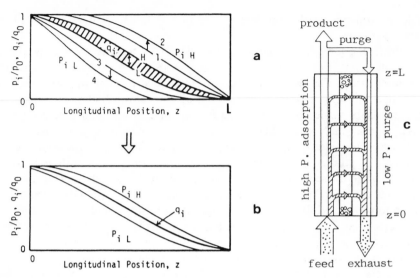

Figure 8.11   (a) Partial pressure (P_i) and amount adsorbed (q_i) profiles at the ends of four steps: (1) repressure, (2) feed, (3) blowdown, and (4) purge. Frozen solid profiles are assumed for (1) and (3); (b) approximate profiles for small adsorbate i throughput per cycle; (c) representation of the Skarstrom cycle by a continuous countercurrent-flow contactor. Source: Suzuki [28]. Reprinted with permission.

The mass balance equations for the steady-state contactor are:

$$N_H \frac{dC_{iH}}{dz} + M_i = 0 \tag{8.55}$$

$$N_L \frac{dC_{iL}}{dz} + M_i = 0 \tag{8.56}$$

where M_i is the mass transfer rate expressed in moles/m^3/s, and C_i is the molar ratio between component i and the inert carrier, thus related to pressure by:

$$P_{iH} = \frac{C_{iH}P_H}{1 + \Sigma C_{iH}} \tag{8.57}$$

$$P_{iL} = \frac{C_{iL}P_L}{1 + \Sigma C_{iL}} \tag{8.58}$$

The quantity N is the molar flux of the inert carrier entering or leaving the bed. The mass transfer rate, following Figure 8.11b, is:

$$2M_i = k_{iH}(P_{iH} - P_i^*)/RT = k_{iL}(P_i^* - P_{iL})/RT$$
$$= \bar{k}_i(P_{iH} - P_{iL})/RT \tag{8.59}$$

where $\bar{k}$ is the overall coefficient:

$$\frac{1}{\bar{k}_i} = \frac{1}{k_{iH}} + \frac{1}{k_{iL}} \tag{8.60}$$

In the preceding and following derivations, the high-pressure feed and low-pressure purge steps are assumed to be equal in duration. Thus the values of N_H and N_L are one-half of their respective values in the actual Skarstrom cycle. The same reason holds for the factor of 2 entered in equation 8.59. The profile for the amount adsorbed is then determined by the extended Langmuir isotherm:

$$q_i = q_i(P_i^* \ldots) \tag{8.61}$$

where P_i^* is obtained from equation 8.59:

$$P_i^* = \frac{2M_i RT}{k_{iL}} + P_{iL} \tag{8.62}$$

The boundary conditions are:

$$\text{At } z = 0,\ C_{iH} = C_{if} \tag{8.63}$$

$$z = L,\ C_{iL} = C_{iPurge} \text{ or} \tag{8.65}$$

$$C_{iL} = (C_{iH})_{z=L} \tag{8.66}$$

When equation 8.66 is used, mass balance around the bed yields:

$$(C_{iL})_{z=0} = [C_{if} - (C_{iH})_{z=L}](N_H/N_L) + (C_{iH})_{z=L} \tag{8.67}$$

The second boundary condition may be approximated by assuming complete cleanup (i.e. $C_{iH} = 0$ at $z = L$). Thus, from equation 8.67, equation 8.65 is replaced by:

$$\text{At } z = 0,\ C_{iL} = C_{if}(N_H/N_L) \tag{8.68}$$

Equations 8.55 and 8.56 are numerically integrated with the aid of the foregoing equations to yield the steady-state bed profiles of P_{iH}, P_{iL}, and q_i for the ith component. An example of the application for hydrogen purification using the Skarstrom cycle is given in Figure 8.12, although the Skarstrom cycle is not commercially used for this application (see Chapter 7, section 7.2.2). This approximation model has been verified for air drying, where a good agreement was obtained between this and the isothermal model results obtained at the cyclic steady state [17, 28]. As may be expected, the results from the approximate model are highly sensitive to the mass transfer coefficients [28]. It is difficult to judge whether an independently measured pore diffusivity (D_e) can be used to yield a

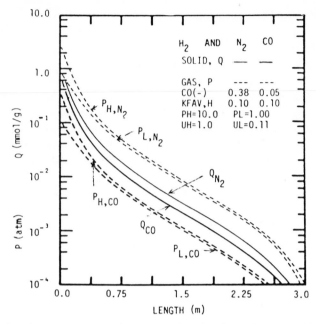

Figure 8.12 Steady countercurrent-flow approximation for hydrogen purification with 5A zeolite using the Skarstrom cycle. Feed mixture: N_2, 26.5% or $C_{if} = 0.38$; CO, 3.5% or $C_{if} = 0.05$ and the balance H_2. Operation conditions: $P_H = 10$ atm, $P_L = 1$ atm, $N_H = 2.0$ mol/m^2/s, $N_L = 0.22$ mol/m^2/s (H_2 inert). $k_{iH} = 0.1$ s^{-1}, $k_{iL} = 1.0$ s^{-1} for all i. $L = 3$ m. Half-cycle time → zero.

mass transfer coefficient ($k \cong 15D_e/R_p^2$) in this model, since both isothermality and frozen solid phase are assumed. These two assumptions, as already discussed, have opposite effects on the predicted separation results.

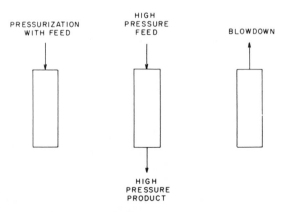

Figure 8.13 Steps in the single-bed PSA-parametric pumping process.

8.2   MODELS FOR PSA-PARAMETRIC PUMPING

The PSA-parametric pumping process [29–31], also referred to as *rapid PSA*, is a single-bed process, as fully described in section 7.2.4 of Chapter 7. The process is commercially used for small-volume oxygen generation [31–33].

A simplified schematic of the process is given in Figure 8.13, which does not include the product surge tank and continuous product withdrawal. The cycle schematic is identical to the first three steps of the Skarstrom cycle, with the omission of the purge step. The modeling of this process is, therefore, similar to the Skarstrom cycle, except when a varying time cycle and product surge tank are included for consideration.

8.2.1   Analytic Model

In contrast to the Skarstrom cycle, which is used to recover the inert (or weakly adsorbed) carrier, the single-bed process is used to recover the weakly adsorbed "impurity" — for example, separating oxygen from air with zeolites. In the ensuing derivation, A and B are still used to refer to impurity and carrier, respectively, except that A is the weakly adsorbed component.

An analytic solution can be derived under the same idealized conditions as given in section 8.1.1. The major assumptions are: linear isotherms, isothermality, and trace amounts of A, hence constant velocity in the adsorption step. Hill's derivation [34] will be followed here.

Following section 8.1.1, the depth of penetration by the feed mixture after step I (pressurization) is:

$$Z_p = (P_H/P_L)^{-\beta}L \tag{8.69}$$

where $\beta = \beta_A/\beta_B$, which approximates the reciprocal of the separation factor. Thus impurity originally within the column is found in the length $0 \leqslant z \leqslant Z_p$, and the pressurizing feed in the length $Z_p \leqslant z \leqslant L$. Also, impurity originally present in the column at position z_L will be found after pressurization at

$$z_H = (P_H/P_L)^{-\beta}z_L, \; 0 \leqslant z_H \leqslant Z_p \tag{8.70}$$

and its mole fraction will have become

$$Y_H = (P_H/P_L)^{\beta-1}Y_L, \; 0 \leqslant z_H \leqslant Z_p \tag{8.71}$$

Impurity introduced in the feed will have the mole fraction distribution:

$$Y_H(z_H) = (z_H/L)^{1/\beta-1}Y_f, \; Z_p \leqslant z_H \leqslant L \tag{8.72}$$

During the high-pressure feed, the penetration is

$$Z_H = \beta_A u_B \Delta t \qquad (8.73)$$

and no change in impurity mole fraction will accompany this movement. The resulting gas-phase mole fraction profile after pressurization is shown in Figure 8.14. The profiles (for $\beta > 1$) are similar to those shown in Figure 8.9 for pressurization of a 5A zeolite bed with air, except in Figure 8.9, where the flowrate is allowed to change as a result of adsorption. Hence no analytic solution is available. The value of β for oxygen (A)/nitrogen (B) on zeolites is nearly 2–3.

Practical interest in the three-step cycle depends on the impurity enrichment ratio, Y_{prod}/Y_f, attainable in the high-pressure product together with the product recovery, ρ_A. The best result will be for the case when no feed breakthrough is allowed into the product in the cycle operation. The conditions for such an operation are given as follows.

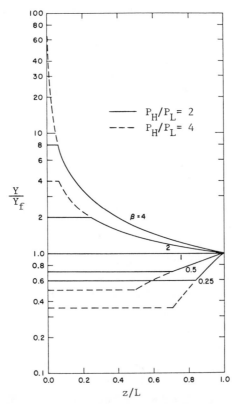

Figure 8.14 Impurity mole fraction profiles after pressurization. Bed equilibrated with feed before pressurization. $\beta \cong 2$–3 for O_2/N_2 on zeolites. Source: Hill [34]. Reprinted with permission.

Feed introduced during the feed step will not break through into the product stream during that step if

$$Z_H \leqslant (P_H/P_L)^{-\beta} L \qquad (8.74)$$

It will not break through in a later step if

$$Z_H \leqslant [1 - (P_H/P_L)^{-\beta}] L \qquad (8.75)$$

Movement of impurity characteristics through a column for a situation in which these inequalities are obeyed is shown in Figure 8.15. The high-pressure product is made up by two contributions with average mole fractions $\bar{Y}_1$ and $\bar{Y}_2$ for the sections, respectively, between $(P_H/P_L)^{-\beta} L$ and Z_H, and Z_H and $(P_H/P_L)^{-\beta} L + Z_H$. The product mole fraction is given by the weighted sum:

$$Y_{\text{prod}} = \frac{1}{Z_H} \left[\int_{(P_H/P_L)^{-\beta} L}^{(P_H/P_L)^{-\beta} L + Z_H} (z/L)^{1/\beta - 1} dz \right] Y_f$$

$$= \frac{\beta L}{Z_H} \left[\left(\frac{P_H^{-\beta}}{P_L^{-\beta}} + \frac{Z_H}{L} \right)^{1/\beta} - \frac{P_L}{P_H} \right] Y_f \qquad (8.76)$$

The product recovery can be obtained by a mass balance around the column, and

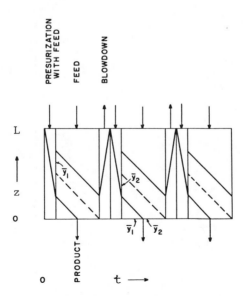

Figure 8.15 Movement of impurity characteristics through column in the three-step cycle under conditions when no feed breakthrough into product occurs. Source: Hill [34]. Reprinted with permission.

similar to equation 8.27, we have:

$$\rho = \left(\frac{Y_{prod}}{Y_f}\right)\frac{P_H/P_L}{(\beta L/Z_H)(P_H/P_L - 1) + P_H/P_L} \tag{8.77}$$

The results are graphically shown in Figure 8.16, where the product cut is defined as the total fraction of feed removed as product.

8.2.2   Numerical Models

Numerical models as well as experimental results on the single-bed process have been published by three different groups: Kadlec et al. [29, 35]; Fernandez and Kenney [20]; and Cheng and Hill [36, 37].

In all three models, the isothermal condition and instantaneous gas-solid equilibrium are assumed. The other idealized assumptions listed in section 8.1.1 have all been relaxed to various extents (except that the ideal gas law is also used, which is a good approximation). A major difference in the three models is in the form of isotherm equations.

The separation of a mixture containing 28.6% N_2 in CH_4 (N_2 is the weakly adsorbed component) with 5A zeolite was studied by Kadlec et al. [29, 35]. The isotherms were expressed by a Freundlich isotherm for the total amount adsorbed

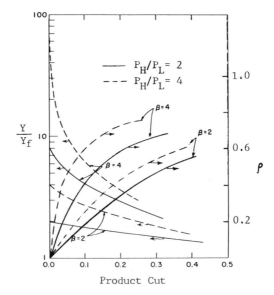

Figure 8.16   Dependence of enrichment (Y/Y_f) and recovery (ρ) of the weakly adsorbed impurity on product cut in the single-bed PSA-parametric pumping process. Source: Hill [34]. Reprinted with permission.

plus a constant separation factor (α) between the two components. The total amount adsorbed was assumed to be independent of the composition, based on experimental data on this system. A unique feature of this model is that the pressure gradient in the bed is allowed through the use of Darcy's law. As discussed in Chapter 7 (section 7.2.4), the single-bed process employs a fine particle size (40–60 mesh) in order to create a significant pressure gradient, which is a key factor in the success of the process. The pressure gradient, however, is not accounted for in the other models. Fernandez and Kenney studied the separation of oxygen from air with 5A zeolite. The adsorption of nitrogen was assumed to follow the Langmuir isotherm, whereas that for oxygen was linear, and the two were noninterfering. These are reasonable assumptions for the system under commercial operating conditions. Cheng and Hill [37], in their study of helium-methane separation with activated carbon, approximated the Langmuir form by a stepped linear isotherm:

$$q = B_1 C + B_2 \tag{8.78}$$

Other various process complexities were also simulated by these models, such as the delay step, constant product withdrawal, and the inclusion of surge tanks. Although a detailed description of these numerical models is beyond the scope of the ensuing discussion, the results which are of direct industrial interests are summarized:

Oxygen Enrichment

The governing equations are equations 8.41–8.44 for two linear isotherms. The isotherms are now modified [20] to allow the Langmuir form for N_2, while that for O_2 remains linear. Thus for nitrogen (which is the strongly adsorbed carrier component):

$$q_B = \frac{B_B C_B}{1 + B'_B C_B} \tag{8.79}$$

The coefficients a_2 and a_3 in equations 8.41 and 8.42 are now modified to concentration-dependent forms through equations 8.42a–c, and

$$\beta_A = \frac{\varepsilon}{\varepsilon + (1 - \varepsilon)B_A} \qquad \text{(unchanged for } O_2) \tag{8.80}$$

$$\beta_B = \frac{\varepsilon}{\varepsilon + (1 - \varepsilon)B_B/[1 + B'_B C(1 - Y_A)]^2} \qquad \text{(for } N_2) \tag{8.81}$$

while a_1 remains unchanged.

Equations 8.41 and 8.42, with the coefficients defined by equations 8.42a–c and 8.80–8.81, have been solved by a Runge-Kutta method for a three-step single-bed process [20]. The three steps are of equal time intervals, Δt. The boundary conditions are:

Step 1   (pressurization), $0 \leqslant t < \Delta t$:

$$Y_A(t = 0, z) = 0.21 \qquad \text{(bed initially contains air)}$$

$$Y_A(t, z = 0) = Y_f = 0.21$$

$$u(t, z = L) = 0$$

$$P = P(t) \qquad \text{(given as measured pressure history)}$$

Step II   (feed and product release), $\Delta t \leqslant t < 2\Delta t$:

$$\frac{\partial P}{\partial t} = 0 \text{ in equation 8.41, } P = P_H = \text{constant}$$

$$Y_A(t = \Delta t, z) = Y_A(z) \qquad \text{(from end of I)}$$

$$Y_A(t, z = 0) = Y_f = 0.21$$

$$u(t, z = L) = u_{prod} = \text{constant}$$

Step III   (blowdown), $2\Delta t \leqslant t < 3\Delta t$:

$$Y_A(t = 2\Delta t, z) = Y_A(z) \qquad \text{(from end of II)}$$

$$\frac{\partial Y_A}{\partial t}(t, z = L) = - \left[\frac{a_3(1 - Y_A)Y_A}{a_1 - a_3 Y_A} \right] \frac{1}{P} \frac{\partial P}{\partial t}$$

(derived from equations 8.41 and 8.42)

$$u(t, z = L) = 0$$

$$P = P(t) \qquad \text{(measured pressure history)}$$

The mole fraction profile, $Y_A(z)$, from the end of step III is then used as the initial profile for step I in the next cycle, and the cycle is repeated until a cyclic steady state is reached. The product flowrate is specified while the product concentration and feed flowrate are calculated as Y_A (at $z = L$) and u (at $z = 0$) from step II, both a function of time. The volume-averaged product purity at cyclic steady state is shown in Figure 8.17, as compared with experimental data. The agreement between theory and experiment are: within 10% for product purity, 15% for feed flowrate, and 12% for product recovery [20]. The agreement improves, as seen in Figure 8.17, at long cycle times (which favors gas-solid equilibration). The longest step time in this investigation was $\Delta t = 42.25$ seconds. This may indicate that in the rapid PSA process instantaneous gas-solid equilibrium is not approached, but isothermality is nearly established since both conditions are assumed in the model.

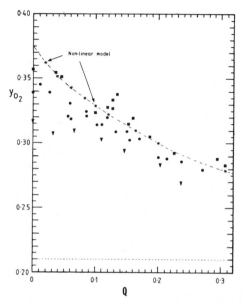

Figure 8.17 Experimental and predicted O_2 product mole fraction as a function of dimensionless product flowrate (Q) for a cycle with three equal time (Δt) steps. $Q = (u \varepsilon A C \Delta t)/(a_2 P_H L)$, $P_L = 1$ atm. Source: Fernandez and Kenney [20]. Reprinted with permission.

Effects of End Volume or Surge Tank on Separation

A cell model was used by Cheng and Hill [36, 37] for predicting bulk separation results. The cell model is essentially identical to the finite-difference method, both reducing the partial differential equations into first-order ODEs for numerical integration. For instance, the backward finite-difference method is identical to the cell model in which effluent from the ith well-mixed cell is used as the influent for the $i + 1$ cell. Axial dispersion is accounted for by virtue of the finite number of cells used [38]. The cell model of Cheng and Hill [37] is the backward finite-difference formulation for the mass balance equations (eqs. 8.41 and 8.42), with instantaneous gas-solid equilibrium given by the stepped linear isotherm (eq. 8.78). The separation being studied was He/CH_4 with activated carbon. An interesting result obtained in this study was the effect of a dead volume attached to either end of the bed. Such a dead volume is equivalent to a surge tank, differing only in the degree of mixing. The volume of the dead volume added outside the feed end is expressed as the fraction of the total interparticle voids:

$$v_{FD} = \frac{\text{dead vol.}}{\varepsilon A L} \qquad (8.82)$$

Similarly, the fraction of the dead volume added outside the product end is:

$$v_{PD} = \frac{\text{dead vol.}}{\varepsilon AL} \tag{8.83}$$

The predicted results of both types of dead volume are shown in Figure 8.18. Perfect mixing in the dead volume is assumed. Curve 1 in the figure is typical of the single-bed process without dead volume [34, 36]. A plateau is found at small cuts. Curve 2 is for the same bed with a dead volume only at the product end. This dead volume is equivalent, depending on the degree of mixing, to a surge tank for oxygen production from air. It is seen that the dead volume improves the separation, by generating a gas in the dead volume enriched in the light component which is used to purge the bed during blowdown. Curve 3 is for a bed only with feed-end dead volume. Such a dead volume decreases the separation. This occurs because methane-rich gas from the exhaust step is left in the dead volume at the end of that step. This gas is richer in methane than the feed, and it becomes the first feed gas to be treated in the following pressurization step. Thus the process must actually separate a mixture richer in the heavy component than in the feed. Curve 4 has dead volume at both ends. The effect of the product-end dead volume appears to be stronger than that of the feed-end volume. These effects have been verified experimentally.

The effect of the degree of mixing in the dead volume on separation was also studied by increasing the number of well-mixed cells in the dead volume. One cell indicates perfect mixing, which is the case shown in Figure 8.18. A large number indicates poor mixing. The results are shown in Figure 8.19. The degree of mixing is compared for one cell and fifteen cells, which are assumed for both feed-end and

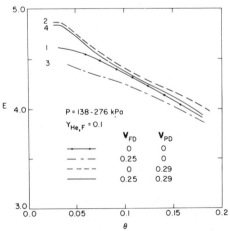

Figure 8.18   Effects of dead volumes on both the feed (v_{FD}) and product end (v_{PD}) (expressed as fraction of interstitial bed voids) on helium enrichment ($E = Y/Y_f$) as a function of product cut (θ = moles product/moles feed). $\Delta t = 25$ s. Source: Cheng and Hill [37]. Reprinted with permission.

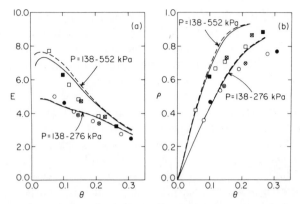

Figure 8.19 Experiment and model predictions for helium enrichment ($E = Y/Y_f$, $Y_f = 0.1$) and recovery (ρ) as a function of product cut ($\theta =$ moles product/moles feed). In all cases, the dead volumes are $v_{FD} = 0.25$ and $v_{PD} = 0.29$. The dashed lines are predictions for well-mixed dead volumes, and the solid curves represent those that are poorly mixed. Source: Cheng and Hill [37]. Reprinted with permission.

product-end dead volumes. It is seen that the degree of mixing is not important. The practical implication of the preceding results is that a dead volume added to the product end is desirable, whereas the dead volume on the feed end should be avoided. The same effects should be expected in PSA processes other than the single-bed process.

Hydrogen Isotope Separation

The separation of trace amounts of deuterium and tritium from hydrogen presents a difficult problem; yet it is of considerable importance in the nuclear industry [39]. PSA processes have been investigated for this separation. As discussed in section 8.1.2, an enrichment factor of nearly 3 was obtained for the hydrogen-deuterium separation using a Skarstrom cycle with palladium beds [15]. Gas-solid equilibrium was nearly reached in the cyclic process. The separation of hydrogen-tritium was investigated by using several PSA cycles in which vanadium metal in the form of pellets was used as the sorbent. The feed mixture contained 4 ppb tritium in the form of HT. The sorption is a bulk process where a bulk vanadium hydride is formed. The thermodynamic equilibrium between the hydrogen isotope and vanadium is well established [40]. The equilibrium uptake of tritium is slightly higher than that of hydrogen. The equivalent separation factor, α, of tritium (HT) over hydrogen is 1.2 at 25°C, decreasing to 1.05 at approximately 300°C. There is, however, a kinetic isotope effect; that is, the hydrogen atom diffuses in the solid at a higher rate than the tritium atom. The separation was studied using the single-bed process with the following operating conditions [41]: $P_L = 1$ atm, $P_H = 4$–10 atm, $T = 60$–150°C, $Y_f = 4 \times 10^{-9}$, and $\Delta t = 10$–20 seconds. (The time for pressurization was included in the feed step.)

It was expected that the high-pressure product would be depleted in tritium. However, in all experiments performed under these conditions, the high-pressure effluent was enriched in tritium. The enrichment factor was approximately 2 at small product cuts. The result indicated that with the rapid PSA cycle, the kinetic factor dominated the process. Nevertheless, qualitative agreement was obtained between experimental data and a pseudoequilibrium model, in which tritium was assumed to be the less strongly adsorbed component. In a later study it was shown that the situation was reversed in a slow PSA cycle that yielded a depleted tritium product [39]. The mixture was purified from 4 to 2 ppb tritium under the best conditions. In this study a Skarstrom cycle was employed with a cycle time of 30 minutes. In addition, a temperature swing was imposed on the cycle by using a cold feed during the high-pressure adsorption step and a hot purge during the low-pressure purge step. An equilibrium model for the combined temperature and pressure swing was formulated [39], which agreed well with the experimental results.

8.3   MULTIBED PROCESS FOR BULK SEPARATION OF BINARY AND MULTICOMPONENT MIXTURES

As discussed in detail in Chapter 7, the majority of commercial PSA processes involve bulk separations — for example, hydrogen "purification" where the hydrogen contents are in the neighborhood of 70%, air separation, normal and iso-paraffin separation, CO/H_2 separation, CO_2/CH_4 separation, and so forth. For these separations, multibed processes are used where the PSA cycles are more complex than the Skarstrom cycle since additional steps are required. The additional cycle steps typically used in the multibed processes are cocurrent depressurization or heavy component purge preceding the countercurrent blow-down and purge steps. More than two beds are usually needed to accommodate and synchronize these cycle steps.

Besides the use of more cycle steps, bulk separations differ from purifications in two ways: Bulk separations are highly nonisothermal, and the equilibrium isotherms are strongly dependent on the composition. In addition, the flow velocity is not constant during the adsorption and purge steps. Given these differences, an analytic solution similar to that in sections 8.1.1 and 8.2.1 would be entirely meaningless. Therefore, modeling of the bulk separation processes must resort to a numerical solution.

8.3.1   Experimental Method

Considerable experimental simplification can result by the use of a single-bed apparatus for the purpose of simulating multibed processes. A typical single-bed apparatus is shown in Figure 8.20. Solenoid valves located at the feed, cocurrent, and countercurrent end points are used to direct the flow alternately into and out of

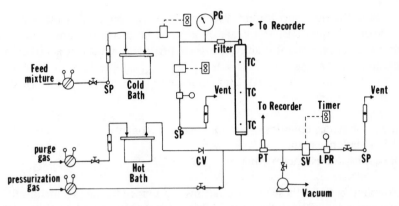

Figure 8.20 Schematic diagram of a single-bed apparatus for studying PSA processes. SP: sampling port; PG: pressure gauge; CV: check valve; PT: pressure transducer; SV: solenoid valve; TC: thermocouple; LPR: line pressure regulator. Source: Yang and Doong [42]. Reprinted with permission.

the column. The solenoid valves are activated by electronic timers. The timers are preset according to a time schedule that corresponds to the PSA cycle. All PSA cycles can be simulated by the single-bed apparatus.

Gas storage cylinders can be added to the apparatus for simulating the steps that employ the process-derived gases, such as the repressure (pressure equalization) and purge steps. The high-pressure product is fed into the storage cylinders. The separation is not influenced significantly, however, by the purity of the high-pressure product used in repressure and purge, at a purity above approximately 95%, except for obtaining ultrahigh purity product. Thus pure gas cylinders can be used for these cycle steps without a significant influence on the separation results.

A major difference between laboratory and plant results is caused by the heat effects in the process. A nearly adiabatic condition is approached in the large plant-size beds, whereas the heat capacity of the vessel and the heat exchange with the ambient air are significant for small laboratory beds. A small heat transfer rate through the walls, even when insulations are used, can have a significant influence on the separation [43, 44].

8.3.2 Equilibrium Model, LDF Model, and Pore-Diffusion Models

The following assumptions are made:

1. Ideal gas behavior
2. Negligible axial dispersion and pressure gradient in the bed
3. Negligible radial gradients in temperature and composition
4. Instant thermal equilibrium between fluid and solid particles

In addition, the transport (diffusivities and heat transfer coefficient) and physical (heat capacities, densities, and heats of adsorption) properties are assumed to be independent of temperature since the PSA process operates in a rather narrow temperature range.

The PSA process for separating an *n*-component mixture is governed by the following equations:

1. *n* mass balance equations, one for each component
2. 1 heat balance equation
3. *n* equilibrium isotherm equations

The coupling between these three equations is provided by the expressions for mass transfer rates. In the equilibrium model, mass transfer is assumed to be instantaneous, and hence no additional equations are needed. In the LDF model, the rates are approximated by a set of *n* LDF equations (section 4.3, Chapter 4), one for each component. In the pore-diffusion model, the mass transfer rates are the actual fluxes at the pore mouths of the sorbent particles. The fluxes at the pore mouths are calculated by solving the diffusion equations for the porous particle — again, one for each component. As will be shown in detail, the diffusion equation can be substantially simplified by assuming a parabolic concentration profile within the particle, thereby eliminating the need for integration along the radial distance in the particle. Consequently the computation for the pore-diffusion model is not significantly more than that for the LDF model. The advantages of the pore-diffusion model will also be described.

The mass balance equations for the bed (or for the interparticle voids) are:

$$\frac{\partial C_i}{\partial t} + \frac{\partial u C_i}{\partial z} + \frac{1-\varepsilon}{\varepsilon}\frac{\partial \bar{q}_i}{\partial t} = 0, \qquad i = 1, 2, \ldots, n \tag{8.84}$$

The heat balance equation is:

$$(\varepsilon_t \rho_g C_{pg} + \rho_B C_{ps})\frac{\partial T}{\partial t} + \varepsilon \rho_g C_{pg} u \frac{\partial T}{\partial z} - \sum_{i=1}^{n}(1-\varepsilon)H_i\frac{\partial \bar{q}_i}{\partial t} + \frac{2h}{R_b}(T - T_w) = 0 \tag{8.85}$$

where ε_t is the total void fraction $= \varepsilon + (1-\varepsilon)\alpha$, and α is the intraparticle void fraction. The wall temperature, T_w, is given by:

$$\rho_w C_{pw} A_w \frac{\partial T_w}{\partial t} = 2\pi R_b h(T - T_w) \tag{8.86}$$

where subscript *w* denotes wall properties. In equations 8.85 and 8.86, the heat transfer to the ambient air is neglected. Thus a high h value is used for simulation purposes. Alternatively, the last term in the LHS of equation 8.85 can be replaced by $2h(T - T_0)/R_b$ and the heat capacity of the wall is included in C_{ps} [44]. In this case, equation 8.86 is not necessary. This last term may be neglected for commercial scale adsorbers.

The loading ratio correlation (LRC) equations are used for the equilibrium amounts adsorbed:

$$q_i^* = \frac{q_{mi} B_i (C_i/\eta_i)^{b_i}}{1 + \Sigma\, B_i (C_i/\eta_i)^{b_i}}, \qquad i = 1, 2, \ldots, n \tag{8.87}$$

This is a four-constant correlation, discussed in detail in section 3.1 of Chapter 3. Accurate correlations are essential to all PSA models because of the high sensitivity of the models to the equilibrium isotherms.

Equations 8.84–8.87 constitute the governing equations for the PSA bed. For numerical computations, the n mass balance equations (eq. 8.84) are recast into an overall mass balance equation and $n - 1$ species equations, as shown below. Here the ideal gas law is used, $C_i = PY_i/RT$ and $\Sigma\, Y_i \equiv 1$.

$$\frac{1}{RT}\frac{\partial P}{\partial t} - \frac{P}{RT^2}\frac{\partial T}{\partial t} + \frac{P}{RT}\frac{\partial u}{\partial z} - \frac{uP}{RT^2}\frac{\partial T}{\partial z} + \frac{1-\varepsilon}{\varepsilon}\sum_{j=1}^{n}\frac{\partial \bar{q}_j}{\partial t} = 0 \tag{8.88}$$

$$\frac{P}{RT}\frac{\partial Y_i}{\partial t} + \frac{uP}{RT}\frac{\partial Y_i}{\partial z} + \frac{1-\varepsilon}{\varepsilon}\left[\left(Y_i\sum_{j=1}^{n}\frac{\partial \bar{q}_j}{\partial t}\right) - \frac{\partial \bar{q}_i}{\partial t}\right] = 0, \qquad i = 1, 2, \ldots, n-1$$

$$\tag{8.89}$$

Equations 8.88 and 8.89 replace equation 8.84 in all numerical models.

Equilibrium and LDF Models

The coupling between the $2n + 1$ governing equations are:

$$\text{Equilibrium model:} \quad \frac{\partial \bar{q}_i}{\partial t} = \frac{\partial q_i^*}{\partial t} \tag{8.90}$$

$$\text{LDF model:} \quad \frac{\partial \bar{q}_i}{\partial t} = k_i(q_i^* - \bar{q}_i) \tag{8.91}$$

The equilibrium amount adsorbed, q_i^*, is a function of T, P, and composition Y_i. Thus,

$$\frac{\partial q_i^*}{\partial t} = \frac{\partial q_i^*}{\partial P}\frac{\partial P}{\partial t} + \frac{\partial q_i^*}{\partial T}\frac{\partial T}{\partial t} + \sum_{j=1}^{n-1}\frac{\partial q_i^*}{\partial Y_j}\frac{\partial Y_j}{\partial t}, \qquad i \neq j \tag{8.92}$$

which can be used in the equilibrium model. In the LRC equations the substitution of $C_i = PY_i/RT$ is also made and the isotherm constants, q_{mi} and B_i, are temperature-dependent:

$$q_m = k_1 + k_2 T \qquad (8.93)$$

$$B = k_3 \exp(k_4/T) \qquad (8.94)$$

For each component there are four empirical constants, $k_1 - k_4$. The constants b and η in the LRC may be assumed to be independent of temperature.

A note should be made regarding the value of the mass transfer coefficient, k_i. In Glueckauf's LDF equation, k_i is approximated by 15 D_e/R_p^2 [23]. However, as noted in section 4.3 of Chapter 4, D_e is a solid-phase diffusivity (based on the solid diffusion equation, without the $\alpha \partial C/\partial t$ term for the voids), and not the effective pore diffusivity reported in the literature. Thus the value for k_i may be considered a fitting parameter, which can be empirically obtained by fitting the separation results to the model.

The governing equations in the equilibrium model are equations 8.88, 8.89 (n mass balance equations), 8.85 (heat balance), and 8.87 (n equilibrium isotherms). Equation 8.92 is substituted directly for $\partial \bar{q}_i/\partial t$ into the heat and mass balance equations. There are $2n + 1$ governing equations in the equilibrium model.

For the LDF model, the same mass balance, heat balance, and equilibrium isotherm equations are used. In addition, n rate equations (eq. 8.91) provide the coupling for these equations. Thus the $3n + 1$ equations constitute the LDF model.

A number of numerical methods can be used to solve these two models. The mass and heat balance equations are a set of hyperbolic differential equations. For solving these hyperbolic equations, the stability of the implicit finite difference methods is guaranteed [45]. The governing equations can be solved by these methods with given boundary conditions. The boundary conditions are determined from the PSA cycle. Illustrations of the boundary conditions will be given later along with the PSA cycles. A set of boundary conditions is associated with each step of the cycle. An initially clean bed is usually assumed to start the computation, which ends until a cyclic steady state is reached. The final bed condition in each cycle step is automatically used as the initial condition for the next step. Two finite-difference schemes are outlined as follows.

In one scheme [46], the computation starts from the species mass balance (eq. 8.89) (having substituted equations 8.90, 8.92, and 8.87 for the equilibrium model, and equations 8.91 and 8.87 for the LDF model). Equation 8.89 represents $n - 1$ PDE with $n - 1$ unknowns, $\partial Y_i/\partial t$. A standard Gaussian elimination method may be used to solve these equations. With the values of $\partial Y_i/\partial t$, the values of the velocity, u, at different bed positions are obtained by integrating the total mass balance equation (eq. 8.88) (having incorporated equations 8.90, 8.92, and 8.87 for the equilibrium model, and equations 8.91 and 8.87 for the LDF model). In equation 8.89, the coefficients containing the q_i derivatives have isotherm and bed properties. These coefficients may be conveniently evaluated by numerical differentiation using the conditions in the previous time step. Therefore, an explicit scheme is actually used here for solving equations 8.89 and 8.88. The heat balance equations (eqs. 8.85 and 8.86) may be solved in a similar manner using the values of $\partial \bar{q}_i/\partial t$ evaluated from equations 8.87 and 8.90–8.92.

An iterative scheme using implicit finite difference has been used to solve these model equations for separating a five-component mixture using a four-step PSA cycle [47]. Equations 8.87 (incorporating equations 8.90, 8.92, and 8.87 or equations 8.91 and 8.87, depending on the model); 8.89 (incorporating the same equations); and 8.85–8.86 are expressed in implicit finite-difference forms. Temperature and composition are iterated in two separate loops. First, a set of Y_i and T is assumed for each space segment. The values of q_i are calculated from equations 8.87 and 8.90 or 8.91, depending on the model. The value of u is then evaluated from equation 8.88. With these values, a new set of Y_i is calculated from equation 8.89, which is compared with the assumed set. The iteration is continued until Y_i are within a preset fraction (e.g., 10^{-4}), of the assumed values. Equations 8.85 and 8.86 are used to calculate a new T, which is iterated until it reaches a point within a preset fraction (e.g., 10^{-3}) of the assumed T. A typical computation time in a minicomputer such as VAX 780 for the separation of a five-component mixture for each PSA cycle is 10 minutes [47].

Monodisperse Pore-Diffusion Model

This is an exact model in which experimentally measured pore diffusivities, D_e, can be used. The sorption rate term, $\partial \bar{q}_i/\partial t$, in the heat and mass balance equations is evaluated by solving the mass balance equation within the sorbent particle. Gas-solid equilibrium is assumed within the pores, thus providing the link between the equilibrium isotherms and the heat and mass balance equations.

The pore structure is monodisperse. Sorbents in this category include activated carbon, alumina, and silica gel. The model does not apply to zeolites, since they have bidisperse pores.

The mass balance for component i inside the pores of a spherical particle at axial location z in the bed yields:

$$\alpha \frac{\partial C_{ip}}{\partial t} + \frac{1}{r^2} \frac{\partial}{\partial r}(r^2 N_{ir}) + \frac{\partial q_i}{\partial t} = 0, \qquad i = 1, 2, \ldots, n \qquad (8.95)$$

where α is the intraparticle void fraction and N_i is the flux of component i.

Equation 8.95 can be simplified by employing the following particle volume-averaged quantities:

$$\bar{C}_{ip} = \frac{3}{R_p^3} \int_0^{R_p} C_{ip} r^2 \, dr, \qquad i = 1, 2, \ldots, n \qquad (8.96)$$

$$\bar{q}_i = \frac{3}{R_p^3} \int_0^{R_p} q_i r^2 \, dr, \qquad i = 1, 2, \ldots, n \qquad (8.97)$$

By integrating equation 8.95 with respect to r, using the volume-averaged quantities and noting that $N_i = 0$ at $r = 0$, we get:

$$\alpha \frac{\partial \bar{C}_{ip}}{\partial t} + \frac{3}{R_p} N_i^s + \frac{\partial \bar{q}_i}{\partial t} = 0, \qquad i = 1, 2, \ldots, n \qquad (8.98)$$

where N_i^s is the flux at the particle surface.

To further simplify the model, parabolic concentration profile within the particle is assumed, which is a good assumption when compared with computed profiles (see section 4.3, Chapter 4). Thus we have

$$C_{ip} = E_i + F_i r^2, \qquad i = 1, 2, \ldots, n \qquad (8.99)$$

where the constants E and F can be evaluated by using the surface condition:

$$C_{ip} = C_{ip}^s \text{ at } r = R_p$$

$$E_i = C_{ip}^s - F_i R_p^2$$

By integrating equation 8.99 and using the volume-averaged quantity:

$$F_i = (C_{ip}^s - \bar{C}_{ip}) \frac{5}{2R_p^2}$$

Therefore,

$$\left(\frac{\partial C_{ip}}{\partial r} \right)_{r=R_p} = (C_{ip}^s - \bar{C}_{ip}) \frac{5}{R_p} = \frac{P}{RT} (Y_{ip}^s - \bar{Y}_{ip}) \frac{5}{R_p}, \qquad i = 1, 2, \ldots, n \qquad (8.100)$$

The sorption rate term in the heat and mass balance equations can be related to the flux at the pore mouths, or N_i^s:

$$N_i^s = Y_{ip}^s \Sigma N_i^s - D_e \left(\frac{\partial C_{ip}}{\partial r} \right)_{r=R_p}, \qquad i = 1, 2, \ldots, n \qquad (8.101)$$

where N_i is flux defined in the outward direction. The first term on the right-hand side is the convective contribution, and the second term is the diffusive contribution. The first term applies only to molecular and transition diffusion. If the diffusion is in the Knudsen regime, only the second term is needed. The diffusivity, D_e, may be replaced by a pseudobinary diffusivity for diffusion in a multi-component mixture [48].

The convective flux term in equation 8.101 can be obtained by summing equation 8.98 over all components:

$$\sum_{i=1}^{n} N_i^s = - \frac{R_p}{3} \frac{\alpha}{RT} \frac{\partial P}{\partial t} + \frac{R_p}{3} \frac{\alpha P}{RT^2} \frac{\partial T}{\partial t} - \frac{R_p}{3} \sum_{i=1}^{n} \frac{\partial \bar{q}_i}{\partial t} \qquad (8.102)$$

where the relationships $C_i = PY_i/RT$ and $\Sigma Y_i = 1$ have been used.

Combining equations 8.95, 8.100, 8.101, and 8.102, and using the ideal gas law, we get:

$$\frac{\partial \bar{Y}_{ip}}{\partial t} = (Y_{ip}^s - \bar{Y}_{ip})\frac{1}{P}\frac{\partial P}{\partial t} - (Y_{ip}^s - \bar{Y}_{ip})\frac{1}{T}\frac{\partial T}{\partial t}$$

$$+ (Y_{ip}^s - \bar{Y}_{ip})\frac{15D_e}{\alpha R_p^2} - \frac{RT}{\alpha P}\frac{\partial \bar{q}_i}{\partial t} + \frac{RT}{\alpha P}Y_{ip}^s \sum_{j=1}^{n}\frac{\partial \bar{q}_j}{\partial t} \qquad (8.103)$$

where $\partial \bar{q}_i/\partial t$ is obtained from equation 8.92, assuming gas-solid equilibrium inside the pores.

Equations 8.87 (isotherms) and 8.92 are substituted into equation 8.103. Equation 8.103 is a working equation for the pore-diffusion model. It requires integration only with respect to time, while eliminating integration in the radial distance. It gives the values of $\bar{Y}_{ip}$ upon integration. The local sorption term in the heat and mass balance equations is then calculated from $\bar{Y}_{ip}$:

$$\frac{1-\varepsilon}{\varepsilon}\frac{\partial \bar{q}_i}{\partial t} = \frac{3\rho_B}{\varepsilon\rho_p}\frac{1}{R_p}N_i^s \qquad (8.104)$$

The flux at the pore mouths, N_i^s, is calculated from equations 8.100, 8.101 and 8.102. Equation 8.104 is used to indicate the substitution of the right-hand side for the sorption rate term, $[(1-\varepsilon)/\varepsilon]\partial \bar{q}_i/\partial t$.

The governing equations for the pore-diffusion model are: equations 8.88; 8.89 (n mass balance equations); 8.85 (heat balance equation, along with 8.86); 8.87 (n isotherm equations); and 8.103 (n pore-diffusion rate equations, along with 8.87 and 8.92). Equation 8.104 relates equation 8.103 (from which $\bar{Y}_{ip}$ is obtained) to the sorption rate term in the heat and mass balance equations. The model is thus complete.

The procedure of the numerical solution for the model is outlined below. The boundary conditions are determined by the PSA cycle. A set of boundary conditions is associated with each cycle step. A clean bed is usually used to initiate the computation, which ends when a cyclic steady state is reached. The final bed condition in each step is automatically used as the initial condition for the next step. Equations 8.103 (incorporating 8.87 and 8.92) and 8.86 are first integrated to obtain, respectively, $\bar{Y}_{ip}$ and T_w at the next time step by using any finite difference scheme. Equation 8.104 is then used to calculate the values of the sorption rate term, $[(1-\varepsilon)/\varepsilon](\partial \bar{q}_i/\partial t)$, for the heat and mass balance equations. With the values of the sorption rate term, the interstitial velocity, u, is calculated from equation 8.88 for all space segments in the bed. Here, $\partial T/\partial t$ may be evaluated at the last time step since the influence of $\partial T/\partial t$ on u is smaller than that of $\partial P/\partial t$ and the sorption rate terms. Finally, with the values of u and sorption rates, equations 8.89 and 8.85 are solved separately for Y_i and T by using a suitable finite difference scheme. The typical computer time for binary mixture separation using a five-step PSA cycle [42] is approximately 1 minute per cycle in a VAX 780 minicomputer.

Bidisperse Pore-Diffusion Model for Zeolites

As discussed in Chapter 2, zeolite sorbents consist of crystals, in the size range of 1–9 μm, which are pelletized with a small amount of binder. The sorption of gases is entirely due to the crystals. Diffusion rates in both the binder phase (which contains macropores) and the crystals (which contain micropores) can be important in determining the overall sorption rate. A schematic of the pellet is shown in Figure 8.21, assuming spherical crystals.

Mass balance for gas component i in the bed gives:

$$\varepsilon \frac{\partial C_i}{\partial t} + \varepsilon \frac{\partial u C_i}{\partial z} - S_i = 0, \qquad i = 1, 2, \dots, n \qquad (8.105)$$

where S_i is the sorption rate per unit volume of bed.

Mass balance in the macropores within the pellet that is located at position z in the bed yields:

$$\alpha \frac{\partial C_{ip}}{\partial t} + \frac{1}{R^2} \frac{\partial}{\partial R}(R^2 N_{iR}) + \frac{\partial \bar{q}_i}{\partial t} = 0, \qquad i = 1, 2, \dots, n \qquad (8.106)$$

where α is the void fraction of the macropores and C_{ip} is the concentration in the macropores. The quantity $\bar{q}_i$ is the volume-averaged amount adsorbed at a radial location, R, within the pellet. Thus $\bar{q}_i$ is averaged over an entire crystal. The flux is:

$$N_{iR} = Y_{ip} \sum_{j=1}^{n} N_{jR} - D_{im} \frac{\partial C_{ip}}{\partial R}, \qquad i = 1, 2, \dots, n \qquad (8.107)$$

where D_{im} is the pseudobinary diffusivity of i in the multicomponent mixture [48]. The first term on the right-hand side is not negligible since molecular diffusion prevails in the large macropores of commercial zeolites under normal conditions.

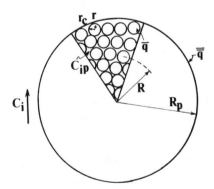

Figure 8.21   Schematic of a model zeolite pellet containing a binder phase and crystals, and the notation used in modeling.

By assuming a parabolic concentration profile within the pellet and using the volume-averaged quantities, an equation similar to equation 8.103 can be derived from equation 8.106:

$$\frac{\partial \bar{Y}_{ip}}{\partial t} = (Y_{ip}^s - \bar{Y}_{ip})\frac{1}{P}\frac{\partial P}{\partial t} - (Y_{ip}^s - \bar{Y}_{ip})\frac{1}{T}\frac{\partial T}{\partial t}$$

$$+ (Y_{ip}^s - \bar{Y}_{ip})\frac{15}{R_p^2}\frac{D_{im}}{\alpha} - \frac{RT}{\alpha P}\frac{\partial \bar{\bar{q}}_i}{\partial t}$$

$$+ \frac{RT}{\alpha P}Y_{ip}^s \sum_{j=1}^{n}\frac{\partial \bar{\bar{q}}_i}{\partial t}, \qquad i = 1, 2, \ldots, n \qquad (8.108)$$

where $\bar{\bar{q}}_i$ is the value averaged over the entire pellet:

$$\bar{\bar{q}}_i = \frac{3}{R_p^3}\int_0^{R_p} \bar{q}_i R^2 dR \qquad (8.109)$$

where $\bar{q}_i$ is the average amount over the crystal. As mentioned, the amount adsorbed by the binder is negligible. The value of Y_{ip}^s is equal to that in the bulk flow, Y_i, since film resistance is negligible.

Mass balance in the crystal is given by the following solid diffusion equation since the gas phase in the crystal voids is not considered (and, based on the equation, the values of D_i given in the literature were determined):

$$\frac{\partial q_i}{\partial t} = \frac{D_i}{r^2}\frac{\partial}{\partial r}\left(r^2 \frac{\partial q_i}{\partial r}\right) \qquad (8.110)$$

As shown in section 4.3 of Chapter 4, a parabolic concentration profile $q_i(r)$ combined with the solid diffusion equation leads directly to the LDF equation:

$$\frac{\partial \bar{q}_i}{\partial t} = \frac{15 D_i}{r_c^2}(q_i^s - \bar{q}_i) \qquad (8.111)$$

where q_i^s is in equilibrium with C_{ip} at radial location R in the pellet.

The following dimensionless variables are defined:

$$Y_i' = \frac{Y_i}{Y_{i0}}, \qquad \bar{Y}_{ip}' = \frac{\bar{Y}_{ip}}{Y_{i0}}, \qquad Y_{ip}^{s\prime} = \frac{Y_{ip}^s}{Y_{i0}}, \qquad u' = \frac{u}{u_0},$$

$$Z = \frac{z}{L}, \qquad \tau = \frac{u_0 t}{L}, \qquad \bar{\bar{q}}_i' = \frac{\bar{\bar{q}}_i}{q_{i0}},$$

$$P' = \frac{P}{P_0}, \qquad T' = \frac{T}{T_0}, \qquad S_i' = \frac{S_i}{\dfrac{15 D_{im}}{R_p^2}\dfrac{\rho_B}{\rho_P}\dfrac{Y_{i0}P_0}{RT_0}}$$

where subscript 0 denotes the feed mixture condition, except for u_0, which is defined as the effluent velocity in the high-pressure adsorption step. The quantity q_{i0} is the amount adsorbed at T_0 and P_0 for each pure component. With these dimensionless variables, equations 8.108, 8.109, and 8.111 are recast into:

$$\frac{\partial \bar{Y}'_{ip}}{\partial \tau} = \frac{1}{P'}(Y^{s\prime}_{ip} - \bar{Y}'_{ip})\frac{\partial P'}{\partial \tau} - \frac{1}{T'}(Y^{s\prime}_{ip} - \bar{Y}'_{ip})\frac{\partial T'}{\partial \tau}$$

$$+ \frac{1}{\alpha}(Y^{s\prime}_{ip} - \bar{Y}'_{ip})\beta_i - \frac{\eta_i}{\alpha}\frac{T'}{P'}\frac{\partial \bar{\bar{q}}'_i}{\partial \tau}$$

$$+ \frac{Y^{s\prime}_{ip}}{\alpha}\frac{T'}{P'}\sum_{j}^{n} Y_{j0}\eta_j\frac{\partial \bar{\bar{q}}'_j}{\partial \tau} \qquad (8.112)$$

$$\frac{\partial \bar{\bar{q}}'_i}{\partial \tau} = 3\int_0^1 \frac{\partial \bar{q}'_i}{\partial \tau}\left(\frac{R}{R_p}\right)^2 d\left(\frac{R}{R_p}\right) \qquad (8.113)$$

$$\frac{\partial \bar{q}'_i}{\partial \tau} = \gamma_i(q^{s\prime}_i - \bar{q}'_i), \qquad \bar{q}'_i = \bar{q}_i\left(\frac{R}{R_p}, Z, r\right) \qquad (8.114)$$

where

$$\beta_i = \frac{L}{u_0}\frac{15D_{im}}{R_p^2}, \gamma_i = \frac{L}{u_0}\frac{15D_i}{r_c^2}, \eta_i = \frac{q_{i0}}{Y_{i0}}\frac{RT_0}{P_0}$$

Using the ideal gas law, equation 8.105 is recast into a total mass balance equation and $n-1$ species equations:

$$\frac{\partial u'}{\partial Z} - \frac{1}{T'}\frac{\partial T'}{\partial \tau} - \frac{u'}{T'}\frac{\partial T'}{\partial Z} - \frac{\rho_B}{\varepsilon\rho_p}\frac{T'}{P'}\sum_j^n S'_j Y_{j0}\beta_j + \frac{1}{P'}\frac{\partial P'}{\partial \tau} = 0 \qquad (8.115)$$

$$\varepsilon\frac{\partial Y'_i}{\partial \tau} + \varepsilon u'\frac{\partial Y'_i}{\partial Z} + \frac{\rho_B}{\rho_p}\frac{T'}{P'}Y'_i\sum_j^n S'_j\beta_j Y_{j0} - \beta_i\frac{\rho_B}{\rho_p}\frac{T'}{P'}S'_i = 0, \qquad i = 1, 2, \dots, (n-1)$$

$$(8.116)$$

The dimensionless sorption rate, S'_i, through which the bulk flow mass balance and the macropore mass balance equations are coupled, is:

$$S'_i = -\frac{P'}{T'}(Y^{s\prime}_{ip} - \bar{Y}'_{ip}) - \frac{Y^{s\prime}_{ip}}{\beta_i}\sum_j^n Y_{j0}\eta_j\left(\frac{\partial \bar{\bar{q}}'_j}{\partial \tau}\right)$$

$$+ \frac{\alpha}{\beta_i}Y^{s\prime}_{ip}\frac{P'}{T'^2}\frac{\partial T'}{\partial \tau} - \frac{\alpha}{\beta_i}\frac{Y^{s\prime}_{ip}}{T'}\frac{\partial P'}{\partial \tau} \qquad (8.117)$$

The dimensionless form of the heat balance equation for an adiabatic adsorber is:

$$\frac{\partial T'}{\partial \tau} + \delta_1 u' \frac{\partial T'}{\partial Z} - \sum_{j}^{n} \delta_{2j} \frac{\partial \bar{\bar{q}}'_j}{\partial \tau} = 0 \tag{8.118}$$

where

$$\delta_1 = \frac{\rho_g C_{pg}}{\varepsilon \rho_g C_{pg} + \rho_B C_{pg} \sum \bar{\bar{q}}'_j q_{j0} + \rho_B C_{ps}}$$

$$\delta_{2j} = \frac{\rho_B q_{i0} H_i}{\rho_g C_{pg} T_0} \delta_1$$

The model is complete with the isotherm equations (eq. 8.87). Furthermore, D_{im} may be assumed to be inversely proportional to P.

The model has been solved for the PSA separations of methane-carbon dioxide [49] and hydrogen-methane [50] mixtures with 5A zeolite. The inclusion of the micropore diffusion (eq. 8.114) renders the system of equations stiff, and a long computation time would be necessary for an accurate solution if a simple Euler's method is used. Gear's [10] method is suitable for solving ODEs with stiffness. Thus, although the same numerical procedure for solving the monodisperse pore diffusion model may be used, Gear's method (by the package from the IMSL Library) has been used to solve this model [49]. Equations 8.112, 8.114, 8.116, and 8.118 may be written as ODEs expressed in terms of, respectively for the four equations, $d\bar{Y}'_{ip}/d\tau$, $d\bar{q}'_i/d\tau$, $dY'_i/d\tau$, and $dT'/d\tau$. This set of equations may be solved by the Gear package. Equation 8.113 may be integrated by, for example, Simpson's rule. The values of $q_i^{s'}$ are calculated from the isotherms (eq. 8.87) based on the concentration profile in the macropores within the pellet. Although the Gear method can self-adjust the integration order and time step, the velocity, u', appearing in equation 8.116 must be evaluated at a small time interval (0.1 second in a case for binary separation, reference 49). Euler's method may be applied to solve equation 8.115 for the velocity distribution in the bed. The sorption rate, S'_i, is given by equation 8.117. The computation is initiated with a clean bed. The boundary conditions for each cycle step are given by the PSA cycle and cycle operating conditions. The time steps in the computation are continued through the cycle steps until a cyclic steady state is reached.

8.3.3   Bulk PSA Separations

Except for air drying, all major commercial PSA processes involve bulk separations — for example, air separation, normal and iso-paraffin separation, and hydrogen "purification" — in which a typical feed contains 70% hydrogen. The commercial multibed processes typically consist of the following steps in each cycle:

Step I: Repressurization with the light product or feed

Step II: High-pressure feed

Step III: Cocurrent depressurization

Step IV: Countercurrent blowdown

Step V: Purge with the light product

The five-step PSA cycle can be used to represent the multibed processes. Step I in this cycle is actually accomplished by a succession of pressure equalization steps in many commercial processes (see section 7.1.3 and Figures 7.14, 7.15, and 7.17 in Chapter 7). The results by these processes will lie between those using light-product repressurization and using feed repressurization. In most processes, however, the bed is clean upon repressurization and the results closely resemble those of light-product repressurization. The commercial zeolite PSA processes frequently employ a small desiccant (silica gel or activated alumina) section at the feed end of the beds. The desiccant section is used to adsorb water vapor and other highly polar gases while the actual separation is performed by the zeolite beds. These processes can be simulated in the laboratory, in both modeling and experiments, by using a dry feed or one pretreated with desiccant. The following discussion will be based largely on the five-step cycle. Discussion will also be given to the separation characteristics of some different cycles — for example, cycles involving vacuum desorption and heavy-component purge.

Boundary Conditions and Result Presentation

The following are the boundary conditions for the five-step cycle where $z = 0$ is the feed end:

Step I: Feed pressurization: $Y_i(t, z = 0) = Y_{i0}$, $T(t, z = 0) = T_0$, $u(t, z = L) = 0$
             Light-product pressurization: $Y_i(t, z = L) = 1$ (light component) or 0 (others), $T(t, z = L) = T_0$, $u(t, z = 0) = 0$

Step II: $Y_i(t, z = 0) = Y_{i0}$, $T(t, z = 0) = T_0$, $u(t, z = L) = u(t)$

Step III: $u(t, z = 0) = 0$, $u(t, z = L) = u(t)$

Step IV: $u(t, z = L) = 0$, $u(t, z = 0) = u(t)$

Step V: $Y_i(t, z = L) = 1$ (light component) or 0 (others), $T(t, z = L) = T_0$, $u(t, z = 0) = u(t)$

All steps: $P = P(t)$

Only one boundary condition between $P(t)$ and $u(t)$ is needed. For convenience in numerical computation, $P(t)$ is used as the input to the model while the effluent velocity, $u(t)$, is computed. Alternatively, $u(t)$ may be used as the input while the pressure history of the cycle may be computed from the model.

The separation results are expressed by three interrelated sets of results at cyclic steady state: product purity, product recovery, and sorbent productivity. The raw data obtained from both model and experiment are the time-dependent effluent composition and flowrate. The sorbent productivity is expressed as the rate of feed processed per unit amount of sorbent. The product purity of a given component is calculated as its volume-averaged concentration taken over the entire step that the component is obtained. *Product recovery* is defined as the amount of component contained in the product stream divided by the amount of the same component in the feed to the process.

Temperature Excursion

In purification processes, such as air drying, the temperature excursion in a steady-state PSA cycle is usually below 5°C. In bulk separation, the temperature variation at a fixed point in the bed can exceed 100°C during the cycle. The experimental and theoretical temperature excursion in separating a 50/50 H_2/CO mixture with activated carbon is shown in Figure 8.22. This temperature excursion is obtained with a small-bed (2 inch diameter) laboratory unit where adiabatic conditions are

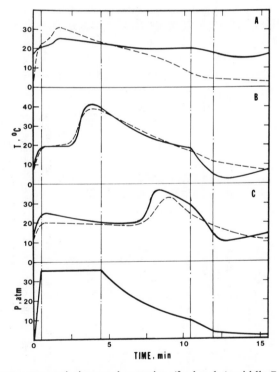

Figure 8.22 Temperature variations at three points (feed end *A*, middle *B*, and outlet end *C*) in the bed during a steady-state PSA cycle (steps I through V) for the separation of a 50/50 H_2/CO mixture with activated carbon. Experimental (solid curves); equilibrium model (dashed curves). Other conditions: volumetric H_2 purge/feed fraction = 0.05, H_2 pressurization in step I. Source: Yang and Cen [51]. Reprinted with permission.

Table 8.3 Steady-State PSA Separation of 50/50 H_2/CO with Activated Carbon under Various Thermal Conditions

Step	Isothermal	Adiabatic	Laboratory[b]	Inerts Added[c]		Heat Exchange[d]	
				5%	10%	Bed 1	Bed 2
I Input H_2, l[a]	14.64	14.35	14.93	14.54	14.59	13.69	13.72
II Output, l	21.90	22.64	22.72	22.57	22.50	22.06	22.07
H_2, %	99.91	99.84	99.84	99.85	99.86	99.90	99.90
III Output, l	11.98	12.74	12.59	12.71	12.66	12.11	12.14
H_2, %	87.03	71.62	76.07	73.76	75.30	76.08	76.09
IV + V Output, l	16.94	15.13	15.78	15.41	15.60	15.73	15.72
CO, %	91.65	90.52	90.54	90.64	90.74	90.98	90.94
H_2 recovery, %	92.58	92.37	92.07	92.34	92.34	92.53	92.50
CO recovery, %	90.79	78.96	82.40	80.56	81.75	81.77	81.67

Note: Conditions are the same as shown in Figure 8.22. Source: Yang and Cen [51].
[a]All volumes are at STP conditions. Amount of sorbent = 420 g.
[b]Laboratory unit with a small heat exchange with the surroundings.
[c]High heat-capacity inerts added (e.g., weight-percent iron particles).
[d]Heat exchange between two beds allowed (e.g., by a shell [bed 1]-and-tube [bed 2] configuration).

not achieved. The temperature excursion will be greater under adiabatic conditions.

The large temperature excursion is detrimental to separation because both adsorption and desorption are hampered by, respectively, the temperature rise and drop that accompany these steps. The separation results, in terms of product purity and recovery, are shown in Table 8.3 for various thermal modes. The best separation is accomplished by the isothermal condition which is hypothetical. The adiabatic operation yields the worst separation.

Various remedial techniques have been suggested to alleviate the adverse effects caused by the large temperature excursion. Internal heating of the cold region in the bed by using inserted heaters has been suggested for oxygen generation from air with zeolites [52]. A small amount of inert additive that has a high heat capacity, such as iron particles, will increase the mean heat capacity of the bed and can significantly improve the separation, as shown in Table 8.3 [51]. The separation can also be improved by allowing heat exchange between the beds that are undergoing different steps in the cycle, also shown in Table 8.3 [51].

The heat of adsorption on zeolites is generally higher than that on carbon because of both the electrostatic and the van der Waals forces. Consequently, the temperature excursion in a zeolite bed can be substantially greater than that in a carbon bed. This is not always the case, however, since the temperature excursion also depends on the equilibrium amount adsorbed as well as the throughput per cycle. Figure 8.23 shows the temperature variations in a steady-state adiabatic PSA

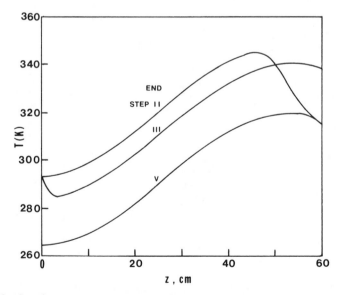

Figure 8.23 Steady-state temperature profiles at the end of steps II (adsorption), III (cocurrent depressurization), and V (countercurrent blowdown and purge) for separating a 50/50 H_2/CH_4 mixture with 5A zeolite, predicted for adiabatic PSA. Source: Doong and Yang [49].

cycle for H_2/CH_4 (50/50 feed mixture) separation with 5A zeolite [49]. A smaller temperature swing, by about 20°C, was observed experimentally with a 2 inch adsorber, which was not adiabatic [50].

Factors Controlling the Light Product

The purity of the light product depends entirely on the degree of bed cleanliness prior to the adsorption step. This, in turn, depends on a number of interrelated factors: the repressurization step, the purge/feed ratio, the pressure history, and other factors involved in desorption.

Bed repressurization by the light product from the end opposite to the feed direction can sharpen the wavefront in the subsequent adsorption step, thereby yielding a high-purity light product. When using pressure equalization steps, it is essential that the final equalization is accomplished with the high-purity light product. Lower-purity streams may be used in the initial equalization steps. The impurities will be eluted toward the feed end during final equalization, preventing their early breakthrough in the adsorption step.

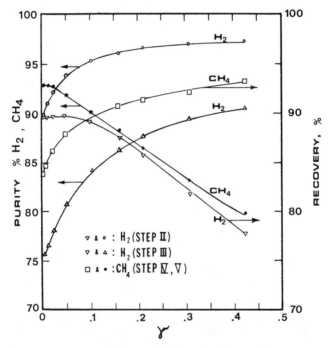

Figure 8.24   Effects of purge/feed fraction (γ) on separation of a 50/50 H_2/CH_4 mixture with carbon using a five-step PSA. Conditions: pressure between 5 and 300 psig, repressurization by feed, CH_4 front coverage in adsorption ($u_0 t_a/L$) = 2.48, and pore-diffusion parameter ($D_e t_c/R_p^2$) = 10.71, where t_a = adsorption time and t_c = cycle time. Source: Doong and Yang [53]. Reprinted with permission.

The purge/feed ratio (or fraction) in bulk separation is defined as the ratio of the light product amount used in the purge step over that contained in the feed. The effects of purge/feed (P/F) fraction on bulk separation has been intensively investigated. The general feature of the effects is shown in Figure 8.24. The light product purity increases and levels off with increasing P/F fraction. In contrast, the light-product recovery and heavy-product purity both decrease with an increasing P/F fraction. The optimum value for the P/F fraction is usually near 0.1.

The relationship shown in Figure 8.24 involves a relatively high pressure ratio (i.e., feed pressure/purge pressure). As the pressure ratio is reduced, more purge is needed to produce the same light-product purity. The qualitative relationship shown in the figure is still valid, except that the light-product purity levels off at a higher P/F fraction. Conversely, at a higher pressure ratio, 500/5 (psig), it is found that the light-product purity levels off at a much reduced P/F fraction (i.e., $\gamma < 0.06$) [44].

Other cycle steps can also effectively regenerate the bed and produce a pure product. The purity of oxygen in air separation can be increased by replacing the purge step by an evacuation step, as shown in the Guerin-Domine cycle (section 7.1.1 of Chapter 7). The models given in section 8.3.2 of this chapter are applicable for the vacuum-swing cycle by using the appropriate boundary conditions [47, 54].

Factors Controlling the Heavy Product

It is shown in Figure 8.24 that the purity of the heavy product declines with an increasing P/F ratio because of dilution by the purge stream. Thus a low P/F ratio is desirable for the purity of the heavy component. However, the gas remaining in the void space in the bed prior to the desorption step is the predominant factor limiting the heavy-product purity. The gas remaining in the void space of a saturated bed has the same composition as the feed. Because of the high feed pressure and large void fraction, the amount of gas in the void space is comparable to that in the adsorbed phase. Thus if the heavy component is a desired product, it is essential to reduce the gas mixture remaining in the voids. This can be accomplished in two ways: (1) by cocurrent depressurization, and (2) by purging the bed with the heavy component. The function of the cocurrent depressurization step has been discussed in section 7.1.2 of Chapter 7 and illustrated by Figure 7.6. By purging with the heavy component, the gas mixture in the voids can be totally displaced, and a high-purity heavy product will be obtained. By using this step in the PSA cycle, Tamura claimed that products containing 91% oxygen and 99.96–99.98% nitrogen were obtained with a zeolite [55].

Using the heavy-component purge cycle, the separation of H_2/CH_4 with activated carbon has been recently studied in this author's laboratory [57]. A set of results is shown in Table 8.4. A reasonable comparison is obtained between the experiment and equilibrium model. Since the methane purge pressure is the same as the feed pressure, a high purge/feed ratio for methane is needed to displace the mixture remaining in the voids. However, this methane is almost entirely recovered during desorption. Two factors are favorable for a high methane product purity in

Table 8.4 Steady-State Separation of a 50/50 H_2/CH_4 Mixture with Activated Carbon by the PSA Cycle

| Step | Product Purity, % | | | | Total Amount, ISTP | |
| | Hydrogen | | Methane | | | |
	Experiment	Model	Experiment	Model	Experiment	Model
II	99.77	99.60			26.11	29.07
III	79.37	68.70			8.73	8.90
IV			99.33	99.96	33.65	32.18
V			93.52	92.52	6.41	6.31
Recovery, %	61.59	71.80	91.66	85.29		

Sorbent productivity = 10.62 ISTP feed/min/kg carbon

Note: I: Repressure with H_2 (0.5 min); II: feed at 300 psig (3 min); III: cocurrent CH_4 purge (3 min); IV: countercurrent blowdown (to 5 psig, 2.5 min); V: H_2 purge (1 min). $P/F(H_2)$ = 0.036; $P/F(CH_4)$ = 0.85; sorbent = 420 g. Experiments and equilibrium model. Source: Cen and Yang [57].

this PSA cycle: a high methane purge/feed ratio and a low hydrogen purge/feed ratio. These two factors, meanwhile, result in a lower hydrogen product purity. Thus, if the strongly adsorbed component is the only desired product, the two P/F ratios may be optimized to maximize this product. Furthermore, the sorbent productivity of this PSA cycle is high because it is allowable to saturate nearly the entire bed during the feed step. Since the heavy product is obtained at a low pressure, the costly compression of this product is required for the heavy-product purge step.

Other Factors Affecting Product Purity and Recovery

The effects of two other variables on separation will be discussed: cycle time and temperature. To facilitate discussion, their effects will be considered for given throughput and bed size. Other variables such as P/F ratio and pressure ratio are also fixed.

A commercial PSA cycle consists of steps which have the same time length. The four-bed process, for example, consists of four equal-time steps, as shown in Figure 7.14. When cycle time is increased, the light-product purity will decrease, because the beds become more contaminated. Meanwhile, the light-product recovery will increase for the following reason. The unrecovered light component is contained in the effluent during the countercurrent blowdown and purge steps. The amount of this effluent for a given amount of feed is reduced when the cycle becomes longer; that is, less frequent throwaway of the light component. The opposite effects apply to the heavy product, for both purity and recovery. Thus, qualitatively, the effects of decreasing cycle time are similar to those of increasing P/F ratio. A quantitative example of the effects of cycle time is given by Doshi et al. [59] for hydrogen purification.

Little is known about the effects of the ambient temperature (that is, the temperature of the feed and purge streams) and the feed temperature on PSA separations. Some qualitative results are summarized here, based on model simulations. For separations where desorption is not a limiting factor, such as H_2/CH_4 and H_2/CO separations, a lower temperature will increase both product purity and recovery for the light (H_2) product, because of the enhanced adsorption. But the increases are usually small. For separations involving strongly adsorptive gases, such as the separation of CH_4/CO_2 with zeolite, desorption is a limiting factor for separation, and an increase in temperature will improve the separation.

Influence of Diffusional Resistance on Separation

There are no criteria available that predict conditions when diffusional resistance is important in a PSA process. Such conditions can be found, without recourse to experiment, by a comparison of the results calculated from the equilibrium and pore-diffusion models.

For the separation of binary mixtures using a monodisperse sorbent with the five-step PSA cycle, the product purity is determined by the following parameters [53]:

$$Y_i = Y_i \left[\frac{u_0 t_a}{L}, \frac{D_e t_c}{R_p^2}, Y_{i0}, \frac{P}{F}, P(t) \right] \qquad (8.119)$$

where t_a is the time for the adsorption step, t_c is the total cycle time, and subscript 0 denotes feed conditions. Under a wide range of all other parameters, a threshold value of approximately 100 for the parameter $D_e t_c / R_p^2$ was empirically found [53]. Pore diffusion was important below this value, whereas the equilibrium model was useful above this value. This empirical criterion was supported by experimental data on activated carbon for a number of binary mixtures [42–44]. Under the experimental as well as industrial operating conditions, these values of $D_e t_c / R_p^2$ are indeed close to the threshold value. Thus equilibrium is approached. However, the

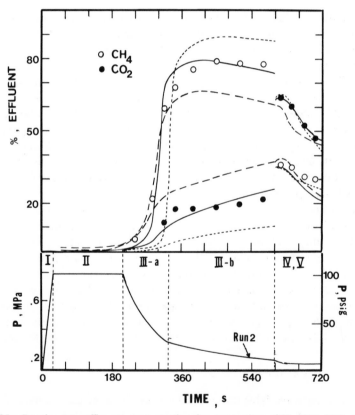

Figure 8.25   Steady-state effluent concentration for separation of $H_2/CH_4/CO_2$ (one-third each) with activated carbon by the five-step PSA cycle. Comparison of experimental data with equilibrium model (short-dash lines), Knudsen diffusion model (long-dash lines) and Knudsen plus surface-diffusion model (solid lines). Source: Doong and Yang [46]. Reprinted with permission.

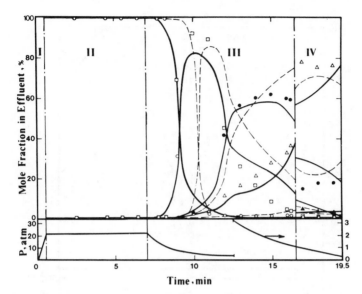

Figure 8.26 Steady-state separation of $H_2/CO/CH_4/CO_2/H_2S$ (1% H_2S, 24.75% all others) with carbon by PSA. Comparison of experimental data: $H_2(\bigcirc)$, $CO(\square)$, $CH_4(\bullet)$, $CO_2(\triangle)$, and $H_2s(\blacktriangle)$ with models: equilibrium (dashed lines) and LDF model (solid lines). Source: Cen and Yang [47]. Reprinted with permission.

empirical criterion only applies to binary mixtures. For multicomponent mixtures subjected to the same PSA cycle, pore-diffusion resistance becomes important. The multicomponent separation results are shown in Figure 8.25 for a three-component mixture and in Figure 8.26 for a five-component mixture. These results may be compared directly to the binary separations of hydrogen/methane [42] and hydrogen/carbon monoxide [44] with the same sorbent and PSA cycle. Equilibrium is approached for both binary mixtures. When the number of components is increased, Figures 8.25 and 8.26 show that the diffusional resistance becomes important. In both figures, the equilibrium model predicts a late breakthrough in desorption for all components. The reason for the increasing importance of diffusional resistance in PSA separation as the number of components in the mixture is increased is not understood. A probable explanation is that the interference and overlapping of wavefronts are enhanced as the number of components increases. These effects are accumulated over cycles, resulting in the observed early breakthrough during desorption.

The situation is more complex for zeolites which have a bidisperse pore structure. The results for a binary mixture, hydrogen/methane on 5A zeolite, using the five-step PSA cycle are shown in Figure 8.27 for various pellet and crystal sizes. It is expected that pore-diffusion resistances would become more important as the number of components increase. The results shown in Figure 8.27 are predicted by the nonadiabatic bidisperse pore-diffusion model, which has been verified experimentally [49, 50]. The results clearly show that although resistance to crystalline

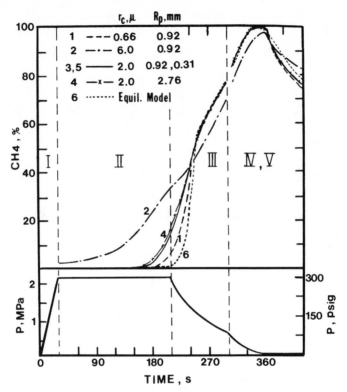

Figure 8.27 Effluent composition in a steady-state PSA cycle for separating a 50/50 H_2/CH_4 mixture using 5A zeolite with different crystal (r_c) and pellet (R_p) sizes. Feed = 39.2 lSTP/cycle; purge/feed = 0.036. Source: Doong and Yang [49].

diffusion is important in PSA separation, resistance to diffusion in the binder is not important. However, for PSA processes requiring an ultra-high-purity product (H_2 in step II in the present example), the operating conditions are adjusted such that all curves in steps II and III in Figure 8.27 are low and near zero. Under such circumstances, the differences among all curves are small, and the equilibrium model can give a good prediction. For processes where an ultra-high-purity product is not required, the resistance to crystalline diffusion should be considered.

NOTATION

A cross-sectional area of bed
b constant in the loading ratio correlation
B Langmuir or Henry's constant
C gas-phase concentration in the bulk flow; interpellet concentration
C_{ip} gas-phase concentration within pores for component i
C_0 feed or initial concentration

C_p	heat capacity, with subscripts g and s denoting, respectively, gas and solid
D_e	effective diffusivity
D_i	crystalline diffusivity in zeolites
D_z	axial dispersion coefficient
E	enrichment of the strong adsorptive component
G	fraction of light component introduced during the high-pressure feed step that is used as purge
h	heat transfer coefficient
H	heat of adsorption (negative) or desorption (positive)
k	mass transfer coefficient
k_{ez}	axial thermal dispersion coefficient
L	total bed length
M	molar flux
n	number of components in gas mixture; number of PSA cycles from startup
N	number of moles entering or leaving the bed per half-cycle; molar flux entering or leaving bed
N_i	gas flux for component i through the porous particle (outward being positive)
P	total pressure
Pe	Peclet number $= uL/D_z$
q	amount or equilibrium amount adsorbed per unit volume of pellet
$\bar{q}$	average amount adsorbed in pellet (per unit volume of pellet)
q^*	equilibrium amount adsorbed per unit volume of pellet
q_m	"monolayer" amount adsorbed per volume pellet
q_0^*	q^* at C_0
r	radial distance in pellet
R	gas constant or radial distance in zeolite pellet
R_b	radius of bed
R_p	radius of pellet
S	sorption rate per unit volume of bed
t	time
T	temperature
T_w	wall temperature
u	interstitial velocity
u_H	interstitial velocity during high-pressure feed
u_L	interstitial velocity during low-pressure purge
X	mole fraction in the adsorbed phase
Y	mole fraction in the gas phase
Y_{ip}	gas mole fraction of component i within the pores
z	axial distance in bed
Z	penetration distance by concentration wavefront
α	void fraction within the pellet or intrapellet void fraction
α_{ij}	separation factor $= X_i Y_j / X_j Y_i$
β_i	equilibrium ratio of gas-phase capacity to total capacity of a sorbent ($= \varepsilon/[\varepsilon + (1-\varepsilon)B_i]$)

β $\beta_A/\beta_B(\approx 1/\alpha_{AB})$

ε interstitial or interpellet void fraction in bed

η constant in loading ratio correlation

γ purge/feed ratio. For Skarstrom cycle with equal purge/feed times, $\gamma = u_L/u_H$. For other cycles, $\gamma =$ fraction of feed used as purge.

ρ density or product recovery

ρ_B bed density

ρ_g gas density

ρ_p pellet density

Δt half-cycle time; time or a step in the cycle

Subscripts

A, B components A and B

f feed

g gas

H high-pressure step (adsorption)

i component i in mixture

L low-pressure step (purge)

n nth cycle

s solid

∞ after ∞ cycles (i.e., at cyclic steady state)

Superscripts

s surface of pellet

—   volume-averaged quantities

=   volume-averaged quantities for zeolite pellets

′   dimensionless quantity

REFERENCES

1. R.L. Pigford, B. Baker III, and D.E. Blum, *Ind. Eng. Chem. Fundam.*, *8*, 144 (1969).
2. H.T. Chen and F.B. Hill, *Separa. Sc.*, *6*(3), 411 (1971).
3. L.H. Shendalman and J.E. Mitchell, *Chem. Eng. Sc.*, *27*, 1449 (1972).
4. Y.N.I. Chan, F.B. Hill, and Y.W. Wong, *Chem. Eng. Sci.*, *36*, 243 (1981).
5. C.W. Skarstrom, in *Recent Developments in Separation Science* (N.N. Li, ed.), Vol. 2 (Cleveland, Ohio: CRC Press, 1972), pp. 95–106.
6. K.S. Knaebel and F.B. Hill, *Chem. Eng. Sc.*, in press (1986).
7. C.D. Holland and A.I. Liapis, *Computer Methods for Solving Dynamic Separation Problems* (New York: McGraw-Hill, 1983).
8. J. Villadsen and M.L. Michelson, *Solution of Differential Equations Models by Polynomial Approximation* (Englewood Cliffs, N.J.: Prentice-Hall, 1978).

9. B.A. Finlayson, *The Method of Weighted Residuals and Variational Principles* (New York: Academic Press, 1972).
10. C.W. Gear, *Numerical Initial Value Problems in Ordinary Differential Equations* (Englewood Cliffs, N.J.: Prentice-Hall, 1971).
11. B. Carnahan, H.A. Luther, and J.O. Wilkes, *Applied Numerical Methods* (New York: Wiley, 1969).
12. D.U. von Rosenberg, *Methods for the Numerical Solution of Partial Differential Equations* (New York: Elsevier, 1969).
13. R.D. Richtmyer and K.W. Morton, *Difference Methods for Initial-Value Problems*, 2nd ed. (New York: Interscience, 1967).
14. J.E. Mitchell and L.H. Shendalman, *AIChE Symp. Ser.*, *69*(No. 134), 25 (1973).
15. K. Weaver and C.E. Hamrin, Jr., *Chem. Eng. Sc.*, *29*, 1873 (1974).
16. J.W. Carter and M.L. Wyszynski, *Chem. Eng. Sc.*, *38*, 1093 (1983).
17. K. Chihara and M. Suzuki, *J. Chem. Eng. Japan*, *16*, 53 (1983).
18. K. Chihara and M. Suzuki, *J. Chem. Eng. Japan*, *16*, 293 (1983).
19. N.S. Raghavan, M.M. Hassan, and D.M. Ruthven, *AIChE J.*, *31*, 385 (1985).
20. G.F. Fernandez and C.N. Kenney, *Chem. Eng. Sc.*, *38*, 827 (1983).
21. E. Richter, J. Strunk, K. Knoblauch, and H. Juntgen, *German Chem. Eng.*, *5*, 147 (1982).
22. E. Glueckauf and J.E. Coates, *J. Chem. Soc.*, 1315 (1947).
23. E. Glueckauf, *Trans. Faraday Soc.*, *51*, 1540 (1955).
24. S. Nakao and M. Suzuki, *J. Chem. Eng. Japan*, *16*, 114 (1983).
25. K. Chihara and M. Suzuki, *Proc. 2nd World Cong. of Chem. Eng.*, Vol. IV, p. 234, Montreal, October (1981).
26. S. Nakao and M. Suzuki, *J. Chem. Eng. Japan*, *16*, 330 (1983).
27. K.S. Knaebel and F.B. Hill, *Separ. Sc. and Tech.*, *18*, 1193 (1983).
28. M. Suzuki, *AIChE Symp. Ser.*, *81*(No. 242), 67 (1985).
29. P.H. Turnock and R.H. Kadlec, *AIChE J.*, *17*, 335 (1971).
30. R.L. Jones, G.E. Keller II, and R.C. Wells, U.S. Patent 4,194,892 (1980).
31. G.E. Keller II and R.L. Jones, *ACS Symp. Ser.*, *135*, 275 (1980).
32. G.E. Keller II, in "Industrial Gas Separation," *Am. Chem. Soc. Symp. Ser.*, No. 223, p. 145 (1983).
33. R.T. Cassidy and E.S. Holmes, *AIChE Symp. Ser.*, *80*(No. 233), 68 (1984).
34. F.B. Hill, *Chem. Eng. Commun.*, *7*, 33 (1980).
35. D.E. Kowler and R.H. Kadlec, *AIChE J.*, *18*, 1207 (1972).
36. H.C. Cheng and F.B. Hill, "Recovery and Purification of Light Gases by Pressure Swing Adsorption," *Am. Chem. Soc. Symp. Ser.*, No. 223, p. 195 (1983).
37. H.C. Cheng and F.B. Hill, *AIChE J.*, *31*, 95 (1985).
38. C.Y. Wen and L.T. Fan, *Models for Flow Systems and Chemical Reactors* (New York: Marcel Dekker, 1975).
39. F.B. Hill, Y.W. Wong, and Y.N.I. Chan, *AIChE J.*, *28*, 1 (1982).
40. Y.W. Wong and F.B. Hill, *AIChE J.*, *25*, 592 (1979).
41. Y.W. Wong and F.B. Hill, *Chem. Eng. Commun.*, *15*, 343 (1982).
42. R.T. Yang and S.J. Doong, *AIChE J.*, *11*, 1829 (1985).
43. R.T. Yang, S.J. Doong, and P.L. Cen, *AIChE Symp. Ser.*, *81*(No. 242), 84 (1985).
44. P.L. Cen and R.T. Yang, *Ind. Eng. Chem. Fundam.*, in press (1986).
45. R.D. Richtmyer and K.W. Morton, *Difference Methods for Initial-Value Problems,"* 2nd ed. (New York: Interscience, 1967), p. 233.
46. S.J. Doong and R.T. Yang, *AIChE J.*, *32*, 397 (1986).
47. P.L. Cen and R.T. Yang, *Separa. Sc. Tech.*, *20*, 725 (1985).

48. C.R. Wilke and C.Y. Lee, *Ind. Eng. Chem.*, *47*, 1253 (1955).
49. S.J. Doong and R.T. Yang, paper presented at the Annual AIChE Meeting, Chicago, November (1985).
50. S.J. Doong, J.A. Ritter, and R.T. Yang, unpublished results (1985).
51. R.T. Yang and P.L. Cen, *Ind. Eng. Chem. Proc. Des. Dev.*, *25*, 54 (1986).
52. J.J. Collins, U.S. Patent 4,026,680 (1977).
53. S.J. Doong and R.T. Yang, *Chem. Eng. Commun.*, *41*, 163 (1986).
54. P.L. Cen, W.N. Chen, and R.T. Yang, *Ind. Eng. Chem. Proc. Des. Dev.*, *24*, 1201 (1985).
55. T. Tamura, U.S. Patent 3,797,201 (1974).
56. N.S. Raghavan, M.M. Hassan, and D.M. Ruthven, *Chem. Eng. Sc.*, in press (1986).
57. P.L. Cen and R.T. Yang, *Separa. Sc. Tech.*, in press (1986).
58. J.C. Kayser and K.S. Knaebel, *Chem. Eng. Sc.*, in press (1986).
59. K.J. Doshi, C.H. Katira, and H.A. Stewart, *AIChE Symp. Ser.*, *67*(No. 117), 90 (1971).

Author Index

339

Subject Index

Activated alumina, 10, 17, 18
Activated carbon, 10
  manufacturing processes for, 11
  pore structure of, 14
  surface properties of, 12
Activity coefficients of mixed adsorbates, 65, 68, 69, 85
Adsorbent productivity, 238. *See also* Productivity
Adsorption, 1
Adsorption azeotrope, 72, 77
Adsorption of gas mixtures. *See* Mixed-gas adsorption
Adsorption isotherm, 26
  classification of, 27
Affinity coefficient, 41, 57, 58, 84
Air, adsorption of, in 5A zeolite, 263
Air drying, 238
Air separation, 239, 240, 246, 248, 252, 253, 263–272, 323
Asymptotic solution for adsorber dynamics, 158–161
Axial dispersion, 102, 106, 107, 124–126, 148

BET isotherm, 35
  for mixed-gas adsorption, 52
Bidisperse pore diffusion model, 152–156
  for adsorber breakthrough curves, 152–156
  for PSA, 320–323
Bidisperse pore structure, 113, 121
Biot number, 123–124
Blowdown step in PSA, 294–296
  amount discharged during, 295
Boundary, 173
Break point, 207, 212, 241
Breakthrough curves, 141
  from adiabatic absorber, 161–165
  asymptotic solution, 158–161
  constant-pattern solution, 158–161
  desorption, 169
  effect of axial dispersion on, 148

equilibrium theory for, 142
nonequilibrium theory for, 148
nonisothermal models for, 161–165
stage model for, 157
for zeolite beds, 152–156
Bulk separation, 3, 193, 201, 249
Bulk separation by PSA, 312–334

Carbon canister in automobile, 255
Carbon number, 260
CD step in PSA. *See* Cocurrent depressurization
Cell model for PSA, 309
Chapman-Enskog equation, 109
Characteristic curve, 28, 39–43, 59, 177
Characteristic temperature. *See* Reversal temperature
Characteristic movement in column during PSA, 305
Chemical-kinetic model for adsorber dynamics, 149
Chemisorption, 26
Chromatography, 212–217
  column packing for, 213
  equilibrium stage or theoretical plate for, 213
  elution, 215
  eluto-frontal, 216
  plate theory for, 212
  preparative, 212
Cocurrent depressurization (or blowdown) (CD), 241–243
Coherence condition, 162, 173, 177, 187
Coherent fronts, 173, 174
Combined temperature and pressure swing, 312
Compressive wave, 144
Concentration wavefront, 126, 142
Constant-pattern solution, 158–161, 161–165
Constant-state zone, 173
Contact discontinuity, 192
Crank-Nicolson method, 285

diffusional resistances, 331
pressure ratio, 329
purge/feed ratio, 328
equilibrium model for, 313
heavy product in, 329–331
LDF model for, 313
light product in, 328–329
pore diffusion models, 313
purge with heavy product in, 329
Pressurization of bed. *See*
Repressurization in PSA
Pretreatment beds in PSA, 245–247
Product cut, 310. *See also* Product
recovery
Product purity, 238, 324
Product recovery, 238, 310, 324
Productivity, 238, 324
Proportionate pattern type wavefront.
See Dispersive wavefront
PSA-parametric pumping, 265–267,
303–312
analytic model for, 303–306
comparison of with PSA, 267
enrichment of weakly adsorbed
impurity product, 306, 310
numerical models for, 306–309
oxygen generation by, 303, 307–309
recovery of weak adsorptive impurity
by, 303, 306, 310
Pulse injection, 215
Purasiv HR process, 217
Pure temperature (thermal) wave, 161,
163, 164
condition for the existence of, 164
Purge by strong adsorptive gas in PSA,
247–248
Purge/feed ratio (P/F), 254, 279
definitions of, 279
on air drying, effect of, 289
Purge gas consumption, 169
minimum, 172
Purge gas temperature, characteristic,
171
Purification, 3, 201

Raffinate, 202, 238
Rapid PSA (or PSA-parametric
pumping), 263–267
Recurrence formula, 180
Regeneration with cold purge, 170
condition for, 170
Regeneration of sorbent, 2, 202
optimal temperature for, 206
purge time for, 206

Relative transport resistance inside and
outside sorbent particle, 104, 107,
123–124
Relative transport resistance of
micropore and macropore, 152
Relative resistance of film, micro- and
macropores, 155
Relative volatility, 2
Repressurization in PSA, 292–294,
304–305
with feed mixture, 304
Resolution for Gaussian elution bands,
215
Reversal temperature, 165, 171, 206, 207
Riemann's problem, 176, 188
Roll-over or roll-up, 173
Rosen model for adsorber dynamics,
149–151

Self-sharpening wave, 144
Separation, 1
of carbon dioxide for enhanced oil
recovery, 271
of carbon dioxide from hydrocarbons, 6
of carbon dioxide from methane, 6
of landfill gas, 271
of natural gasoline into n-paraffins and
branched/cyclic hydrocarbons, 242
of normal paraffins from isomers,
260–262, 323
Separation factor, 2, 61, 186, 222, 303
for air in zeolite, 304
Shock wave, shock transition or shock
discontinuity, 143, 144, 167, 168,
180, 181, 182, 189
Silica gel, 10, 18, 19
Simulated moving-bed adsorption
processes, 216–221
Single-bed PSA process, *see* PSA-
parametric pumping
Skarstrom cycle, 237–241, 243, 254, 275
air drying by, 297
analytic model for, 275–284
complete purification by, conditions
for, 280
critical purge/feed ratio for complete
purification by, 281–284
cyclic steady state in, 298
effect of dispersion on, 291
effect of mass transfer resistance on, 291
effect of temperature swing on, 298